THE AGE OF LINCOLN AND THE
ART OF AMERICAN POWER, 1848–1876

Also by William Nester

The Revolutionary Years, 1775–1789:
The Art of American Power during the Early Republic (2011)

The Hamiltonian Vision, 1789–1800:
The Art of American Power during the Early Republic (2012)

The Jeffersonian Vision, 1801–1815:
The Art of American Power during the Early Republic (2012)

The Age of Jackson and the Art of American Power, 1815–1848 (2013)

THE AGE OF LINCOLN

AND THE ART OF AMERICAN POWER,

1848–1876

WILLIAM NESTER

Potomac Books
An imprint of the University of Nebraska Press

Manufactured in the United States
of America.

Library of Congress Cataloging-in-Publication
Data
Nester, William R., 1956–
The age of Lincoln and the art of American
power, 1848–1876 / William Nester.
pages cm
Includes bibliographical references and index.
ISBN 978-1-61234-658-8 (cloth: alk. paper)
1. United States—Politics and government—
1849–1877. 2. Lincoln, Abraham,
1809–1865—Influence. 3. Power (Social
sciences)—United States—History—19th
century. 4. Manifest Destiny. 5. United States—
History—Civil War, 1861–1865. 6. Reconstruction (U.S. history, 1865–1877) I. Title.
E415.7.N37 2014
973.7—dc23
2013034651

Set in Adobe Garamond Pro by Hannah Gokie.
Designed by Laura Wellington.

CONTENTS

Introduction

Abraham Lincoln and the Art of Power

Let us have faith that right makes might, and in that faith let
us to the end dare to do our duty as we understand it.

ABRAHAM LINCOLN

The legitimate object of government is to do for a community of people
whatever they need to have done, but cannot do at all, or cannot so
well do for themselves—in their separate and individual capacities.

ABRAHAM LINCOLN

I shall not surrender this game leaving any available card unplayed.

ABRAHAM LINCOLN

Power is essential to everyone's daily life but usually lurks in the background until a conflict flares. We recognize power when we assert it or fall prey to that of others in a clash of interests. Defining the art of power is as simple as it is profound; it is the ability to get what one wants.

Wielding that art is tough enough at the interpersonal level; the challenges rise with the level of politics. The head of a country obviously asserts and faces arrays of power far greater than that of any individual asserting his or her own interests. Ideally a sovereign government wields power to defend or enhance the interests of the country in which it is embedded. Each country has its own distinct traditions and institutions of power.

America's art of power is grounded in the Declaration of Independence, which expresses the nation's ideals, and the Constitution, which provides a system of government designed to realize these ideals. Ultimately the success or failure of a president and his administration can be measured by how well or poorly they advance American interests within the parameters of American ideals and institutions.[1]

Abraham Lincoln was a master of the art of American power.[2] Politics, psychology, and power are distinct but inseparable; to understand and act decisively in one realm is to understand and act decisively in the others. Lincoln knew that power is ultimately rooted not in gun barrels but in human intellects, feelings, and characters and that the most effective way to wield power is through persuasion rather than coercion. Although he probably never heard of let alone read Sun Tzu, he acted on that ancient Chinese philosopher's core teaching that victory in any struggle is virtually impossible if one fails to know one's foe or oneself.[3]

Understanding one's limits is essential to mastering the art of power. Lincoln was well aware of how the course of human events constrains even the seemingly mightiest positions. Looking back at his years as president, he admitted, "I claim not to have controlled events, but confess plainly that events have controlled me."[4] Yet he was never a fatalist. He simply distinguished between what was possible and what was not and strove to wield "smart power," or all the appropriate "hard" physical and "soft" psychological powers at his disposal to alleviate or overcome the problems before him.

Lincoln's art of power was innate rather than trained. When he entered the White House, he had served twelve years in the Illinois assembly but only two years as a congressman in Washington. His managerial experience was limited to being the senior partner in a two-man law firm. When he was twenty-three, he captained a militia company for all of three months. Then for four years, from his inauguration as president on March 4, 1861, to his murder on April 14, 1865, he brilliantly governed, developed the economy, crushed the rebellion, liberated four million people from slavery, and reunified the nation.

He accomplished all that by tapping deep into his profound intelligence, instinct for wielding power, and ability to learn from his mistakes and think outside the box. Had he played chess he would have been a grand master, as he out-thought his opponents in multiple moves ahead in multiple directions and combinations. He always searched for new ways to finesse a problem and did not give up until he succeeded, insisting that "I shall not surrender this game leaving any available card unplayed."[5] He continually distinguished primary from secondary interests, or castles from pawns. His law partner William Herndon marveled at his skill at "giving away six points and carrying the seventh . . . [with] the whole case hanging on the seventh. Any man who took Lincoln for a simple-minded man would very soon wake up with his back in a ditch."[6]

Lincoln's art of power ultimately reflected his unswerving devotion to the Declaration of Independence's principles and the Constitution's institutions, or, as he so elegantly expressed it, "to a government of the people, by the people, and for the people." He understood that the struggle for hearts and minds was the essence of politics in a democracy: "In this age and this country, public sentiment is everything. With it nothing can fail; against it nothing can succeed. Whoever molds public sentiment goes deeper than he who enacts statutes or pronounces judicial decisions. He makes possible the enforcement of these, else impossible."[7]

His favorite leadership technique was to set the example. He did so hoping to inspire others to emulate the integrity and reason that guided his search for practical solutions to problems whereby everyone with a stake wins something but not necessarily everything. He asserted power mostly by appealing to people's hopes rather than their fears. No one exceeded his power to master a complex subject and reduce it to values and analogies that most people could instantly understand and accept. For instance, how does one argue against this notion: "Those who deny freedom to others deserve it not for themselves."[8]

All along he tried to shape rather than reflect prevailing public opinions that differed from his own. To that end, he was brilliant at bridging the gap between progressives and conservatives by reining in the former and urging on the latter. As such he was careful that his own principles did not pull his policies faster or further than was prudent. He reported triumphantly in September 1864 that "the public interest and my private interest have been perfectly parallel because in no other way could I serve myself so well as by truly serving the Union."[9]

Lincoln's appreciation for life's complexities and paradoxes led him to forgo some conventional sources of power. Throughout history, rulers have mobilized the masses by insisting that God is on their side. People who believe that are generally willing to make greater sacrifices than those who do not. But Lincoln thought that resorting to such gross deceptions ultimately weakened rather than strengthened one's cause. A liberal democracy survives and, ideally, thrives on reason rather than blind faith. His duty as the American president was to educate rather than delude the people. As for God's will, he wrote, "In great contests each party claims to act in accordance with the will of God. Both may be, and one must be, wrong. God cannot be for and against the same thing at the same time. In the present civil war it is quite possible that God's purpose is different from the purpose of either party."[10]

For Lincoln, the core philosophical and political problem that he faced as president was "whether in a free government the minority have the right to break up the government whenever they choose." His answer, of course, was a resounding no. Yet while he insisted on majority rule, he just as adamantly championed minority rights. And that raised his administration's second great philosophical and political question, "whether the nation could endure, permanently, half slave and half free."[11]

The nature of national power and the nature of government are inseparable. The American debate over the purposes and thus the powers of government is as old as the republic. By the mid-nineteenth century, nearly all Americans adhered to one of three philosophical positions. Hamiltonianism called for a muscular government that worked with the private sector to develop the nation, overcome problems, and promote the potential of all people to better themselves. Jeffersonism and Jacksonism both espoused a bare-bones government but differed on the details. Jeffersonians wanted little more in government than a medium for dealing with foreigners and Indians and delivering the mail, while leaving defense largely in the hands of local militia companies and gunboats in ports. Jacksonians parted with them by insisting on a powerful national army and navy. Both asserted that prosperity spreads best when government lets markets and private enterprise alone.

Abraham Lincoln was a lifelong, fervent Hamiltonian. For him, "the legitimate object of government is to do for a community of people whatever they need to have done, but cannot do at all, or cannot so well do for themselves—in their separate and individual capacities."[12] That principle was rooted in his acute observations of the world. Without constraints, the powerful few repress and exploit the weak many. A government's role is not just to protect the weak from the world's bullies, both foreign and domestic, but to strengthen the weak so that they can eventually take care of themselves. To that end in the early 1790s, Alexander Hamilton devised a set of specific policies designed to enhance the wealth and thus the power of all Americans and the entire nation. He and his Federalist Party fought to enact a national bank to regulate the money supply, establish a sound currency, and pay off the national debt; investments in canals, roads, and ports, the skeleton of an economy; a high tariff that provided the government with revenues and manufacturers with protection from predatory foreign rivals; and an army and navy strong enough to deter foreign aggression. For complex reasons, Thomas Jefferson and his Republican Party vanquished the Federalists, and Jeffersonism largely prevailed for the next couple of decades. During the 1820s, Jefferson's Republican Party morphed into Jackson's Democratic Party, and Jacksonism competed with Jeffersonism to dominate the party and the nation. Hamiltonianism reemerged with Henry Clay's "American System" and his Whig Party that he founded in 1832. Lincoln joined the Whigs that year and remained a devoted member until the party's demise in 1854. He then joined the Republican Party that emerged that year and espoused Hamiltonianism enhanced with a homestead act to help families settle farms in the West, a transcontinental railroad to the Pacific Ocean, schooling for all children, and land-grant colleges for the gifted. As president, Lincoln not only succeeded in enacting every item on the Hamiltonian agenda except a national bank, he did so as he struggled to overcome a far greater challenge to the nation's fate.

A distinct age of American history unfolded between the Mexican War's end in 1848 and Reconstruction's end in 1876.[13] The future of slavery and black Americans was the core political question during those nearly three decades. Politicians failed to overcome a series of crises over those questions that culminated with the South's secession, followed by a catastrophic Civil War, abolition, and the South's "Reconstruction."

While that age's central issues and bookends are clear enough, what is it best called? The Age of Jackson (1815–48) that preceded it was clearly overshadowed by its namesake's commanding personality, ideology, and policies.[14] Did such a larger-than-life leader dominate the next twenty-eight years?

How about the Age of Lincoln? Although Abraham Lincoln was among seven men who served as president during those years, history has been just if not kind to his colleagues. Zachary Taylor, Millard Fillmore, Franklin Pierce, James Buchanan, Andrew Johnson, and Ulysses Grant have been rated either mediocrities or much worse. To varying degrees, each failed to comprehend let alone overcome the crucial challenges that he faced.[15]

In contrast, Abraham Lincoln was a giant in character and deeds. While the others mostly provided lessons in what not to do, Lincoln alone mastered the art of American power during this era. No president has ever faced a worse threat to America. Eleven states rebelled and warred against the United States. Lincoln decisively confronted and eventually overcame this crisis. Most Americans adore Abraham Lincoln for two truly great accomplishments: "he saved the Union and freed the slaves." Yet he also found time to work with congressional leaders to enact virtually the entire Hamilton agenda. As such he represented that age's progressive zeitgeist or spirit. No one during these nearly three decades was a more eloquent voice for moderation, reason, compromise, and wisdom in addressing the nation's divisive issues, with slavery and its legacy their core. And in doing so he persistently excelled at the art of American power even if he only briefly wielded it.

Abraham Lincoln proved to be a brilliant master of the art of power because he was as pragmatic as he was progressive. Indeed, the two are inseparable. It is impossible truly to be one without being the other. One crucial principle underlay all others and guided Lincoln throughout his life: "Let us have faith that right makes might, and in that faith let us to the end dare to do our duty as we understand it."[16] He excelled in all of the president's duties, not just as the chief commander but as America's chief diplomat, economist, educator, humanist, moralist, and nationalist.

After Jesus, Abraham Lincoln is history's most written about character. He is America's most celebrated and beloved national icon. Much larger than life, a statue of him is enthroned within a marble temple facing Washington's obelisk a mile away and the Capitol an equal distance beyond. His profile on the copper penny at once recalls his lowly origins and his stunning rise to power. Yet, despite his familiarity and the millions of words written about him by hundreds of authors, Lincoln remains elusive, enigmatic. His character was a labyrinth. Tragedies deepened his natural melancholy. Although no president was more introspective, he loved swapping tales with others even as he emotionally kept them at arm's length. He could crack the most ribald remark one moment and the most profound one the next. His happiest moments were spent romping with his children or riding the court circuit with his fellow lawyers.

The history that we read about was not inevitable. Decisions matter. Different leaders facing the same problem may make completely different choices and thus wrench history in unexpected directions. Any leader's decisions are the outcome of a struggle between his character and circumstances; they depend on how he defines what interests are at stake and what means are at hand to best assert them. *The Age of Lincoln and the Art of American Power* explores how Abraham Lincoln and other key leaders from 1848 to 1876 reacted to the crises and opportunities that they faced and in doing so decisively shaped American history.

he was an experienced and skilled orator, he was likely a bit nervous. He was about to launch one of the most blistering attacks on a president ever uttered in that chamber. For the next forty-five minutes, he systematically picked apart "Mr. Polk's War" as grounded upon, "from beginning to end, the sheerest deception" and "the half insane mumbling of a fever dream." He condemned the president's shifting and contradictory statements on the war, insisting that "his mind, taxed beyond its power, is running hither and thither, like some tortured creature on a burning surface, finding no position on which it can settle and be at ease." Among the war's worst evils was that Polk was surely "deeply conscious of being in the wrong," yet stayed the course come what may. Even so, Lincoln could not help but feel compassion for such "a bewildered, confounded, and miserably perplexed man."[3]

Lincoln's ire was partly aroused by the Polk administration's silence toward his maiden speech of December 22, 1847, when he eschewed the customary expression of gratitude and dedication to his constituents and the nation. He chose instead to raise a contentious issue whereby he took an unpopular minority stand. He proposed a resolution that required the president to prove that Mexican troops had invaded and shed American blood on American soil, Polk's key justification for asking Congress for a war declaration in May 1846.[4]

If the White House ignored Lincoln's proposal, Congress did not. On January 3, 1848, George Ashmun of Massachusetts was inspired to offer a more explicit resolution that the war had been "unnecessarily and unconstitutionally begun by the president of the United States."[5] Lincoln joined eighty-five fellow Whigs in voting for this resolution.

Lincoln and the war's other opponents defied the views of most Americans, including William Herndon, Lincoln's law partner. Herndon upheld the Polk administration's position that the border of Texas rested on the Rio Grande, not the Nueces River 150 miles farther north, as Mexico claimed. Thus the Mexicans invaded American territory by crossing the Rio Grande and started the war when they attacked part of Gen. Zachary Taylor's army. In his reply to Herndon and other critics, Lincoln argued that the land between those rivers remained Mexican because its mostly Mexican inhabitants had not joined the Texas rebellion. He cited the terrible precedent cast by the Polk administration: "Allow the president to invade a neighboring nation, wherever he shall deem it necessary to repel an invasion . . . and you allow him to make war at pleasure."⁶

Although Lincoln condemned the war, he lauded the soldiers who fought it: "Our arms have given us the most splendid successes, every department and every part, land and water, officers and privates, regulars and volunteers, doing all that men can do, and hundreds of things which it had ever before been thought men could not do."⁷ He dutifully voted for every war appropriation bill.

Lincoln, then an obscure freshman congressman, was not the only war opponent who would eventually rise to the political pinnacle. Ulysses S. Grant was then a young army captain who had no doubt over just who started the war: "The presence of United States troops on the edge of the disputed territory furthest from the Mexican settlements was not sufficient to provoke hostilities. We were sent to provoke a fight, but it was essential that Mexico should commence it." After Congress declared war, Grant was "bitterly opposed to the measure and to this day regard[s] the war which resulted as one of the most unjust ever waged by a stronger against a weaker nation."⁸

It takes a powerful will and sense of principle to oppose a war that one's government and most fellow citizens zealously favor, at least initially. Grant understood that: "Once initiated there were but few public men who would have the courage to oppose it. Experience proves that the man who obstructs a war in which his nation is engaged, no matter right or wrong, occupied no enviable place in history."⁹

In opposing the war with Mexico, Lincoln boldly set himself against the literal march of American history. If imperialism is the conquest of one people by another, then America has been imperialistic from its beginning. The English colonists took land from the Indians and over the next century and a half expanded their holdings to the Appalachian Mountains and in some places beyond. After winning its war of independence, the United States carried on that imperialism. Most Americans at once exalted in their nation's swelling borders while denying the often deceptive, brutal, and dishonorable means whereby it unfolded. Proponents justified expansion in various ways. Thomas Jefferson proclaimed America "an empire of liberty" that benefited all peoples within its embrace. In 1845 John O'Sullivan, the *New York Tribune*'s editor, justified that imperialism with the expression "Manifest Destiny," or the inherent American right to expand. The war with Mexico was simply the latest stage of American history illuminated by Manifest Destiny.[10]

The Treaty of Guadeloupe Hidalgo, signed on February 2, 1848, split the difference between the extremes of those who wanted nothing and those who wanted everything. Mexico agreed to recognize America's previous annexation of Texas with a frontier on the Rio Grande and to cede the provinces of New Mexico and California—522,000 square miles of territory that today includes not just those two states but Arizona and parts of Nevada, Utah, and Colorado. In return, the United States agreed to pay Mexico $15 million and assume the roughly $3.25 million in debts that Mexico's government and citizens owed Americans.

President Polk received the treaty on February 21 and sent word to Congress. Later that day in the House of Representatives, the Speaker submitted a resolution to thank the generals for leading the nation to victory. John Quincy Adams, among the war's most stalwart critics, struggled to his feet, red-faced and fuming, muttered "no," then collapsed. He lingered two days before dying on the evening of February 23. His last words were, "This is the end of the earth, but I am composed."[11]

This same day Polk sent the treaty to the Senate. The subsequent debate raged for two and a half weeks. A majority voted down a proposal by Democrat Jefferson Davis of Mississippi that the treaty be amended to include northern Mexico. George Badge, a North Carolina Whig, lost his bid that the United States take no territory from Mexico. Other resolutions were aired and rejected. Of the fifty-eight senators, twenty-six voted at least once against an attempt to amend the treaty. It was not until March 10 that opponents exhausted their alternatives and the Senate voted on the original treaty. The Treaty of Guadeloupe Hidalgo was ratified by a tally of thirty-eight to fourteen, with four abstentions. The treaty was promptly sent to Mexico, whose government eventually also ratified the original version after a bitter congressional debate. The ratifications were formally exchanged on May 30.[12]

President Polk tried to give Americans special cause to rejoice that Fourth of July by formally declaring the treaty in effect that day. The treaty's celebration was hardly universal. Although the debate over what to take from Mexico was over, the debate over what to do with what was taken had only just begun.[13]

America's triumph in the Mexican War had already literally begun to pay off. James Marshall was a carpenter for John Sutter, who owed a vast cattle and horse ranch in California's Central Valley and had founded the settlement of New Helvetia, guarded by Sutter's Fort on the Sacramento River, in 1840. On the chilly morning of January 24, 1848, Marshall was supervising a team of men building a sawmill when he spotted a gold-colored speck glittering in the millrace. He plucked it out, rubbed it between his fingers, and pondered a moment. "Boys," he announced in a classic laconic western drawl, "I believe I have found a gold mine."[14]

Marshall hurried to his boss with his find. Sutter excitedly concluded that his land appeared to have yielded a new source of wealth. They tried to keep the discovery secret but word was already racing through New Helvetia and other ranches across the region. Scores of workers quit their jobs, scoured streambeds for gold, and exchanged what they found for goods at Sam Brannan's store. In May Brannan journeyed down to San Francisco with a vial full of gold flakes and announced the strike. That set off a rush to Sutter's land and elsewhere along the Sierra foothills. As more of their crews deserted, captains ordered their vessels' anchors raised and sails lowered while they still had any men left. Word eventually reached the eastern United States. President Polk trumpeted that news as part of his December 1848 address to Congress.

As a national and international phenomenon, the gold rush did not begin until the next year. The "Forty-Niners" had two ways to reach California, neither easy nor quick. A ship from the east coast took seven or eight months of straight sailing to reach San Francisco. A shortcut across the narrow waists of the Americas through Nicaragua or Panama to a vessel on the Pacific coast might cut that journey's time in half. The overland trail from Independence, Missouri, took from four to five months. Most people went overland, with perhaps forty thousand reaching California by that route in 1849 alone. California's population soared from fourteen thousand in 1848 to over one hundred thousand in 1850, when it received statehood.[15]

For foreign diplomats accredited to the United States, Washington City appeared not just an unlikely but a dismal place for the capital of an empire that now stretched across the continent. Indeed, the British government deemed America's capital a hardship post until the twentieth century. Charles Dickens charitably called it a "city of magnificent intentions," referring to Pierre L'Enfant's design of interconnecting squares, ovals, and institutions.[16] In 1848 the city had barely begun to fulfill the vision that L'Enfant had outlined nearly seven decades earlier. There were still more empty than developed lots. Even the two most prominent buildings were either forlorn or unfinished. Depending on the weather, a muddy or dusty field surrounded the White House. The Capitol was missing its dome. Throughout the town, shanties and taverns clustered near handfuls of elegant mansions. Although the winters were mild, the summer air was filled with sweltering heat and hordes of mosquitoes. Among Washington's forty thousand inhabitants were eight thousand free blacks and two thousand slaves. To the shame of some people and the pride of others, auction blocks stood literally in the Capitol's shadow.

The United States looked impressive on a map but was anything but a unified nation in 1848. The people were split among a spectrum of political, economic, social, religious, racial, and ethnic lines. The most glaring differences were, of course, black and white, slave and free. The 1850 census revealed that more than four million Americans, or one in six, were black, with nine of ten slaves and nineteen of twenty living in the South.

Although an industrial revolution was increasingly fueling America's economy, 85 percent of the population still lived in the countryside while only 15 percent resided in towns with twenty-five hundred or more people. America remained a largely Protestant nation—36,534 Protestant churches with 14 million parishioners starkly overshadowed 1,227 Catholic churches and 37 Jewish synagogues, with their respective 676,000 and 19,000 members.[17]

A growing distinction was between native and foreign born. Of the 23,191,000 people counted in the 1850 census, 2,244,000, or one in ten, were immigrants, of whom 1,470,000 had stepped ashore in just the previous decade. The potato famine in northern Europe, most severely in Ireland, was the most powerful push behind all those immigrants. Then, in 1848, a surge of political refugees swelled the year's wave as mass revolts erupted in most of Europe's capitals and largest cities. The underlying causes were worsening poverty, famines, and repression, whose injustices revolutionary leaders illuminated through the ideologies of liberalism, nationalism, or socialism. In most countries, the governments crushed those rebellions. France, however, did experience a short-lived revolution that overthrew the monarchy and briefly established a liberal republic.[18]

In upstate New York that year a small group of mostly women announced their own peaceful revolution. The first Women's Rights Convention in human history took place in six sessions at Seneca Falls on July 19 and 20.[19] At the gathering's conclusion, exactly one hundred people, sixty-eight women and thirty-two men, of the several hundred who attended, signed a Declaration of Sentiments that revised America's Declaration of Independence to read, "We hold these truths to be self-evident: that all men and women are created equal."

That convention and declaration were inspired by the abolition movement. During the 1840s, more women who fervently championed the emancipation of slaves came to realize that equality should prevail between genders as well as races. Elizabeth Cady Stanton and Lucretia Coffin Mott, the convention's organizers, leaders, and keynote speakers, first met in 1842 and for the next half-dozen years developed this ideal among themselves and a growing network of followers. The abolitionist and women's rights movements complemented each other. Frederick Douglass, the only African American to attend the convention, rose to declare that the liberation of blacks and women should be inseparable and to condemn the "denial of the right to participate in government" that led "not merely [to] the degradation of women and the perpetuation of a great injustice . . . but the maiming and repudiation of one-half of the moral and intellectual power of the government of the world."[20]

Two progressive events in New York prompted Stanton and Mott to call for the convention. In April the state assembly passed the Married Women's Property Act that for the first time gave women the right to keep the property they brought to a marriage along with what they acquired during the marriage. Then in June, during the Liberty Party convention in Buffalo, Mott received five votes to be Gerrit Smith's vice presidential running mate, the first time a woman was officially considered for a position of national power. These two votes at once illuminated how far women trailed men in rights and opportunities while hinting that a vigorous mass movement could narrow and one distant day eliminate that gap. Like black men, women struggled for decades before they achieved legal equality, although they continue to trail in wealth and power.

Had James Polk not been a perfectionist, he might have derived enormous satisfaction during his last year in the White House. He had fulfilled all four promises that he had made when he became president. He signed a tariff bill that reduced the rate to a level that produced revenues but did not strongly protect American industries and a banking bill that helped stabilize financial markets. Far more spectacularly, he took the Oregon Territory from Britain and the Southwest Territory from Mexico.

Yet each of these triumphs provoked acrimonious debates between Democrats and Whigs that presidential year, none more so than whether slavery should be allowed in the Mexican War conquests.[21] In his speech announcing his latest run for the presidency, House Speaker Henry Clay condemned "Mr. Polk's War" as "unnecessary and . . . offensive" and predicted that the conquests "might prove a fatal acquisition, producing distraction, dissension, division, possibly disunion."[22]

The Democratic Party nominated Senator William Cass of Michigan for the presidency during its convention at Baltimore in May. Cass's supporters won only after a long, hard fight against those of Martin Van Buren, the president from 1838 to 1842. The Cass and Van Buren factions were bitter enemies. After Cass won, Van Buren and his faction bolted the convention, vowing to form their own party. Cass and his supporters called the defectors Barnburners, claiming they were so single-minded that they would burn down their own barn to rid it of mice. In retort, Barnburners called their critics Hunkers for allegedly being so venal that all they "hunkered" after in politics was to fill their pockets with "campaign contributions." Genuine disputes over policies lay behind the name-calling. Barnburners were "free soilers" who upheld both the 1820 Missouri Compromise and the Wilmot Proviso limits on slavery's expansion. Hunkers championed the "popular sovereign" right of territorial and state governments to determine whether they would be free or slave.

The Whig Party had last won a presidential election in 1840 by nominating a victorious general as president. Alas, William Henry Harrison lasted little more than a month in the White House before he died of pneumonia. He was succeeded by Vice President John Tyler, who was such a fervent slavocrat that the Whigs eventually expelled him from their party. Now the Whigs hoped to duplicate their win of a presidential election with the same strategy. At their June convention in Philadelphia, the Mexican War's two best commanders dueled for the nomination along with several other candidates. Although Winfield Scott was a far more skilled general than Zachary Taylor, he lost. Their nicknames help explain why "Rough and Ready" Taylor beat "Old Fuss and Feathers" Scott. Taylor led on the first ballot with III votes to Henry Clay's 97, Scott's 43, Daniel Webster's 22, and 6 split among two others. He won a majority on the fourth ballot. Clay declined Taylor's request to serve as his running mate. Millard Fillmore, a New York senator, was picked instead.

After the convention, Abraham Lincoln enthusiastically backed Taylor's campaign. Although as a loyal Whig he would have done so anyway, he was jubilant when Taylor endorsed a platform that embraced Henry Clay's American System of a protective tariff, internal improvements, and a national bank. Although Taylor owned a Louisiana plantation worked by over a hundred slaves, he upheld the Wilmot Proviso that forbade slavery from a territory taken from Mexico.

Another party emerged that year to compete with the Whigs for many of the same voters and states. The Free Soil Party was an amalgam of dissatisfied Whig, Democrat, and Liberty Party adherents who rallied around the slogan "Free Soil, Free Speech, Free Labor, and Free Men."[23] The National Free Soil Convention met at Buffalo, New York, and on August 9 nominated Martin Van Buren for president and Charles Francis Adams as his running mate. In this gathering were men who either were or would be national progressive leaders, including senators William Seward, Salmon Chase, and Benjamin Wade and newspaper editors Horace Greely, Walt Whitman, and Frederick Douglass, respectively of the *New York Tribune, Brooklyn Daily Eagle*, and *Rochester North Star*. A small group of fellow black abolitionists accompanied Douglass, who was already a celebrity for his autobiography, *The Narrative of the Life of Frederick Douglass, An American Slave*, which was published in 1845.[24]

This year's election was the first wherein states chose their electors on November's first Tuesday, and all but South Carolina did so by a popular vote. Taylor won a solid plurality with 1,361,393 votes, or 47.3 percent, compared to Cass with 1,223,400, or 42.5 percent, and Van Buren with 291,616, or 10.1 percent. In the Electoral College, Taylor garnered 163 to Cass's 127 and none for Van Buren. With about 10 percent of the popular vote, the Free Soilers made a respectable showing for a third and new party but also provoked the wrath of the second-place candidate and his supporters for being a spoiler that robbed the Democratic Party of victory. The Liberty Party, dedicated to slavery's abolition, got only 2,245 votes.

As Taylor prepared to move to Washington and assemble a cabinet, Abraham Lincoln struggled with mixed feelings over returning to his family, friends, and law career at Springfield, Illinois. He tried to reconcile himself to the reality that his brief sojourn on the crowded national political stage was over, most likely forever.

2

Young Lincoln

"The short and simple annals of the poor." That's my life,
and that's all you or any one else can make of it.

ABRAHAM LINCOLN

I range the fields with pensive tread,
And pace the hollow rooms,
And feel (companion of the dead)
I'm living in the tombs.

ABRAHAM LINCOLN

Every man is said to have his peculiar ambition. . . . I can say . . .
that I have no other so great as that of being truly esteemed of
my fellow-men, by rendering myself worthy of their esteem.

ABRAHAM LINCOLN

I don't think much of a man who is not wiser
today than he was yesterday.

ABRAHAM LINCOLN

When a journalist offered to write his biography for his 1860 presidential campaign, Abraham Lincoln dismissed the notion as "a great piece of folly." He characterized his early decades as "'the short and simple annals of the poor.' That's my life, and that's all you or any one else can make of it."[1]

Lincoln, of course, cannot be understood without exploring the time from his birth to his twenty-second year, when he literally and figuratively turned his back on his family and set forth in search of a better life. He was indeed born into poverty on February 12, 1809, on the hardscrabble farm of his parents, Thomas and Nancy, and elder sister, Sarah, near Elizabethtown, Kentucky. Thomas was a stern, penny-pinching taskmaster who had witnessed Indians murder his own father when he was six. Nancy was reserved but bright and kind. Both parents were barely literate. The Lincolns migrated to Indiana in 1816. After Nancy died when Lincoln was nine, his father left his two children to fend for themselves while he returned to Elizabethtown in search of a new wife. He eventually reappeared with Sarah Bush Johnston, a widow with three small children aged nine to five.

Starved for affection, Lincoln soon loved his sweet and nurturing stepmother, who taught him to read and write. During his teens he voraciously devoured every book he could get his hands on. He later cited the family Bible, William Scott's *Lessons in Elocution*, Parson Weems's *Life of George Washington*, John Bunyan's *Pilgrim's Progress*, William Shakespeare's tragedies, William Grimshaw's *History of the United States*, and *Aesop's Fables* as the most influential books of these years.

Thomas resented the time Lincoln spent reading, partly because it distracted him from his work but perhaps more because he could not understand let alone control his son's ever-expanding mind. So he redoubled his efforts to fill his son's life with unrelenting, exhausting physical labor. When Lincoln was done with the myriad of tasks on their own farm, Thomas hired him out to neighbors and pocketed what little coin his son earned. He increasingly favored his obedient stepson John over his natural son Abraham. The father and son became so deeply estranged that decades later Lincoln declined to visit him on his deathbed, reasoning that "if we could meet now, it is doubtful whether it would not be more painful than pleasant."[2]

In his thirty-seventh year, he looked back and wrote a revealing poem about his youth.

My childhood's home I see again,
And sadden with the view;
And still as mem'ries crowd my brain,
There's pleasure in it too . . .

Where things decayed and loved ones lost
In dreamy shadows rise,
And freed from all that's earthly vile . . .
Near twenty years have passed away
Since here I bid farewell
To woods and fields and scenes of play
And playmates loved so well . . .
How changed, as time has sped!
Young childhood grown, strong manhood grey
And half of all are dead . . .
I range the fields with pensive tread,
And pace the hollow rooms,
And feel (companion of the dead)
I'm living in the tombs.[3]

The single most important event of Lincoln's young life occurred in 1828, when he and his cousin John Hanks poled a flatboat piled with goods all the way to New Orleans, sold them off, then took a steamboat home. Lincoln's hatred of slavery dates from that journey. He was morally repelled by the sight of blacks chained, whipped, prodded, and disdained. His most haunting experience was witnessing a young mulatto woman on an auction block surrounded by leering bidders. He later wrote that "I am naturally antislavery. If slavery is not wrong, nothing is wrong. I cannot remember when I did not think so."[4]

Lincoln emerged from his first two decades with an enduring legacy. From an early age, he deplored the bullying of the weak by the strong and cruelty to animals. Although outwardly gregarious, he encased his deepest feelings, turtle-like, within a hard, impenetrable shell. He hated physical labor and constantly sought to expand his mind through reading and discussion. He extolled reason and developed the ability to express himself through finely crafted arguments. Lincoln's childhood was not all ceaseless toil. He enjoyed telling stories, pulling pranks, and performing feats of strength. He reached his height of six foot, four inches by his late teens.

At age twenty-two, Lincoln was determined to cut loose from his family and begin life as an independent man.[5] He decided where to settle during a second journey to New Orleans, when his flatboat got stuck on the milldam across the Sangamon River at New Salem, Illinois, in April 1831. For some complex of reasons this hamlet appealed to him. In July he returned to New Salem, where he became a store clerk. A year later he was jobless when the store went bankrupt. He resorted to hiring himself out as a day laborer.

Abraham Lincoln won his first election in 1832, when most men in his militia company voted for him as their captain. Illinois's governor had mustered the militia for Black Hawk's War, caused when that chief led his Sauk and Fox people from west of the Mississippi River into the state in a desperate search for food. Lincoln's company never fired a shot in the campaign that eventually crushed Black Hawk and his followers. Indeed, during his three-month stint as a soldier, his only decisive action was to save rather than take a life. One evening an old Indian man appeared in their camp with an official safe-conduct pass. Some of the militia called for murdering him. At that "Lincoln jumped between our men & the Indian and said we must not shed his blood." In a typical expression of how twisted frontier values could get, "some thought Lincoln was a coward because" he saved the Indian's life. To this Lincoln replied, "If any one doubts my Courage let him try it."[6]

This fleeting leadership experience whetted his appetite for more. Later that year he ran for the state legislature. Although he came in eighth in a thirteen-man race, he saw his loss not as a failure but an opportunity for its insights in how to do better the next time. His first public speech revealed a remarkable maturity of thought and emotions for someone so young. He embraced the Whig Party platform of a government that nurtured the nation's development by building roads, canals, railroads, and ports; a protective tariff that encouraged investments in industry and raised federal revenues; and universal education for children.[7]

He sought a comfortable middle-class life by scrapping together his savings and investing in a store with William Berry. Unfortunately Berry was an alcoholic who drank himself to death and drained the store's profits; he left Lincoln with a $1,100 debt that took him fifteen years to pay off. Once again, Lincoln reverted to earning money by splitting rails, cutting firewood, and performing other hard manual work.

An important opportunity arose for Lincoln in May 1833, when he was appointed New Salem's postmaster. No available local job was then better suited for him. Post offices were community centers in early America. People gathered there to chat, swap tales, make friends, cut deals, and peruse newspapers. It was the perfect place for an ambitious young man at once to develop his mind and a political following. It was also the perfect place to read when customers were scarce. His most influential books during those years were Thomas Paine's *Age of Reason* and Constantin de Volney's *Ruins of Civilization*, each critical of organized religion. He honed his speaking and thinking skills by attending the debate club. Most importantly, he studied law informally by reading texts, most notably William Blackstone's *Commentaries* and the *Revised Laws of Illinois*. He passed the bar in September 1836.[8]

Most ambitious men get their law licenses before they venture into politics. Not Lincoln, who launched his political career four years earlier in 1832, when he was just twenty-three years old, then won his first campaign to be an Illinois assemblyman in 1834 and reelection campaigns in 1836, 1838, and 1840.[9] His most critical act during those eight years came on March 3, 1837, when he joined five other dissidents to vote against an overwhelming seventy-six-member majority who resolved that "we highly disapprove of the formation of abolition societies," upheld as "sacred" the "right of property in slaves," and asserted that Congress "cannot abolish slavery in the District of Columbia, against the consent of its citizens."[10]

As a politician, Abraham Lincoln modeled himself after Whig Party leader Henry Clay. He described Clay as "my beau ideal of a statesman" and added, "during my whole political life I have loved and revered him as a teacher and leader."[11] In his 1852 eulogy, he lauded Clay as "that truly national man" who "loved his country because it was a free country" and "saw in such the advancement, prosperity, and glory of human liberty, human rights, and human nature." Lincoln may have also found in Clay a father figure who was everything that his own ignorant and at times brutal father was not.[12] In Clay, Lincoln saw reflected a highly intelligent, largely self-taught, self-made man who eloquently advocated progressive, pragmatic policies to strengthen the nation economically, politically, and morally.[13]

Lincoln championed Clay's American System, whose three key policies were designed to develop America's economy—a protective tariff, internal improvements, and a U.S. bank to regulate the monetary system. That Whig agenda was the latest incarnation of the political philosophy articulated by Alexander Hamilton and his Federalist Party in the 1790s. Lincoln was a Whig as much for the image it conveyed as the policies it espoused. Whigs represented self-made, worldly, sophisticated American men. There was also a very practical reason: "The man who is of neither party is not—cannot be of any consequence."[14]

Lincoln rose steadily in the state's Whig Party ranks. From its birth in 1832 until its demise in 1854, the Whig Party battled the Democratic Party across much of the nation, although its strength lay mostly in the North. Illinois mirrored the national distribution of party power. Like Indiana and Ohio, Illinois was split politically north and south. Northerners from back east had settled the state's northern half and southerners the southern half. Not surprisingly, Whigs and later Republicans tended to dominate northern Illinois and Democrats, southern Illinois.

Lincoln moved to Springfield on April 15, 1837, and the same day found lodging with Joshua Speed above his store.[15] Speed became Lincoln's most intimate friend, with whom he shared his innermost thoughts and a bed for four years. Most of this time two other young men, William Herndon and Charles Hurst, crowded into the same room. His first law partner was John Stuart, but in 1844 he established a partnership with Herndon that continued seventeen years, until he entered the White House. Herndon had recently passed the bar and was nine years younger than him. They remained friends until Lincoln's death. Herndon would later write a book that provided deep insights into Lincoln's character and early life.[16]

Lincoln's legal and political skills were interchangeable. He spoke with simple words and told engaging stories spiced with wit and wisdom that any voter or juror could understand. His advice to would-be lawyers reveals his core values: "Discourage litigation. Persuade your neighbors to compromise whenever you can. Point out to them how the nominal winner is often a real loser—in fees, expenses, and waste of time. As a peace-maker the lawyer has a superior opportunity of being a good man."[17]

He expressed key elements of his political philosophy in a speech before the Young Men's Lyceum in Springfield on January 27, 1838.[18] A vicious crime inspired his oration. Just two months earlier, a mob had murdered the outspoken abolitionist Elijah Lovejoy and destroyed his printing press in Alton, Illinois. Lincoln titled his speech "The Perpetuation of Our Political Institutions." He began by asking his audience to appreciate how fortunate they were to live in such a rich and free country due to the ability of the nation's founders "to display before an admiring world . . . the capability of a people to govern themselves." America's prosperity and democracy, however, faced a dire and worsening threat. This danger "cannot come from abroad. If destruction be our lot we must ourselves be its author and finisher. As a nation of freemen we must live through all time or die of suicide." Violent mobs would be the weapon whereby the nation self-destructed. Fortunately there was an antidote to this deadly poison: "Let every American, every lover of liberty, every well wisher to his posterity, swear by the blood of the Revolution never to violate in the least particular the laws of the country, and never to tolerate their violation by others. . . . Let reverence for the laws . . . become the political religion of the nation."[19]

Lincoln committed an act in September 1842 that was completely out of character. Had he gone through with it, he would have violated the very laws and institutions that he swore to uphold. Had he lost, the course of American and world history might have decisively shifted. What Lincoln did was to accept a challenge to a duel. The challenge arose after he anonymously ridiculed James Shields, a local Democratic Party leader, in the *Sangamon Journal*. He had no desire to duel but was egged on by several prominent Whig leaders. Fortunately the duel was averted when the seconds struck a deal whereby both men repudiated the fighting words that provoked them to "the field of honor." Lincoln typically drew life-changing lessons from this experience. He resolved that henceforth reason would command his emotions and he would never anonymously criticize anyone.[20]

What of Lincoln's love life? He was awkward among women and was said to be "deficient in those little links which make up the chain of woman's happiness."[21] He may have scared off many a potential mate with his gangly height and crude behavior. Shortly after moving to Springfield, he confessed that "I am quite as lonesome here as I ever was anywhere in my life. I have been spoken to by but one woman since I have been here and should not have been by her if she could have avoided it. I've never been to church yet and probably shall not be soon. I stay away because I am conscious I should not know how to behave."[22] Herndon recalled that "Lincoln had terribly strong passions for women—could scarcely keep his hands off them," but "his honor and a strong will . . . enabled him to put out the fires of his terrible passion."[23] Although he could be bumbling in words and demeanor around the fair sex, he was a man far ahead of his time when it came to women's rights. During his 1836 run for the Illinois assembly, he courageously aired the then-outlandish belief that women who paid taxes should be allowed to vote.[24]

Ann Rutledge became his life's first and perhaps only romantic love in 1835. He later recalled that "I did honestly—& truly love the girl & think often . . . of her now."[25] They planned to marry after Lincoln was admitted to the bar. Tragically, she contracted "brain fever," perhaps encephalitis, and died on August 25. Lincoln was crushed and for months was mired in deep depression.

The next year he began courting Mary Owens, who came from Kentucky to live with her sister, Lincoln's friend, in New Salem. His heart was not in it. He broke off the relationship by arguing that she would not be happy in Springfield and being with him would only compound her misery.[26] His reluctance is understandable given that her girth made her "a fair match for Falstaff" and with her he could not "avoid thinking of my mother . . . not from withered features—for her skin was too full of fat to permit of its contracting into wrinkles—but from her want of teeth." He got involved with her in the first place because of his rash promise to her sister that he would marry Owens sight unseen. The experience was so unsettling that he concluded "never again to think of marrying, and for this reason I can never be satisfied with anyone who would be blockhead enough to have me."[27]

Mary Todd became the wife if not the love of Lincoln's life.[28] She had grown up in wealth, with house slaves and finishing schools as the pampered daughter of a leading merchant of Lexington, Kentucky. In 1837 she came to Springfield to escape a mean stepmother and stay with her older sister. She later enjoyed recalling her first encounter with Lincoln at a ball. He mustered his courage, strode up to her, and admitted that he wanted to dance with her "in the worst way." And so, she would add with a laugh, he did.[29]

What attracted Lincoln to Mary? She was bright, educated, vivacious, and voluptuous. Perhaps as important, her father was a rich Whig and friend of Henry Clay. Mary appeared to be the ideal trophy wife for an ambitious politician. But as he courted her he saw the flaws behind her appearance. Vain, spoiled, and nervous, she craved to be constantly the center of attention and the belle of the ball. Whenever stymied she could erupt with tantrums or burrow in bed with splitting headaches.

Understandably Lincoln got cold feet not long after he initially proposed and she accepted. The break came in December 1841, when he told Mary that he did not love her. She burst into tears. His resolve melted: "I found the tears trickling down my own cheeks. I caught her in my arms and kissed her."[30] That reconciliation was fleeting. He ended their relationship on New Year's Day 1841. Yet, rather than feel relief, he fell into a deep depression. To his law partner John Stuart he revealed that "I am now the most miserable man living. . . . To remain as I am is impossible; I must die or be better." He finally roused himself and visited his friend Joshua Speed, who had returned to his family's home in Kentucky and was himself torn over whether to wed his fiancée. Eventually both men reluctantly decided that wedlock was the lesser evil over a lifetime of bachelorhood.[31]

At age thirty-three, Lincoln married Mary on November 4, 1842. A week later he wrote a friend, "Nothing new here except my marrying, which to me is matter of profound wonder."[32] Their first child, Robert Todd, was born on August 1, 1843. With time they would have three more sons, Edward Baker on March 10, 1846, William Wallace on December 21, 1850, and Thomas, nicknamed Tad, on April 4, 1853.

Lincoln ran for his district's seat in the House of Representatives in 1846.[33] His opponent was Peter Cartwright, a Methodist circuit rider. Among the charges that he and his supporters leveled against Lincoln was that he scorned religion. To this, Lincoln offered an honest and heartfelt reply: "That I am not a member of any Christian Church is true, but I have never denied the truth of the Scriptures; and I have never spoken with intentional disregard of religion in general, or of any denomination of Christians in particular." He asserted that he could not "support a man for office whom I knew to be an open enemy of, and scoffer of, religion" and that no "man has the right thus to insult the feelings, and injure the morals of the community in which he may live."[34]

After he won on August 3, 1846, Lincoln and his family had plenty of time to prepare for their move to Washington and his new duties. The next Congress was not scheduled to open for another year and a half, in

December 1847. The Lincolns reached Washington City on December 2, 1847, just days before Congress reconvened. After settling his family into a boardinghouse, Lincoln got to work. His most notable acts were the eight resolutions that he introduced on December 22, 1847, calling on the Polk administration to submit all documents to prove their assertion that Mexico initiated the war, and when those were not forthcoming, his blistering condemnation of the president and his war on January 12, 1848. Although he opposed the war, he supported the troops by voting for every military appropriation bill.

What was it like to attend a Lincoln speech? He was a first-rate orator. Like Jesus, he liked to illustrate his points with parables and folksy images that penetrated his listeners' hearts and minds. At times he conveyed the loftiest of thoughts or most daunting of challenges through haunting, poetic phrases that will enrich humanity to the end of time. Yet, while nearly all enjoyed the substance and style of his words, some were confounded by his delivery of them:

> His voice was not musical, rather high keyed . . . [yet] had an exceedingly penetrating, far reaching quality. The looks of the audience convince me that every word he spoke was understood at the remotest edges of the vast assemblage. His gesture was awkward. He swung his long arms sometimes in a very ungraceful manner. Now and then he would bend his body with a sudden downward jerk, and then shoot up again with a vehemence that raised him to his tiptoes and made him look much taller than he really was. There was, however, a tone of earnest truthfulness, of elevated noble sentiment, of kindly sympathy, which added greatly to the strength of his arguments. . . . Even when attacking his opponent . . . there was still a certain something in his utterances making his hearers feel that those thrusts came from a reluctant heart, and that he would much rather have treated his foe as a friend.[35]

Then there was his appearance. Lincoln's face and tall, lean body are instantly recognizable to those familiar with the iconic photographs. Yet these images fail to convey how he moved and how his contemporaries saw him. Herndon leaves this brilliant description: "He was thin, wiry, sinewy, raw-boned; thin through the breast through the back, and narrow across the shoulder; standing he leaned forward. . . . The whole man, body and mind, worked slowly, as if it needed oiling. . . . When he walked he moved cautiously but firmly; his long arms and giant hands swung down by his side."[36]

Lincoln was incessantly reminded of his gangly, homely appearance by opponents and well-wishers alike. He typically tried to disarm with self-deprecating humor one excuse not to vote for him. He liked to tell the story of the woman who stops an ugly man and calls him "the homeliest man I ever saw." The man agrees but explains that "I can't help it." To that the woman retorts, "No, I suppose not, but you might stay at home!"[37] One can imagine the mirth with which Lincoln told that story but also the twinge of inner hurt. After being elected to the White House, he famously followed a young girl's advice that a beard might make him look more appealing.

What of the statesman behind his unforgettable voice and appearance?[38] Two powerful forces, pragmatism and principles, or what was doable and what was ideal, guided Lincoln. Principles provided the parameters within which he practiced politics as the art of the possible. He deconstructed any problem, examined how all the parts fit together, then proposed ways to right what was wrong: "If we could first know where we are and whither we are tending, we could better judge what to do, and how to do it."[39] If one proposal failed to inspire enough support to win approval, he devised another. The best example of this was his approach to slavery. From a young age he hated slavery and believed that ideally it should be abolished. Yet as a politician he adjusted his positions to what was feasible, with four distinct phases: tolerating its legality under the Constitution; preventing its expansion to new territories; asserting a limited emancipation justified by military necessity; and finally, supporting a constitutional amendment that completely abolished slavery. When a congressman complained, "Mr. President, you have changed your mind entirely within a short time," he replied, "I don't think much of a man who is not wiser today than he was yesterday."[40]

Hard reason rather than lofty sentiment was Lincoln's political and intellectual rudder. Young Lincoln honed his thinking to the highest levels by studying the six books of Euclid's geometry. Bolstering his command of reason was an emotional maturity rarely attained by most so-called adults. He had the power to check his sorrows and convert his anger into humor and wisdom. His self-deprecating wit helped endear him to many people. He was a teetotaler, an attribute that was a political encumbrance in that hard-drinking age. Yet his abstinence reflected his character. The power of reason obviously diminishes with each tip of the jug. His obsession with self-control had many sources, of which watching a teenage friend go insane was certainly the most haunting, followed by his first business partner drinking himself to death.

Work pressures strained his marriage. In April 1848 Mary and the boys returned to Springfield. In perhaps his most intimate surviving letter to Mary, he confessed, "In this troublesome world, we are never quite satisfied. When you were here, I thought you hindered me some in attending to business; but now, having nothing but business . . . it has grown exceedingly tasteless to me. . . . I hate to stay in this old room by myself." It took a couple of months before Mary expressed a wish to return. Lincoln's reply reveals whose behavior prompted their separation: "Will you be a good girl in all things if I consent? Then come along . . . as soon as possible."[41]

Melancholy, or enduring feelings of profound wonder and sadness for life's mingled beauties, tragedies, and intransigence, shadowed Lincoln throughout his life. These feelings were natural to him but were exacerbated by the early deaths of his beloved mother, sister, and Ann Rutledge and his father's unrelenting attempts to harness and exploit him. Lincoln described his melancholy as "a misfortune not a fault."[42] He tried to sublimate his "misfortune" with learning, writing, and speaking about the world's most pressing issues, along with sharing the wit and wisdom for which he became renowned. He was perhaps most happy when he was playing with his sons or riding the court circuit with his fellow lawyers. Yet at times these diversions failed and his melancholy morphed into outright depression that deprived him of sleep through chronic insomnia and bad dreams and several times in his twenties pushed him to the brink of self-destruction.

Lincoln's religious beliefs heightened his melancholy.[43] Like such notable earlier Americans as Benjamin Franklin, George Washington, Alexander Hamilton, and Thomas Jefferson, he was a Deist who believed that God and nature's universal laws were one. There was no personal God, miracles, or afterlife, only the infinite universe and the laws that governed it. When asked if he believed in life after death, he replied,

"I'm afraid there isn't. It isn't a pleasant thing to think that when we die that is the last of us."[44]

This outlook changed after he assumed the presidency and the crushing burdens of fighting a civil war. He increasingly appealed to a personal God for help in his endeavors. He came to believe that "without the assistance of the Divine Being I cannot succeed."[45] Early in the war, he explained that

> I am not a man of a very hopeful temperament. . . . But believing
> . . . that our cause is just, and relying on God for help, I firmly
> believe we shall conquer. . . . I am sometimes astonished at the
> part I am playing in this terrible drama. I can hardly believe I am
> the same person I was a few months ago when I was living my
> humble way . . . in Springfield. . . . I would gladly take my neck
> from under this yoke, and go home . . . to Springfield. . . . But
> . . . it has pleased Almighty God to put me in my present posi-
> tion, and looking to him for divine guidance, I must work out
> my destiny as best I can.[46]

Lincoln tended to believe that free will was an illusion in a world where everything was predetermined. This fatalism was imbedded from his earliest years by his parents and backwoods preachers who were Separate Baptists committed to a strict Calvinist predeterminism. He explained that "early in life I was inclined to believe in . . . the 'Doctrine of Necessity' that . . . the human mind is impelled to action, or held in rest by some power, over which the mind itself has no control."[47] Shortly before entering the White House, Lincoln anticipated himself as president as merely "an accidental instrument, temporary, and to serve but for a limited time."[48] Looking back through his presidency, he concluded that he had not "controlled events, but confess plainly that events have controlled me. Now at the end of three years struggle the nation's condition is not what either party or any man devised or expected. God alone can claim it."[49]

Lincoln's fatalism appears to refute his extraordinary life whereby he rose from poverty to the presidency and during four years in the White House provided decisive, hands-on leadership that won a war, reunited the nation, and ended slavery. He was a self-made man who insisted that the "way for a young man to rise is to improve himself every way he can" and that he "must not wait to be brought forward by the older men."[50]

How did he reconcile this contradiction between fatalism and drive? His answer was that for reasons far beyond human understanding some powerful universal force popularly called Providence or God directed each step of his life or anyone else's. Today, of course, analysts find answers not in the stars but deep in one's psyche. However, in the pre-Freudian age in which Lincoln lived, a Deist explanation of life was about as sophisticated as any available.

Lincoln supplemented his Deism with a bleak view of human nature. He believed that "all human actions were caused by motives, and at the bottom of these motives was self."[51] Each self was inherently selfish even if individual motives differed. Providence then combined with circumstances to work through one's motivation to determine what one did in life. Providence was at once fickle, inexplicable, and all powerful. This left "the human mind . . . impelled to action or held in rest by some power over which the mind itself has no control."[52] Human nature stirred empathy rather than cynicism in him. He was a deeply compassionate, forgiving, and nurturing man who sought to channel the self-interest of others into beliefs and acts that benefited humanity.

In Lincoln's first political speech in 1832, he revealed the motivation that drove him: "Every man is said to have his peculiar ambition. . . . I can say . . . that I have no other so great as that of being truly esteemed of my fellow-men, by rendering myself worthy of their esteem."[53] From this motivation came astonishing achievements that changed the world.

3

Uncle Tom's Cabin

So this is the little lady who made this big war.

ABRAHAM LINCOLN

Liberty for the few—Slavery, in every form, for the mass!

GEORGE FITZHUGH

Enslave but a single human being and the liberty of the world is put
in peril. . . . The war [against slavery] is a war of extermination
and I will perish before an inch shall be surrendered, seeing that
the liberties of mankind and harmony of the universe, and the
authority and majesty of Almighty God, are involved in the issue.

WILLIAM LLOYD GARRISON

The state of Georgia will . . . resist . . . any action of Congress
upon the subject of slavery . . . incompatible with the safety
and domestic tranquility, the rights and honor of the slave-
holding states, or any refusal to admit as a state any
territory . . . because of the existence of slavery.

GEORGIA CONVENTION

If destruction be our lot we must ourselves be its author and finisher.
As a nation of freemen we must live through all time or die of suicide.

ABRAHAM LINCOLN

Freedom is not possible without slavery.

RICHMOND (VA) ENQUIRER

Abraham Lincoln made perhaps the most awkward greeting of his life when he hosted Harriet Beecher Stowe at the White House in 1862. To the author of the antislavery novel *Uncle Tom's Cabin; or, Life among the Lowly*, he exclaimed, "So this is the little lady who made this big war." Stowe's reaction was not recorded, but acute embarrassment and irritation would have been understandable.[1]

Stowe was inspired to write her novel after the 1850 Fugitive Slave Act forced free state and local governments and their citizens to aid masters in recovering their escaped slaves or else suffer fines and prison. She then lived in Cincinnati, just across the Ohio River from slavery's northern boundary. Cincinnati had a swelling black population, of whom many were escaped slaves. Her novel undoubtedly changed more minds about slavery's evils than all the editorials and speeches by abolitionists over the decades. The story first reached a mass audience as a weekly serial in the newspaper the *National Era* from mid-1851 to spring 1852, during which time speculation over what would happen next in the story animated countless conversations across the North and beyond. When *Uncle Tom's Cabin* appeared as a book in 1852, it swiftly broke the existing best-seller record, with three hundred thousand copies snatched up the first year alone and two million by the time eleven slave states rebelled against the United States nine years later.[2]

The political impact of *Uncle Tom's Cabin* far exceeded its literary qualities. Even then critics noted its melodrama, sentimentality, and clichés of character and plot. Yet this novel forced ever more northerners to contemplate slavery's moral and economic costs, and southerners to conjure up ever more tortured "logic" to defend their "peculiar institution."

It is often remarked that slavery was America's original sin, although the continent's original inhabitants might dispute this.[3] Nonetheless, the tragic matrix of race, slavery, wealth, and power extends back nearly to the nation's beginning. It remains unclear whether the shipload of blacks sold by a Dutch sea captain to Jamestown's leaders in 1619 ended up as slaves or indentured servants. Regardless, this transaction decisively altered the course of what would become American civilization. Ironically, given New England's later leading role in the abolition movement, slavery was first legalized in Massachusetts in 1641 and in Connecticut in 1650 but in Virginia not until 1661, two generations after that first fatal shipload of chained Africans dropped anchor. Although slavery eventually existed in every colony, the proportion of whites to blacks widened the farther north and narrowed the farther south one journeyed. For nearly two and a half centuries, nine of ten blacks throughout first the colonies and then the states were slaves. Slavery was best suited to large-scale plantations producing commodities like tobacco, cotton, sugarcane, indigo, and rice.

Americans justified their war of independence from Britain by declaring the self-evident truth "that all men are created equal, that they are endowed by their Creator with certain inalienable rights, that among these are life, liberty and the pursuit of happiness." Morally developed individuals thereafter deplored the discrepancy between these ideals and the reality that slaves numbered one of five people then living in the new United States.

This hypocrisy troubled most of the nation's founders, among whom many themselves were masters. George Washington and Thomas Jefferson were the most prominent leaders who at once hated slavery yet kept slaves all their lives. Jefferson admitted in *Notes on the State of Virginia* that "the whole commerce between master and slave is a perpetual exercise of the . . . most unremitting despotism on the one part, and degrading submission on the other. Our children see this and learn to imitate it." He described slavery's moral dilemma as "holding the wolf by its ears," in which dangers lurked in both holding on and letting go. He feared that these pent-up, raging hatreds "will probably never end but in the extermination of one or the other race."[4]

A few founders did more than deplore the institution. In 1784 Benjamin Franklin, Alexander Hamilton, and John Jay founded the Pennsylvania Society for the Abolition of Slavery. The following year Hamilton and Jay formed the New York Society for the Manumission of Slaves. In 1794 these two groups established the American Convention for Promoting the Abolition of Slavery and Improving the Condition of the African Race.

The Constitution's framers at once upheld slavery's legality and assumed that the institution would eventually die a natural death. Out of shame they barred the word *slave* from the Constitution. Yet they alluded to and allowed the institution by counting three slaves for every five white people in a state's population to determine how to apportion representatives and taxes, requiring states where slaves had escaped to assist masters in recovering their chattel, and delaying to 1808 any law outlawing the importation of slaves.

Congress first asserted its power to regulate slavery with the 1787 Northwest Ordinance that forbade slavery north of the Ohio River, then the 1790 Southwest Ordinance that permitted slavery south of the Ohio River. From 1789 to 1854, most politicians struggled to uphold a balance between slave and free states. To this end, they tried to admit pairs of free and slave states, like Indiana and Mississippi, Illinois and Alabama, Maine and Missouri, and Michigan and Arkansas. With this balance, slavocrats could block in the Senate, where each state has two senators regardless of its population, any antislavery bill that emanated from the House of Representatives, where more seats were apportioned each decade to the North, with its rapidly growing population. Congress's power to regulate slavery culminated with the 1820 compromise that let in Missouri and Maine as a slave and free state, respectively, and drew a line at 36°30′ north latitude from Missouri to the Rocky Mountain watershed, with slavery permitted south and forbidden north of that line.

At the time or soon after America won independence most states acted on the Revolution's ideals by granting limited political rights to free black men. By 1790 free blacks could vote in Vermont, New Hampshire, Massachusetts, Rhode Island, Connecticut, Pennsylvania, New York, New Jersey, Delaware, Maryland, and North Carolina. Free blacks received that right in Kentucky in 1792 and Tennessee in 1796.

Tragically, this revolution provoked a counterrevolution. In 1799 Kentucky became the first state to rescind its rights for free blacks and, one by one, nearly every state enacted similar laws that imposed varying degrees of political, economic, and social discrimination. Laws segregated blacks in schooling, housing, public transportation, marriage, and most jobs. Some states tried to limit the presence of blacks. Ohio, Indiana, Illinois, Iowa, and Oregon forbade any new blacks from residing within their borders or required them to post expensive bonds to guarantee good behavior. By 1850 blacks had equal voting rights and could serve on juries only in Maine, Massachusetts, Vermont, and New Hampshire.[5]

This racist backlash split abolitionists. Those of the revolutionary era believed in freeing, improving, and integrating blacks within white society, and countless abolitionists in the nineteenth century upheld these values. But a different approach appeared with the American Colonization Society's founding in 1816 by Henry Clay, John Marshall, James Madison, and James Monroe, among others, who sought to liberate blacks and expatriate them to Africa. Abolitionists also split over whether emancipation should be gradual or immediate and compensated or not.[6]

Divisions among abolitionists reflected their different backgrounds. Those favoring the gradual compensation of owners and the expatriation of blacks tended to be slaveholders who sought government's aid in ridding themselves of their moral dilemma. During the nineteenth century, those advocating eventual abolition and integration, like Theodore Weld, James Birney, the brothers Arthur and Lewis Tappan, the sisters Angelina and Sarah Grimke, Gerrit Smith, Charles Finney, Benjamin Lundy, Theodore Parker, Lydia Maria Child, and Harriet Beecher Stowe, enjoyed abundant wealth and education and were members of liberal Christian sects like the Unitarians and Quakers. This did not hold true for abolitionism's most celebrated and reviled advocate.

Probably no abolitionist was more influential than William Lloyd Garrison.[7] He began his life in poverty after his father abandoned his family and a fire destroyed their home along with much of the rest of Newburyport, Massachusetts. As a young teenager Garrison became an apprentice printer at a newspaper, where he learned literally and figuratively how to construct arguments on the era's leading issues. His powerful intellect, ambitions, and sense of justice led him swiftly to master the trade and, when he was twenty-one, launch his own newspaper, the *Free Press*. His printing skills and impassioned essays inspired Benjamin Lundy, who asked him to coedit Lundy's monthly newspaper, the *Genius of Universal Emancipation*, in Baltimore. During his half-year sojourn, Garrison converted from believing in gradual, compensated emancipation to immediate, uncompensated, and integrated emancipation. Among the millions of words he wrote or spoke, these perhaps best capture his core beliefs: "Enslave but a single human being and the liberty of the world is put in peril. . . . The war [against slavery] is a war of extermination and I will perish before an inch shall be surrendered, seeing that the liberties of mankind and harmony of the universe, and the authority and majesty of Almighty God, are involved in the issue."[8]

This uncompromising moral stance repeatedly got Garrison into trouble with lawsuits or clubs wielded by slavocrats and into squabbles with moderate abolitionists. In 1830 he was jailed for libeling a local slaveholder. This precipitated his split with Lundy, who was a gradualist. Garrison moved to Boston, where, on New Year's Day 1831, he printed the first edition of his newspaper, the *Liberator*, which would appear weekly until 1866, and in 1832 founded the New England Anti-Slavery Society. Then, on December 4, 1833, Garrison was a leading force among sixty-two delegates who established the American Anti-Slavery Society in Philadelphia. Membership soared to 250,000 members among 1,350 branches by 1838.[9]

Black abolitionists were just as divided.[10] David Walker helped found the Massachusetts General Colored Association, edited the *Freedom's Journal*, and in 1829 issued his "Appeal to the Colored People of the World," whereby he called on blacks to revolt against their oppressors. In contrast, Frederick Douglass all along emphasized the peaceful liberation of blacks from slavery, poverty, and discrimination, although with time he shifted from being a gradualist into an immediatist. After escaping from slavery as a young man, he eventually became the leading black abolitionist. He first achieved fame with the publication in 1845 of his *Narrative of the Life of Frederick Douglass: An American Slave, Written by Himself*. He proved to be as skilled a speaker as a writer as he traveled the abolitionist circuit. His home was Rochester, New York, where he published his weekly abolitionist newspaper, the *North Star*.[11]

Being an abolitionist was a dangerous vocation for blacks and whites alike. Slavocrats beat, tarred and feathered, jailed, and at times murdered abolitionists and wrecked their offices and printing presses. The most notorious terrorist act was the murder of Elijah Lovejoy and destruction of his printing press at Alton, Illinois, in November 1837. Violence and even riots of white supremacists against blacks and abolitionists erupted throughout the antebellum era, with 21 during the 1820s, 115 during the 1830s, 64 during the 1840s, and 46 during the 1850s.[12]

With time the power balance among abolitionists shifted from grad-
ualists to immediatists, and the movement itself from America's radical fringe to the political mainstream. By the end of the Civil War's
fourth blood-soaked year, the immediate, uncompensated abolition of
slavery was grounded in American policy, law, and the Constitution as
demanded by majorities in Congress and among the public.

Over time slaveholders developed an ideology to justify their way of life
that is best called slavocracy and its adherents slavocrats, terms coined
in the 1830s.[13] Slavocracy, however, suffered from two fatal flaws—it
was grounded in legal and moral quicksand. Slavocrats compounded
these flaws by reacting with rage rather than soul-searching when critics
exposed the depravity of their beliefs and lifestyles. They pummeled
their critics with increasingly extreme demagoguery and eventually with
violence. This, of course, only provided critics with more ammunition
to expose slavocracy's pathologies.

Slavocrats tried to build a legal wall around slavery with the notion
of states' rights, the belief that the United States was merely a confed-
eration of sovereign states with each reserving the right to nullify any
federal law and even secede. This belief, however, is rooted in wishful
thinking rather than the law. One searches in vain for any hint of this
dogma in the Constitution, the Federalist Papers, or other expressions
of the framers' original intent. Indeed, the overwhelming evidence is
that those who designed and approved the Constitution sought to
establish an enduring, sovereign national and republican government.
Chief Justice John Marshall explained this in the Supreme Court's
1821 *Cohens v. Virginia* decision: "In war we are one people. In making
peace we are one people. In all commercial regulations we are one and
the same people. In many other respects the American people are one,
and the government which is alone capable of controlling and manag-
ing their interests in all these respects is the government of the Union.
It is their government and in that character they have no other."[14] Yet
the resounding refutation of states' rights by history and the Supreme
Court did not stop countless people from fervently believing in it and
just as fervently acting on this belief.

The "moral" arguments of slavocrats were just as delusional and dog-
matically asserted. If eighteenth- and early nineteenth-century slavehold-

ers tended to defend their way of life as "a necessary evil," subsequent generations insisted that slavery was "a positive good" for everyone, especially childlike blacks who would be helpless savages without their masters' paternal care.[15] Senator John Calhoun of South Carolina explained that "the two great divisions of society are not the rich and the poor, but white and black; and all the former, the poor as well as the rich, belong to the upper class." Senator William Yancey of Alabama insisted that the nation's founders "built this government on two ideas. The first is that the white race is the citizen, and the master race. . . . The second is that the negro is the inferior race." No one developed slavocracy as an ideology further than George Fitzhugh. In his 1854 book *Sociology for the South; or, the Failure of Free Society*, he tried to prove with tortured logic that slave labor was far more humane than free labor and that a privileged elite was morally and mentally entitled to rule over everyone else. He summed up slavocracy with the phrase "Liberty for the few—Slavery, in every form, for the mass!" Slavocracy's justification for enslaving blacks was best summarized in the title of his 1857 book, *Cannibals All!; or, Slaves without Masters*.[16] Slavocracy's sheer Orwellian "logic" was most succinctly expressed by the *Richmond (va) Enquirer*: "Freedom is not possible without slavery."[17]

A pathological mindset upheld a pathological economic system. To justify slavery, slavocrats had to dehumanize their chattel. How else could they justify enchaining and beating, sometimes raping, and occasionally outright murdering their slaves if they were fellow humans? At best blacks were at the mental and moral level of children who forced their masters to care for them, and at worst they were nothing but beasts tamable only with the lash.

Slavocracy was rooted in cultural as well as racial stereotypes. Slavocrats romanticized themselves and their region as characterized by honor and chivalry that contrasted with Yankee coldheartedness and greed.[18] From a psychological perspective, this utterly deluded view is understandable. Slaveholders were at the apex of two overlapping economic, social, and political hierarchies grounded respectively in the exploitation of black slaves and white tenants. What could be more coldhearted and greedy? Few people have the strength of character to admit such a harsh truth about themselves. To do so would logically and morally demand a revolution in one's way of life. So rather than come to terms with their own pathologies, slaveholders projected them onto hated others—Yankees and especially abolitionists.

Slavocrats condemned abolitionists for provoking thoughts of liberation among their chattel, then assisting their escape. They were enraged by the antislavery pamphlets smuggled into the South and the antislavery petitions introduced in Congress. Each slave state passed laws that harshly punished anyone guilty of distributing abolitionist literature. In Congress, slavocrats succeeded in grossly violating the Constitution by imposing a formal gag rule in the House of Representatives from 1836 to 1844, and an informal gag rule in the Senate throughout the antebellum era, on any debate of antislavery petitions. This merely provoked abolitionists to increase the number of petitions and number of signatures on each that they submitted to Congress.

The growing movement of those who would limit or abolish slavery provoked the worst primordial existential fears and challenged the basest interests of slavocrats. Only one event worried slavocrats more than being deprived of their slaves, and that was being murdered by their slaves. Each decade or so, an aborted or realized slave revolt reinforced this deep fear. Southerners pointed to the thwarted plots of Gabriel Prosser in Virginia in 1800 or Denmark Vesey in South Carolina in 1822, or Nat Turner's bloody revolt in Virginia in 1831 in which fifty-seven white men, women, and children were murdered before it was crushed. Then there were the occasional murders of masters by individual slaves. These horrendous crimes must be weighed against the reality that they were extremely rare, statistical near nullities amid four million slaves. But in this as in all related issues, slavocrats spotlighted anything that justified their beliefs and obscured the rest.

Perversely, this fear provoked slaveholders to cling all the more tightly to their way of life rather than discard it. They became increasingly frantic not just to defend but to expand slavery as widely as possible. The most zealously outspoken slavocrats—Robert Barnwell Rhett, who published the *Charleston (sc) Mercury*; George Fitzhugh, the best-selling author; and the senators Edmund Ruffin of Virginia, Robert Barnwell Rhett of South Carolina, and William Yancey of Alabama—became known as the "fire-eaters." Inspired by John Calhoun's speeches and writings, they shrilly advocated nullification and secession if necessary to defend slavery. The fire-eaters demanded that slavery be free everywhere and that the African slave trade be reinstated, which would overturn existing American law and defy international law.[19]

Even this was not good enough for fire-eaters, who increasingly advocated breaking away from the United States and forming their own country. Senator Alexander Stephens of Georgia noted as early as December 1849 that "the feeling among the Southern members for a dissolution of the Union—if the antislavery [measures] should be pressed to extremity—is becoming much more general. . . . Men are now beginning to talk of it seriously, who, twelve months ago, hardly permitted themselves to think of it."[20] This vision first peaked on June 3, 1850, when delegates from fourteen slave states met in a states' rights convention at Nashville. Over the next nine days, although they vented their rage at anyone who disputed the God-given right of slaveholding, majorities upheld the 1820 Missouri Compromise and rejected secession. When this states' rights group reconvened in November, only seven delegations attended; elsewhere Unionists blocked the efforts of extremists to get state governments officially to join the proceedings. Nonetheless, these states' rights conventions were dress rehearsals for the Confederacy's birth little more than a decade later.

Slaveholders were increasingly aware that history was rapidly turning against their way of life as more governments and people in the Western world viewed slavery as evil. Britain outlawed the international slave trade in 1808 and abolished slavery in 1833. The countries that won independence from the Spanish Empire all ended slavery during the 1820s. By 1860 the United States, Brazil, and Cuba were the only Western Hemisphere countries where slavery was legal. Carl Schurz of Wisconsin spotlighted the reality that slavocrats were fighting an increasingly powerful current of history: "Slaveholders of America . . . Are you really in earnest when you speak of perpetuating slavery? . . . You stand against a hopeful world, alone against a great century, fighting your hopeless fight . . . against the onward march of civilization."[21]

Slavocrats grew more extreme and zealous in defending their institution as the proportion of slaveholders diminished. While more than one of three, or 36 percent, of southern whites owned slaves in 1830, that ratio plummeted to only one of four, or 26 percent, in 1860. That the slavocrats led their region into secession, rebellion, and war against the United States in 1860 is at once ironic and understandable.[22]

The thirteen years between the Mexican War's end in 1848 and the Civil War's beginning in 1861 differed in a crucial way from the Jacksonian era that preceded them.[23] The most obvious was that a new generation of political leaders replaced the Great Triumvirate—Henry Clay, Daniel Webster, and John Calhoun—that had dominated the Age of Jackson. The halls of the Senate resounded with the heated and eloquent words of Stephen Douglas, William Seward, Jefferson Davis, and Charles Sumner. Although slavery remained the toxic core of American politics, the political center increasingly frayed toward its extremes—abolitionism and secessionism. A series of events radicalized more northerners and southerners, with the former angrily pointing to the 1850 Fugitive Slave Act, 1854 Kansas-Nebraska Act, and 1857 Dred Scott Supreme Court decision, the latter to John Brown's 1859 Harpers Ferry raid, and both to Bloody Kansas.

When Zachary Taylor took the presidential oath on March 4, 1849, Americans celebrated him as a national hero but had no idea what he might do in the White House.[24] He had been a professional soldier since he received a second lieutenant's commission in 1808, had fought in the War of 1812, the Black Hawk War, and the Seminole War, and during the Mexican War commanded an army that won every battle— Resaca de la Palma, Palo Alto, Monterrey, and Buena Vista—that it fought. As a tactician, he preferred the massed bayonet charge straight at the enemy. He was renowned for his utter calm as bullets or arrows whizzed past. He was a soldier's soldier who shared his men's discomforts. He was anything but pretentious. As a general, he got away with wearing civilian work clothes and a straw hat rather than a uniform.

What did Taylor believe in? Politics really did not interest him; he never voted in an election before 1848. His views and choices came from his gut and heart rather than his mind. Indeed, he was malleable to the point of being contradictory. He at once championed the Union and states' rights. He was a Whig who mildly opposed a protective tariff, internal improvements, and a national bank. He was a slaveholder who opposed slavery's expansion in the newly conquered territories. From the Whig Party's perspective, these paradoxes along with his distinguished army career made him a winning candidate. For voters he was an inkblot test upon which to project their own views. He was a down-to-earth man of the people who could be nearly all things to nearly all people.

As president, Taylor was notable not for any enduring achievements but for a couple of "lasts"—he was the last slaveholder and Whig to live in the White House. Nonetheless he did advocate clear positions on issues that tended to split the difference between extremes. He favored the admission of California, Utah, and New Mexico as states, with their respective peoples to decide whether or not to permit slavery. He not only opposed but tried to stop filibustering expeditions launched from American soil. He backed a treaty whereby the United States and Britain agreed not to build a canal across Nicaragua without the other's approval. He did not live long enough to realize these views. Taylor died painfully of acute gastroenteritis on July 9, 1850, after overindulging on a sweltering summer day with too much iced milk, cherries, and raw vegetables.

Millard Fillmore took Taylor's place in the White House. The Whigs had tapped him as vice president for two compelling reasons. He provided some of the intellectual and political ballast lacking in Taylor and, as a New Yorker, geographically balanced the southerner. Atop that, Fillmore enjoyed an impeccable reputation for integrity. He was born into a working-class family and as a young teen labored for a textile manufacturer. His intelligence won him admission to a private academy, then a law apprenticeship. He passed the bar and began practicing law in 1826. Two years later he won election as an Anti-Masonic Party candidate to New York's state assembly, where he served three one-year terms. Like most Anti-Masons, he soon switched to the Whig Party. In 1832 he was elected to the House of Representatives, where he served until 1843. He stepped down to prepare himself for what became an unsuccessful run for New York's governorship in 1844. After being elected the state's comptroller in 1848, he achieved fame for reforming New York's banking system. This gave him the buzz at the Whig convention that led to his selection as Taylor's running mate.[25]

Fillmore began his presidency shorn of any political baggage lingering from his predecessor. After taking the oath on July 9, he accepted the entire cabinet's resignation, then filled those chairs with men that he trusted and respected. He would need all the unity and support he could get as the nation faced its latest political crisis.

A dispute arose that threatened to tear the Whig Party apart. After the Mexican War, an array of contentious issues had built up over whether the newly won western territories along with the District of Columbia should be free or slave. The party's liberal wing advocated a bill that would hold a plebiscite for the capital's residents over whether to abolish slavery and let free black men vote along with qualified whites. Moderates sought to table this bill as too incendiary at the time. Then Daniel Gott, a New York representative, got a majority to endorse a resolution that slavery in Washington was "contrary to natural justice and the fundamental principles of our political system, . . . notoriously a reproach to our country through Christendom, and a serious hindrance to the progress of republican liberty among the nations of the earth."[26]

Abraham Lincoln was still in Congress when these measures arose. He voted against both, arguing that while he agreed that Congress was empowered to abolish slavery in Washington City, "that power ought not to be exercised unless at the request of the people of said District."[27] On January 10, 1849, he introduced an alternative to Gott's resolution. He called for a referendum on slavery whereby only qualified white males could vote. If a majority struck down slavery then the federal government would compensate all owners who agreed to free their slaves with "full cash value," while all children born to slave mothers after 1850 would be freed. Washington officials would remain bound to return any slaves who escaped to the District of Columbia.[28] Radicals from both sides denounced Lincoln's plan. Abolitionists condemned it for not going far enough, slavocrats because even a voluntary, compensated, gradual abolition was abhorrent to them. Lincoln backed off from this array of critics and never presented his proposal as a carefully drafted bill.

Passions became so heated that slavocrat leaders warned that their states would secede if they did not get their way. On January 20, 1850, Senator Henry Clay of Kentucky, who was a key player in resolving the crises of 1820 and 1833, proposed a compromise package of eight resolutions that he hoped would overcome the latest crisis. He paired the first six, with each couple offering a concession to each side. The first resolution admitted California as a free state, while the second organized two territories, New Mexico and Utah, without reference to slavery. The third resolution favored New Mexico in its boundary with Texas, but the fourth consoled irate Texans with the federal assumption of that state's outstanding debts. The fifth resolution abolished slave auctions in the District of Colombia while the sixth upheld slavery's legality there.

The last two resolutions favored slavocrats, with the seventh forbidding Congress to restrict the interstate slave trade and the eighth calling for a tougher fugitive slave law. The Senate voted to establish a committee chaired by Clay to study these and any other proposals.

Slavocrats and Free Soilers alike found plenty to dislike about Clay's resolutions. Free Soilers objected that the bulk favored slavocrats. Slavocrats objected to any that favored Free Soilers. Together they forced Clay's bundle of proposals to be unraveled and voted on separately on July 31. The result was that majorities voted down each proposal in turn.

Stephen Douglas of Illinois recognized that no package deal would ever pass since most senators and representatives would find far more to oppose than support. So he devised six separate bills that together constituted a grand compromise that would attract majorities on separate votes. That strategy was a resounding success. The first to be approved was a Texas boundary bill, passed on August 9, that gave that state far more land than Clay had proposed, yet drew its western boundary several hundred miles east of the Rio Grande claim. This passage provided momentum for the swift passage of five more: the admission of California as a free state, separate bills that put no restrictions on introducing slavery in the territories of New Mexico and Utah, the Fugitive Slave Act, and the abolition of the slave trade in the District of Columbia. President Fillmore signed those bills into law on September 20.[29]

The abolition of slave auctions in Washington City incensed most southerners. Georgia actually held a convention to debate whether or not to secede. In the end, unionists edged out secessionists, but the convention did call for all states to "resist . . . any action of Congress upon the subject of slavery in the District of Columbia or in places subject to the jurisdiction of Congress" that were "incompatible with the safety and domestic tranquility, the rights and honor of the slave-holding states, or any refusal to admit as a state any territory . . . because of the existence of slavery."[30]

Meanwhile the 1850 Fugitive Slave Act outraged not only abolitionists but also many northerners previously indifferent to the issue. The Constitution clearly let masters retrieve slaves who escaped to other states. The Supreme Court acknowledged that in its 1842 *Prigg v. Pennsylvania* decision, when the 1793 Fugitive Slave Act was challenged. This ruling, however, required only the federal government, not state and local officials, to cooperate with slave catchers. The 1850 Fugitive Slave Act was designed to overcome what slavocrats believed were weaknesses in the 1793 version. The 1850 law empowered federal officials to deputize people from free states to assist any efforts by masters to recapture their slaves and imposed fines of up to $1,000 and six months in prison if they refused. The federal government rather than the masters paid any expenses involved in recapturing escaped slaves. The status of anyone accused of being an escaped slave was determined not by a jury but by federal commissioners, who were paid ten dollars if they certified and only five dollars if they denied a master's accusation that a black person was an escapee.

The 1850 Fugitive Slave Act was far more provocative than effective. In the decade leading up to the Civil War, enraged masters wielded its powers to capture and carry back into slavery only 332 blacks, or about one in twenty of those they pursued. Nonetheless, the courts almost invariably upheld this process; judges freed only eleven blacks who contested their masters' claims.[31]

Each case that made the news inspired more people to condemn slavery as evil even if they differed over just what to do about it. Yet, given the harsh penalties, few people were principled enough to resist the slave catchers. Virtually all witnesses looked on in grim silence. As might be expected, liberal Boston, Massachusetts, was the epicenter of resistance. Led by Theodore Parker and William Garrison, abolitionists protested so fiercely the extradition of first William and Ellen Craft in 1850, then Thomas Sims in 1851, and finally Antony Burns in 1854 that state officials never again cooperated with slave catchers. In doing so Massachusetts clearly violated not just federal law but the Constitution itself.

The Supreme Court ruled in the 1851 *Strader v. Graham* case that slave states could determine whether any fugitive who reached a northern state was actually free under the slave state's laws. That was a potentially revolutionary decision, as it empowered the slave states to violate with impunity the laws of free states. This was not the most tortured interpretation of the Constitution that Chief Justice Roger Taney made.

Northerners noted the hypocrisy of those who so fervently insisted on states' rights for themselves yet were so swift to deny it to others. Abolitionists had a more subtle way to defy the hated Fugitive Slave

Act. The Underground Railroad was a system of safe houses that led escaped slaves to freedom in the northern United States and often all the way to Canada. How many slaves escaped will never be known, but estimates vary from about sixty thousand to one hundred thousand.[32]

Northern protests and civil disobedience against the law in turn provoked the rage of southern fire-eaters, who called for secession. The secessionists, however, did not explain how breaking away from the United States would ease the process of recovering their escaped slaves.

After leaving Congress, Abraham Lincoln spent the next four years developing a flourishing law practice with his partner, William Herndon, in Springfield and on the circuit.[33] He became renowned across the state for the powerful reason and oratory with which he defended his clients in hundreds of cases. He took on virtually all those who requested his services, including masters who sought to regain their slaves and slaves who sought to escape their masters.

The Lincolns suffered a tragedy on February 1, 1850, when their son Edward Baker, who had always been sickly, died of pulmonary tuberculosis. They rejoiced at the birth on April 4, 1853, of Thomas, nicknamed Tad, short for tadpole. After Edward's death, Abraham and Mary cherished their children all the more, perhaps too much, since they pampered them. As with so many dimensions of his life, in his relationship with his sons Lincoln used his own father as a model for how not to be. When Lincoln was old enough he had fled his smothering father. This taught him a priceless lesson: "Love is the chain to lock a child to its parent." He was devoted to creating a loving home for his children that made them "free, happy, and unrestrained by paternal tyranny."[34]

The Lincolns were immensely proud of their offspring and loved to show them off to visitors by dressing them up and having them sing, dance, quote poetry, and perform other feats. Lincoln enjoyed taking care of the boys even at work, to the point where neighbors gossiped that he was "henpecked." Yet Lincoln at times got lost in his thoughts and did not notice what his sons were doing. One memorable time he was pulling them in a wagon around Springfield's streets when a passerby hollered that one of the boys had fallen out.[35]

Herndon was among many who disliked the Lincoln boys as spoiled brats. He wrote that "I wanted to wring their little necks and yet out of respect for Lincoln I kept my mouth shut." He was just as venomous toward their mother, whom he had hated since Lincoln began to court her. He blistered her as "imperious, proud, aristocratic, insolent, witty, and bitter" and once compared the glide of her dancing technique to "the ease of a serpent."[36] Mary openly harbored a similar animus toward Herndon and never once invited him to dinner at their home. Herndon was hardly the only target of her wrath. She was spitefully jealous of any of her husband's closest friends and associates.

Even though he no longer held an elected office, Lincoln remained a Whig Party leader. In his search to expand the party, he saw a natural "union of the Whigs proper and such of the Liberty men who are Whigs in principle on all questions save only that of slavery."[37] On this issue the Whig Party opposed slavery's extension to new territories while the Liberty Party sought its abolition everywhere. Lincoln insisted that it was "a paramount duty of us in the free States, due to the Union of the States, and perhaps to liberty itself (paradox though it may seem), to let the slavery of the other States alone, while, on the other hand, I hold it to be equally clear that we should never knowingly lend ourselves, directly or indirectly, to prevent . . . slavery from dying a natural death—to find new places for it to live in."[38]

The animosities stirred by the Compromise of 1850 animated the 1852 national election. The Democratic Party was more diverse than the Whig Party and thus took longer to reach a consensus on controversial issues. During their convention at Baltimore, the delegates were still deadlocked after forty-nine roll call votes among four Democratic heavyweights—Stephen Douglas, Lewis Cass, William Marcy, and James Buchanan. With each of them far from earning the needed two-thirds majority, they finally turned to a compromise candidate.[39]

Franklin Pierce was personable, easygoing, handsome, and very well connected.[40] As a boy his wealthy and aloof father sent him to a series of elite boarding schools, culminating with Philips Exeter, then to Bowdoin College, where he got involved in political, debate, and literary clubs. These activities apparently distracted him from his studies—he graduated last in his class. But throughout his life Pierce compensated for his intellectual shortcomings with his engaging personality. He attracted patrons who eventually assisted his way to the White House. He studied law at a college in Northampton, Massachusetts, then apprenticed under that state's Governor Levi Woodbury before returning to New Hampshire and stints under judges Samuel Howe and Edmund Parker. In 1827 he passed the bar and began practicing law in Concord, New Hampshire. The following year he won a seat as a Democrat in the state assembly's lower house, where he was elected speaker in 1832. He moved on to national politics, serving in the House of Representatives from 1833 to 1837 and the Senate from 1837 to 1842. He then abruptly cut short his promising political career to appease his wife, who hated Washington. During the Mexican War, he pulled political strings in the Democratic Party first to be appointed a colonel, then a brigadier general. He served under Gen. Winfield Scott. With all this behind him, Pierce appeared to be an excellent nominee for the presidency.

The Whigs were just as divided as the Democrats. Their convention at Baltimore in May became an epic, exhausting, and ultimately self-destructive battle between President Millard Fillmore and Gen. Winfield Scott. The first vote was a dead heat between them, with Fillmore's 133 edging out Scott's 132 votes. Not much changed in vote after vote until the general finally surpassed the two-thirds hump with 159 votes on the fifty-third ballot. The deadlock, disarray, and split in the Whig Party prompted many of its followers to search for another party that better reflected their beliefs and hopes.[41]

Once again the Free Soilers competed for many of the same liberal voters and states as the Whigs. They held their convention at Pittsburgh and renominated John Hale as their presidential candidate. Much more notably, the Free Soil leaders embraced Frederick Douglass, naming him the party's secretary.

That year another fringe party emerged. Like the abolitionist Liberty Party, the Order of the Star-Spangled Banner, also known as the American or Know Nothing Party, was largely devoted to a single issue, but it differed from the Liberty Party by calling for the restriction rather than the liberation of others. The issue was unfettered immigration—2,939,000 foreigners stepped ashore in the United States just from 1845 to 1854, with Irish Catholics composing around 1,200,000, or 40 percent, of the total.[42] The party was founded in 1849 to resist what its adherents called an immigrant horde that carried with it worsening wages, disease, ignorance, crime, poor morals, and an alien religion—Catholicism. In northern cities, Democrats mobilized immigrants into political machines of patronage, corruption, and one-party government. The American Party was best known as the Know Nothing Party because its early organizers claimed to know nothing about their own efforts. The party was most popular in northeastern cities with large, swelling immigrant populations.[43]

The main contest was between the Democrats and the Whigs. Personality appears to have been the presidential election's deciding factor. Scott's victory over Fillmore at the Whig convention proved to be pyrrhic. While Scott may have been brighter and braver than Franklin Pierce, his critics dismissed the abrasive, easily irritated general as "Old Fuss and Feathers," a glaring contrast to his affable opponent.

Pierce won 1,601,274 votes, or 50.9 percent of the popular vote, and twenty-seven of the thirty-one states, while Scott got 1,386,580, or 44.1 percent. The rest—155,825, or 5.0 percent—fell to Free Soil candidate John Hale. Pierce racked up an even more lopsided victory in the Electoral College by winning 254 votes to Scott's 24.

When Franklin Pierce was inaugurated as president on March 4, 1853, he was the youngest man and the first born in the nineteenth century to hold that office. Pierce's critics denounced him as a "doughface," a northerner with southern principles. That was an apt description. Pierce soon acted decisively on these principles in a way that provoked the latest national crisis.

4

Bleeding Kansas

Our progress in degeneracy appears to me to be pretty rapid. As a
nation we began by declaring that "all men are created equal." We
now practically read it "all men are created equal, except Negroes."
When the Know Nothings get control, it will read "all men are
created equal, except Negroes and foreigners and Catholics."

ABRAHAM LINCOLN

Let North and South—let all Americans—let all lovers of liberty
join in the great and good work. If we do this, we shall not only
have saved the Union, but we shall have so saved it as to make
and to keep it forever worthy of the saving. We shall have so saved
it that the succeeding millions of free, happy people, the world
over, shall rise up and call us blessed in the latest generations.

ABRAHAM LINCOLN

Arguably, no one was more politically divisive during the 1850s than
Stephen Douglas, the chief architect behind the Compromise of 1850
and the 1854 Kansas-Nebraska Act.[1] His nickname, the "Little Giant,"
was inspired not just by his political deeds but by his booming voice
and arguments resounding from a large head framed with a mane of
dark hair atop a barrel-chested body and stubby legs. He was born in
Vermont and emigrated to Illinois in 1833 at age twenty. There he stud-

ied law while supporting himself by teaching school. His brilliant gifts of oratory and reason as a lawyer soon carried him into politics as a fervent Democrat. He rose through a series of state elected and appointed posts until 1842, when he won a seat in the House of Representatives. He served two terms there before, in 1846, being sent to the Senate, where he remained until his death from typhoid in June 1861.

Douglas dedicated his career to boosting the interests of his state and himself, and he articulated values that reinforced both. His political creed's core was "popular sovereignty," or letting the peoples of territories and states decide the issues that directly affected them, including whether or not to permit slavery. The virulent racism that he expressed in many of his speeches reflected the prevailing attitudes of his time as well as his ownership for years of a Mississippi plantation worked by scores of slaves. He became a slaveholder when his first wife inherited her childhood plantation. That he was a Democrat supposedly opposed to internal improvements did not keep him from championing federal land grants to underwrite a transcontinental railroad that would stretch west from Chicago to San Francisco and in which he would be a partner. He first began propounding this vision as a freshman congressman in 1843 and persisted until his death. He gained the perfect platform to do so after becoming chair of the Senate Committee on Territories. Meanwhile he invested heavily in real estate and railroad companies that would enrich him if his idea was approved.

Douglas joined his interests in slaves and railroads in a bill that he introduced in the Senate on January 4, 1854.[2] When he did so he could not imagine that the bill's passage would exacerbate sectional passions and propel the nation toward secession and civil war, but this is exactly what it did. Under the 1820 Missouri Compromise, slavery was banned above and legal below 36°30′ north latitude from Missouri to the Rocky Mountain watershed, then the nation's western boundary. With what became known as the Kansas-Nebraska Act, Douglas destroyed this compromise by splitting all this land between the territories of Kansas and Nebraska and leaving the question of free or slave in the hands of the people actually living in each territory. He justified this policy with the notion of "popular sovereignty."

By holding out the possibility to southerners of slavery's expansion across all the territories, Douglas sought their support for federal land grants for his railroad scheme. It did not quite work out as he hoped. Douglas was hardly the only proponent of a transcontinental railroad emanating from his home state. Senators from Missouri, Tennessee, Mississippi, and Louisiana called for terminals at St. Louis, Memphis, Vicksburg, and New Orleans, respectively. Most senators and representatives elsewhere did not support the railroad plan because it did not directly help their states. The most that Douglas and other boosters got was a $150,000 appropriation for a survey of possible routes.

If Douglas's railroad plan fizzled, enthusiasm for his Kansas-Nebraska Act spread like wildfire, at least among southerners. After two months of debate the bill passed the Senate by thirty-seven to fourteen votes on March 3, an unsurprising passage since the southern states and Democrats had the edge there. But the outcome in the House was uncertain since most representatives were northerners. For the next two months this bill was Congress's most hotly debated issue. The final vote was close, with 113 to 100 in favor on May 22. President Franklin Pierce signed the Kansas-Nebraska Act into law on May 30, 1854.

Word of the Kansas-Nebraska Act filled Abraham Lincoln with revulsion and dread. He later explained that "I have always hated slavery, I think as much as any Abolitionist . . . but I have always been quiet about it until this new era of the introduction of the Nebraska bill."[3] He decided to harness these powerful feelings by reentering the political arena and challenging the bill's author head on. Douglas was then traveling around Illinois making speeches justifying his act. Lincoln first replied at Springfield, then elaborated his views in a three-hour address at Peoria on October 16, 1854. This speech was among the most brilliant that Lincoln ever devised.[4]

Typically, Lincoln was conciliatory rather than judgmental toward Douglas and others who championed the Kansas-Nebraska Act: "I do not propose to question the patriotism or to assail the motives of any man or class of men, but rather to confine myself strictly to the naked merits of the question."

The future of slavery was this age's core question. Central to confronting that question was distinguishing "between the existing institution and extension of it." Lincoln regretted that he was forced to accept slavery since the Constitution protected it, but he opposed the spread of this "evil." He was filled with "hate" for slavery both because of its "monstrous injustice" and "because it deprives our republican example of its just influence in the world; enables the enemies of free institutions . . . to taunt us as hypocrites; causes the real friends of freedom to doubt our sincerity; and especially because it forces so many good men among ourselves into an open war with the very fundamental principles of civil liberty, criticizing the Declaration of Independence, and insisting that there is no right principle of action but self-interest."

Yet here, too, Lincoln was conciliatory. He insisted that "I have no prejudice against the Southern people. They are just what we would be in their situation. If slavery did not now exist among them, they would not introduce it. If it did now exist among us we should not instantly give it up. Doubtless there are individuals on both sides who would not hold slaves under any circumstances, and others who would gladly introduce slavery anew if it were out of existence."

He then asserted an extended argument, grounded in the nation's founding documents and history, that the framers intended and hoped that slavery would eventually die out. He expounded the Declaration of Independence's most critical passage: "all men are created equal; that they are endowed by their Creator with certain inalienable rights; that among these are life, liberty, and the pursuit of happiness." The framers intended that universal right to embrace all men in all times and places, including black men. Thus slavery was not the "moral right" claimed by slavocrats but was solely a legal right that violated the natural rights of black men. He distilled that argument to its essence: "If the negro is a man, why then my ancient faith teaches me that 'all men are created equal' and that there can be no moral right in connection with one man's making a slave of another."

He called on Americans to return the Declaration of Independence "to the position that our fathers gave it. . . . Let North and South— let all Americans—let all lovers of liberty join in the great and good work. If we do this, we shall not only have saved the Union, but we shall have so saved it as to make and to keep it forever worthy of the saving. We shall have so saved it that the succeeding millions of free, happy people, the world over, shall rise up and call us blessed in the latest generations."

Lincoln was elected to the state assembly in 1855. He no sooner took his seat than he spread word of his interest in winning an open U.S. Senate seat.[5] His three Democratic Party rivals were James Shields, with whom he had nearly fought a duel thirteen years earlier; his friend Lyman Trumbull; and Governor Joel Matteson. The election was held on February 8. In the hundred-seat assembly, a Senate candidate needed fifty-one votes to win. On the first ballot, Lincoln garnered the largest share with forty-five votes, while Shields got forty-one and Trumbull got five. Lincoln's supporters failed to talk Trumbull into sending his supporters to Lincoln. Instead Shields threw his support to Matteson and a series of ballots ensued with Lincoln's share peaking at forty-seven on the ninth. On the tenth ballot Lincoln chose to throw the race to Trumbull as the lesser of two evils—Trumbull opposed and Matteson supported the Kansas-Nebraska Act. Lincoln also astutely reckoned that Trumbull would thereafter be his devoted political ally.[6]

Under the Kansas-Nebraska Act, settlers could begin staking claims on May 30, 1854. This inspired fervent abolitionist and slavocrat groups alike to try to ensure that the territories reflected their own beliefs and interests.[7] Congressman Eli Thayer of Massachusetts formed the New England Emigrant Aid Company to help organize and finance parties of Free Soilers to settle in Kansas and Nebraska. Horace Greeley, the *New York Tribune*'s editor, called repeatedly for Free Soilers to transplant themselves to those western lands. Meanwhile Senator David Atchinson of Missouri led slavocrat efforts to take over those territories. He promised Secretary of War Jefferson Davis of Mississippi that he and his followers would "shoot, burn, & hang" to assert a slavocracy over Kansas, and "the thing will soon be over."[8] He emphasized that his intention was "to 'Mormonize' the Abolitionists," or to mass murder Free Soilers as Missourians had murdered Mormons who tried to settle in the state during the 1830s. Atchinson eventually would be good to his word.

The slavocrats enjoyed a decisive geographic and thus political edge since Missouri was adjacent to the disputed territories while New England was far away. Andrew Reeder, Kansas's first appointed governor, held an election for the territory's delegate to Congress on November 29, 1854. Atchinson led hundreds of Missouri border ruffians into Kansas to pack the polls and elect a slavocrat to that post. Reeder then scheduled an election to choose a legislature for Kansas Territory on March 30, 1855. At that time a census counted 8,501 residents, of whom 2,905 were registered voters and only 242 were slaves. Atchison again rallied several thousand followers to cross the border and stuff ballot boxes and bully Free Soilers at each polling place. The number of recorded votes was 6,307, or 2,003 more than those officially registered. An investigation later found that all but 500 of the 5,427 votes cast for slavery were invalid.[9]

Although Governor Reeder knew that the election was fraudulent, he certified it anyway. The Pierce administration promptly recognized the proslave government that was set up at Lecompton, while the Democrats introduced a bill in Congress upholding the recognition. The result was a territorial legislature packed with thirty-six slavocrats and only three Free Soilers. The legislature promptly passed laws that forced each man in the territory to take an oath to support slavery or else forgo his right to hold any public office or serve on juries; made it a felony to criticize slavery; and condemned to death anyone who helped escaped slaves or distributed abolitionist literature.

Free Soilers denounced the slavocracy and organized their own government at Topeka in October 1855. The constitution they wrote was approved in a referendum by 1,731 to 46 in December. In January 1856 the Free Soilers elected a legislature and Charles Robinson as their governor. In Congress the Republican Party introduced a bill recognizing the Free Soil government as legitimate.

Upon taking office, Robinson sent an urgent plea to backers in New England for firearms to resist the border ruffians. Of the dozens of churches and groups that responded, none was more generous than the congregation headed by Henry Ward Beecher, a fiery liberal minister and Harriet Beecher Stowe's father. He preached an impassioned sermon to his well-heeled followers, passed the collection plate, bought 325 rifles with the proceeds, and shipped them west in boxes labeled "Bibles"; those rifles became affectionately known as "Beecher's Bibles."

These weapons did not reach Free Soilers in time to help deter a slavocrat invasion. On May 21, 1856, seven hundred border ruffians rode into Lawrence, the closest large Free Soil town to Missouri, and terrorized that community by burning the hotel and the Free Soil governor's home, destroying the two newspaper presses, and plundering businesses and homes. They did not, however, kill anyone. Two nights later, John Brown and seven followers retaliated by murdering five slavocrats along Pottawatomie Creek.

The worsening terrorism by slavocrats was not confined to Kansas. Massachusetts senator Charles Sumner was an articulate advocate for free soil and abolition.[10] He delivered a brilliant oration entitled "The Crime against Kansas" on May 19 and 20, 1856. Among those whom Sumner criticized for the violence and anarchy in Kansas was Senator Andrew Butler of South Carolina. On May 22, Preston Brooks, Butler's cousin and a South Carolina representative, entered the Senate, strode over to Sumner, and viciously beat him with his cane.

This crime split the nation, with most northerners condemning Brooks as a thug while slavocrats lauded him as a hero. The House of Representatives voted 121 to 95 to expel him, short of the necessary two-thirds majority. Brooks resigned and was promptly reelected by his constituents in a special election. Charges were filed in a federal district court; Brooks was found guilty of assault and fined $300. The beating so physically and emotionally crippled Sumner that he needed two and a half years before he was ready to return to the Senate.

The heinous sack of Lawrence and beating of Sumner were turning points for many northerners. They were appalled that southerners cheered rather than condemned such atrocities. Swelling violence, anarchy, and extremism were eating away the nation's political and moral foundations. In light of these events, the president and many in Congress appeared not just callous but complicit.

It takes power to get power. President James Polk at once asserted and greatly expanded American power by besting Britain and Mexico in showdowns. Through diplomacy alone he won a contest with Britain over the Oregon Territory that had begun with American sea captain Robert Gray's discovery of the Columbia River mouth in 1792. A joint occupancy compromise deal between the United States and Britain lasted from 1818 to 1848. After an exchange of war brinksmanship rhetoric, the British caved to Polk's demand that the United States take exclusive control of the Oregon Territory by extending America's northern frontier with Canada along the forty-ninth parallel from the Rocky Mountains to the Pacific Ocean. "Mr. Polk's War" succeeded where his diplomacy failed to get Mexico to recognize America's annexation of Texas and to sell New Mexico and California to the United States. After expanding American territory by nearly a quarter, all the way to the Pacific coast, over a mere two years, Polk was a tough foreign policy act to follow.

This mattered little to either Zachary Taylor or Millard Fillmore, who were disinterested in foreign policy. Fortunately Daniel Webster filled this void as the secretary of state from July 1850 to October 1852. He was well acquainted with his duties and foreign relations, having previously held that post from March 1841 to May 1843. He initiated two policies of lasting importance during his first stint: the 1842 Webster-Ashburton Treaty settled the northeastern boundary between the United States and Canada, and the 1842 Tyler Doctrine asserted Hawaii as a sphere of American influence worth defending should any foreign power dispute it. His most important policy during his second stint was to uphold the Tyler Doctrine.

Although American merchants and missionaries dominated Hawaii's economy and government, their British and French counterparts were also contenders. In 1850 the French minister to Hawaii's monarchy threatened to land troops to assert the French community's interests in a dispute with King Kamehameha. When Webster learned of this threat, he protested to the French minister in Washington, had the American minister in Paris echo that protest, and sent word to America's Pacific flotilla commander and minister in Hawaii to assure the king that the United States would defend him. The grateful monarch sent word to Washington that he was actually prepared to raise the American flag and declare his realm's annexation to the United States should the French invade. In the face of American resolve, the French backed down in July 1851. Webster resisted calls by the American community in Hawaii for the United States to exploit the situation by annexing the kingdom. He insisted that American interests were better advanced by upholding Hawaii's sovereignty while expanding informal power over the islands. The United States would eventually take over Hawaii, but not for nearly another five decades.

Unlike his two immediate predecessors, President Franklin Pierce took an active role in foreign policy. He had good political and ideological reasons for doing so. As a "doughface," or northerner with southern sympathies, he did everything he could to benefit slavocrats within the

Democratic Party. This interest lay behind his most important initiative. He authorized James Gadsden, America's minister to Mexico, to buy a swath of territory across northern Mexico. The rationale was to provide land for a future transcontinental railroad to run from New Orleans to San Diego. Gadsden first offered President Antonio López de Santa Anna $50 million for 250,000 square miles of northern Mexico. Santa Anna bluntly rejected the offer. After weeks of haggling they finally agreed that Mexico would sell 54,000 square miles of land south of the Gila River, which runs west from southern New Mexico through Arizona to the Colorado River, for $15 million, the same price that the United States had paid for all of upper California and New Mexico under the 1848 Treaty of Guadeloupe Hidalgo. A version of the treaty barely squeaked by with a thirty-three to twelve Senate ratification vote, reflecting solid southern support and a divided North. Those who favored the purchase enticed a few key votes by agreeing to sever 9,000 square miles from the territory, thus reducing the acquisition to 45,000 square miles while slashing the price to $10 million.

Slavocrats were united in the desire to expand slavery but differed over where and how. Many looked far beyond the horizon southward as well as westward for potential conquests. During the Mexican War, a vocal minority demanded that the United States conquer all of Mexico, whereupon slavery would be reimposed throughout the country; they were enraged when the winnings were limited to New Mexico and California. They then began scanning the Caribbean islands and Central America for potential conquests. Cuba and Nicaragua appeared especially ripe for the plucking; Cuban nationalists sought to overthrow Spanish rule, while near anarchy prevailed in Nicaragua as factions vied for power across a land that provided a transit route between the oceans.

In bowing to the slavocrat demand for Cuba, Secretary of State William Marcy penned on April 3, 1854, one of the more controversial letters in the nation's diplomatic history. In it he authorized Pierre Soulé, America's minister in Madrid, to buy Cuba from Spain for up to $130 million. If talks failed Soulé was authorized to "direct your efforts to detach that island from the Spanish dominion and from all dependence on any European power."[11] Just why did the Pierce administration desire Cuba? Slavery was legal and pervasive in Cuba. If Cuba were acquired and split up into states, slavocrats would dominate the Senate indefinitely.

However unlikely that Madrid would have agreed to the sale, Soulé could not have been a worse man for that mission. He was a hothead and troublemaker. He had fought a duel with the French ambassador for gazing at Soule's wife's décolletage, and he freely passed bribes to officials and others who might advance his interests. Not surprisingly, the Spanish government rejected any notion of selling Cuba to the United States. This enraged Soulé, who in October hurried to Ostend, Belgium, where he rendezvoused with two other American diplomats, James Buchanan and James Mason, the respective ministers to Britain and France. Together they journeyed to Aix-la-Chapelle and there issued the Ostend Manifesto, which declared that "Cuba is as necessary to the North American republic as any of its present members," called for the island's purchase for no more than $120 million, and warned that "by every law, human and Divine, we shall be justified in wrestling it from Spain" if Madrid refused to sell.[12]

The Ostend Manifesto was the most explicit public declaration by high-ranking officials of Manifest Destiny's essentially imperialist nature. It provoked a political firestorm in America and Europe when newspapers published the text. In the United States, northern liberals denounced it while conservatives split, with some silently embarrassed and others either tepidly or enthusiastically supportive. Although Marcy had issued Soulé instructions that differed little from the Ostend Manifesto, the last thing he or others who backed such a blatantly aggressive policy wanted was its revelation to the world. Marcy had no choice but to repudiate the Ostend Manifesto and recall Soulé. These gestures could not begin to repair the diplomatic damage abroad and political damage at home. The result was a shelving of the most overt efforts of American imperialists until the Spanish American War of 1898.

As for Nicaragua, the 1849 gold rush transformed American interests there. The country provided relatively easy transit by river and flat land from the Caribbean to the Pacific. American steamship companies, most notably Cornelius Vanderbilt's, dominated the route. Visionaries spoke of one day linking the oceans with a canal across either Nicaragua or Panama.

Americans were not the only foreigners with growing ties related to travel and trade in the region. Unlike the United States, Britain had colonies across the Caribbean and resented American meddling in what it considered its sphere of interest. Yet the British recognized that America's crushing defeat of Mexico revealed that it was no longer the second-rate military power that Britain had fought in the War of 1812. Indeed, while the United States remained a second-rate global power, it was clearly North America's number-one military power. British power was stretched thinner as it expanded its empire in regions around the world. The last thing British policymakers needed was a war with the United States.

To avoid a future fatal clash of interests, Secretary of State John Clayton and British minister Henry Bulwer signed on April 19, 1850, what became known as the Clayton-Bulwer Treaty, which prevented either country from building a canal across any Central American country without the other's permission. Bilateral relations improved further when Marcy and James Bruce, the Earl of Elgin and Canada's governor general, signed on June 5, 1854, the Marcy-Elgin Treaty that opened for Americans the St. Lawrence River for transit, Canada for trade, and Canadian waters beyond three miles of shore for fishing.

Nicaragua's endemic political instability and violence threatened America's transit and growing commercial interests there. This threat was personified when Solon Borland, America's minister to Nicaragua, was hurt by an angrily thrown bottle as he addressed a crowd at Greytown. Upon hearing of that insult, the Pierce administration decided that a show of force was essential. Capt. George Hollins, who commanded the uss *Cyrene*, received orders to steam to Greytown and demand an apology from local authorities. In July 1854, after his demands were ignored, Hollins ordered his gunners to bombard the port. Then, in the eyes of Nicaraguans and others, the White House compounded this act of war by at once publicly disclaiming and privately encouraging a series of aggressive acts by Americans.

If Washington's direct purchase or conquest of any more lands for the potential expansion of slavery was too controversial at home and abroad, slavocrats advocated an alternative strategy. A private venture would conquer a country and impose a constitution that established democracy for whites and slavery for blacks. The new government would then ask for annexation to the United States. This private venture version of imperialism became known as "filibustering," from the Spanish word *filibustero*, which means freebooter or pirate.[13]

No filibusterer was a more vivid, persistent, fleetingly successful, and ultimately spectacular failure than William Walker.[14] By all accounts he had a brilliant, obsessive intellect. He was born in Nashville in 1826, graduated from the University of Nashville at age fourteen, got a medical degree from the University of Pennsylvania, then moved to New Orleans where he passed the bar, practiced law, and edited the *New Orleans Crescent*. In 1849 he joined the frenzied rush to California's gold, but he never panned a stream or dug a mine. Instead, he settled briefly in San Francisco, where he became a leader in the vigilante movement, exposed crime and corruption through newspaper articles, and fought three duels in which he was twice wounded.

None of these adventures satisfied such a restless mind and spirit. In 1853 an obsession seized him to conquer and rule his own country. He embarked with forty-five heavily armed followers to take over Baja California. Upon capturing La Paz, the provincial capital, he proclaimed himself president. This was just the first step. He aimed eventually to vanquish all of Mexico, one province after another. He led his men to invade neighboring Sonora. Although Mexican troops decimated the filibusterers, Walker managed to escape to the United States.

Rather than let that defeat humble him, Walker instead was inspired by his brief grasp of power as Baja's "president." In 1855 he sailed with fifty-seven men for Nicaragua, where he joined and soon led an insurrection against the government. By July 1856 he had routed his foes and proclaimed himself the president. He then legalized slavery and granted land to southerners who brought their slaves and started plantations. All went well until Walker tried to overthrow Cornelius Vanderbilt as president of the Accessory Transit Company, which controlled the transportation route across the country. Vanderbilt threw his money and organizational support behind the rebel forces and eventually forced Walker and his surviving followers to flee to New Orleans in May 1857.

Across the southern United States, slavocrats celebrated Walker as a hero, "the grey-eyed man of destiny." He soon massed enough men and money for a second expedition against Nicaragua. In November 1857 he sailed from Mobile but the navy intercepted his vessel, arrested him on federal charges of violating U.S. neutrality laws, and took him to New Orleans for trial. A sympathetic jury acquitted him in May 1858. Walker soon set forth on his third expedition to Nicaragua but his ship wrecked on a reef sixty miles from shore; a British vessel rescued the castaways and returned them to the United States. Despite his string of defeats, Walker did not give up but simply changed his strategy. Rather than launch his fourth expedition with fiery speeches and parades before adoring crowds, he and ninety-eight men quietly embarked in small groups aboard different vessels bound for Honduras, where they planned to assemble and invade neighboring Nicaragua. A British warship intercepted the ship that Walker was sailing on, arrested him, and turned him over to Honduran authorities. On September 12, 1860, Walker faced a firing squad at Trujillo.

Narciso Lopez was that era's second most notorious filibusterer. He was a Cuban nationalist who fled to New York City in 1848 after the Spanish crushed his effort to provoke a revolt. There he recruited several hundred mercenaries for an expedition to liberate his homeland. Recognizing that he lacked the status, men, and funds to pull off his campaign, he asked Senator Jefferson Davis to lead the effort. Davis declined the leading role even though he was an outspoken proponent of conquering Cuba to expand American slavery; he did, however, introduce Lopez to his slavocrat network of politicians and businessmen. With this backing, Lopez packed men and supplies aboard a small flotilla of vessels and prepared to sail for Cuba in September 1849. Getting wind of the expedition, the Taylor administration ordered the navy to interdict it for violating America's neutrality law. Lopez switched his base to New Orleans, which was geographically and ideologically far more conducive to realizing his dreams. In May 1850 he and six hundred followers sailed from New Orleans. To the filibusterers' dismay, Cubans fled rather than joined the invaders after they landed on the island's northwest coast. As an overwhelming force of Spanish troops neared, Lopez reembarked his men and they escaped to Key West.

Despite Lopez's failure, southerners toasted him as a hero. Within a year he had attracted enough men, money, munitions, and provisions for another expedition. Second in command was William Crittenden, the attorney general's nephew. The Fillmore administration was aware of the plot but succumbed to political pressure to turn a blind eye to it. In August 1851 Lopez sailed with 420 men for Cuba. This time the Spanish army moved quickly, attacked, slaughtered about two hundred of the invaders, and captured the rest, including Lopez and Crittenden.

In the subsequent trials, the court sentenced 160 filibusterers to prison in Spain, condemned 50 men, including Crittenden, to execution by firing squad, and had Lopez garroted in the public square.

The grim fate of Lopez's expedition provoked rather than deterred the slavocrats. They were outraged that President Fillmore apologized to Spain rather than backing the filibusterers. They reaped their vengeance in 1852 by helping elect Franklin Pierce to the White House. In his inaugural address, Pierce asserted that the "policy of my Administration will not be controlled by timid forebodings of evil from expansion. Our position on the globe renders the acquisition of certain possessions . . . eminently important for our protection. . . . The future is boundless."[15]

Pierce was good to his word. In July 1853 he actually encouraged Mississippi governor John Quitman to fulfill his own dreams of conquest. By early 1854 Quitman had signed up a thousand or so Americans, Cuban exiles, and adventurers from an array of other nationalities. In May Senator John Slidell of Louisiana introduced a resolution to suspend the neutrality law. Everything was set to go. But the president got cold feet and provoked slavocrat rage when he issued on May 31 a proclamation that Washington would prosecute filibusterers under the neutrality law. The reasons for Pierce's flip-flop were rooted in politics rather than the law or morality. His administration and party had spent enormous political capital in pushing the Kansas-Nebraska Act through Congress. Pierce and most other leading Democrats feared that they would destroy their party's northern wing if they openly backed Quitman's expedition to conquer Cuba.[16]

News soon reached the United States of an American foreign policy triumph that most northerners and southerners alike applauded. American interests in the Far East originated when the merchant ship *Empress of China* sailed from Boston for Canton in 1784. This inaugurated a steadily growing trade with China as a key link in a global trade network where canny American sea captains exchanged goods for ever-greater profits in ports along the way during voyages that lasted years and, after their return to their home port, made them and their investors very rich. Until 1842, only Canton was open to foreign traders. That year Britain imposed the Treaty of Nanjing on China after winning the Opium War that began in 1839. Under its terms, China ceded Hong Kong Island to Britain and opened five more ports to trade.

The United States joined other foreign powers in negotiating access to the ports. All this boosted trade across the Pacific basin that included buying hides and tallow at California ports, sea otter pelts along the Oregon coast, sandalwood at the Hawaiian Islands, then known as the Sandwich Islands, and most profitably, Chinese silk, porcelain, and tea. But a vital link was missing in that network.

Japan had severed itself from virtually all trade relations shortly after 1600 when the Tokugawa clan vanquished their rivals and took over the country. The new rulers blocked trade fearing that the European powers posed an insidious threat to their rule by arming their enemies and converting the population to Christianity. American and European merchants alike fantasized about selling their wares to a nation of thirty million consumers. Profit was not the only reason to convince the Japanese to open their country. In their long circuit around the Pacific basin, merchant and whaling captains alike longed to drop anchor in Japanese ports to buy food, water, and coal but dared not do so knowing that Tokugawa officials imprisoned and at times executed any foreigners who violated their isolation policy.

The Opium War and Treaty of Nanjing gave America's diplomatic and international business communities hope that Japan could be pried open. The Japanese kept a window open to the world through the port of Nagasaki, where the Chinese and Dutch were permitted to trade. The Tokugawa regime was well aware that China's humiliating defeat had made the western powers dominant in the Far East. Determined to avoid China's fate, some within the regime leaned toward opening Japan to a secondary power like the United States through diplomacy rather than to the world's greatest military power, Britain, through war. The Japanese knew that they could not long resist a naval blockade that cut off their ports from food supplied by the coastal trade or bombarded their wooden cities to ashes.

For these reasons, President Fillmore ordered Commodore Matthew Perry to organize and launch an expedition to convince the Tokugawa to establish trade and diplomatic relations with the United States. Perry was an excellent choice. During his more than two decades in the navy, he had sailed the world and fought in the Mexican War. Upon receiving his mission, he at once massed the necessary vessels, sailors, and supplies and gathered all available information on that mysterious realm.

En route to Japan, he honed his diplomatic skills by negotiating trade and diplomatic treaties with the kingdoms of first Thailand and then the Ryukyu, or Okinawa, Islands. He adapted to the time-consuming consensus-building style of Japanese decision making. After his flotilla dropped anchor in what is now called Tokyo Bay in July 1853, he remained patient during a tense deadlock that lasted several weeks as Japanese authorities demanded that the Americans leave and he requested that they simply accept a letter from President Fillmore to their ruler. After the Japanese finally yielded, Perry announced that he would return for an answer within a year, then sailed away to winter in the Ryukyu Islands. During the intervening nine months before he reappeared in March 1854, the Tokugawa forged a consensus that it was better to trade than fight. The Treaty of Kanagawa, signed on March 31, required Japan to open two small ports to American merchants and diplomats on a "most favored nation" foundation whereby the United States automatically received any benefits that Japan bestowed on other countries. From this limited beginning, Japan was eventually brought fully into the global system through a series of subsequent treaties with the United States and other foreign nations.

Perry's opening of Japan was a triumph of American power and a turning point in American foreign policy. Although he never once threatened Japan with military force, this was not necessary. The threat was implicit in the four gunboats bristling with huge cannons among his nine-ship flotilla. Ever since then the United States has wielded "gunboat diplomacy" to assert its interests in ever more disputed places around the world.

As American power expanded abroad, the two-party political system collapsed at home. In 1854 the Whig Party dissolved after twenty-two years of vigorous existence as virtually all of its leaders and followers abandoned that political vessel for others, like the Free Soil, American, Liberty, and Republican Parties. Abraham Lincoln was among the loyal Whigs who suffered a political identity crisis after the party's demise. To his old friend Joshua Speed he explained,

> You inquire where I now stand. That is a disputed point. I think I am a Whig, but others say there are no Whigs, and that I am

an Abolitionist. When I was at Washington, I voted for the Wilmot Proviso as good as forty times, and I never heard of anyone attempting to unwhig me for that. I now do no more than oppose the extension of slavery. I am not a Know Nothing, that is certain. How could I be? How can anyone who abhors the oppression of Negroes be in favor of degrading classes of white people? Our progress in degeneracy appears to me to be pretty rapid. As a nation we began by declaring that "all men are created equal." We now practically read it "all men are created equal, except Negroes." When the Know Nothings get control, it will read "all men are created equal, except Negroes and foreigners and Catholics.[17]

A new party soon emerged to serve as the vehicle for Lincoln's beliefs.

The Republican Party proverbially rose phoenix-like from the Whig Party's carcass.[18] With Whigs as their core, Republicans also enticed Free Soilers, Know Nothings, and moderate Democrats. Use of the "Republican" label to designate the new party was first proposed at a meeting in Ripon, Wisconsin, in February 1854, was approved by a group of like-minded congressmen in Washington in May, and was adopted by a state convention in Michigan on July 6. Within months Republican Parties mushroomed in all the northern states. Philosophically, the Republican Party was the latest incarnation of the Federalist Party that Alexander Hamilton formed in the early 1790s to battle Thomas Jefferson's Republican Party over just what kind of nation America would become. For diverse reasons, the Federalist Party died as a national force during the first decade of the nineteenth century, then was reincarnated in the mid-1820s as the National Democrats and in the early 1830s as the Whigs. Each version advocated a national bank, protective tariff, and internal improvements as policies and celebrated enterprise, creativity, free labor, education, and equality before the law for all. In addition, the Republicans called for a homestead act that gave away western public lands to settlers, a transcontinental railroad, and land-grant colleges that promoted higher education and agrarian improvements. Like Alexander Hamilton, their intellectual and political progenitor, Republicans insisted that these policies would promote a virtuous cycle of economic development that provided a higher standard of living and quality of life for more Americans.

The Republicans advocated not abolishing slavery but preventing its extension to new territories in hope that it would eventually die a natural death. They believed that would happen as the North's free-labor system widened the economic chasm between the regions and more impoverished southern whites recognized and struggled against the reality that slavery shackled them as well as blacks. Republicans at once accepted and lamented that the Constitution legalized slavery. Yet they also pointed to the Constitution's clauses that empowered Congress to outlaw the international slave trade and to limit or outright abolish slavery in federal lands, like the District of Columbia and the western territories. Most Republicans cared far more about the fate of white workers than black slaves. Henry Carey, a Pennsylvania economist, was the intellectual powerhouse behind the Republican Party platform. He justified each of these policies in his books: *The Harmony of Interests: Agricultural, Manufacturing, and Commercial* and *The Slave Trade, Foreign and Domestic*, both published in 1856, *The Principles of Social Science*, in 1858, and *Financial Crises: Their Causes and Effects*, in 1863.

During the 1856 convention the Republican Party's political giants were William Seward of New York and Salmon Chase of Ohio. Yet the delegates spurned them and instead chose a popular hero as their presidential candidate. John Frémont was renowned for his exploring expeditions across the West and role in conquering California. Most Republicans hoped that Frémont's image could carry him to the White House much as two other heroes, Whig candidates William Henry Harrison and Zachary Taylor, had beaten their more prosaic Democratic Party rivals in the respective elections of 1840 and 1848. But Frémont had some crucial flaws as a person and thus as a leader—he was mercurial, pompous, overbearing, hardheaded, and not noted for his intellect.[19] Nonetheless, most Republicans enthusiastically chanted the campaign slogan of "Free Soil, Free Speech, Free Men, Frémont!"

Abraham Lincoln was gratified to receive 110 votes for the vice presidential slot, although eventually William Dayton of New Jersey won it. From then until the election, Lincoln campaigned tirelessly for Frémont and other Republicans. As he gave speeches around Illinois, his toughest challenge was refuting the charge that the Republicans were abolitionists who would break up the United States into free and slave countries.

Like a judo master, Lincoln took that charge and threw it back against slavocrats by citing and expounding key tenets of the Declaration of Independence. He argued that Republicans upheld and Democrats violated the document's letter and spirit. America's founders believed "that all men are created equal" and enjoyed rights to "life, liberty and the pursuit of happiness." Thus a black woman has the "natural right to eat the bread that she earns with her own hands without asking leave of anyone else" and in that "she is my equal, and the equal of all others." An essential difference split the political parties: "The Republicans inculcate . . . that the Negro is a man, that his bondage is cruelly wrong, and that the field of his oppression ought not to be enlarged. Democrats deny his manhood; deny or dwarf to insignificance the wrong of his bondage; so far as possible crush all sympathy for him, and cultivate and excite hatred and disgust against him; compliment themselves as Union-savers for doing so; and call the indefinite outspreading of his bondage 'a sacred right of self-government.'"[20] The United States was founded on the Declaration of Independence, and anyone who rejected the values and aspirations of this document rejected America.

Once again a third party siphoned votes from the latest party grounded in Hamiltonian principles and policies. The American, or Know Nothing, Party nominated Millard Fillmore as its presidential candidate. Although the Republican and American party platforms overlapped, they did not ally but instead fought for the votes of many of the same constituents.

The Democrats faced a dilemma in choosing their presidential candidate, as their two most prominent leaders—President Franklin Pierce and Senator Stephen Douglas—were tainted by the northern uproar over the Kansas-Nebraska Act, the slavocrat takeover of Kansas, and worsening violence. The party settled on James Buchanan, who like Pierce was a "doughface" sympathetic to slavocrat interests but had avoided the Kansas political tar baby.

Although three men ran for the presidency, there were only two genuine races—Frémont versus Buchanan in the North, and Fillmore versus Buchanan in the South. In the popular vote, Buchanan received 1,838,169 votes, or 45.34 percent, Frémont a respectable 1,341,264, or 33.09 percent, and Fillmore 872,534, or 22.57 percent. This translated into 174 electoral votes for Buchanan, 114 for Frémont, and 8 for Fillmore. The eleven states that Frémont won were all in the upper North; his vote counts faded the closer they were cast to Dixie. In the South, Frémont's name appeared on ballots in only four states, where he got less than 1 percent of the vote. Yet had Fillmore been Frémont's running mate rather than his rival they would have won by a landslide.[21] Instead, the winner was the man who is generally rated among the worst presidents in American history.

5

Dred Scott and Harpers Ferry

"A house divided against itself cannot stand." I believe this
government cannot endure, permanently, half slave and half free.
I do not expect the Union to be dissolved—I do not expect
the house to fall—but I do expect it will cease to be
divided. It will become all one thing or all the other.

ABRAHAM LINCOLN

I know and you know that a revolution has begun. I know, and
all the world knows that revolutions never go backward.

WILLIAM SEWARD

The cause of civil liberty must not be surrendered at
the end of one or even one hundred defeats.

ABRAHAM LINCOLN

We have a means provided for the expression of our belief
in regard to slavery—it is through the ballot box—the
peaceful method provided by the Constitution.

ABRAHAM LINCOLN

James Buchanan took the oath as president of the United States on March 4, 1857. He had an impressive resume, having graduated from Dickinson College; passed the law exam and opened a practice in Lancaster, Pennsylvania, in 1812; served two terms in Pennsylvania's legislature; been elected in 1820 to Congress for the first of five terms in the House of Representatives; been appointed by President Jackson to be minister to Russia in 1831; been elected to the Senate in 1833, where he stayed until President Polk tapped him to be his secretary of state; and been appointed by President Pierce to be minister to Britain. Along the way he revealed his ambitions in his failed attempts to become the Democratic Party's presidential nominee in 1844, 1848, and 1852. He was a stout sixty-six years old when he entered the White House and remains the only "confirmed bachelor" to serve as president. Politically he was a Jacksonian Democrat and described himself as "a northern man with southern principles." These appear to have been the only principles that guided him. He was among those countless persons whose essential mediocrity, incompetence, and venality lurk behind worldly achievements, natty attire, and chatty familiarity.[1]

His administration was among the more corrupt in American history.[2] A House of Representatives investigation uncovered massive and widespread kickbacks for contracts, votes, and offices. The president himself shamelessly wielded public resources to enrich his private fortune and political power. The worst miscreant, however, was Secretary of War John Floyd, a Mississippi slavocrat who not only juggled books and personnel to extract a fortune in public resources and divvy it up among himself and his cronies, but as the Confederacy was forming, passed crucial intelligence to the rebels and dispersed American military forces to prevent them from reacting promptly against the rebellion.

With such massive and shameless malfeasance the president and his men became known as the "Buccaneers." Yet Buchanan and his coterie got away with all that without any of them being prosecuted, let alone serving time. Congress turned a deaf ear to any allegations of wrongdoing. This was partly because Democrats controlled the Senate by 37 to 23 and the House by 128 to 92 Republicans and 14 Whigs. But more importantly, Congress and the nation faced a series of crises that overshadowed any scandals.

The first controversy to rock the nation during Buchanan's presidency came not from his administration but from the Supreme Court, and a mere two days after he took office. After the 1854 Kansas-Nebraska Act, no act incensed morally sensitive Americans more than the Supreme Court's 1857 *Dred Scott v. Sandford* decision.[3] Dred Scott was a slave who accompanied his master, army surgeon John Emerson, first to Fort Armstrong, at Rock Island, Illinois, then to Fort Snelling in Wisconsin Territory. In all, Scott spent three years in free states or territories. After his master died, Scott became the property of Emerson's wife, Eliza. In April 1846 Scott filed for emancipation in Missouri's court system on the grounds that, according to the state's law, a master who took his slaves into free territory automatically emancipated them. He won his case in the lower court but lost in the superior court when Eliza appealed. Meanwhile Eliza remarried and moved to Massachusetts with her husband, Calvin Chafee, leaving Scott in the hands of her brother John Sanford. In 1853 Scott appealed Missouri's decision to the federal circuit court, which accepted it, although in designating the case *Scott v. Sandford*, the court misspelled one of the principal's names. When these judges ruled against him, Scott once again appealed. The opposing lawyers argued the case before the Supreme Court in February 1856. The justices did not get around to reaching a decision for another year.

In *Scott v. Sandford*, the Supreme Court, like the three lower courts, pondered questions with potentially revolutionary constitutional, political, and moral answers. Had Scott's years of residence in a free state freed him? Even if he were free, as a black man was Scott a citizen with the right to sue in a federal court? Had Congress acted unconstitutionally when it passed the 1787 Northwest Ordinance forbidding slavery in the Northwest Territory and the 1820 Missouri Compromise forbidding slavery above 36°30′ north latitude?

The Supreme Court's 1851 *Strader v. Graham* decision provided a powerful precedent that had already guided the decisions of Missouri's superior court and the federal circuit court. This case involved two Kentucky slaves who escaped to Ohio. Chief Justice Roger Taney ruled that the "once free, always free" doctrine was unconstitutional and the law of the state from which slaves escaped determined their fate. Thus federal courts had no jurisdiction over such cases and a slave state's laws could trump a free state's laws. At first Taney and a majority mulled using *Strader v. Graham* to dismiss the Dred Scott case, then changed their mind. The chief justice and his fellow slavocrats on the court saw the Dred Scott case as a powerful weapon by which to advance their cause.

The justices ruled seven to two against the plaintiff. Chief Justice Taney was eighty when he read this crucial decision on March 6, 1857, and his age showed. Yet, while his voice quavered and waned, his words could not have been more striking in their impact. He began by asserting slavocracy's "once a slave, always a slave" doctrine and attacking the concept of "once free, always free." Slaves by definition had no rights and thus could not sue. He could have ended his case there but instead asserted a broader opinion that he hoped would imbed slavocracy forever in the nation's legal foundations. Turning a blind eye to the Constitution's "diversity of citizenship" clause, he insisted that the framers intended that even free blacks could not be federal citizens. Each state or territory had the sole right to determine the question of slavery for itself. He repudiated the 1787 Northwest Ordinance and 1820 Missouri Compromise by ruling that Congress had no power to restrict slavery in any way, anywhere. Slaves were property and thus their masters were protected by the Fifth Amendment's clause that prevented anyone from being deprived of his or her property without due legal process. Finally, Taney argued that these legal principles were embedded in the loftiest morality, since blacks were "altogether unfit to associate with the white race . . . and so far inferior that they had no rights which the white man was bound to respect." This permitted any black to be "justly and lawfully . . . reduced to slavery for his benefit."[4]

The Supreme Court's 1857 Dred Scott decision had revolutionary implications. Blacks, whether slave or free, were not and never could be citizens. Congress could not impose any restrictions on slavery. Only the states and territories could determine whether slavery was legal. Thus, theoretically, slavery could be extended or reestablished anywhere.

As slavocrats and most Democrats cheered, Republicans and abolitionists harshly condemned the Dred Scott decision. Abraham Lincoln was among countless people who excoriated Taney's court for grounding their decision in the ideology of slavocracy rather than decades of legal and political precedents. The first session of Congress under the

Constitution reaffirmed the 1787 Northwest Ordinance that forbade slavery in that territory. In 1808 Congress passed a bill outlawing the importation of slaves. The 1820 Missouri Compromise was grounded on these precedents. None of the framers then living denied the constitutionality of these laws. The Constitution's institutions are rooted in and shaped by the Declaration of Independence's values that "all men are created equal" and "liberty and justice for all." Lincoln was appalled by the "obvious violence" that Taney and the six other justices had inflected on "the plain unmistakable language of the Declaration"; in doing so they had shamelessly violated the nation's founding document to the point where, "if its framers could rise from their graves, they could not recognize it."[5]

The Dred Scott decision's blatant miscarriage of justice sullied Lincoln's faith in the Supreme Court as the impartial judicial institution that the framers intended. Thereafter he believed that judicial rulings were valid as far as they concurred with the beliefs of the president and majorities in Congress: "If the policy of the government, upon vital questions affecting the whole people, is to be irrevocably fixed by decision of the Supreme Court, the instant they are made . . . the people will have ceased to be their own rulers, having . . . resigned their government into the hands of the . . . tribunal."[6] In rejecting the concept of judicial review, Lincoln abandoned a key constitutional principle of Hamiltonianism and embraced its opposed doctrine in Jeffersonism.

Kansas was the Buchanan administration's most pressing political issue.[7] The territory was split between the slavocrat Lecompton and Free Soil Topeka governments and was ravaged by worsening violence. Buchanan was determined to uphold the Lecompton government as recognized by his Democratic predecessor and the Democratic-controlled Congress and to crush the upstart Topeka government. For this mission he appointed as governor his friend Robert Walker, a Democratic senator and slaveholder from Mississippi who favored slavery's extension and Cuba's acquisition.

Although Walker clearly had the ideological, political, and economic credentials for this hatchet job, he lacked a crucial ingredient—amorality. He soon learned that the slavocrats had rigged the elections and initiated the cycle of violence. He understood that the territory's legally approved government would never achieve legitimacy without the support of most Kansas citizens. To this end he implored Free Soilers to vote in the territory's legislative elections scheduled for October 1857.

The Free Soilers ignored Walker's pleas and continued to boycott anything associated with the Lecompton government. As a result, voter turnout was low, with only 2,200 of 9,250 registered voters actually showing up at the polls. But once again the slavocrats made up for that with thousands of fraudulent votes. The cheating was astonishingly blatant. Over 1,200 names came from a Cincinnati residential directory, while 2,900 were cast in two rural districts that had only 130 registered voters between them.

Walker threw out these returns even though Buchanan pressured him to certify the election no matter how rigged it was. The fraudulent vote made an utter mockery of Stephen Douglas's notion of "popular sovereignty." In what may have been his finest hour, on December 3, Douglas strode angrily into the White House and confronted President Buchanan with the cheating. Buchanan not only denied this reality but he and other leading Democratic slavocrats vowed to do all they could to undercut Douglas's prominence within the party. The resulting split in the Democratic Party would bring the Republicans to power three years later.

Meanwhile the Lecompton government ignored Walker's directives and, on November 7, held a convention that approved a proslavery state constitution to be submitted for approval in a referendum scheduled for December 21. Free Soilers once again sat out the vote. Slavocrats approved their handiwork by 6,226 to 569; an investigation later found 2,720 fraudulent votes. The Topeka government held its own referendum on January 4, 1858. The result was 10,226 against and 138 for the Lecompton constitution.

Although clearly several thousand more people opposed than approved the Lecompton constitution, Buchanan sent it as a bill to Congress on February 2. The Senate approved it by 33 to 25 on March 23, but it died in the House with only 112 to 120 votes on April 1, 1858. A conference committee devised a compromise bill that on April 30 passed the Senate by 31 to 22 and the House by 112 to 103 and was signed into law by Buchanan. But this had to be approved by Kansas voters. Buchanan promised that federal officials would carefully monitor the referendum scheduled for August 2, 1858. Free Soilers turned out and rejected the revised Lecompton constitution by 11,300 to 1,788. In its efforts to establish a legitimate government, Kansas was back at square one, but this time the seesaw of political power had shifted decisively toward Free Soilers.

Violence between groups with starkly opposed ways of seeing the world was not confined to Kansas. The Mormons, or Church of Latter-Day Saints, began suffering persecution not long after Joseph Smith gathered his first disciples in 1830.[8] Although Mormons insisted that they were faithful followers of Jesus Christ, most Christians viewed their religion as heretical, especially their practice of "plural marriage" for men. The conflict was not confined to theology. A vicious cycle pursued the group everywhere they tried to settle. The Mormons would seek to protect themselves by dominating their region's business and politics, which would provoke reactions that would turn violent and drive them into another exile. In 1839 a mob killed seventeen Mormons at Haun's Mill, Missouri. In 1844 officials arrested Smith and his brother for destroying the printing press of a Mormon dissenter. A mob broke into the jail at Nauvoo, Illinois, where the Smiths were incarcerated and murdered them.

Brigham Young assumed the Mormon leadership and, Moses-like, in 1846 led the first of a series of groups westward to refuge in the Great Salt Lake valley. There they built a small, flourishing civilization in the desert. Salt Lake City became the metropolis for a cluster of settlements. In 1849 the Mormons held a constitutional convention and applied to Congress to become a state named Deseret.[9]

Congress rejected that petition in 1850 and instead designated as Utah Territory a vast swath of the Great Basin where the Mormons had settled. Although President Fillmore appointed Young as the territory's governor and Indian superintendent, he also tapped three non-Mormons as federal judges. These judges were appalled by Young's cult-like theocracy, with its polygamy and discrimination against non-Mormons. In 1854 President Franklin Pierce pointedly did not renew Young's appointment as governor, but he could not initially find any non-Mormon willing to take that post. Legally this let Young retain the governorship until someone officially replaced him.

Young and the Mormon ruling council decided to try to pressure Washington into granting them the autonomy they had long sought. They initiated a series of aggressive acts that culminated not in autonomy but in a quasi-war between them and the federal government. In December 1856 a mob broke into the office of Judge George Stiles, whom the Mormons had excommunicated, burned his law books, and stole the court records. In early 1857 the Mormons intimidated a federal surveying party into withdrawing from the territory. Around the same time Mormons murdered an apostate father and son.

The worsening anarchy in Utah Territory forced the Buchanan administration to act. The consensus was for Buchanan to appoint a new governor and three new judges and send them to the territory under a military escort large enough to restore order. Col. Albert Sidney Johnson commanded the fifteen-hundred-man expedition.

Learning of the expedition, Young gathered twenty-five hundred militia and fortified Echo Canyon, through which the main trail led to the Mormon homeland. As Johnson's force neared, Young sent out a raiding party that attacked three separate supply trains and altogether burned seventy-four wagons and stole fourteen hundred head of cattle and horses. Without supplies, Johnson and his men had to winter at Fort Bridger on the Green River, 115 miles east of Salt Lake City. Mormon raiders attacked an emigrant wagon train that was passing through the territory en route to California, murdered over 120 men, women, and children, and took 18 babies back for adoption, a vicious atrocity that became known as the Mountain Meadows Massacre.[10]

The Mormons escaped prosecution for these horrendous crimes. Buchanan and his cabinet agreed to appease rather than crush their rebellion. The Mormons were far away, while the administration faced a worsening crisis across the rest of the country.

In 1857 a speculation-fueled financial bubble burst and plunged the U.S. economy into a prolonged depression. Over the proceeding half-dozen years the number of banks had more than doubled, to fifteen hundred. No federal bank or laws existed to regulate the industry to deter reckless financial gambles and fraud. Only states could charter and oversee banks; they competed with each other to charter ever more banks while turning a blind eye to excesses and irregularities.[11]

The immediate trigger for the financial panic was the collapse of several New York banks when European investors liquidated their holdings and demanded hard coin in exchange. With virtually all banks in debt to each other, the collapse of some either bankrupted or devastated the others. The panic coincided with sharp cutbacks in European purchases of American wheat, which was no longer needed after the Crimean War ended the previous year. The collapse of the financial and farm markets in turn dragged down other economic sectors in a domino effect of failed businesses. Increasingly more people had less income and thus bought fewer goods or started fewer new enterprises.

The depression prompted Republicans to try to push through Congress their economic agenda. They proposed bills for internal improvements, a protective tariff, a central bank, a homestead act, a transcontinental railroad, and a land-grant college act. The Democrats killed every one of these proposals. For now the Hamiltonian agenda appeared dead. Within a few years it would experience a stunning revival.

Abraham Lincoln made his latest attempt at a political comeback in 1858 when the Illinois Republican Party nominated him to run against Stephen Douglas for his Senate seat. Upon learning who would oppose him, Douglas worried that "I shall have my hands full." He generously described Lincoln as a man who was "as honest as he is shrewd and if I beat him, my victory will be hardly won."[12]

Lincoln opened his campaign with some of his most famous words: "'A house divided against itself cannot stand.' I believe this government cannot endure, permanently, half slave and half free. I do not expect the Union to be dissolved—I do not expect the house to fall—but I do expect it will cease to be divided. It will become all one thing or all the other."[13]

Shortly thereafter he challenged Douglas to join him on the campaign trail for a series of debates around the state.[14] To his credit, Douglas accepted even though as the favored candidate he was better off ignoring than debating his lesser-known opponent. The result was seven debates, starting at Ottawa on August 21, then Freeport on August 27, Jonesboro on September 15, Charleston on September 18, Galesburg on October 7, Quincy on October 13, and ending at Alton on October 15. The format was to alternate who spoke first, with the lead speaker allowed an hour, his opponent an hour and a half to reply, then back to the first for a half-hour rebuttal. Douglas opened four and Lincoln three of the debates.

The men clashed in more than an ideological sense. At a very lean six foot four inches tall, Lincoln towered above the "Little Giant," who at a stout five foot six inches rose only to his rival's shoulder. Douglas's baritone voice boomed while Lincoln's high-pitched voice twanged. Douglas's gestures were fluid and theatrical; Lincoln's were awkward. Douglas's clothing was tailored and stylish; Lincoln's was rumpled and ill-fitting.

Between debates the candidates did not quietly rest up for the next. During the campaign, Douglas made 130 campaign speeches and journeyed 5,227 miles around the state; Lincoln made 63, or half as many, speeches but traveled 4,350 miles—3,400 by train, 600 by carriage, and 350 by boat.[15] All along Lincoln was essentially his own campaign manager, secretary, and fund-raiser. He was aided, of course, by each local Republican Party branch that turned out to cheer, feed, and lodge him before sending him onward.

During the Freeport debate, Lincoln asked the crucial constitutional and political question that the Supreme Court answered with its Dred Scott decision: "Can the people of a United States territory in any lawful way, against the wish of any citizen of the United States, exclude slavery from its limits prior to the formation of a state constitution?"[16]

That question forced Douglas to face a philosophical and political dilemma. If he agreed and cited his "popular sovereignty" doctrine, he would repudiate the Dred Scott decision and alienate potential southern Democrats for his intended presidential campaign in 1860. If he flip-flopped on popular sovereignty he would alienate northern Democrats and might lose his current reelection campaign. He tried to bridge this chasm with generalities that praised both state and congressional authority. He then counterattacked by accusing Lincoln of being a radical abolitionist who "believes that the Almighty made the Negro equal to the white man. He thinks that the Negro is his brother. . . . I believe that this government of ours is founded on the white basis. It was made by the white man for the benefit of the white man, to be administered by white men. . . . Preserve the purity of our Government as well as the purity of our race; no amalgamation, political or otherwise, with inferior races!" He condemned "any mixture or amalgamation with inferior races" as leading to "degeneration, demoralization, and degradation."[17]

Three powerful forces shaped Lincoln's views on race: the Declaration of Independence, the Constitution, and his own conscience.[18] He presented overwhelming evidence that the nation's founders hated slavery, tried to contain it, and looked forward to its eventual demise: "The framers of the Constitution found the institution of slavery amongst their other institutions at the time. They found that by an effort to eradicate it, they might lose much of what they had already gained. They were obliged to bow to the necessity. They gave power to Congress to abolish the slave trade at the end of twenty years. They also prohibited slavery in the Territories where it did not exist. They did what they could and yielded to the necessity for the rest."[19] He distinguished between slavery in the existing states, which he believed was constitutional, and slavery's extension to new territories, which he opposed and believed that Congress was empowered to determine. He also believed that Congress was empowered to abolish slavery in the District of Columbia.

For Lincoln, the debates boiled down to one crucial issue—"the differences between the men who think slavery is wrong and those who do not think it wrong."[20] He condemned slavery as simply evil: "If slavery is not wrong, nothing is wrong." He explained the stark and unbridgeable chasm between himself and his opponent: "It is the eternal struggle between these two principles—right and wrong—throughout the world. They are two principles that have stood face to face from the beginning of time; and will ever continue to struggle."[21] He demolished the slavocrat arguments for slavery. As for the allegation that slaves are better off than white laborers, he noted that "we never hear of the man who wishes to take good of it by being a slave himself." He pointed out that even "the most dumb and stupid slave that ever toiled for a master does constantly know that he is wronged." And if skin color is the criteria for slavery then by "this rule, you are to be slave to the first man you meet with a fairer skin than your own." As for the argument that an alleged superior intelligence gives whites the right to enslave blacks, by "this rule you are to be slave to the first man you meet with an intellect superior to your own."[22] The Declaration of Independence made no racial distinction in asserting that "all men [are] created equal—equal in 'certain inalienable rights, among which are life, liberty, and the pursuit of happiness.'" He argued that "there is no reason in the world why the Negro is not entitled to all the natural rights enumerated in that Declaration."[23]

Yet, having said all that, Lincoln nonetheless believed that the white and black races should remain separate. Like his hero Henry Clay, he favored the voluntary resettlement of blacks in Liberia or Latin America.[24] As for the vast majority of blacks who remained in the United States, he could not imagine let alone promote a time when they would be accepted as politically equal and socially and economically integrated with whites. He reassured the public that "I am not nor ever have been in favor of making voters or jurors of Negroes, nor of qualifying them to hold office, nor to intermarry with white people." He believed that the "physical difference between the white and black races . . . will forever forbid the two races living together on terms of social and political equality." To those who condemned abolition for leading to miscegenation, he dismissed that "counterfeit logic which concludes that because I do not want a black woman for a slave I must necessarily want her for a wife."[25] Yet he was never recorded as expressing the common belief of his time that blacks were intellectually or morally inferior to whites.

The election was virtually a dead heat, with about 125,000 votes for the Republicans, 121,000 for the Douglas Democrats, and 5,000 for the Buchanan Democrats. It was the gerrymandered districts that decided the contest, allocating fifty-three seats to the Democrats and forty-seven to the Republicans. In the legislative election for the Senate seat on January 5, 1859, Douglas beat Lincoln by fifty-four to forty-six votes.[26]

Lincoln was at once disappointed and philosophical about his defeat: "I am glad I made the last race. It gave me a hearing on the great and durable question of the age, which I have had in no other way; and though I now sink out of view, and shall be forgotten, I believe I made some marks which will tell for the cause of civil liberty long after I am gone." He insisted that the "fight must go on. The cause of civil liberty must not be surrendered at the end of one or even one hundred defeats."[27] And so it would, but for progressives this struggle increasingly seemed a lost cause.

Abolitionists were all but powerless. They were only a sliver of the North's population. Over the decades all their petitions, pamphlets,

and protests, along with their aid to escaped slaves, inspired few con-
verts to their cause. Instead, as slaveholders felt more morally besieged,
they became more extreme in defending their way of life. For decades
nearly all slaveholders upheld a country half slave and half free, while
only a handful of fire-eaters demanded secession. This balance tilted
during the 1850s until by 1861 most slaveholders zealously insisted on
having their own country.[28]

Southern paranoia swelled in 1857, when Hinton Rowan Helper's
book *The Impending Crisis of the South: How to Meet It* appeared, arguing
that slavery stunted and distorted the South's economic as well as moral
development; that the southern aristocracy repressed and exploited both
slaves and poor whites; and that slavery was an inefficient and wasteful
economic system that caused the South to fall ever further behind the
North. Southern states censored the book when they learned about it.
North Carolina's law was the severest—anyone caught distributing the
book would be publicly whipped and imprisoned for a year the first time
and hanged the next. Of course, sales soared with the southern condemnation as bold and curious natives sought to peek into its forbidden text.[29]

Slavocrats insisted that popular sovereignty and states' rights permitted the holding and selling of slaves anywhere. In January 1859
Buchanan endorsed this view when he declared that the Dred Scott
decision resolved "the question of slavery in the territories" by con-
firming "the right . . . of every citizen . . . to take his property of
any kind, including slavery, into the common territories" and "have
it protected . . . under the Federal Constitution." Senator Jefferson
Davis of Mississippi followed this up with a resolution holding that
it was the federal government's duty to protect the property rights of
slaveholders in the territories. In May the southern states held a convention at Vicksburg, Mississippi, during which the delegates voted
forty to nineteen for a resolution that called for repealing the 1808
law that outlawed the importation of slaves. If one accepted slavery's
legality and morality, it was hard to dispute Georgia senator William
Goulden's argument that there was no difference "between buying
a man in Virginia, who was a slave there, and buying one in Africa,
who was a slave there."[30]

Southerners became increasingly obsessed, indeed paranoid, over
destroying any real or imagined threats to slavery. Then Harpers Ferry

realized their worst nightmares of a slave revolt whereby they were murdered in their beds by their vengeful chattel.

John Brown had a messiah complex.[31] He believed that God endowed him to crusade against the abomination of slavery and destined him to die as a martyr in this glorious cause. He acquired this vision at a young age and devoted his life to fulfilling it. Along the way he failed at such occupations as farming, sheep raising, cattle driving, and land speculating and sired half a dozen children with his long-suffering wife. His morality stretched thin when it came to money—he was jailed for a fraudulent land deal and was sued twenty-one times. He was among the idealists called to win Kansas as a free state. However, unlike virtually all other Free Soilers, he backed his beliefs with violence. After the border ruffians sacked Lawrence, he led seven men, including two of his sons, to murder five slavocrats along Pottawatomie Creek in May 1856.

This mass murder was the dress rehearsal for a far more ambitious plan in Brown's tormented mind. He intended to provoke a slave rebellion by capturing the federal arsenal at Harpers Ferry and distributing the weapons to blacks. For this operation he gathered nineteen "soldiers," including three of his sons and five blacks, who joined him in the attack. Brown and his men did not act alone. Backing the plot with money and fervor were wealthy abolitionists known as the "Secret Six": Thomas Higginson, Theodore Parker, Samuel Howe, George Stearns, Franklin Sanborn, and Gerrit Smith. Brown, his men, and the Secret Six were an anomaly within the abolitionist movement; virtually all abolitionists advocated nonviolence.

Brown and his men took over the Harpers Ferry arsenal on the evening of October 16, 1858. Although they cut the telegraph wires, word soon spread of the takeover. The next morning militia surrounded the arsenal and a contingent of marines arrived that afternoon. Ironically, the two ranking federal army officers who captured the raiders—Col. Robert E. Lee and Lt. J. E. B. Stuart—would themselves soon commit treason against the United States. Sporadic gunfire echoed through the town and surrounding hills as each side sniped at the other. Lee ordered Stuart and twelve men to storm the arsenal. One marine and two of Brown's followers died in the fighting before Brown and his six surviving men surrendered. These deaths were atop the four citizens and eight raiders previously killed. Five of Brown's followers posted outside the arsenal managed to escape. The subsequent trial culminated with death sentences for Brown and his men; four were carried out on December 16, 1859, and the other two, after failed appeals, on March 16, 1860. On December 2, 1859, John Brown strode to the scaffold as fearlessly as he fought against slavery.

Harpers Ferry had an enormous impact on the 1860 election and thus America's fate.[32] Although the vast majority of northerners, including most abolitionists, abhorred and denounced the raid, a few, like William Garrison, Wendell Phillips, Frederick Douglass, Ralph Waldo Emerson, Henry David Thoreau, Herman Melville, Walt Whitman, and John Greenleaf Whittier, publicly responded by denouncing slavery and admiring Brown's courage. William Seward inspired abolitionists and enraged slavocrats by declaring that "I know and you know that a revolution has begun. I know, and all the world knows that revolutions never go backward."[33] The violence and fanaticism of Brown and his followers appalled Abraham Lincoln, who wrote, "We have a means provided for the expression of our belief in regard to slavery—it is through the ballot box—the peaceful method provided by the Constitution."[34]

Once a zealous, outspoken minority, Democratic Party fire-eaters who exalted slavery and secession swelled their ranks after Harpers Ferry. The *Richmond (VA) Enquirer* summed up the raid's impact: "The Harpers Ferry invasion has advanced the cause of disunion more than any other event that has happened since the formation of the national government."[35] John Brown would be the grim reaper ominously standing before countless southern men as they cast their ballots in 1860.

6

The Election

If slavery is right, all words, acts, laws, and constitution against it
are themselves wrong, and should be silenced and swept away. If it is
right, we cannot justly object to its nationality—its universality;
if it is wrong, they cannot justly insist on its extension.

ABRAHAM LINCOLN

Our new government . . . rests on the great truth, that the negro
is not equal to the white man; that slavery—subordination to
the superior race—is his natural and normal condition.

ALEXANDER STEPHENS

America was undergoing revolutionary economic and demographic changes in 1860.[1] Over the preceding decade, the nation's population had soared by more than a third, from 23.2 million to 31.5 million. Of those 8.2 million new people, 5.5 million were native born and 2.7 million were immigrants. Although every state had more people, the North carried most of that growth. This led to the latest shift in the House of Representative's regional power imbalance, with slave states accounting for only 83 of 233 members, or 36 percent. Yet slavery was hardly the dying institution that many hoped or feared it to be. In 1860 the census counted 3,953,760 slaves worth $3.059 billion, up from 1,191,354 slaves worth $291 million in 1810.[2]

The economic changes were even more stunning. Related industrial, transportation, and communications revolutions were rapidly transforming mid-nineteenth-century America. Factories mass produced more goods at cheaper prices. Railroads and steamboats transported these goods at cheaper rates. The telegraph tried the nation together literally if not figuratively with nearly instantaneous communications. These greater efficiencies and economies of scale dropped commodity and consumer prices by 45 percent and 50 percent, respectively, from 1815 to 1860. Meanwhile wages and wealth rose with the greater demand for labor and the cheaper prices. The result was a virtuous economic cycle whereby increasingly cheaper goods led to greater demand that led to greater production that led to cheaper prices. Thus did these revolutions feed each other.[3]

Nonetheless, every region of the nation remained rural, with only one in four Americans living in a town with twenty-five hundred or more people. Six of ten Americans, or 59 percent, were farmers while less than one in five, or 18 percent, were manufacturers. Farms produced 75 percent of the nation's exports, with cotton the most important crop.[4]

The North benefited far more from the industrial revolution than the South. Of the national economy in 1860, the North accounted for 73 percent and the South 26 percent. A comparison between industries reveals startling disparities:

> In 1860, the North had produced $167,295 worth of flour and meal as compared with the South's $55,849,000. The North had 19,770 miles of railway track; the south, 10,513. . . . The North . . . had 109,000 manufacturing establishments to the South's 31,300. The capital investment in Northern manufactures was $842,000,000 to the South's $167,855,000. The number of workers in Northern manufactures was 1,131,600 to the South's 189,000. The values of the manufactured products turned out in the North was $1,594,486,000 compared to the South's $291,375,000. . . . The capital stock of the North's banks was put at $292,594,000; of the South's banks, at $129,287,000. The total bank deposits in the North stood at $1,877,678,000; in the South, at $66,124,000. In the North money in circulation totaled $119,826,000; in the South, $87,276.000.[5]

Indeed, the South harbored only 5 percent of the nation's industrial capacity and three in ten of its white people. These would be enormous if not insurmountable disadvantages in the coming Civil War.

Yet if each region's wealth were divvied up equally among its people, each southerner would be richer than each northerner. In 1860 the average slaveholder was ten times wealthier than the average northern farmer, by $33,906 to $3,858, and owned five and a half times more land, valued at $46.74 an acre compared to $13.47 an acre. The regional gap was actually widening, as cotton and slave prices doubled during the 1850s. Cotton exports soared from $681,176 to $1,739,893 from 1850 to 1860, while the assessed value of four million slaves rose from $1.5 billion to $3 billion. Those regional disparities are grossly misleading without an understanding of how wealth was actually distributed in the North and South.[6]

The American Dream of upward economic, social, and educational mobility was largely confined to the North. Most northerners enjoyed solid middle-class incomes and lifestyles with relatively well-paying jobs, well-furnished homes, good schooling, and ease in embarking on new careers if need be. Most southerners were trapped and exploited by the elite at the top of either a feudal or slave socioeconomic pyramid, depending on whether they were white or black.

Northerners who journeyed beyond the Mason-Dixon Line were appalled by what they found. Senator William Seward of New York made three fact-finding trips across swaths of the South, in 1835, 1846, and 1857, and each time despaired at the "exhausted soil, old and decaying towns, wretchedly neglected roads, and, in every respect, an absence of enterprise and improvement. . . . Such has been the effect of slavery." Frederick Law Olmstead observed that "for every rich man's house . . . I passed a dozen shabby and half furnished cottages and at least a hundred cabins—mere hovels, such as none but a poor farmer would house his cattle in at the north." Cassius Clay of Kentucky, Henry Clay's cousin, suffered the same despair when he traveled north and contrasted that region's "industry, ingenuity, numbers, and wealth" with his own state's stagnation and mass poverty amid rich planters. In favoring slavery's eventual demise, Republicans like George Weston argued that "to destroy slavery is not to destroy the South, but to change its social organization for the better."[7]

Abraham Lincoln was doing quite well himself. Then fifty-one years old, he and his family lived a comfortable upper-middle-class life in a

$5,000 home and owned $12,000 in other property. The Lincolns had three living sons, Robert, Willie, and Thomas or Tad, respectively aged sixteen, nine, and seven. Two servants helped Mary care for the house, cooking, and boys.[8]

Lincoln worked incessantly behind the scenes to promote the Republican Party. The party was split between moderates who were willing to compromise on the issues and radicals who were not. Lincoln was a moderate who continually sought to convince others that pragmatism was better for the party and nation than idealism. For instance, he wrote Salmon Chase, then Ohio's Radical Republican governor, advising him that introducing "a proposition for repeal of the Fugitive Slave law, into the next Republican National Convention, will explode the convention and the party. Having turned your attention to the point, I wish to do no more."[9]

Although Lincoln denied his interest in one day running for president, his movements after he lost his 1858 Senate campaign called this into question. In 1859 he journeyed four thousand miles and gave twenty-three speeches in Ohio, Michigan, Wisconsin, and Kansas. Then, in midwinter 1860, he traveled from Springfield all the way to New York City to give a speech at the Cooper Union Institute. What he said on February 27, 1860, ranks among his greatest orations.[10] William Cullen Bryant, the poet and newspaper editor, introduced him.

Lincoln was well aware that his audience extended far beyond the several hundred people sitting before him, that his words would resonate across the nation. He explored the breadth and depth of the founders' intentions and the nation's worsening divisions over slavery. The result for every American was a stark moral choice: "If slavery is right, all words, acts, laws, and constitution against it are themselves wrong, and should be silenced and swept away. If it is right, we cannot justly object to its nationality—its universality; if it is wrong, they cannot justly insist on its extension." Lincoln urged his audience to share his conclusion that slavery was indeed a terrible evil and that it must be not be allowed to spread. Yet to preserve the Union it was equally essential that, for now, slavery must be tolerated where it currently existed.[11]

No election in American history was more consequential than that of 1860.[12] The first party to name candidates for the presidency and vice presidency was brand new. The Constitutional Union Party was composed mostly of older Whigs and Know Nothings who sought a middle ground between Democrats and Republicans. Shortly after their convention opened at Baltimore on May 9, the delegates nominated senators John Bell of Tennessee and Edward Everett of Massachusetts as their presidential and vice presidential candidates.

The Republican Party was the next to name its contenders. Abraham Lincoln, the eventual winner, had enormous handicaps compared to his rivals. His only experience at the national political level was a single two-year term in the House of Representatives. He had lost both of his attempts to be elected to the U.S. Senate. His campaign committee, brilliantly headed by David Davis, tried to obscure his inexperience by promoting Lincoln as "the rail-splitter," a self-made man who rose from poverty to prosperity through hard work, good humor, and keen intelligence. They mass-marketed Lincoln with an official biography, slogans, songs, and rallies.[13]

The Republicans held their convention at the Wigwam, a recently completed meeting hall in Chicago, from May 16 to 18. This venue was perfect for Illinois Republicans to promote the nomination of their native son. Like the other candidates, Lincoln stayed home to await the verdict. He sent one key message to David Davis, his campaign manager in Chicago: "Make no contracts that will bind me."[14] Davis did not obey that order. He promised a cabinet post to Simon Cameron, the party's most prominent Pennsylvanian, if he deferred running for the nomination and instead delivered his state to Lincoln.

Although he faced such political giants as William Seward, Salmon Chase, Simon Cameron, and Edward Bates, Lincoln was no dark horse candidate. For those who followed politics, he was either renowned or reviled for the positions he had articulated during his debates with Stephen Douglas two years earlier. His speaking tour in the northeast in 1859 and his Cooper Union speech in February 1860 further promoted his image and views. He was a small town "man of the people" and westerner unsullied by the political tar baby of Washington or big-city machines. Illinois and Indiana were swing states that the midwesterner Lincoln would likely carry. If elected he would be the first president born west of the Appalachian Mountains and thus would symbolize how much the nation's center of population and political and economic gravity had shifted over the previous century.

Lincoln's cousin, John Hanks, contrived an effective bit of political theater. He carried into the Wigwam two fence rails that he claimed Lincoln had split thirty years earlier. Hanks and other supporters then proclaimed Lincoln the "Rail-Splitter Candidate" for president.

On the first ballot of 466 votes cast, Lincoln won a solid second place with 102 votes, behind Seward's 173½ but with twice as many as the next three candidates, Cameron with 50½, Chase with 49, and Bates with 48. The rest of the votes were spread among a host of minor figures. It was then that Davis cut that deal with Cameron. On the second ballot Pennsylvania's delegation along with many other delegates cast their votes for Lincoln, who with 181 votes was just behind Seward with 184½, while the other candidates all lost votes. On the third ballot, Lincoln surged ahead of Seward with 231½ votes, just a few shy of a majority. Then, with a nod from Chase, Ohio's leader rose and announced that the state was shifting its votes to Lincoln; others followed, giving Lincoln 364. In a show of party unity, Seward's supporters threw their votes to Lincoln, who won unanimously. Senator Hannibal Hamlin of Maine was chosen as Lincoln's running mate.

That afternoon a delegation of party leaders took the train down to Springfield and officially offered Lincoln the nomination. Lincoln gratefully accepted. Governor John Wood lent Lincoln a room in the state capitol for his campaign headquarters. Although Lincoln was tempted to launch a speaking campaign across the states, etiquette insisted that he should not seem to want the White House too eagerly. Prominent Republicans across the country championed Lincoln in their speeches whether they were running for reelection or not. Spearheading Lincoln's campaign at the grassroots level were Wide Awake clubs that rather ominously dressed in black and paraded with split rails and flaming torches through the streets.

As the Republicans unified around Lincoln, the Democrats tore apart between two bitterly opposed factions. Of all the possible sites for the Democratic convention in 1860, none could have been worse than Charleston, the epicenter of slavocracy, nullification, and secession. A rancorous deadlock ensued after the convention opened on April 23. Although a minority in numbers, the fire-eaters dominated the proceedings, shouted down their rivals, and did all they could to castigate front-runner Stephen Douglas for opposing the Lecompton constitution and Dred Scott decision. The result after fifty-nine votes over nine grueling days was Douglas stuck far from the required support of two-thirds of delegates. Slavocrats rallied around Vice President John Breckinridge of Kentucky, who advocated spreading slavery anywhere and suppressing freedom of speech and freedom of the press for anyone who opposed slavery. One by one the southern delegations walked out. Those left finally agreed to call it quits and reconvene at Baltimore after the Republican convention.

The change of locale failed to dilute the passions and positions of the fire-eaters. Yet word that the Republican Party had nominated Lincoln gave moderate and extreme Democrats alike a common enemy against whom to vent their rage. After convening at Baltimore on June 18, they nominated Douglas on the second ballot and soon tapped Herschel Johnson of Georgia as his running mate. That outpouring of Democratic Party unity, however, swiftly collapsed. The following day Breckinridge's supporters met in a separate hall and unanimously declared him the Democratic Party's candidate, then nominated Joseph Lane of Oregon as his running mate.

This four-man race broke down into two parallel contests, Lincoln versus Douglas in the North and Breckinridge versus Bell in the South. The November 6 election results reflected the nation's political fragmentation. Lincoln won a plurality with 1,866,452 votes, or 35.4 percent of the total, over Douglas with 1,376,957, Breckinridge with 849,781, Bell with 588,849, and the Fusion Party, which lacked a nominee, with 595,846. Of course, the American people do not elect presidents, special electors do based on who wins which states. The results put Lincoln over the top with 180 electors—107 northern, 73 western, and none from the South—compared to 72 for Breckinridge, 39 for Bell, and 12 for Douglas. The victory was lopsided regionally as well, with nearly all of Lincoln's votes coming from northern states while he carried only 2 of 996 southern counties.[15]

A national crisis immediately followed the election.[16] On November 10 South Carolina's legislature voted unanimously to hold a state convention on December 6 to consider secession. Within a month every state across the Lower South scheduled its own convention.

The lame-duck president did nothing to stem that tide. In the annual address that he sent to Congress on December 3, Buchanan admitted that secession was unconstitutional but blamed the nation's breakup on "the long continued and intemperate interference of the northern people with the question of slavery in the Southern States." Other than that he fatalistically accepted secession and offered no suggestions for how to entice the rebel states back into the Union. Indeed, he declared that "I am the last president of the United States."[17]

Most Congressional leaders acted more responsibly. Each chamber set up committees to debate and propose compromises that might resolve the crisis. The House's Committee of Thirty-Three, with each state represented, eventually hammered out bills to enforce the Fugitive Slave Act and protect slave states from any federal government interference. The Senate Committee of Thirteen was chaired by John Crittenden, a Kentucky Unionist and slave master, and included William Seward of New York. Crittenden and Seward searched for a deal in a series of meetings with political leaders from both houses. The result was called the Crittenden proposals: the federal government would continue not to interfere in any state's practice of slavery; the Missouri Compromise line, which allowed slavery south of 36°30′ north latitude from western Missouri to the Rocky Mountain watershed, would be revived and extended to the Pacific Ocean; slavery would remain legal in the District of Columbia unless Virginia and Maryland agreed to its abolition; and masters would be compensated for any slaves that escaped north and could not be recovered.[18] In both houses, leaders talked about but never formally submitted a Thirteenth Amendment that forbade the federal government from interfering with any state's practice of slavery.

All along, moderate politicians and newspaper editors tried to dilute southern zealotry and paranoia with reason. They explained that the election had changed nothing of substance. While President-Elect Lincoln and Congress's pending Republican majority opposed slavery's extension, they had foresworn challenging slavery where it existed or the constitutional right of masters to recapture their escaped slaves wherever they ran.

Not just southerners condemned and feared Lincoln. Exacerbating northern dread over the secession crisis was uncertainty over the man who had been elected president. Charles Francis Adams, whose father and grandfather had been president, expressed that deep concern: "I must . . . affirm, without hesitation, that in the history of our government down to this hour, no experiment so rash has ever been made as that of elevating to the head of affairs a man with so little previous experience for his task as Mr. Lincoln."[19]

In the end, all the compromise efforts in Congress came to naught. Most men in the Lower South's states were hell-bent to secede and no appeals to reason could stop their lemming-like rush. South Carolina declared its independence on December 20, followed by Mississippi on January 9, Florida on January 10, Alabama on January 11, Georgia on January 19, Louisiana on January 26, and Texas on February 2. The secession of Texas came too late for its delegates to join a convention of the other six states that met at Montgomery, Alabama, on February 4. Over the next week, the delegates wrote a constitution, elected Jefferson Davis the president of the Confederate States of America on February 9, and sent envoys to the other slave states to urge them to secede and join them. Davis was inaugurated as president on February 28. His first decisive act came on March 6, when he called for one hundred thousand volunteers to join the Confederate army.

Slavery was the cause for which the southerners had seceded and would war if need be. Mississippi's declaration of the "Immediate Causes which Induce and Justify the Secession" was typical: "Our position is thoroughly identified with the institution of slavery. . . . A blow at slavery is a blow at commerce and civilization. . . . There was no choice left us but submission to the mandates of abolition, or a dissolution of the Union. . . . It is not a matter of choice, but of necessity. . . . We must either submit to degradation . . . or we must secede from the Union." The Texans expressed more graphically the racist ideology that shaped every dimension of their lives and justified their rebellion: "We hold a as undeniable truths that . . . all white men are and of right ought to be entitled to equal civil and political rights; that the servitude of the African race . . . is mutually beneficial to both bond and free, and is abundantly authorized and justified by the experience of mankind, and the revealed will of the Almighty Creator."[20] Slavocrats saw their region as a separate nation. On the war's eve, Jefferson Davis expressed the outlook of most southerners when he denounced as "political heresy" the idea that "ours is a union of the people, the formation of a nation, and a supreme government charged with providing for the general welfare." Vice President Alexander Stephens most succinctly expressed the Confederate cause: "Our new government . . . rests on the great truth, that the negro is not equal to the white man; that slavery—subordination to the superior race—is his natural and normal condition."[21]

Although most northerners viewed with mingled sorrow and outrage the breakaway of seven states, there were exceptions. Horace Greely, the *New York Tribune*'s outspoken editor, was among those who waved good riddance to the rebels. Like most of his fellow abolitionists, he believed that a truncated United States whose members lived up to American ideals was superior to one that tolerated the evil of slavery among nearly half the states.

Not every slave state embraced secession when the motion was raised. In the first months of 1861 majorities of either legislators or voters rejected drives for secessionist conventions in the Upper South of Virginia, Arkansas, Tennessee, and North Carolina and the border states of Missouri, Kentucky, Maryland, and Delaware. After Lincoln called for seventy-five thousand volunteers to put down the rebellion, each of those states would reopen the debate over whether or not to secede.

As each state in the Lower South rebelled it seized any federal forts, arsenals, warehouses, dockyards, and other federal property in its territory. Louisiana stole a fortune when it appropriated the U.S. mint in New Orleans. Texas alone took over nineteen federal forts. Only two federal strongholds held out, because they were sited on islands guarding the entrances to bays, Fort Sumter at Charleston and Fort Pickens at Pensacola.

The Civil War's first shots exploded on January 9, when South Carolina gunners opened fire on the *Star of the West*, flying the American flag and packed with supplies and 250 troops, as it sailed to Fort Sumter. The vessel's captain prudently reversed course and sailed back to New York. In firing on the American flag, the gunners and the officials who ordered them to do so committed treason, the first of countless such acts over the next four years.[22]

2

Civil War,
1861–1865

7

Limited War

The Union is older than any of the States,
and in fact created them as States.

ABRAHAM LINCOLN

We are not enemies, but friends. We must not be enemies. . . .
The mystic cords of memory, stretching from every battlefield
and patriot grave to every living heart and hearthstone all over
this broad land will yet swell the chorus of the Union, when again
touched, as surely they will be, by the better angels of our nature.

ABRAHAM LINCOLN

Forward to Richmond!

NEW YORK TRIBUNE

We have had no war; we have not even been playing at war.

EDWIN STANTON

Retreat? No, I propose to attack at daybreak and lick them.

ULYSSES S. GRANT

As the secession crisis unfolded Abraham Lincoln remained at Springfield. Like any president-elect, he faced a tedious four-month wait until the inauguration. Yet this interval was anything but uneventful. He viewed the secession of one southern state after another with increasing alarm. As someone who revered the Declaration of Independence, Lincoln certainly believed in the right to revolt against tyrants, but without "a morally justifiable cause . . . revolution is no right but simply a wicked exercise of physical power."[1] And this was exactly how Lincoln viewed the secessionists.

Lincoln mulled various compromise proposals that might entice the rebel states back into the Union. He tentatively endorsed the one proposed by the House and Senate committees to strengthen the Fugitive Slave Act, promise not to abolish slavery in the District of Columbia, and even support a Thirteenth Amendment that forbade the federal government from intervening in any state's practice of slavery, but he adamantly opposed any extension of slavery to the western territories: "Let there be no compromise on the question of extending slavery."[2] In the end, he and his advisors deemed it best that he not publicly say anything until after he took the presidential oath. He would leave it to the lame-duck Buchanan administration and Congress to deal with the worsening crisis.

He spent most of these months assembling his administration. His first step was to choose John Nicolay and John Hay as his secretaries.[3] Their initial task was to screen the hordes of office seekers who lined up outside Lincoln's office on the second floor of the capitol at Springfield. He was determined to have an administration loyal from top to bottom. To this end he eventually purged 1,520 of 1,195 high-ranking Buchanan appointees and replaced them with Republicans. This was just the top of the bureaucratic pyramids. The federal government employed 40,621 civilians in 1861, a number that soared to 195,000 by 1865.[4]

Lincoln's most important job was to assemble his cabinet, later dubbed his "team of rivals" since it included many who had opposed him for the Republican Party nomination along with three Democrats.[5]

The first man Lincoln tapped was his greatest rival. William Seward gratefully accepted the post of secretary of state.[6] He was Lincoln's senior by eight years of life and countless worldly experiences. He had graduated from Union College, soon passed the bar exam, and developed a brilliant career as a lawyer. Like Lincoln he was a once-fervent Whig who became an equally fervent Republican. In all he served four years in New York's senate, twelve years in the U.S. Senate, and four years as New York's governor. He was as good-hearted as he was self-confident, intelligent, and politically savvy. He was a Renaissance man who loved the theater, painting, literature, travel in Europe, fine meals and wines, and horticulture. Initially he disdained Lincoln and sought to be the administration's real power behind a figurehead president. This swiftly changed as Seward saw the political genius, indomitable will, and sterling character behind Lincoln's homespun façade. They became close friends who shared many an evening in amiable conversation after spending the day in terse discussions about how to win the war and then the peace.

Lincoln next chose Salmon Chase as treasury secretary.[7] Chase followed up a Kenyon College education with a law career and a succession of public offices that led him into Ohio's governor's mansion. As an outspoken abolitionist, he was the cabinet's most radical Republican. While he claimed to love humanity, he found individual relationships irksome. This natural tendency was compounded by the overwhelming sorrow of having to bury three wives in succession. Lincoln tried hard to like him and eventually failed. Chase compensated for his dour personality with genuine achievements, most notably by devising an elaborate constitutional case for abolition and spearheading the enactment of the Republican Party's economic agenda. In return, Lincoln rewarded Chase by naming him the Supreme Court's chief justice.

Among all those he asked to join his cabinet, Lincoln was reluctant to give anything, let alone the War Department, to Simon Cameron.[8] Cameron was a two-term senator whose Pennsylvania political machine was notorious for corruption, and a former moderate Democrat who had defected to the Republicans. When asked about Cameron's character, Senator Thaddeus Stevens quipped that he had once believed that Cameron would not steal a red-hot stove but recently had to apologize for changing his mind on the question.[9] Although Lincoln had warned his campaign manager not to cut any deals at the Republican convention, he felt honor-bound to fulfill Davis's promise of a cabinet post to Cameron for the vote of his state's delegation.

The personalities Lincoln chose to fill the big three cabinet positions—the secretaries of state, treasury, and war—tended to overshadow the four second-tier posts. Edward Bates agreed to be Lincoln's attorney general. He was a moderate Missouri Democrat who had served in that state's assembly and courts and as a representative to Congress. Gideon Welles was another Jacksonian Democrat who had evolved toward the political center. He proved to be an excellent secretary of the navy. For postmaster general, Lincoln chose Montgomery Blair. His father was Francis Blair, a political master who once had been a Jacksonian but had recently converted to Republicanism. Blair was an outstanding postmaster general. He turned a $10 million deficit into an $861,000 surplus by 1865, largely by raising fees and cutting waste.[10] The least distinguished cabinet member was Caleb Smith, who headed the Interior Department; Smith was a former Indiana Whig and current Republican.[11]

The day before his fifty-second birthday, Lincoln gave a poignant farewell address in Springfield:

> My Friends: No one . . . can appreciate my feeling of sadness at this parting. To this place and the kindness of these people, I owe everything. Here I have lived a quarter of a century, and have passed from a young to an old man. Here my children have been born and one is buried. I now leave, not knowing when or whether ever I may return, with a task before me greater than that which rested on Washington. Without the assistance of that Divine Being who ever attended him, I cannot succeed. With that assistance, I cannot fail.[12]

Then Lincoln and his family boarded the first of a series of trains that carried them from Springfield to Washington. He turned that journey into a twelve-day whistle-stop tour across the northern states to rally them for national unity and against secession. In all, he traveled 1,904 miles on eighteen different trains, with daily stops along the way to speak or spend the night, most notably at Indianapolis, Cincinnati, Columbus, Pittsburgh, Cleveland, Buffalo, Albany, New York, and Philadelphia.[13]

His most haunting sojourn and remarks were at Independence Hall in Philadelphia, where the Founders crafted and approved the Declaration of Independence and Constitution. As he spoke there on George Washington's birthday, he was "filled with deep emotion at finding myself standing in this place from which sprang the institutions under which we live." He expressed his political philosophy's essence: "I have never had a feeling, politically, that did not spring from the sentiments embodied in the Declaration of Independence. . . . It was that which gave promise that in due time the weights would be lifted from the shoulders of all men, and that all should have an equal chance." He then asked the key question of their time: "Now, my friends, can this country be saved on that basis?"[14]

An overnight train brought the Lincolns to Washington City before dawn on February 23. At the station entrance the weary travelers climbed into a carriage that clattered through the dark, nearly deserted streets to the Willard Hotel, where they resided for the next ten days. From then until his inauguration, the president-elect visited Buchanan at the White House, spoke with key members of Congress, and conferred with his cabinet.

By noon on March 4, 1861, the inauguration day was clear skied but chilly; a shower early that morning had dampened the dust. Outgoing president James Buchanan arrived by carriage before the Willard Hotel and President-Elect Abraham Lincoln climbed in beside him. They rode the few blocks to the East Portico of the Capitol with its unfinished dome. This was not the city's only uncompleted symbol of American aspirations for greatness. Midway down the mall the Washington Monument was half done; the project started in 1848 but halted abruptly in 1854 as funds ran out and patriotic supporters failed to muster majorities willing to renew them in a bitterly divided Congress.

Irony and tension permeated the swearing-in ceremony. Chief Justice Roger Taney, who authored the Dred Scott decision, administered the oath to Abraham Lincoln, an outspoken critic of the ruling. Taney's voice and hand quavered from his eighty-four years. Lincoln's voice was high pitched but powerful and reached most of the thirty thousand listeners crowded before the Capitol.

In his inaugural address, Lincoln faced his life's most formidable oratory challenge. Somehow he had to walk a tightrope between appearing too tough or too soft with the rebel states. His foremost point was that "in contemplation of universal law and of the Constitution, the

Union of these States is perpetual." Of the many reasons upholding this essential truth, the most important was "the history of the Union itself. The Union is much older than the Constitution." Beyond America's own past the history of humanity reveals "that no government proper ever had a provision in its organic law for its own termination." He then exposed "the central idea of secession" as "the essence of anarchy. A majority held in restraint by constitutional checks and limitations, and always changing easily with deliberate changes of popular opinions . . . is the only true sovereign of a free people. Whoever rejects it does, of necessity, fly to anarchy or to despotism." Thus he held that "no State can lawfully get out of the Union; that resolves and ordinances to that effect are legally void; and that acts of violence within any State or States against the authority of the United States are insurrectionary or revolutionary."

Nonetheless, for now he foresaw the need for only modest defensive measures against the secessionists. He promised that the "power confided to me, will be used to hold, occupy, and possess the property and places belonging to the government, and to collect the duties and imposts; but beyond what may be necessary for these objects, there will be no invasion, no using of force against, or among the people anywhere." Yet ultimately what he did depended on rebel decisions: "In your hands, my dissatisfied fellow-countrymen, and not in mine, is the momentous issue of civil war." He soon learned their decision.

He starkly contrasted the differences splitting the nation: "One section of our country believes slavery is right, and ought to be extended, while the other believes it is wrong and ought not to be extended. This is the only substantial dispute." While acknowledging that he upheld the latter values, he tried to reassure the rebels that "I have no purpose, directly or indirectly, to intervene with the institution of slavery in the States where it exists. I believe that I have no lawful right to do so, and I have no intention to do so."

Lincoln ended his speech with an eloquent appeal for national unity: "We are not enemies, but friends. We must not be enemies. . . . The mystic cords of memory, stretching from every battlefield and patriot grave to every living heart and hearthstone all over this broad land will yet swell the chorus of the Union, when again touched, as surely they will be, by the better angels of our nature."[15]

Lincoln no sooner settled into the White House than he faced the first of an unrelenting series of hard choices over the next four years. The day after the inauguration he read an urgent message. Maj. Robert Anderson, Fort Sumter's commander, reported that his eighty-man garrison faced the exhaustion of supplies within six weeks and overwhelming rebel forces ringing Charleston Bay. South Carolina gunners had turned back the supply ship *Star of the West* on January 9. Fort Sumter was not the only imperiled federal garrison in the Confederate states. Fort Pickens guarded Pensacola Bay's entrance but was less vulnerable since it was beyond artillery range of the surrounding shores and held several months' worth of supplies.

Lincoln turned to Winfield Scott, the army's commanding general, and asked him to calculate just what was needed to mount a relief expedition for Fort Sumter. He learned to his dismay that the United States lacked the hard military power to do anything for now. On paper the American army numbered 17,133 men, but it was scattered in small detachments across the United States, including 3,894 in the Department of the East, 3,584 in the Department of the West, 2,258 in Texas, 3,624 in the Department of the Pacific, 685 in Utah, and 686 elsewhere.[16] Desertion and disease brought the real figures much lower. Then there was the steady stream of southern officers who resigned their commissions and headed home as their states seceded. Eventually 313 of 1,108 officers joined the rebel cause.[17]

After conferring with his staff, Scott reported to the president and his cabinet on March 9 that the mission would demand five thousand regular and twenty thousand volunteer troops packed aboard a vast flotilla of vessels filled with provisions and munitions and that would take months to assemble. As if mustering this expedition was not daunting enough, Scott pointed out that sending it against Charleston would most likely provoke the Upper South and possibly the border states to secede. In the short term, he could dispatch a vessel or two that could simply try to run past the rebel batteries to resupply Fort Sumter.[18] The meeting broke up in indecision.

Scott took the initiative to draft an evacuation order to Anderson that he submitted for the secretary of war's approval. Cameron showed it to the president, who told him to put it away for now. The fading hope was that, having vented their passions and made their point, the rebels would come to their senses. Meanwhile the middle course of neither withdrawing nor reinforcing Fort Sumter's garrison seemed the most prudent. The fort's steadily dwindling supplies conflicted with this policy.

Lincoln convened his cabinet on March 15 and posed the crucial question: "Assuming it to be possible to now provision Fort Sumter, is it wise to attempt it?"[19] Seward, Cameron, Welles, and Bates called for abandoning the fort. Chase wanted to send supplies if it did not provoke war. Only Blair supported a relief expedition no matter what. Faced with these divisions, they agreed to shelve a decision for the time being, hoping that reason might prevail with the rebels. Instead, to their chagrin they learned that South Carolina's pressure on Anderson to surrender mounted as Fort Sumter's provisions diminished toward the vanishing point.

Scott submitted his latest plan on March 28, this time urging the abandonment of both Fort Sumter and Fort Pickens to "soothe and give confidence to the eight remaining slave-holding states, and render their cordial adherence to the Union perpetual."[20] The following day Lincoln convened his secretaries to discuss this and other proposals. Now everyone but Seward rejected any notion of appeasing the rebels and instead called for resupplying Fort Sumter; Seward advocated leaving Fort Sumter and holding Fort Pickens. Lincoln came down on the side of holding the line. He asked Welles to ready the navy's three most powerful warships—the *Powhatan*, *Pawnee*, and *Pocahontas*, then at the Brooklyn Naval Yard—to escort supply vessels to Fort Sumter.

Seward was determined to stop the expedition by any possible means. Although he offered the proposal on April Fool's Day, he could not have been more earnest in what he proposed. Under the title "Some Thoughts for the Consideration of the President," Seward advocated reunifying the nation by provoking crises with Spain, France, and possibly Britain. The excuse would be Spain's annexation, with France's connivance, of Santo Domingo just a few days earlier and the threat the two nations posed to Haiti. Seward sincerely believed that the nation would reunite if the Lincoln administration evoked the Monroe Doctrine against such blatant European imperialism.[21]

The utter absurdity of his most trusted advisor's proposal was a shrill wake-up call for Lincoln. He realized that he had to firmly grasp and wield whatever power was available to act decisively. To yield to Seward would set a precedent that would make Lincoln's assertion of power over subsequent issues increasingly problematic. He realized that "I can't afford to let Seward take the first trick." He politely asked Seward to shelve his proposal for now and urged Welles to redouble his efforts to mobilize the relief expedition.[22]

Seward's machinations revealed a challenge that Lincoln initially faced with his entire cabinet. Somehow he had to gain their respect and compliance when each thought himself superior in intellect and decisiveness to someone so deficient in experience and formal schooling. Typical was Attorney General Bates's belief that Lincoln was "an excellent man, and, in the main wise, but he lacks will and purpose, and I greatly fear he has not the power to command."[23] There was a measure of truth in this criticism, at least at first. But as Lincoln steadily grew into his role as president, one by one his secretaries came deeply to respect and follow him.

Lincoln informed South Carolina governor Francis Pickens on April 6 that "an attempt will be made to supply Fort Sumpter [*sic*] with provisions only. . . . If such attempt be not resisted no effort to throw men, arms, or ammunition will be made without further notice or in case of an attack on the fort."[24] He then notified the press of his decision. This posed a tough choice to the rebels. If they fired on unarmed ships carrying food to hungry men, they would not just start a war but do so inhumanely rather than honorably. Thus could a military defeat become an American propaganda triumph.

Seward then undermined Lincoln's policy by ordering the *Powhatan* to sail for Fort Pickens rather than Fort Sumter. However, he did so with the president's unwitting approval. Lincoln signed the order without bothering to ask or read just what he was signing.

The rebels soon rendered the administration's confusion moot. Upon receiving Lincoln's notice that he intended to supply Fort Sumter, Confederate leaders in Charleston and Montgomery agreed to capture the fort before the supply expedition arrived. On April 9 President Jefferson Davis authorized Gen. Pierre Beauregard to open fire as soon as his batteries were ready. On April 12 Beauregard ordered his artillery crews to bombard Fort Sumter. Anderson and his men valiantly held out until April 14, when the major agreed to surrender.

The following day Lincoln called for seventy-five thousand three-month military volunteers and a special session of Congress to meet on July 4. He knew that the war would last much longer than ninety days but was advised that the 1795 Militia Act bound him to that narrow period. He hoped this stopgap measure would mobilize an army in time for Congress to pass a bill to organize a volunteer army for three years or the war's duration. But why not convene Congress immediately? Here Lincoln may have deliberately sought a three-month interim whereby he could devise and implement policies through the bureaucracy without Congress tying his hands.

The question was what to do with all those troops. On May 3 Gen. Winfield Scott proposed what was eventually dubbed the Anaconda Plan, which included a blockade of the rebel ports, capture of the Mississippi River Valley to split the Confederacy, and the massing elsewhere of armies to overrun and occupy the rest of the South. This, of course, would take a long time to implement. Meanwhile the Union would rest on the defensive in hopes that reasonable southerners would retake power from the radicals.

Scott's Anaconda Plan involved a tightening blockade of southern ports and the penetration of the interior by armies transported by steamships and protected by gunboats. This would be possible only with the steady expansion of the American navy. Navy Secretary Gideon Welles brilliantly fulfilled this mission. The first step was a massive naval buildup. The navy numbered 42 vessels when the rebellion erupted. By the end of 1861 he had brought the number of vessels to 260, with another hundred in construction.

Lincoln endorsed the blockade but shelved the rest for now. He worried that Scott's reticence to support an immediate effort to crush the rebellion reflected conflicted loyalties. Scott was a genuine American hero, having worn an army uniform for nearly five decades, fought valiantly at the head of a regiment during the War of 1812, and during the Mexican War, led an army in a brilliant campaign that defeated the enemy in a series of battles, culminating with Mexico City's capture. But Scott was Virginia-born and his state would be among the first battlegrounds. Although he claimed old age and ill heath as to why he did not lead the army in the field, not wanting to war against his homeland may have been just as important.[25]

Lincoln's first constitutionally questionable measure came on April 19, when he declared a blockade of the rebel states. According to international law, a blockade is an act of war. According to the Constitution, only Congress can declare war. Lincoln would cite "military necessity" in fulfilling his role as commander in chief and his oath to preserve and protect the Constitution to justify this and other legally dubious acts: "It became necessary for me to choose whether, using only the existing means, agencies, and processes which Congress had provoked, I should let the government fall into ruin, or whether, availing myself of the broader powers conferred by the Constitution I would make an effort to save it with all its blessings for the present age and posterity."[26]

The first crucial task was to secure the nation's capital. Lincoln ordered the volunteer regiments being formed to head for Washington as soon as possible. The Sixth Massachusetts was the first to embark. All went well until those troops tried to change trains in Baltimore on April 18 and a mob waving guns and rebel flags assaulted them. In the melee four soldiers and twelve rioters were killed and thirty-one on both sides were wounded. This was no isolated incident of rebellion. Elsewhere in Maryland rebels tore up railroad tracks, cut telegraph lines, and burned bridges to sever Washington from the rest of the United States. Rumors abounded that Maryland's assembly was about to convene and secede.

Yet these rebels represented a minority of Maryland's population. Slaves accounted for about one of nine people living in the state, and most slaves worked plantations and smaller farms in the tidewater region. As in other eastern seaboard southern states, slavery thinned in the piedmont and all but disappeared in the mountains. Only 1 percent of Baltimore's 212,418 inhabitants were slaves while 11 percent were free blacks. As elsewhere, gerrymandered electoral districts gave slaveholders far more power than they would have merited had the principle of one person, one vote prevailed.[27]

Lincoln responded on April 27 by declaring the suspension of habeas corpus along the transportation and communication lines between Washington and Philadelphia, then on July 2 extended that to New York City. On May 3 he acted on new advice that he was not bound by the 1795 Militia Act after all, so he called for 43,034 three-year volunteers and the regular army's expansion by 22,714 troops and the navy's by 18,000 sailors.[28] He also ordered Postmaster General Blair to purge the mails of any seditious literature. All along, he carefully referred to the "rebellion" or "insurrection" rather than a "war," which might confer some legal status on the Confederacy.

Nothing that Lincoln did as president was more legally controversial than suspending habeas corpus. He justified the act by pointing to the Constitution's line that read, "The privilege of habeas corpus shall not be suspended unless when in cases of rebellion or invasion the public safety may require it." This clearly characterized the present with its insurrection and threat to public safety.

The constitutionality of Lincoln's suspension of habeas corpus was challenged in court.[29] The first case involved John Merryman, an outspoken secessionist who led his militia company to tear down telegraph wires. Merryman was arrested on May 25 and held without charges. He petitioned the circuit court in Baltimore, presided over by Roger Taney, the Supreme Court chief justice. Taney ruled that only Congress could suspend habeas corpus and thus Lincoln was guilty of violating the Constitution. To this Lincoln rhetorically asked whether "all the laws . . . and the government itself" should "go to pieces, lest the one [habeas corpus] be violated?"[30]

The measures Lincoln took after Fort Sumter's surrender played into secessionist hands across the Upper South. Six of the eight slave states bluntly refused to render any support to the United States. Four outright seceded, Virginia on April 17, Arkansas on May 6, Tennessee on May 7, and North Carolina on May 20.

Virginia's secession was the most threatening. Richmond promptly had militia seize all federal property, including the Norfolk naval yard and the Harpers Ferry arsenal. Virginia invited the Confederate Congress to change the capital from Montgomery to Richmond. The rebel Congress approved the transfer on May 21. This transfer of power made sense. Virginia's population and industrial production were the South's largest; being just across the Potomac from the enemy capital gave the Confederate army an enormous advantage.

Lincoln reacted swiftly to word of Virginia's secession by ordering federal troops to occupy and fortify Alexandria, across the Potomac River and a half-dozen miles south of Washington. At this point the nation's unfolding tragedy first struck Lincoln personally. Among the troops that marched into Alexandria was a New York regiment recruited by his law clerk and friend Elmer Ellsworth. Spotting a rebel flag flying defiantly above the Marshall Hotel, Ellsworth entered and tried to tear it down. The proprietor shot Ellsworth dead, then was killed by the New York troops. Lincoln wrote the young man's parents that "promised usefulness to one's country and of bright hopes for one's self and friends, have rarely been so suddenly dashed, as in his fall."[31]

In his Fourth of July speech, Lincoln presented Congress and the American people with a stark choice: "This is essentially a People's contest. On the side of the Union, it is a struggle for maintaining in the world, that form and substance of government whose leading object is to elevate the condition of men . . . to afford all an unfettered start, and a fair chance in the race of life. . . . This is the leading object of the Government for whose existence we contend." The rebel states sought to destroy all that. He condemned the notions of states' rights and secession as unconstitutional and ahistorical: "The States have their status in the Union and they have no other legal status. . . . The Union, and not themselves separately, procured their independence and their liberty. . . . The Union is older than any of the States, and in fact created them as states." He called on Americans to fulfill the vision of the founders to answer affirmatively "to the whole family of man, the question whether a constitutional republic or a democracy—a government of the people by the same people—can or cannot maintain its territorial integrity against its own domestic foes." The southern state rebellion threatened these ideals. The only way to defend them and the government that upheld them was to crush the rebellion. To this end, he called for the "legal means for making this [war] a short, and a decisive one; that you place at the control of the government, for the work, at least four hundred thousand men, and four hundred millions of dollars."[32]

The speech certainly rallied majorities in Congress, which responded the next day by appropriating $50 million for a one-hundred-thousand-man army and soon approved earlier measures that Lincoln had taken to secure the nation. With just five Democrat votes short of unanimity, Congress resolved that "all the acts, proclamations, and order of the President . . . respecting the army and navy of the United States, and calling out or relating to the rebellion are hereby approved and in all respects legalized and made valid . . . as if they had been issued and done under the . . . express authority of the Congress of the United States."

However, they did draw the line at Lincoln's suspension of habeas corpus, the legality of which they left for the Supreme Court to decide.

The vast majority of Americans were just as inspired. Tens of thousands of volunteers lined up across the northern states to enlist in the cause of restoring the Union. These troops had to be organized into regiments, trained, equipped, supplied, and transported where they were needed. All this demanded the mobilization of enormous resources. A one-hundred-thousand-man army on campaign was accompanied by thirty-five thousand riding or draft animals and daily consumed six hundred tons of supplies hauled by twenty-five hundred wagons. The tooth-to-tail ratio was approximately one to twelve. In other words, each soldier armed with a rifle needed roughly two other uniformed men and ten civilians to support him in the field. Corruption and incompetence compounded this challenge. Many contractors sold the federal government shoddy, overpriced provisions, munitions, uniforms, shoes, tents, rifles, medicine, and scores of other essential items. Many quartermasters did not know how to properly store or transport those goods. The result was enormous waste and profiteering.[33]

Another major weakness was the Union practice of organizing volunteers into new regiments rather than replenishing the ranks of existing regiments. With time, disease, desertion, and combat whittled each regiment's ranks. In 1862, of the 421,000 men who volunteered for three years in the American army, only 50,000 joined existing regiments where veterans could swiftly teach them the rudiments of army life and warfare. Each new regiment had to suffer the same brutal learning curve.[34]

During the war's first few weeks, as camps swelled with volunteers, the number of experienced officers capable of turning them into soldiers steadily diminished. By one estimate, three of four officers in the American military in 1860 were Democrats, among whom many were southerners who defected to the rebels. In early 1861, 313 of 1,080 army officers and 373 of 1,554 navy officers resigned. Among the War Department's civilian employees, thirty-four of ninety departed. No defection to the rebel cause would be more calamitous for America than that of Robert E. Lee. General Scott actually offered Lee command of the American army, but the Virginian put his state before his country. Scott himself was also a Virginian, but he put America first. When a delegation from Richmond asked him to commit treason, he angrily warned them, "Go no farther. It is best we part before you compel me to resent a mortal insult."[35]

Lincoln was under enormous pressure from Republican politicians, newspaper editors, and the volunteer regiments to launch the army south as soon as possible. The battle cry of "Forward to Richmond!" was penned in Horace Greeley's *New York Tribune* on June 26, 1861, and swiftly resounded through other newspapers and the halls of Congress.

Lincoln's two highest-ranking professional soldiers rejected that notion. Gen. Winfield Scott continued to press Lincoln to enact his Anaconda Plan. To command what would be known as the Army of the Potomac, Lincoln tapped Gen. Irwin McDowell, a forty-two-year-old West Point graduate and Mexican War veteran. McDowell insisted that his thirty-four-thousand-man army was not ready to fight and he pleaded for more time to train and mass more troops. Lincoln tried to reassure him: "You are green, it is true, but they are green, also; you are all green alike."[36]

McDowell dutifully drew up a plan that Lincoln and his cabinet approved on June 29. The strategy was simple enough. Two rebel armies were massing in northern Virginia, one of twenty-four thousand under Gen. Pierre Beauregard at Manassas Junction, about twenty-five miles south of Washington, and the other of eleven thousand under Joseph Johnston at Winchester at the Shenandoah Valley's north end. Facing Johnston were fifteen thousand troops led by Gen. Robert Patterson, a distinguished veteran of the 1812 and Mexican Wars now weighed down by his sixty-nine years. McDowell and Patterson would simultaneously attack the rebel armies before them.

Unfortunately, the enemy soon learned of this plan. Rose O'Neal Greenhow was a society lady who knew many prominent politicians and officers. She was also a rebel spy who extracted intelligence from her loquacious friends and secreted it to the rebel leaders. Beauregard promptly called on Johnston to give Patterson the slip and join him at Manassas.

McDowell did not get his army on the road south until July 16. It took these troops four days to march the twenty-five miles to Bull Run, the stream beyond which the rebel army was encamped. Not just inexperience slowed his army's march. By now his campaign plan had been leaked to the press and a cavalcade of spectators, including entire families of the elite armed with picnic baskets, accompanied the Union army's march.

McDowell launched his attack early on the morning of July 21, with feints at fords across Bull Run, while he sent most of his troops around the enemy's left flank. At first the Union troops drove back the rebels in confusion. But Johnston arrived just in time to counterattack and rout the American forces. The Union and Confederate armies suffered 2,950 and 1,750 casualties, respectively, figures that horrified northerners and southerners alike.[37] The catastrophe sobered most northern politicians, newspaper editors, and other citizens. The war clearly was not going to be an easy, quick, and glorious romp after all. Yet Bull Run's results could have been far worse. Had Beauregard immediately followed up his victory with a swift march against Washington, the rebels might have captured much of the demoralized American army along with the capital.

With General McDowell discredited, Lincoln searched desperately for someone who could transform the demoralized troops into a professional army and lead it south to crush the rebellion. The person he found would be as disastrous at the latter task as he was brilliant at the first. On July 22, the day after the battle of Bull Run, the president ordered George McClellan to hurry to Washington and take command.[38]

For a nation desperate for victories and heroes, McClellan appeared to be the only man then available. As is so often the case, first impressions were highly deceptive, as his initial burst of boldness soon dissolved into an unrelenting timidity. From his headquarters at Cincinnati, he commanded the Department of the Ohio that embraced the states of Ohio, Indiana, and Illinois. On May 26 he sent two forces into western Virginia, sixteen hundred troops under Col. Benjamin Kelly and fourteen hundred under Col. Ebenezer Dumont, to secure the Baltimore and Ohio Railroad. Each of those commands brushed aside much smaller rebel forces along the way and converged at Philippi on May 30. There Confederate colonel George Porterfield awaited them with eight hundred troops that he had scrapped together. With the odds favoring them more than four to one, the Federals attacked and routed the rebels on June 3. McClellan arrived to take command on June 21. By early July, he massed twenty thousand troops to march against forty-five hundred led by Gen. Robert Garnett at Beverly. McClellan sent Gen. William Rosecrans and his brigade to encircle the enemy. Garnett shifted part of his force to block Rosecrans at Rich Mountain. On July 13 Rosecrans launched his troops against thirteen hundred Confederates led by Col. John Pegram. The Federals routed the outnumbered rebels and took 550 prisoners at the cost of 12 killed and 49 wounded. This battle could have been an even more decisive victory had McClellan joined the attack with the troops under his command. But he held back, fearing that Rosecrans had been repulsed. Rosecrans and his men spearheaded the advance up the Kanawha River Valley. By early August, Union forces had secured most of western Virginia. Gen. Robert E. Lee arrived to unite the remnants of Confederate forces into a ten-thousand-man army, but his first campaign of the Civil War ended in defeat as Rosecrans's forces repulsed his probes at Cheat Mountain in mid-September. A month later Lee tried to sidestep Rosecrans in the Kanawha Valley but Rosecrans again blocked his path. Lee withdrew his forces into the Shenandoah Valley.

McClellan took credit for a success that clearly rested on the shoulders of his officers who did all the fighting, especially Rosecrans. Thus did public relations trump hard facts. In retrospect this is hardly surprising. If McClellan was truly gifted at anything it was at projecting images that exalted himself and denigrated his rivals. If one were casting for a photogenic general, McClellan looked the part, with his handsome face, neatly trimmed mustache, lean, erect carriage, and crisply pressed, tailored uniforms. He turned his diminutive height into an advantage by having the word spread that he was the "Young Napoleon." In reality, his snaillike pace of warfare that avoided battle was the antithesis of Napoleon's strategy of rapid movements and overwhelming sledgehammer attacks against the enemy. McClellan was bright, personable, and confident and exuded a charisma that dazzled many an audience. He had an impressive resume. He graduated near the top of his West Point class, served in the Mexican War, and was part of an American delegation that observed the Crimean War at the British and French headquarters. In 1854 he retired from the military to serve as president of the Mississippi and Ohio Railroad, where he proved to be a very able administrator and engineer who often put in fifteen-hour work days. He took these same skills to the Union force that he soon dubbed the Army of the Potomac. Given his genuine attributes, McClellan would have made a very good chief of staff as long as his commanding general kept him on a very short leash.

Then there was the increasingly evident downside. In a profession not known for humility, few commanders have matched and none have exceeded McClellan in egomania and arrogance as vast as his generalship was disastrous for America. He fervently believed that "God has placed a work in my hands. . . . I was called to it; my previous life seems to have been unwittingly directed to this great end."[39] Exacerbating his messiah complex were his political ambitions as a devote Democrat who favored reunification and the continued tolerance of slavery. At some future point he hoped to capitalize on his military fame with a run for the White House. Of course, before he did that he actually had to win fame on a grandiose scale. And there his wretched generalship trumped his ambitions.

McClellan's first probe south of the Potomac ended in a humiliating defeat that he typically blamed on others. After months of pressure from the White House, Congress, and newspapers to advance south, he finally authorized several regiments to cross the river at Ball's Bluff on October 21. The Confederates immediately massed, attacked, and routed the Union forces, inflicting eight hundred casualties. Once again Lincoln suffered a personal loss when Col. Edward Baker, his old friend and fellow Springfield lawyer, recent Oregon senator, and deceased son's namesake, was killed.

But rather than fire McClellan, Lincoln promoted him. When Gen. Winfield Scott resigned on November 1, Lincoln assigned McClellan to command the entire American army. When the president asked him whether those duties might be too much, McClellan jauntily replied, "I can do it all."[40]

Meanwhile the Union chalked up victories elsewhere, although not without controversy. Having secured Maryland, Lincoln sought to anchor the other two critical border slave states of Kentucky and Missouri to the United States. He recognized that, so far, unique political circumstances had kept each state loyal. Any federal measures that worked in one state might well push the others into the Confederacy's arms. Nor were these three states equally important, although events in one reverberated to the others. He explained, "To lose Kentucky is nearly the same as to lose the whole game. Kentucky gone, we cannot hold Missouri nor . . . Maryland. These all against us, and the job of our hands is too large for us. We would as well consent to separation at once, including the surrender of this capital."[41]

This was no exaggeration. The strategic position of these three states was crucial. Together they presented a wedge of hard power to whoever won them over. Had these states seceded, the Confederacy's manpower would have risen by 45 percent and its factory output by 80 percent. These states also had 420,000 slaves. With 19.5 percent of its population enslaved, or nearly one in five people, Kentucky had the largest proportion of slaves to the total population, followed by Maryland with 12.7 percent, and Missouri with 9.7 percent.[42]

Throughout the early spring, Missouri teetered at the brink of violence between Union- and rebel-leaning forces.[43] The governor was Claiborne Jackson, a slaveholder and former border ruffian, and the militia general was Sterling Price, a slaveholder and former governor. While they tried to mass a secessionist army in Jefferson City, the capital, they assigned seven hundred militiamen to occupy Camp Jackson on St. Louis's outskirts.

Gen. William Harney commanded the vast Department of the West, headquartered at St. Louis. Shortly after arriving with a small contingent of regular troops from Fort Leavenworth, Capt. Nathaniel Lyon urged Harney to round up any armed secessionists, first in St. Louis, then around the state. Harney refused, insisting that his role was to be a neutral force that tried to reconcile the opposing parties. Lyon complained of Harney to his friend Frank Blair, the attorney general's brother and one of Missouri's representatives in Congress. Montgomery Blair talked the president into recalling Harney to Washington for consultations.

Lyon took advantage of Harney's absence to act. He raised four volunteer regiments devoted to the United States and deployed them around the federal arsenal, with its 60,000 firearms, 1.5 million cartridges, 90,000 pounds of gunpowder, and score of cannons. Then, on May 10, he led his regiments to surround Camp Jackson and force the rebel militia to surrender. Although he pulled this off without a shot being fired, as he paraded his prisoners through the streets a riot broke out that left two soldiers and thirty civilians dead and numerous others wounded. Eventually Lyon restored order. When Harney returned on May 12, he endorsed all of Lyon's decisive acts. On May 29 Lincoln replaced Harney as the Department of the West's commander with Lyon and promoted the captain to brigadier general.

Lyon marched at the head of seventeen hundred troops to Jefferson City. Jackson and Price fled to Booneville, fifty miles up the Missouri River, where they gathered rebel forces and tried to form a government. Lyon pursued and scattered them on June 17, the Civil War's first large-scale skirmish. Jackson and Price found refuge in Springfield, the largest town in Missouri's southwest, leaving the state's central and northern regions in Union hands. Meanwhile, in St. Louis a convention of mostly Republicans and Unionists convened to establish a government and elect Hamilton Gamble the new governor.

Unfortunately, Lyon's tenure as the Department of the West's commander was brief. Lincoln succumbed to political pressure and replaced Lyon with John Frémont, famed for leading four exploration expeditions across the West and being the Republican Party's first presidential candidate, as commander of the Department of the West. Shortly after he reached St. Louis on July 25, the power went to Frémont's head. He set up his headquarters in a mansion for which he billed Washington $6,000 a year. When Frank Blair publicly criticized him, Frémont had him arrested and held indefinitely.

Meanwhile Lyon, who remained the army's field general, cleared rebels from most of Missouri and in early August set up his headquarters at Springfield. For his succession of valiant and decisive acts, Lyon became the war's first northern hero. Tragically, he died a hero's death.

Lyon's army amounted to only fifty-five hundred troops and their supply line stretched 215 miles to St. Louis. Ever more rebel guerrillas infested this route. Meanwhile Gen. Sterling Price commanded thirteen thousand Confederate troops at Fayetteville, Arkansas, seventy-five miles south. In early August Price led his army north and by August 10 was encamped at Wilson's Creek, half a dozen miles from Springfield. Lyon was aware that he was outgunned two to one. With these odds against him, he could have defended Springfield or withdrawn toward St. Louis. Instead he conceived a bold plan to attack the rebels from two directions. Like McDowell at Bull Run, Lyon nearly won the battle of Wilson Creek, but the rebels rallied, counterattacked, and routed the Union troops. The northerners and southerners suffered 1,317 and 1,230 casualties, respectively; Lyon was among the dead. Price followed up his victory by marching north to Lexington on the Missouri River. Although his army swelled with recruits along the way, he eventually withdrew to Springfield as superior Union forces massed at Kansas City and St. Louis.

Rather than lead an army against the invaders, General Frémont remained ensconced in his St. Louis mansion. On August 30 he proclaimed martial law and warned that any rebel civilians caught with firearms would be summarily shot and all slaves of rebels would be liberated. Lincoln feared this policy would provoke rather than deter Missouri's secessionists. On September 2 he wrote Frémont a private letter asking him to rescind the measures, and when the general refused, on September 11 Lincoln issued a public order to do so. He patiently explained the practical and thus moral reasons behind his order. If "you shoot a man, according to the proclamation, the Confederates would very certainly shoot our best men in their hands in retaliation; and so, man for man, indefinitely." Likewise Frémont's emancipation policy "will alarm our southern Union friends and turn them against us." However, Frémont could and should comply with the Confiscation Act that permitted commanders to take any property, including slaves, from rebels.[44]

It was not until October that Frémont finally marched with thirty-eight thousand troops against Price. Outgunned two to one, Price evacuated Springfield and withdrew into northwestern Arkansas. Frémont halted his advance at Springfield, which he entered on October 26. Although he had secured most of Missouri for the Union, he failed to catch up to, let alone defeat, the enemy. But it was continual reports of Frémont's abuses of power that prompted Lincoln to relieve him of command on November 2 and reassign him to head the Department of the Ohio, with its headquarters at Wheeling, West Virginia, where presumably he would do less harm. Lincoln called on Gen. Henry Halleck to head the Department of the West.

While the Civil War engulfed Missouri, Kentucky evaded violence for the time being. Governor Beriah Magoffin was a slaveholder and rejected Lincoln's call for volunteers. The state senate voted on May 24 that Kentucky would be neutral. Yet slowly the political tide shifted toward loyalty to the United States. Unionists prevailed in three elections from May to August, for delegates to a border state convention, for representatives to Congress, and for the state legislature. Unionists dominated the state assembly, with majorities of seventy-six to twenty-four in the House and twenty-seven to eleven in the Senate.

An imprudent rebel act inadvertently shoved Kentucky from neutrality into loyalty to the United States and helped advance the career of America's most successful general during the war. Gen. Leonidas Polk led his army into Kentucky on September 3, 1861, and fortified Columbus on bluffs above the Mississippi River just twenty miles south of its juncture with the Ohio River. A majority in Kentucky's state assembly reacted by condemning this invasion and declaring their support for the United States.

During the war's first few months a counter-secession movement blossomed within one of the rebel states. Virginia extended westward across the Appalachian Mountains to nestle against Kentucky and Ohio. Few masters and slaves lived in the mountainous region, and their presence was resented by nearly everyone else. The regional contrast was startling, with 472,494 slaves in eastern Virginia and 18,571 in the west.[45]

The Virginia assembly's overwhelming vote on April 17 for secession enraged most Appalachians. A grassroots movement to stay in the United States spread across the region. John Carlisle, western Virginia's leading unionist, conferred with Lincoln, who encouraged his efforts. Unionist political leaders gathered for a convention at Wheeling on June 11. Nine days later the delegates declared themselves the state's lawful government, with themselves as the assembly. They promptly elected two senators to send to Washington and Francis Pierpont to serve as their governor. A referendum on West Virginia's secession from Virginia and formation of a new state passed by 18,408 to 781 votes in October. A convention was held in February 1862 to draft a constitution and submit it to Congress for approval. West Virginia was eventually admitted into the United States on July 24, 1863. All along Lincoln encouraged each step.

The potential for a similar secession from a secession existed in eastern Tennessee. There only 27,539 blacks, mostly slaves, existed amid 297,596 whites. As in western Virginia, the Appalachian folks despised slavery and resented being poor and politically unrepresented compared to the rest of the state. In a referendum, most Tennesseans approved secession from the United States, while two of three voters in the eastern region voted against it. Senator Andrew Johnson and three representatives stayed loyal to the United States and retained their seats in Congress. After Union troops overran Tennessee in early 1862, Lincoln named Johnson the state's governor. This kept Tennessee united rather than split into two separate states.[46]

McClellan was a master of organization. By October his Army of the Potomac numbered 120,000 well-equipped and trained troops compared to Beauregard's 45,000 at Manassas. Yet McClellan refused to march, claiming that the rebel army actually numbered 150,000. He contrived those figures with Allan Pinkerton, whom he picked as his intelligence chief. Pinkerton was famed for heading a Chicago detective agency but was a disastrous neophyte at espionage. McClellan and Pinkerton persistently exaggerated rebel troop numbers by two or even three times.

McClellan's most notable act during this time was to defy and insult the president and secretary of state. Having vital issues to discuss, Lincoln and Seward visited McClellan's house the evening of November 13. The general passed them in the parlor without a glance or word and went upstairs. The two continued to wait, assuming that McClellan would soon return to speak with them. After another half hour, they sent word that they were still downstairs. McClellan had his butler reply that he had gone to bed and was not to be disturbed. Seward was incensed but Lincoln tried to calm him by arguing that "it was better at this time not to be making points of etiquette and personal dignity." While this was the last time that Lincoln paid a visit to McClellan's home, he remained cheerfully indifferent to such slights, insisting that "I will hold McClellan's horse if he will just bring us successes."[47]

For now Lincoln kept McClellan but disposed of another worsening liability. Those who had warned him that taking Simon Cameron into his cabinet would result in a scandal could say "I told you so" in early 1862. Under Cameron, the War Department swiftly acquired a reputation for waste, fraud, and incompetence. Yet after learning of this malfeasance, the president hesitated for weeks to fire Cameron, fearing that he might inflict more damage outside than inside the administration. What clinched Lincoln's decision was being told by powerful

New York banker James Hamilton that the Treasury Department could swiftly raise $100 million from private investors if someone of impeccable character and administrative skills headed the War Department. Lincoln gave Cameron notice on January 11, 1862, but covered the blow by nominating him to be minister to Russia.

Lincoln replaced him with Edwin Stanton.[48] In doing so he once again revealed his seemingly endless gift for embracing his foes and converting them into allies. Stanton was not just a devote Democrat but had snubbed and denigrated Lincoln during their first encounter in 1855, when both served on a team of lawyers defending Cyprus McCormick in a patent for his reaper. Stanton childishly referred to Lincoln as a "damned long armed ape" and refused to speak to him, let alone work with him. Lincoln brushed off the snub as he sat "in rapt attention" at Stanton's brilliant performance, having never before "seen anything so finished and elaborated and so thoroughly prepared."[49]

Lincoln did not take Stanton's meanness all that personally then or after he tapped him as his secretary of war. Stanton had a well-deserved reputation for being arrogant and condescending, and Lincoln recognized that he was only one of countless targets. With time Stanton understood the brilliance beneath Lincoln's folksy manners, and they became friends as well as colleagues. Lincoln's most important reason for choosing Stanton was his renowned administrative skills and fierce desire to crush the rebellion. Stanton increasingly vented his venom against McClellan, a fellow Democrat, complaining that "we have had no war; we have not even been playing at war" and that "as soon as I can get the rat holes stopped, we shall move. This army has got to fight or run way. . . . While men are striving nobly in the West, the champagne and oysters on the Potomac must be stopped."[50]

McClellan's leisurely and luxurious approach to war deeply frustrated Lincoln. For months the president prodded the general with gentle humor and suggestions rather than orders. At one point he remarked that if the general did not intend to lead the army on a campaign, he "would like to borrow it, provided he could see how it could be made to do something."[51] Lincoln drafted a plan for half of the Army of the Potomac to feint toward the rebel army at Centerville while launching wide-turning movements that rolled up the enemy's flanks. It was an excellent plan, the first of many that the president submitted to his generals. McClellan contemptuously ignored the plan after receiving it on December 1. Lincoln then asked McClellan to draw up and present his own plan. McClellan ignored this request as well.

In early 1862 even Lincoln's legendary patience reached its limits. The turning point was a cabinet meeting on January 13, when McClellan was invited to explain his campaign plan. He enraged his audience by arrogantly pronouncing that "no General fit to command an army will ever submit his plans to the judgment of such an assembly. . . . There are many people here entirely incompetent to pass judgment. . . . No plan made known to so many persons can be kept secret an hour."[52] McClellan then compounded this gross insult the next day by describing his plan to a reporter for the *New York Herald*, which published the story and thus tipped off the enemy.

Lincoln issued on January 27 the President's General Order Number 1, which required all land and naval forces on February 22, George Washington's birthday, to "threaten all [enemy] positions at the same time with superior force, and if they weakened one to strengthen another seize and hold the one weakened."[53] The frustration that led Lincoln to issue this order is understandable, given the inertia of the field commanders on all fronts along with the growing political and public impatience for offensives that crushed the rebellion once and for all. The trouble was that no grand strategy that coordinated the forces toward the enemy's systematic destruction accompanied the order. Nor did it recognize the challenges posed by launching campaigns in winter, when roads were turned into quagmires and pastures offered only withered plants for horses and draft animals to forage.

As Lincoln anxiously awaited the date for the launch of the forces, he and his family suffered a terrible loss on February 20, when typhoid fever killed their eleven-year-old son, Willie. Now the Lincolns had lost two of their four boys, having buried Eddie in Springfield a dozen years earlier. This latest loss devastated both parents. Lincoln was so grief-stricken that he twice asked that his boy's body be exhumed so that he could gaze again upon his face. Mary went into deep mourning, sometimes barricaded in her bedroom for days at a time. She began consulting spiritualists to contact her dead children and others and insisted that her husband sit with her during the séances. For some reason neither parent could lavish as much love and attention on their two surviving children, who likely felt hurt by the neglect. Lincoln became ever closer to his two secretaries, John Nicolay and John Hay, to the point where he treated them like surrogate sons.

As if the pressures on Lincoln were not crushing enough, Mary heaped more upon him. She quickly exceeded the $20,000 appropriated for refurbishing the White House and ran up huge debts. Lincoln was enraged when he learned what she had done. How could anyone justify these expenditures for "that damned old house," he erupted, when "the poor freezing soldiers could not have blankets." He promised to pay the debts. Congress quietly voted to cover the rest of the costs. Lincoln reluctantly agreed to accept this payment. Mary had become the most hated first lady in the nation's history, and not just because of her snobbery and irresponsible extravagance. Some condemned her as an outright traitor, given that one of her brothers, three half brothers, and three brothers-in-law fought for the rebel cause.[54]

The United States and the Confederacy fought a diplomatic as well as military war. The rebel government sought international recognition, trade, aid, and ideally, allies. The American government was determined to deny the rebels all that.[55]

The most vital diplomatic tug-of-war between Washington and Richmond was over British hearts, minds, and wallets.[56] Britain was not only the world's greatest economic and military power, but many of its textile factories converted southern cotton into cloth. So Whitehall, the complex of London buildings housing the government, had a compelling economic interest in siding with the rebels. Atop that was a strategic interest. It was increasingly evident that America posed a long-term threat to surpass Britain economically and that greater wealth could underwrite greater military power. During both the Revolutionary War and War of 1812, the Americans had tried and failed to conquer Canada. They might well succeed in some future war. So it was definitely in Britain's economic and military interests to assist America in tearing itself apart. Countering this were Britain's moral interests. For more than half a century, Whitehall had led an international campaign against slavery and showed the way by first outlawing the international slave trade in 1808, then slavery itself within its empire in 1833. Aiding the Confederate slavocracy would violate a vital principle of British morality and policy.

Britain's economic and strategic interests initially prevailed. On May 13, 1861, Queen Victoria recognized the Confederacy and declared her empire's neutrality. As if that were not provocative enough, she did so the day before Charles Francis Adams, America's minister to Britain, presented his credentials to Foreign Secretary John Russell. Yet Washington had unwittingly instigated this policy. According to international law, when Lincoln declared a blockade of the Confederacy on April 19, he essentially recognized a legitimate government. Russell explained that Whitehall simply followed Washington's lead.

Secretary of State Seward wanted to get tough with the British. He showed Lincoln a letter that he would send Whitehall that condemned its recognition of the Confederacy and meetings with rebel leaders and warned that Washington would sever its diplomatic ties if the British persisted. Once again Seward seemed happy to play a game of diplomatic brinksmanship no matter what the results. War with Britain would have been disastrous to American interests. Lincoln softened the rhetoric so that the letter expressed sorrow rather than anger at British policy.[57]

Exacerbating the deteriorating relationship with Whitehall was a joint act of aggression by Britain, France, and Spain that violated a nearly four-decade-old principle of American foreign policy. In 1823 President James Monroe had issued what became known as the Monroe Doctrine, warning the European powers not to intervene militarily in the Western Hemisphere. Early in 1861 those three countries did just that when they landed troops at Veracruz. They did so to pressure Mexico's government to resume payments on the debt it owed them.

Relations between the United States and Britain reached a nadir during the Trent Affair.[58] In October 1861 Confederate president Davis dispatched John Slidell and James Mason as envoys to Britain with the mission to gain aid and an alliance. The blockade had already tightened to the point where it was deemed safer to take a roundabout route to London. The envoys sailed first to Havana and there awaited a Britain-bound ship. They finally found passage on the mail packet *Trent*. But before they sailed, spies passed word of their mission and whereabouts to Capt. Charles Wilkes, who commanded the uss *San Jacinto* patrolling the Florida Strait. The *San Jacinto* intercepted the *Trent* on

November 8. Wilkes sent aboard marines to arrest Slidell and Mason. The *Trent* then sailed on its way while Wilkes pointed his vessel north to Boston, where the envoys were jailed at Fort Warren.

Upon learning of the capture, the British and Confederate governments protested what they claimed was a violation of international law. Lincoln and all his cabinet dismissed the charge except Blair, who argued that it had merit. Word arrived from London that Britain was preparing its forces for possible war with the United States. This was confirmed when Lord Richard Lyons, Britain's minister in Washington, handed Seward a formal note from his government, dated December 19, that demanded an apology and the captives' release.

Lincoln convened his cabinet on Christmas Day and insisted that fighting two wars at once would be disastrous. Even then the secretaries split over whether to reject or accept the British demand. The deadlock persisted the following day. Lincoln then debated the issue privately with Seward, with each taking the other's position. Lincoln noted that "I could not make an argument that would satisfy my own mind. That proved to me your ground was the right one."[59]

They jointly composed a diplomatic note for Seward to send Whitehall. Captain Wilkes had acted on his own initiative yet would have been in full accord with international law had he taken the *Trent* to a prize court. He erred legally in arresting the envoys without due process. For this reason, the envoys would be released.

Lincoln's face-saving gesture had a sobering effect in London. War talk faded. Foreign Minister Russell tried to pursue better relations with the United States, via both American minister Charles Adams in London and British minister James Lyons in Washington. A major bilateral conflict disappeared in April 1862, when the British along with the Spanish withdrew their troops from Veracruz after Mexico resumed its debt payments to them. Then, on July 11, 1862, American and British diplomats signed a treaty that committed both countries to suppress the international slave trade.

These acts resolved the worst potential foreign threat to American security. Yet Lincoln somehow found time in early 1862 to commit an important symbolic act of diplomacy and principle that went virtually unnoticed amid the bewildering maze of war, domestic politics, and vital relations with Britain and France. The United States fully recognized the sovereign nations of Haiti and Liberia and exchanged ministers with these countries populated and governed by black people.

McClellan neither acknowledged nor acted on Lincoln's order for all Union forces to attack the closest rebel forces on February 22. He would not get around to launching his offensive until nearly two months after the deadline. However, other generals did obey the commander in chief. Gen. George Thomas attacked first, routed the enemy at Logan's Crossroads near Mills Springs, Kentucky, on January 19, and secured that state's eastern region. An even more decisive campaign was unleashed at Kentucky's western end.

A genuine hero emerged there in the unlikely figure of Ulysses S. Grant.[60] In 1843 he graduated twenty-first in his West Point class of thirty-nine; as a student he was best at drawing and horsemanship and worst at tactics. He was fearless in battle even though he sickened at the sight of blood, let alone masses of gruesomely killed and wounded men. Although assigned to the quartermaster corps during the Mexican War, he repeatedly not just joined but led attacks and was twice breveted for bravery. He was forced out of the army in 1854 for being drunk on duty. Over the course of the next seven years, he failed as a businessman, farmer, rent collector, and real estate agent. When the war broke out he was a clerk in his father's store in Galena, Illinois. He was lean and of medium height, with reddish-brown hair and blue-gray eyes. Indifferent to his appearance, he was often described as seedy and rumpled. The man who commanded vast armies and later became president of the United States was not just taciturn but painfully shy and hated to speak in public. However, behind closed doors he was a devoted, affectionate husband and father. For vices he chain-smoked cigars and at times drank to excess. He repeatedly fell for shysters with get-rich-quick schemes even though he was burned each time. Throughout his life he failed at all but one of his ventures, including being president. The exception was that he was a master of the art of war.

As Grant explained it, this art was profoundly simple: "Find out where your enemy is. Get at him as soon as you can. Strike him as hard as you can and as often as you can and keep moving on." No man knew Grant better than Gen. William Sherman, who shared insights into how his friend waged war: "He fixes in his mind what is the true objective and abandons all minor ones. If his plan goes wrong he is never disconcerted but promptly devises a new one and is sure to win in the end." Grant's dogged refusal to give up and continual search for a better way was epitomized by his attitude after the first day's fighting at Shiloh. The rebels took him by surprise, inflicted heavy casualties, and pushed back his army. Even such brilliant generals as Sherman and James McPherson believed they had been defeated and had to withdraw. To this Grant replied, "Not beaten yet. Not by a damn sight. . . . Retreat? No, I propose to attack at daybreak and lick them."[61]

Grant's memoirs are a classic of military history, prose, and psychology that honestly reveal his fears and mistakes as well as triumphs. In his first action of the Civil War, he provided an insight into himself and the nature of war. In northern Missouri then-Colonel Grant was ordered to march his regiment to attack an enemy regiment. His fear grew as he led his men closer to the enemy position, followed by relief when they found only a deserted camp: "It occurred to me that [rebel Colonel] Harris had been as much afraid of me as I had been of him. This was a view of the question I had never taken before; but it was one I never forgot afterwards. From that event to the close of the war, I never experienced trepidation upon confronting an enemy, though I always felt more or less anxiety. I never forgot that he had as much reason to fear my forces as I had his."[62]

Grant first made headlines after fighting the battle of Belmont on November 7, 1861. He commanded seventeen thousand troops split between two strategic sites: Cairo, Illinois, at the confluence of the Mississippi and Ohio Rivers, and Paducah, Kentucky, forty-five miles up the Ohio and just three and fifteen miles, respectively, downstream from the mouths of the Tennessee and Cumberland Rivers. Twenty miles down the Mississippi from Cairo, Gen. Leonidas Polk was dug in with twenty thousand troops at Columbus, Kentucky. Seeking to probe Polk, Grant packed 3,114 troops aboard riverboats and steamed down to Belmont, Missouri, just across from Columbus. After his troops scattered a small rebel force, Grant deployed them to meet seven thousand Confederates that Polk sent across the river. The Union troops stood their ground and repelled several rebel attacks before Grant withdrew them to the steamboats and back to Cairo. His troops inflicted more losses—642, including 175 prisoners, four spiked cannons, and two captured cannons—than the 485 they sustained. More importantly, this bold raid boosted Grant's confidence and skills to try increasingly ambitious campaigns in the future.[63]

In early 1862 Grant scored twin victories that let Union forces over-run most of central and western Tennessee. Fort Henry and Fort Donel-son stood a dozen miles apart guarding the Tennessee and Cumberland Rivers, respectively. On February 2 Grant packed seventeen thousand troops aboard transports that followed seven gunboats commanded by Capt. Andrew Foote up the Tennessee River. He led his army ashore just beyond range of Fort Henry's cannons on February 6. Faced with over-whelming odds, Fort Henry's commander withdrew his twenty-eight hundred troops to Fort Donelson. After garrisoning Fort Henry, Grant marched his army toward Fort Donelson while the flotilla steamed there. Grant deployed his army in a crescent west of Fort Donelson on Febru-ary 8. Foote's flotilla arrived on February 13 and opened fire. The next day the rebels attacked Grant's lines but were repulsed. Reinforcements swelled Grant's army to twenty-seven thousand troops. The Confederate commander was Gen. Simon Buckner, Grant's old friend from West Point. Sentiment played no role in what happened next. When Buck-ner asked that his army be paroled, Grant replied, "No terms except an unconditional and immediate surrender can be accepted. I propose to move immediately upon your works." Buckner protested the "unchiv-alrous and ungenerous terms" but surrendered his 17,000-man army; only 14,623 troops actually went into captivity, as Gen. Bedford Forrest escaped during the night with 2,500 men.[64]

Grant's capture of Forts Henry and Donelson, and the destruction of the Memphis and Ohio Railroad bridges south of those forts, forced Gen. Albert Sidney Johnson, the region's rebel commander, to with-draw his forces across the region. Grant wanted to follow up his vic-tories promptly by steaming Foote's flotilla up the Cumberland River to capture Clarksville and Nashville, while he pursued and destroyed Johnson's army. Tragically, Gen. Henry Halleck, the Department of the West's commander, forbade him from doing so.

Nonetheless, Grant's victories opened the way for the Federal takeover of the region from the Mississippi River to the Appalachian Mountains. Gen. Don Carlos Buell, who commanded the Army of the Ohio, had languished at his Louisville headquarters despite repeated orders from

Washington to advance, including a pointed one from the commander in chief himself on January 7.[65] Buell's affliction with the "slows," as Lincoln called it, aggravated the president nearly as much as McClellan's. With the adjacent lower Tennessee and Cumberland River Valleys cleared of rebels, Buell finally felt secure enough to lead his own army southward. Union troops marched into Clarksville, the site of the Confederacy's largest iron works after the Tredegar complex in Richmond, on February 21, and into Nashville, the state's capital, on March 1, without fighting a battle along the way as small groups of rebels withdrew before them. But, to Buell's shame and anger, he found that Grant, contrary to orders, had gotten there ahead of him to occupy those strategic sites and secure huge stores of rebel supplies before they were destroyed or withdrawn. On the Mississippi River, Gen. John Pope led an expedition downstream to occupy Columbus, Kentucky, which General Polk hastily evacuated after the fall of Forts Henry and Donelson, and to capture Island Number Ten with its seven thousand defenders on April 7 and Fort Pillow with its one thousand men on May 10, disembarking at an undefended Memphis on June 7.

Meanwhile Grant faced enemies among his "brothers in arms." His victories provoked jealousy in lackluster generals. Halleck actually relieved him on March 6, with several politically motivated excuses, including that by capturing Fort Donelson he had intruded into Army of the Ohio's region, that he had visited Nashville without orders to do so, and that he had failed to send Halleck reports for two weeks after he captured Fort Donelson. Actually Grant had dutifully sent a series of reports, but a telegraph operator with rebel sympathies at Cairo did not forward them. Halleck also appears to have instigated the rumor that Grant had resumed his old, "vile habits" of drunkenness. Lincoln was astonished that anyone would attack Grant just because he happened to win a decisive victory and visited a captured enemy state capital in another army's region. He then found out about the diverted reports and, on March 13, ordered Halleck to reinstate Grant.[66]

Farther west the Union won another victory. In early March Gen. Samuel Curtis and eleven thousand Union troops were encamped along Pea Ridge in northwestern Arkansas. Gen. Earl Van Dorn marched up from Fayetteville and curled around the Union army to sever its supply line and attack its rear on March 7. Curtis maneuvered his troops to repel that first of a series of assaults. The next morning Curtis ordered a charge that routed the rebels. This battle cost each side thirteen hundred casualties but secured the region for the Union after Curtis marched his army into Fayetteville.

In the east, the Union navy scored some key victories. On November 7, 1861, a flotilla of seventy-seven vessels commanded by Flag Officer Samuel DuPont steamed into Port Royal Sound, located about halfway between Charleston and Savannah, pounded two forts to rubble, and disembarked twelve thousand troops to occupy Port Royal. That small port served as the blockading fleet's base for this stretch of coast. Farther north, long, slender, sandy islands shelter North Carolina's coast from the Atlantic Ocean. Behind these barriers are two vast bays, Albemarle Sound northward and the far larger Pamlico Sound southward. Smugglers sailed from a half-dozen small ports around each sound for the open ocean and distant foreign markets, where they sold cotton and bought war supplies and luxury goods for resale in the Confederacy. A fort on Roanoke Island defended the entrance to Albemarle Sound. On February 7 Gen. Ambrose Burnside landed seventy-five hundred troops just beyond cannon shot of this fort. The following day his troops attacked and, at the cost of 264 casualties, forced rebel general Henry Wise to surrender with his 2,675 troops. Using the fort as a base, Burnside led expeditions that captured Elizabeth and Edenton on Albemarle Sound, then steamed down to Pamlico Sound and captured New Bern. This expedition at once sharply curtailed smuggling and provided bases from which to march westward into North Carolina's interior.

Shortly thereafter a battle changed the history of warfare and thus the world.[67] The rebels converted a captured warship, the uss *Merrimack*, into an iron-plated vessel named the css *Virginia*. On March 8 the *Virginia* attacked the Union fleet anchored at Hampton Roads in Chesapeake Bay and sank two warships before returning to its anchorage for more fuel and ammunition. When the *Virginia* steamed out the next morning, the iron-plated uss *Monitor* was waiting. The contrast in design was striking. The 264-foot *Virginia* could be compared to a barn roof with a dozen cannons studding each sloped side. The 172-foot *Monitor* was a cheese box with two cannons in a revolving turret atop a deck just above the waterline. The battle was a draw, as each vessel pounded the other without inflicting more than dents. The *Virginia* withdrew.

The advent of iron warships rendered wooden vessels forever obsolete. The opposing naval secretaries, Gideon Welles and Stephen Mallory, deserve full credit for having the vision and drive to launch this revolution. In July 1861 Welles approved engineer John Ericsson's proposal to build the *Monitor* in the Brooklyn Naval Yard and got Congress to underwrite the project with a $1.5 million appropriation. Fortuitously, the *Monitor* was finished and steamed south just in time to counter the *Virginia* as it began a second day of rampaging against the American fleet.

Once back in command, Grant led his 42,682-man Army of the Tennessee up the Tennessee River to Pittsburg Landing on the west bank, where they camped and awaited Buell's 40,000-man Army of the Ohio; Shiloh church stood near the Union line's center. Once joined, the two armies would march under Grant's command twenty miles south to Corinth, where General Johnson had massed 40,335 troops.

Johnson had retreated to Corinth all the way from Bowling Green, Kentucky, when the armies of Grant and Buell advanced on either side of his own. Deserters brought him word of the enemy plan. This spurred him to strike Grant before Buell reinforced him. He led his army north and unleashed it against Grant's early on the morning of April 6. The attack caught the Union troops by surprise. Some regiments broke and fled while others held their ground or slowly gave way. Gen. William Sherman and his division were among those later acclaimed for their fierce defense. That night Buell's army arrived and bolstered Grant's line. The following morning Grant ordered the combined armies to attack. In late afternoon the rebels retreated to Corinth. Grant's victory came at a huge cost, with the Union suffering 13,447 casualties to the Confederate's 10,699; Johnson was among the dead. Shiloh was bloodier than all the war's previous battles combined.

Once again Grant was the center of controversy. His enemies pilloried him for not detecting the rebel advance and whispered that he was drinking to excess. Lincoln was the most prominent of those who lauded his victory; he dismissed the critics by insisting, "I can't spare the man, he fights."[68] Yet Grant was temporarily eclipsed.

Halleck hurried down from his St. Louis headquarters and on April 11 took command of the two armies that, with reinforcements, reached one hundred thousand troops. Fearful of a surprise attack, he crept his troops toward the enemy at Corinth, twenty miles south. The army progressed less than half a mile a day, partly because of the nearly incessant rains that turned roads into quagmires, but mostly because Halleck kept his men busy mostly fortifying their camps rather than marching. Facing that snail-paced juggernaut were seventy thousand rebels led by Gen. Pierre Beauregard. On May 25 Beauregard and his men abandoned Corinth and withdrew to Tupelo, Mississippi, fifty miles south. The Union army marched into the enemy's deserted entrenchments the next day. Halleck had taken nearly eight weeks to move his troops from Shiloh to Corinth, a distance that with a dry road and no resistance could have been hiked in a day. Grant lamented that Halleck had deprived him of the opportunity "that Corinth could have been captured in a two days' campaign commenced promptly on the arrival of reinforcements after the battle of Shiloh."[69] Halleck compounded his folly by dispersing his army in defensive positions throughout the region rather than pursuing Beauregard.

The Union scored another resounding victory that spring when Adm. David Farragut led a flotilla a hundred miles up the Mississippi River to New Orleans, destroyed several forts en route, and disembarked fifteen thousand troops commanded by Gen. Benjamin Butler into the undefended city on May 1, 1862. Farragut steamed upstream and captured Baton Rouge but was repelled in an assault on Vicksburg and withdrew to Baton Rouge. The rebels began massing troops and building fortifications at Port Hudson, thereby safeguarding a stretch of the Mississippi River from there two hundred miles north to Vicksburg.

While all these decisive events unfolded elsewhere, George McClellan made his own leisurely campaign preparations. In response to the president's queries as to why he was not proceeding quicker, he explained that his duties as both commanding general and general of the Army of the Potomac were enormously time consuming. Lincoln eliminated this excuse when he relieved McClellan as the commanding general on March 11, thus freeing him to concentrate on his campaign; for now, the commander in chief would act as his own general in chief. Another reason for the Army of the Potomac's glacial decision making and movement was McClellan's frequent councils with all twelve of his division commanders. Lincoln hoped to cut some of the time needed to reach consensus by ordering McClellan to organize these divisions into four corps. Although deciding what to do and how to do it was clearly easier with four rather than twelve often outspoken generals, the decisions did not arrive much more swiftly. This initially was because three of the four corps commanders that Lincoln appointed—Edwin Sumner, Samuel Heintzelman, and Irvin McDowell—opposed McClellan's plan, while only Erasmus Keyes approved it. Making critical choices was difficult enough, but implementing them was far tougher. Each corps commander proved to be a mediocre or worse field general and would be replaced during the subsequent campaign.

Lincoln and McClellan disagreed over just where the Army of the Potomac should go and what it should do when it got there. The general intended to outflank Gen. Joe Johnston's Army of Northern Virginia by sailing his army down the Potomac River into Chesapeake Bay, landing it, and marching it against the rebel capital. His first proposed landing site was Urbana, at the tip of the peninsula north of the York River, 120 miles over water from Washington and 50 miles over land to Richmond. Lincoln worried that that strategy would let Johnston launch his army, deployed around Manassas and Centreville, straight at a nearly undefended capital, thirty miles away. He pressed McClellan to envelop the rebel army in northern Virginia and thus defeat the enemy while protecting Washington. Destroying the enemy's army rather than capturing the enemy's capital should be the primary objective.

Lincoln revealed his superior understanding of strategy in a remarkable letter to McClellan dated February 3, 1862. He asked the general to compare their two plans and then answer a series of very pointed questions. Did not McClellan's plan take more time, money, and troops? Was his plan any more certain of victory? Would not the president's plan break the enemy's supply and communications line easier than the general's? Should disaster ensue, which plan offered a safer retreat?[70] McClellan haughtily dismissed Lincoln's plan while insisting that his plan was superb, yet he refused to implement it, claiming he lacked enough troops to do so.

Lincoln was hardly the only person in despair at McClellan's near-traitorous conduct. The president met with the Congressional Committee on the Conduct of the War, chaired by Radical Republican Benjamin Wade, on March 3. The committee members heatedly expressed a litany of charges against McClellan and urged his dismissal. When Lincoln asked who should take his place, Wade insisted that "anybody" would do. To that Lincoln replied that "anybody will do for you, but not for me. I must have somebody."[71]

Rumors abounded that more than timidity explained the general's refusal to act. Some claimed that McClellan was a Democrat who did not want to crush the rebel states let alone abolish slavery as liberal Republicans advocated. That rumor was grounded in truth. In a letter he penned in November 1861, McClellan revealed his true feelings: "Help me dodge the nigger. . . . I am fighting to preserve the integrity of the Union. . . . To gain that end we cannot afford to raise up the negro question."[72]

Johnston meanwhile increasingly feared that the Army of the Potomac would launch just such a plan as conceived by Lincoln. He withdrew his army twenty miles south and centered its deployment at Culpeper, below the Rapidan River. Only then did McClellan advance his army on what he called a "practice march" toward the abandoned enemy lines. What they discovered made McClellan a laughingstock. Although he had claimed that the rebel army far outnumbered his, engineers estimated that the camps held only about half as many troops as those in the Army of the Potomac. And as for all those cannons bristling from the enemy's entrenchments, hundreds were found to be nothing more than black-painted logs, dubbed "Quaker guns" by wags.

The new rebel position did not just stymie Lincoln's envelopment plan. Johnston now could more easily block a Union march from Urbana. This forced McClellan to change his plan. Now the Army of the Potomac would sail all the way to Fort Monroe at the tip of the peninsula between the James and York Rivers, then march toward Richmond. Lincoln reluctantly approved but insisted that McDowell's thirty-thousand-man corps stay in northern Virginia to protect Washington. McClellan shrilly protested that he needed those men for his campaign but the president stood firm.

The Army of the Potomac began disembarking at Fort Monroe on April 1.[73] The only significant enemy force blocking the roads to Richmond was thirteen thousand Confederates led by Gen. John Magruder at Yorktown, a dozen miles away. McClellan inched his army toward Yorktown, where he fired off urgent messages that he was outgunned and desperately needed more troops. Once again McClellan let himself be snookered by "Quaker guns" and Magruder's timeworn ruse of marching the same troops across a clearing in sight of the enemy and then circling them back through woods and again across that clearing. On April 22 Johnston brought his army to Yorktown and was horrified by what he found. Magruder, an amateur thespian, was clearly better at theater than engineering. Johnston reported that the fortifications were weak despite all the labor that had been expended in building them and concluded, "No one but McClellan could have hesitated to attack."[74]

Lincoln had reached the same conclusion. He literally begged McClellan to move and as always grounded his plea in hard strategic logic: "I think it is the precise time for you to strike a blow. By delay the enemy will relatively gain upon you—that is, he will gain faster by fortifications and reinforcements than you can by reinforcements alone. And once more let me tell you it is indispensable to you that you strike a blow. . . . You must act."[75]

Johnston withdrew his army from Yorktown to Williamsburg, a half-dozen miles west, on the night of May 3. The following day McClellan marched his army into empty entrenchments that revealed he faced a foe far inferior in numbers to his own. He continued to claim that he was outnumbered. He did send a corps in pursuit of the retreating rebels. The Union troops caught up to the enemy's rear guard at Williamsburg, attacked, and were repelled, suffering twenty-two hundred losses to the rebels' seventeen hundred.

The defeat bolstered McClellan's timidity. Over the next three weeks he advanced two miles daily toward Richmond. Johnston slowly backed his army westward until he was within the ring of fortifications surrounding the capital. The rebels also withdrew on the south side of the James River. They abandoned Norfolk without a fight on May 9 and two days later were forced to scuttle the css *Virginia* to prevent its capture. This emboldened the Union naval commander to steam his five gunboats, including the *Monitor*, toward the capital; rebel batteries repulsed the flotilla at Drewry's Bluff, eight miles downriver from Richmond, on May 15.

Meanwhile Thomas "Stonewall" Jackson fought one of the most brilliant military campaigns in history.[76] With no more than seventeen thousand troops and often far fewer, he trounced three converging and more numerous Union armies commanded by generals John Frémont, Nathaniel Banks, and James Shields in a whirlwind campaign that engulfed most of the Shenandoah Valley from May 8 to June 9, 1862. In all, his troops fought and won five battles that forced the Union armies, with a combined strength of thirty-three thousand troops, to retreat. He won four of those battles by racing superior numbers of troops against isolated Union forces. Yet another vital reason for Jackson's victories was that the Union forces lacked unity of command.

Lincoln rectified that deficiency by creating the Army of Virginia, comprising all troops in that theater, then looked for an energetic and successful general to command it. He first asked Gen. Ambrose Burnside, whose campaign earlier that year had captured New Bern, North Carolina. Burnside turned down the offer. He then asked John Pope, who had led an expedition down the Mississippi River that captured Island Number Ten and Fort Pillow. Pope accepted and received command on June 27.[77]

Jackson's campaign provoked near-panic in the capital with the fear that he and his victorious army might soon appear near Washington. This prompted Lincoln to fire off his latest plaintive message to McClellan: "I think the time is near when you must either attack Richmond or give up the job and come to the defense of Washington."[78] Nonetheless, the president typically saw a strategic opportunity in any Jackson march on the capital. He hoped to trap Jackson by ordering Pope to dispatch half his sixty-thousand-man army against him. But by then it was too late to catch Jackson, who led his troops east from Gordonsville toward Richmond on June 17. Lincoln then ordered Pope to march on Richmond and join McClellan against the rebel army. But by the time Pope readied his army to march, the Confederate Army of Northern Virginia was moving rapidly to encircle and attack him.

As McClellan's 105,000 troops neared Richmond in late May, Johnston had only 70,000 men to defend the rebel capital. On May 31 Johnston seized an opportunity when McClellan split his troops on both sides of the Chickahominy River, by launching his army against the Federals on Richmond's side of the river at Seven Pines, also called Fair Oaks. The battle raged for two days before the Confederates withdrew in defeat, having lost six thousand men to the Union's five thousand. Johnston was among the wounded and needed months to recover. The battle bought crucial time for the rebels as McClellan typically reacted with indecision, fear, and calls for massive reinforcements.

Meanwhile President Davis made a decision that decisively affected the war—he appointed Robert E. Lee to command the Army of Northern Virginia. Lee readied his army for another offensive, recalled Jackson from the Shenandoah Valley, and sent his cavalry commander J. E. B. Stuart and twelve hundred troopers on a reconnaissance in which they rode entirely around the Union army. Stuart returned with word that Gen. Fitz-John Porter's thirty-thousand-man corps east of the Chickahominy River was vulnerable.

Keeping twenty-seven thousand men in Richmond's trenches and forts, Lee led sixty thousand troops north, then over the Chickahominy River to attack Porter's corps at Mechanicsville on June 26. The Confederates might have crushed the Federals had Jackson brought his men up quickly enough to strike the enemy's right flank. But Porter managed to withdraw his corps after repelling the frontal assault. At Gaines Mills on June 27, Savage Station on June 29, and Glendale on June 30, Lee hurled his army against Porter's corps each time with the same result—the Union troops repulsed the rebels, then Porter withdrew his battered corps a few miles to another defensive position.

Meanwhile, although McClellan had seventy-five thousand troops west of the river facing a thin gray line of rebels defending Richmond, he panicked and chose to retreat rather than attack. He whined to Washington that he faced encirclement and annihilation by two hundred thousand enemy troops if he did not immediately receive massive reinforcements. He wrote Stanton that "if I save this army now I tell you plainly that I owe no thanks to you or any other persons in Washington—you have done your best to sacrifice this army."[79]

McClellan halted his retreat at Malvern Hill, where Lee attacked on July 1. Although Union rifle and cannon fire shattered the rebel assault, McClellan once again turned victory into defeat by withdrawing his army to Harrison Landing on the James River. Although Lee had lost twenty thousand men to the Federals' sixteen thousand in these five battles that became known as the Seven Days, he won a decisive strategic victory.

Lincoln sought to see firsthand whether there was any truth to McClellan's hysterical messages. After arriving at the Army of the Potomac's headquarters on July 8, he carefully debriefed the general and his corps commanders, scanned maps, and reviewed the troops. His conclusion was firm—McClellan should resume the offensive. Despite all contrary evidence, the general continued to insist that the enemy outnumbered his forces by two to one and thus any advance was out of the question.

Lincoln returned to Washington deeply depressed. Although he was the commander in chief, his general refused to follow his instructions. As if stuck in amber, an army of one hundred thousand troops was encamped a score of miles from Richmond. And this was hardly Lincoln's only frustration. Despite his fine grasp of strategy and War Secretary Stanton's administrative talents, without military backgrounds they struggled to direct and supply the deployment of more troops in more commands across the country. The army was in desperate need of a professional commanding general. On July 11 Lincoln tapped Gen. Henry Halleck, the western commander, to come to Washington and take charge of all American soldiers everywhere.

Halleck was a good choice.[80] Known as "Old Brains," he had graduated from and taught at West Point, had written a book titled *The Elements of Military Art and Science*, and was a naturally gifted administrator. He was not just an intellectual. He had served in the Mexican War, commanded the Department of the West at St. Louis, and led a glacial but ultimately successful campaign that took the strategic rail juncture of Corinth, Mississippi.

After arriving on July 23, Halleck immediately got to work with Lincoln and Stanton. Their first decision was to withdraw McClellan's army back to northern Virginia to support Pope. After receiving the order to do so on August 2, McClellan typically dragged his feet in implementing it over the next month.

Satisfied that he had thoroughly cowed McClellan, Lee marched his army north to defeat Pope, with Jackson spearheading the advance. Jackson routed Gen. Nathaniel Banks and his corps at Cedar Mountain on August 9, inflicting 2,353 casualties and losing 1,338. He then quick-marched his corps around Pope's right flank and captured his supply base at Manassas on August 27. Jackson's corps now had cut off Pope from Washington, while the rest of Lee's army was marching to join him. Although the Confederates enjoyed the strategic position, Pope's army still outnumbered Lee's by seventy-five thousand to fifty thousand troops. While Pope had little choice but to attack Jackson on August 29, he could not have been more murderously inept in doing so. Rather than try to outflank Jackson, who deployed most of his men in a deep cut dug in the earth for a railroad, Pope launched a series of piecemeal attacks straight against the rebel line. The result was the latest slaughter. That night both sides swelled with reinforcements, as Lee joined Jackson and the corps of Irwin McDowell and Fitz-John Porter joined Pope. The next morning Lee sent Gen. James Longstreet against the Union's left flank. Pope withdrew his army east and then north around Jackson's position. The Confederates won the second battle of Manassas at a cost of 9,197 men while inflicting 16,054 casualties on the Union army. Lee then led his army in pursuit and caught up to Pope's rear guard at Chantilly on September 1. Once again the rebels routed the Federals, and Pope concentrated his army within twenty miles south of Washington.

Lee was not content with having bloodied and sent reeling two enemy armies within a couple of months. He decided on an even more ambitious goal. He carried the war to the enemy by marching his army north of the Potomac River, where he hoped to win decisive victories that ended the war. The first regiments of the Army of Northern Virginia crossed the river into Maryland on September 4.

Lincoln saw this invasion more as an opportunity than a threat. With superior forces, the Union could at once defend the capital and cut off and destroy Lee's army. And with that victory, Lincoln intended to issue a proclamation that would dramatically transform the cause for which the United States was fighting.

8

Emancipation

If slavery is not wrong, nothing is wrong. I can not remember when I did not so think and feel.

ABRAHAM LINCOLN

My paramount object in this struggle is to save the Union, and is not either to save or destroy slavery.

ABRAHAM LINCOLN

Fellow citizens, we cannot escape history. . . . The fiery trial through which we pass will light us down in honor or dishonor to the latest generation. . . . The dogmas of the quiet past are inadequate to the stormy present.

ABRAHAM LINCOLN

In giving freedom to the slave, we assure freedom for the free . . . and then we shall save the country.

ABRAHAM LINCOLN

Eleven southern states seceded and warred against the United States because of a pathological fear that if they did not do so, the newly elected Republican president and Congress would somehow erode or outright eliminate their "right" to own slaves. They clung to this delusion despite the repeated public reassurances of Abraham Lincoln and most other Republican leaders that they would limit slavery's expansion but continue to tolerate it where it existed. Yet in seceding and warring against the United States, the rebels ended up provoking their worst fear. The abolition of slavery proceeded in a series of small steps driven by military rather than moral necessity that culminated with the Thirteenth Amendment.[1]

The effort did not begin in Congress despite the fact that after the eleven southern states seceded, the Republican Party dominated, with 32 of 48 Senate seats and 106 of 176 House seats. Yet these numbers masked sharp differences among Republicans over principles and policies. While the party was united to crush the rebellion and reunify the nation, it split over the means to that end. Conservatives sought only to rejoin the Union and would continue to tolerate slavery where it existed. The most prominent Senate conservatives were John Sherman, James Grimes, William Fessenden, Schuyler Colfax, and Richard Yates. Liberals, then known as Radicals, believed that reunification and abolition were inseparable. The leading Radical voices in Congress were Charles Sumner, Benjamin Wade, and Zachariah Chandler in the Senate and Thaddeus Stevens, Henry Winter Davis, Owen Lovejoy, and James Ashley in the House. During the war, the power balance within the Republican Party shifted decisively from the conservatives to the Radicals. All along Abraham Lincoln struggled to maintain party unity while he himself gradually evolved from a conservative into a moderate with Radical leanings by the time of his death.[2]

Holding only about one of four seats in each house, the Democrats could protest but not obstruct Lincoln administration policies. They suffered an enormous loss on June 3, 1861, when their most powerful spokesman, Senator Stephen Douglas, died. Rendering the Democrats even more ineffective was their split between "war" and "peace" factions.[3] As the war ground on with no end in sight, some Peace Democrats became so radical in their rhetoric and behavior that Republicans assailed them as traitorous "Copperheads." Lincoln eventually exiled Clement Vallandigham, a prominent Ohio Copperhead and Democrat politician, to the rebel lines.

Lincoln did what he could to entice War Democrats to support Republican policies. Yet at times doing so raised a terrible dilemma in his crusade to crush the rebellion and restore the Union. The political concessions he was forced to make at times contradicted his military strategy. George McClellan, Benjamin Butler, William Rosecrans, and John McClernand were all prominent War Democrats and dismal generals. If he fired them for their at times murderous incompetence, he risked driving War Democrats into the arms of Peace Democrats. Yet by retaining them at the heads of armies, the war dragged on as they either lost battles or lost opportunities to win battles.

The Joint Committee on the Conduct of the War, chaired by Radical Republican Benjamin Wade, was set up in December 1861 to investigate the disasters at Bull Run and Ball's Bluff but swiftly expanded its duties to embrace virtually all aspects of the war. For nearly four years it provided valuable oversight by spotlighting inept generals and corrupt contractors and politicians.[4]

The biggest question that Congress addressed after how to win the war was how to win the peace. The conservative view was reflected in a joint resolution, sponsored by Senator Andrew Johnson of Tennessee and Representative John Crittenden of Kentucky, that passed by huge majorities. The Crittenden-Johnson Resolution proclaimed that "this war is not waged upon our part in any spirit of oppression, nor for any purpose of conquest or subjugation, nor purpose of overthrowing or interfering with the rights or established institutions of these States."[5] Although the words *slave* and *slavery* were nowhere mentioned, everyone understood that the resolution's core message was to reassure slave owners in all the states that they need not fear losing their property. For now, Lincoln publicly echoed this view: "I have no purpose, directly or indirectly, to interfere with the institution of slavery in the States where it exists. I believe I have no lawful right to do so, and I have no inclination to do so."[6] The liberals' reply to the Crittenden-Johnson Resolution came in February 1862, when Senator Charles Sumner of Massachusetts and Representative James Ashley of Ohio submitted resolutions that would transform the rebel states into territories that Congress would remake into states with republican governments; emancipate all slaves without compensation to their owners; confiscate rebel property; and deny political rights to any rebels who were former federal officials or army officers or refused to sign a loyalty oath. These resolutions failed to pass.

While Congress debated the fate of four million enslaved human beings, the army faced a worsening dilemma. Thousands of slaves were escaping to the Union lines. The Fugitive Slave Act was still on the books, requiring that all authorities and citizens aid masters in recovering their chattel. Most commanders followed this law, including most notably generals McClellan, Buell, Halleck, and Burnside; McClellan went so far as to forbid regimental bands from playing the abolitionist song "John Brown's Body."

A few generals, however, saw practical and moral advantages in protecting rather than returning slaves who sought freedom. Slaves were crucial to the Confederate war effort. They not only sowed and reaped crops but dug fortifications and delivered supplies. Depriving the rebels of their slaves would cripple their ability to wage war.

Gen. Benjamin Butler, then commanding Fort Monroe, was the first to recognize and wield this weapon. After three slaves showed up at Fort Monroe on May 23, 1861, and asked for freedom, Butler thought of a way to grant it. He designated the escapees "contraband of war" and put them to work in return for provisions and small stipends. Lincoln accepted that policy when he learned of it, explaining that "the government neither should nor would send back to bondage such as came into our armies."[7] In doing so he repudiated the Fugitive Slave Act, which was grounded in a constitutional tenet, and thus took a significant step on the road to emancipation. Congress codified this policy by passing the Confiscation Act by twenty-four to eleven in the Senate and sixty-one to forty-eight in the House on August 6, 1861.

Gen. John Frémont, who commanded the Department of the West, headquartered at St. Louis, carried this policy a huge step forward. Rather than simply protect and put to work slaves who escaped, he declared martial law in Missouri on August 30 and warned that his forces would liberate any slaves from their masters and execute any rebel civilians bearing arms.

News of Frémont's act alarmed Lincoln, who feared that it might push the border slave states of Kentucky, Missouri, and Maryland into the Confederacy. This was not his only objection. Armies can temporarily requisition property for their needs but must restore it when it is no longer needed. Only legislatures and courts can legally deprive an owner permanently of his property. He assessed Frémont's decree of the "confiscation and liberation of slaves" as "purely political and not within the range of military law or necessity." The result was tyranny: "Can it be pretended that it is no longer the government of the U.S. . . . Constitution and laws—wherein a General or a president may make permanent rules of property by proclamation?" He first privately wrote Frémont on September 2, asking him to cancel his order, and then, when Frémont refused, publicly ordered him to do so on September 11.[8]

Lincoln initially sought emancipation by giving the slave and border states incentives that encouraged manumission. He first targeted the state with the fewest slaves, figuring its government would be the least difficult to convince and that the result could serve as a model for other states. In December 1861 he worked with Delaware representative George Fisher to sponsor a bill whereby his state would emancipate its 1,798 slaves over a decade in return for $719,200 in federal compensation. But Delaware's slaveholders pressured Fisher to break his deal with the president.

Lincoln then asked Congress on March 6, 1862, for a joint resolution that Washington would compensate masters who emancipated their slaves. He grounded his argument on practical rather than moral grounds—the cost of paying masters to free their slaves would be a fraction of the cost of conquering the Confederacy. He followed this up on March 10 by meeting with congressional members of the border states and encouraging them to embrace gradual emancipation over three decades in return for $400 for each freed slave. They bluntly rejected the notion. Nonetheless, on March 13 Congress did amend the Articles of War to forbid officers under pain of court-martial from returning escaped slaves to their masters.[9]

To see whether incentives worked, Lincoln and his congressional allies decided to use the District of Columbia as a laboratory. On April 16, 1862, Lincoln signed into law a bill that abolished slavery in the district, promised to pay masters $300 for each liberated slave, and appropriated $100,000 for any blacks who wished to settle in Liberia in Africa, Chiriqui in Central America, or any other foreign land. Once again he encouraged border state leaders to adapt similar policies but met only with angry refusals.

Having tacked one way, an unexpected event forced Lincoln to tack the other. On May 9, 1862, Gen. David Hunter, the regional commander for South Carolina, Georgia, and Florida, issued an order declaring all slaves in these states freed and calling on black men to join the First South Carolina Colored Regiment that he established. Lincoln rescinded the order on May 19. In doing so, he left himself plenty of room one day to assert his own emancipation proclamation by asserting that only the president, as commander in chief, was empowered to declare slaves free, and only when he deemed it "a necessity indispensable to the maintenance of the government."[10]

New Orleans was the headquarters for the Department of the Gulf, which stretched from Brownsville, Texas, to Pensacola, Florida, and far inland for varying distances. As if the duties of overseeing that region were not daunting enough, the departmental commander also had to run New Orleans itself. Even under the best of circumstances, governing 140,000 people would have been no easy task, but New Orleans was then America's most diverse city. Although most people spoke English, there were communities of French and Spanish speakers from an array of ancestries, while a babble of tongues could be heard along the docks. The black population alone was a microcosm of diversity. Of twenty-five thousand blacks, eleven thousand were legally free and collectively owned $2 million in property. Not only was there a small group of wealthy blacks, but some of them owned slaves. Under these circumstances, those who ruled New Orleans had to be at once sensitive and firm. Although most whites in New Orleans were diehard Confederates, a large minority welcomed liberation by the Union army.

President Lincoln hoped to make Louisiana a reconstruction model.[11] This ambition, however, was problematic as long as Benjamin Butler was in charge.[12] When the war erupted, Butler was a prominent Boston lawyer and Massachusetts Democratic Party political chief who wielded his connections and skill to wrangle a general's commission. Lincoln rewarded his initiative at Fort Monroe with command of the army to take New Orleans. Soon after his troops occupied New Orleans Butler became reviled as "the beast" for mercilessly repressing any rebel resistance. When rebel William Mumford pulled down and ripped into shreds the American flag that Admiral Farragut had raised over New Orleans, then bragged of the deed, Butler had him arrested and tried by a military tribunal. Mumford was found guilty of treason and hanged. Butler replaced the outspoken mayor with Gen. George Shepley. He ordered all six of the city's newspapers shut down for spreading sedition in their columns. He abruptly ended the practice of women hurl-ing insults and spittle upon Union soldiers with this order: "Hereafter when any female shall by word or deed or gesture or movement insult or show contempt for any officer or soldier of the U.S. she shall be regarded and held liable as a woman of the town plying her avocation."[13]

Yet Butler asserted reforms along with the repression. He put the jobless to work by paying them fifty cents a day to clean the streets, ditches, and canals of a century and more of malodorous, disease-fes-tering filth. He distributed provisions to thousands of hungry people. In May 1862 he helped establish the Union Association of New Orle-ans and welcomed into the city's administration anyone who signed a loyalty oath to the United States. He cracked down on criminal gangs that bullied and robbed people in many neighborhoods. New Orleans was never better run than when Butler took over.

The trouble was that Butler had become too controversial and thus a political liability. In December 1862 Lincoln replaced him with Nathaniel Banks, another Democratic Party chief who finagled a general's commis-sion. Banks expanded the reforms while avoiding measures and attitudes deliberately designed to rub salt in rebel wounds. On January 29, 1863, he decreed that those who hired blacks had to sign contracts guaranteeing them ten-hour work days, set wages in coin or kind, provide clothing and shelter if necessary, and promise not to whip their employees for any rea-son. Federal officials could inspect any workplace to ensure compliance with these rules. With the Union army's protection, Louisiana's loyalists wrote, ratified, and implemented a state constitution that established a liberal democracy and abolished slavery. This in turn let them send two senators and five representatives to Congress.

Lincoln and the Republican Party achieved a major and long-sought goal on June 19, 1862, when the president signed a bill forbidding slav-ery in the territories. Nearly a month later, on July 12, and for the third and final time, Lincoln summoned all the border state representatives and senators to the White House and once again tried to talk them into voluntary abolition. He got no takers. This convinced him that eman-cipation could come only through his own leadership. He first revealed his intention to Seward and Stanton on July 13, after they returned in a carriage from the funeral of the war secretary's son. But for the time being that would be their secret.

Over the next few days, Lincoln worked with congressional leaders to draft and pass two bills that he signed on July 17. The Second Confiscation Act empowered the government to confiscate rebel property, including slaves. Due process would prevail—courts rather than soldiers would determine just who was a rebel and thus whether his or her property could be taken. This would obviously be a slow, laborious process, given the nearly 350,000 rebel slaveholders. There was another limitation. Masters in border states loyal to the United States could keep their chattel. Nonetheless, escaped slaves could enjoy relative freedom while their cases worked their way through court. The military could pay escapees to construct fortifications and roads or provide other labor crucial for the war effort. The Militia Act empowered the president to call up three hundred thousand nine-month militia aged from eighteen to forty-five years; a clause let blacks serve in the militia and promised any male slave who enlisted freedom for himself and his family if his master was a rebel.

So far Lincoln had taken a series of small steps that nibbled around slavery's edges and that he later confessed had not "caused a single slave to come over to us."[14] He sought a way to speed the process. After consulting with a number of key abolitionist politicians like Thurlow Weed and Charles Sumner, he drew up the Emancipation Proclamation. He shared his idea with his cabinet on July 21 and the following day submitted the draft to them. They embraced it along with Seward's proposal to issue it only after a major victory to avoid making it seem like an act of desperation rather than triumph.

Lincoln justified freeing slaves in rebel-held territory purely on grounds of "military necessity." If "slaves are property," then declaring them war contraband permits the federal government to seize and use them to help crush the rebellion. This policy obviously had stronger legal and practical than moral rationales. The policy angered liberals who sought immediate and total emancipation on moral grounds.

Lincoln committed a historic first when he invited five leading black abolitionists to the White House on August 14. He reassured them that he completely sympathized with the plight of black people in America: "Your race is suffering . . . the great wrong inflicted on any people. But even when you cease to be slaves, you are yet far removed from being placed on equality with the white race. You are cut off from many of the advantages that the other race enjoys. The aspiration of men is to enjoy equality with the best when free, but on this broad continent not a single man of your race is made the equal of a single man of ours." The only way to escape this tragic fate was to "go where you are treated the best." He then tried to talk them into accepting as the price of abolition for black people immigration to Liberia or someplace in Central America that might welcome them. His argument's essence was that black people should not stay where they were unwanted and could never be accepted as equals: "Your race suffers very greatly, many of them, by living among us, while ours suffer by your presence. There is an unwillingness on the part of our people, harsh as it may be, for you free colored people to remain with us. . . . It is better for us both, therefore, to be separated."[15]

The black delegation firmly rejected any notion of leaving America. What they insisted upon was equality between the races, not the cruel choice of separation and discrimination or exile. Abolitionists were incensed when they read Lincoln's quotes in an article by a *New York Tribune* reporter who attended this meeting. On August 19 Horace Greeley, the *Tribune*'s editor, blistered Lincoln in a column titled "The Prayer of Twenty Millions" and called on him to support slavery's immediate and complete abolition.

Lincoln wrote a reply designed to prepare the public for his upcoming proclamation and that he knew Greely would publish: "My paramount object in this struggle is to save the Union, and is not either to save or destroy slavery. If I could save the Union without freeing any slave I would do it; and if I could save it by freeing all the slaves I would; and if I could save it by freeing some and leaving others alone I would also do that."[16]

A religious delegation met with Lincoln on September 13 and urged him to proclaim emancipation. Of course, he intended to do just that as soon as the Union won a major victory, but he pretended to oppose the notion. He made all the arguments against the idea and let them refute each in turn. He then acknowledged the superiority of their arguments. He said that if he did ever issue a proclamation it would be on practical rather than moral grounds—emancipation would at once deprive the rebels and empower the United States with blacks as laborers and soldiers.

It was through reports of meetings with abolitionists and his own carefully written letters that the newspapers published that Lincoln prepared the public psychologically and politically for emancipation.[17] Yet, paradoxically, most Americans appeared more appalled by the institution of polygamy than slavery. They applauded when Lincoln signed the Morrill Anti-Bigamy Act into law on July 2, 1862. Signing and enforcing a law, however, can involve two very different exercises of power. Lincoln made it clear that suppressing polygamy was not his priority. He needed the Mormon people's cooperation rather than enmity. Specifically, he wanted to call on them to protect the telegraph lines and mail delivery that passed through their territory until federal troops could secure those routes. To a Mormon journalist, Lincoln explained his approach to the antibigamy law: "Occasionally [in clearing timber] we would come to a log that had fallen down. It was too hard to split, too wet to burn, and too heavy to move, so we ploughed around it. That's what I intend to do with the Mormons. Tell Brigham Young that if he lets me alone, I will let him alone."[18] One can imagine the wry expression on Lincoln's face as he passed on this message.

After defeating Pope's Army of Virginia at Cedar Mountain, Second Manassas, and Chantilly, Lee sought to carry the war north of the Potomac River and seek a decisive victory. He marched his army to the head of the Shenandoah Valley, detached Jackson's corps to invest 12,500 Union troops defending Harpers Ferry, and crossed the Potomac with the rest of his men. He used South Mountain, a steep ridge running north-south for twenty miles, to screen his right flank. He detached troops to defend South Mountain's three passes while he spread out most of his other troops to round up provisions.

McClellan, meanwhile, finally obeyed Lincoln's repeated orders to transfer his army from the peninsula to Washington but then typically sat tight rather than seeking the enemy. Then, on September 13, an extraordinary piece of luck gifted the American cause. In an abandoned rebel camp, Union troops found a copy of Lee's Special Order Number 191, wrapped around three cigars, apparently left by a negligent orderly. Officers on the spot recognized the intelligence windfall and hurried it to McClellan's headquarters. What the orders revealed was that Lee had widely dispersed his army behind South Mountain, which was lightly defended, while Jackson's corps was besieging Harpers Ferry.

For the only time in his career, McClellan acted decisively. He ordered his army to march toward and over the South Mountain gaps. The Union troops attacked and routed the rebels at South Mountain's passes on September 15. Lincoln replied to McClellan's triumphant telegraph with congratulations and this admonition: "Destroy the rebel army if possible."[19]

The same day, Harpers Ferry's garrison surrendered to Jackson. After dispatching the prisoners under guard, Jackson led his corps to join Lee, who had massed his army around Sharpsburg behind Antietam Creek. The bloodiest day in American history took place there on September 17, 1862.

McClellan proved to be as utterly inept a tactician as he was a strategist. The Union army outgunned the Confederate by sixty thousand to thirty-seven thousand men. Rather than take advantage of this by launching an overwhelming assault on one or more enemy flanks, McClellan ordered his troops forward in a series of piecemeal attacks directly against the rebel army. This enabled Lee to shift his limited forces to blunt one Federal assault after another. By the day's end, the Union had suffered 13,724 casualties and the Confederates 12,469.

Despite these horrific losses and with no more than twenty-five thousand troops, Lee kept his army defiantly in place the following morning. He had little choice. Rains had swollen the Potomac River and engineers struggled to build a bridge across it so the army could retreat to Virginia. Meanwhile twenty thousand reinforcements joined the Union army, bringing its total to sixty-five thousand troops after subtracting the previous day's losses.

Yet, despite his overwhelming superiority, McClellan refused to attack. Had he done so, Lee's army would have been trapped with its back to the flooded Potomac River and forced to surrender. Nonetheless, Antietam was a decisive Union victory in three ways: it repelled the rebel invasion of Maryland, it undercut the pressure of some in the British government to openly aid the Confederacy, and it gave Lincoln the excuse to issue his Emancipation Proclamation.

McClellan never tested Lincoln's forbearance more severely than during the days and weeks after Antietam. With deepening frustration, the president waited fruitlessly for the general to advance. But McClellan did nothing to prevent or respond to Lee's escape with his army to Virginia a few days after the battle. On October 6 Lincoln bluntly ordered McClellan to "cross the Potomac and give battle to the enemy. . . . Your army must move now." When McClellan made his usual excuses that the rebels were too strong and his own army too weak, Lincoln replied with a long letter that was part pep talk and part military treatise: "You remember my speaking to you of what I called your over-cautiousness. Are you not overcautious when you assume that you cannot do what the enemy is constantly doing? Should you not claim to be at least his equal in prowess, and act upon the claim? . . . Again one of the standard maxims of war, as you know, is to 'operate on the enemy's communications as much as possible without exposing your own.' . . . I say 'try'; if we never try we shall never succeed." McClellan offered the excuse that his horses were worn out and thus he could not pursue Lee. To this Lincoln asked, "Will you pardon me for asking what the horses of your army have done since the battle of Antietam that fatigue anything?" All along Lincoln somehow kept his sense of humor. During a visit to McClellan's headquarters, he pointed to all the soldiers and asked one of his entourage, "What do you suppose all these people are?" To the reply that they made up the Army of the Potomac, Lincoln demurred: "No, you are mistaken. That is General McClellan's body guard."[20]

Shortly after Antietam similar threats erupted in the western theater, with similar results. At his Corinth, Mississippi, headquarters, Gen. Ulysses Grant nipped an invasion in the bud. On September 14 Gen. Sterling Price, with fifteen thousand troops, captured the rail junction of Iuka. Grant sought to encircle and destroy him by sending Gen. Edward Ord due east from Corinth while having Gen. William Rosecrans angle around from the south. Price skillfully shifted his forces, attacked Rosecrans south of Iuka on September 19, then sidestepped him and marched west to join Gen. Earl Van Dorn at Tupelo, Mississippi. Together they led their twenty-two thousand troops north to attack Corinth. Learning of this movement, Grant quick-marched Rosecrans back to defend that vital rail and supply junction. Rosecrans and his men reached Corinth in time to repulse the Confederate attack. Grant then ordered Rosecrans to pursue and destroy the enemy, but the rebels escaped.

Federal troops elsewhere in the west repelled another invasion the same fall. On October 8 Gen. Don Buell's Army of the Ohio blocked Gen. Braxton Bragg's Army of the Tennessee at Perrysville, Kentucky, and after a hard-fought battle forced it to retreat. But, like McClellan, Buell disobeyed Lincoln's order and failed to turn a limited victory into a decisive one by immediately pursuing and destroying the rebel army's remnants. Word of this latest failure prompted Lincoln to despair that "we cannot march as the enemy marches, live as he lives, and fight as he fights, unless we admit the inferiority of our troops and generals."[21]

Swallowing his dismay at McClellan's failure to destroy Lee, Lincoln used the limited victory of Antietam as an excuse to publish, on September 22, his Emancipation Proclamation, which held that from January 1, 1863, all slaves held in any unoccupied states still in rebellion would be "forever free" and that the federal government would employ any able-bodied black man as a laborer, soldier, or sailor.[22]

Lincoln's proclamation was, typically, caught in a cross fire between political extremes. Slavocrats, of course, condemned Lincoln's decree for violating their rights. Abolitionists decried the proclamation as forcing the burden of liberation on the slaves themselves and being limited only to rebel states and not to all states. In the middle were those who traded on Wall Street or showed up at recruiting centers. Lincoln acknowledged that "stocks have declined, and troops come forward more slowly than ever."[23]

Actually, Lincoln's Emancipation Proclamation was a huge step toward abolition everywhere in the United States. While the proclamation did not literally free a single slave on New Year's Day 1863, it embraced 2.9 million slaves, or 82 percent of slaves in the Confederacy and 74 percent of slaves in the United States. Legally breaking the shackles of three of four American slaves was certainly a huge leap toward one day liberating the rest.[24] The deadline imposed a hard choice on each slave state, which had a month to decide whether to abolish slavery with federal compensation or to cling to the institution and most likely get not a penny should Washington one day emancipate all slaves everywhere. For Frederick Douglass, the succession of abolitionist measures revolutionized the conflict's nature: "The war now being waged in this land is a war for and against slavery; and . . .

it can never be effectively put down till one or the other of these vital forces is completely destroyed."[25]

Although his hand trembled slightly as he signed the proclamation, Lincoln had no doubt over its justice. To Seward and his son Fred, he said, "I never in my life felt more certain that I was doing right than I do in signing this paper. If my name ever goes into history it will be for this act, and my whole soul is in it."[26]

In issuing the proclamation, Lincoln took the only constitutional step available to him as president. "Military necessity" empowered him as commander in chief to deprive the enemy of a vital component of their power to resist. Abolition at once depleted the Confederacy and enriched the United States with manpower. In his December 1862 address to Congress, Lincoln called on it to pass a three-part bill promoting a broader emancipation: (1) every state must abolish slavery before January 1, 1900, thirty-seven years in the future; (2) any slaves who escaped during the rebellion would be "forever free," although the government would compensate owners loyal to the United States for their loss; and (3) Congress would appropriate money for any blacks who sought to immigrate to another country. Here again, Lincoln fell short of cutting the Gordian knot of slavery in America by simply advocating a constitutional amendment for its immediate abolition. He had a war to win that would be all the more arduous if the border states joined the rebels.

Having presented his agenda, he tried to sell it on practical grounds. Slaveholders could reason that with nearly four decades until abolition they had plenty of time to extract their money's worth from their chattel. Congressmen and taxpayers could reason that compensating slave states was a lot cheaper than crushing them. Workers could reason that their wages would likely rise once slavery disappeared. Slaves themselves could either try to escape now for guaranteed freedom or stay with their masters and try to learn vital skills to survive after their eventual release.

Lincoln ended his address with some of the most beautiful and profound lines he ever penned: "Fellow citizens, we cannot escape history. . . . The fiery trial through which we pass will light us down in honor or dishonor to the latest generation. . . . The dogmas of the quiet past are inadequate to the stormy present. . . . In giving freedom to the slave, we assure freedom to the free. . . . We shall nobly save or meanly lose the last, best hope of earth."[27]

9

The Hamiltonian Triumph

To secure to each laborer the whole product of his labor, or as nearly
as possible, is a worthy object of any good government. But then
another question arises, How can a government . . . effect this?

ABRAHAM LINCOLN

The legitimate object of government is to do for a community
of people, whatever they need to have done, but cannot
do at all, or cannot so well do for themselves.

ABRAHAM LINCOLN

Upon the subject of education, not presuming to dictate any plan
or system respecting it, I can only say that I view it as the most
important subject which we as a people can be engaged in.

ABRAHAM LINCOLN

I want every man to have a chance.

ABRAHAM LINCOLN

Washington never before more actively mobilized the nation's resources
for war and economic development than from 1861 to 1865.[1] Two factors explain the sweeping measures. One was the Civil War's scale. No
previous war had demanded a fraction of the resources vital for crushing the rebellion. Fortunately, thanks to the industrial revolution, the

economy had developed to the point where it could provide virtually all the goods and money needed to fight and win the struggle. The other was an ideology that provided a blueprint for mobilization, which first Jeffersonian then Jacksonian opponents had previously thwarted. During the 1790s Alexander Hamilton tried to implement his vision of a muscular government dedicated to working with the private sector to develop America's economy through a central bank, a regulated financial system, a national currency, internal improvements, protective tariffs, and education. This agenda's baton was carried first by Hamilton's Federalist Party, then Henry Clay's Whig Party, and then Abraham Lincoln's Republican Party. By the 1860s Hamiltonians controlled all three branches of the American government.

Abraham Lincoln was certainly an outstanding successor for advancing Hamiltonianism. A vision of how to create and distribute wealth was central to his political outlook and efforts for decades before slavery displaced it.[2] His interest stemmed from being born into and struggling free of poverty, combined with his innate sense of right and wrong. Unlike most self-made men, he sought to understand just why poverty existed and how government could work with society and individuals to alleviate it and let ever more people enjoy higher standards of living and a better quality of life. When Lincoln was a young man, Henry Clay, the Whig Party, and such works as Francis Wayland's *Elements of Political Economy* and Henry Carey's *Principles of Political Economy* provided, with their ideas and policies, illuminating answers to his questions.[3]

Lincoln first ran for public office in 1832, the same year that Clay challenged Andrew Jackson in his campaign for reelection to the White House. The contrast between the Whig and Democratic Parties was stark. The Whigs championed and the Democrats condemned the concept of a partnership between the government and the people to develop the economy, grounded in the Bank of the United States, internal improvements, and protective tariffs. Jackson retook the presidency and the Democrats dominated Congress. What happened thereafter reinforced Lincoln's understanding of economics. Jackson's policies of destroying the Bank of the United States, cutting internal improvements and tariffs, and winking at massive corruption and insider trading led to an economic catastrophe—a speculative boom that imploded with the Panic of 1837, followed by a devastating economic depression that ground on for a half-dozen years and left countless people bankrupted, jobless, homeless, or at least substantially poorer. But Jackson's policies simply accelerated an inevitability.

History reveals that markets sooner or later self-destruct; the freer the market, the sooner its self-destruction. The reason is simple. Market Darwinism driven by "survival of the fittest" and "greed is good" values lead either to monopolies or oligopolies that devour all rivals and then gouge consumers with high fixed prices or to booms fueled by speculative bubbles that eventually burst, hurting most producers and consumers alike.

Another lesson of history is equally clear. Federal government policies are crucial to the fate of the economy and thus every American, more or less. As with other elements of his philosophy, Lincoln's economic views appeared simple at first glance but were actually sophisticated and complex. His outlook was grounded in one simple value: "I want every man to have a chance."[4] Foremost he was a libertarian dedicated to "genuine popular sovereignty" in which the relationship between the people and government allowed "that each man shall do precisely as he pleases with himself, and with all those things which exclusively concern him. Applied to government this principle would be that a general government shall do all those things which pertain to it, and all the local governments shall do precisely as they please in respect to those matters which exclusively concern them."[5]

Few Americans of any political stripe could find fault with this view. And this was his intent. He typically wanted to unite his audience on a common ground before he explained just what he believed "all those things" were that "a general government shall do." But before doing that, he sought to expand the common ground so that folks nodded enthusiastically in agreement.

He expressed his understanding of the "relation between capital and labor. . . . That men who are industrious and sober and honest in the pursuit of their interests should after a while accumulate capital, and after that should be allowed to enjoy it in peace, and also if they choose . . . to use it to . . . hire other people to labor for them." Yet a potential problem lurked in this relationship. He noted an unavoidable conflict of interest and class. "The world has never had a good definition of the word liberty. We all declare for liberty but in using the same word we do not all mean the same thing. With some the word liberty may mean for each man to do as he pleases with himself and the product of his labor; while with others the same word may mean for some men to do as they please with other men and the product of their labor. Here are two not only different but incompatible things called by the same name—liberty."[6]

So where does government come in? Government arbitrates conflicts among different interest groups while promoting those that best advance America's "general welfare." The ideal policy "clears the path for all . . . and by consequence, enterprise and hope to all." To Lincoln "the legitimate object of government is to do for a community of people, whatever they need to have done, but cannot do at all, or cannot so well do for themselves—in their separate and individual capacities."[7] Where did the role of government end? He explained, "I do not mean to say that this General Government is charged with the duty of redressing or preventing all the wrongs in the world; but I do think that it is charged with preventing and redressing all wrongs which are wrongs to itself. This government is expressly charged with the duty of providing for the general welfare."[8]

The dilemma for policy makers, of course, is that interests clash. When this happens, government must judiciously weigh the relative merits of all interests involved, then deliver a policy that at once enhances the "general welfare" while ensuring that each individual has a chance to advance. This obviously is no easy task. For instance, Lincoln's belief that "it is best for all to leave each man free to acquire property as fast as he can" had a limit: "Some will get wealthy. I don't believe in a law to prevent a man from getting rich; it would do more harm than good. So while we do not propose any war upon capital, we do wish to allow the humblest man an equal chance to get rich with everybody else."[9] Ideally, "a worthy object of any good government" was "to secure to each laborer the whole product of his labor, or as nearly as possible." But this raises the question, "How can a government . . . effect this?" Lincoln distinguished among "useful labor, useless labor, and idleness," of which "the first only is meritorious." The "remedy" was for government "to drive useless labor and idleness out of existence."[10]

Within four years, Lincoln and congressional progressives enacted nearly the entire Republican agenda into law and policy. In doing so,

Congressional leaders and committees played the decisive role, while the president encouraged their efforts. The number of laws passed by Congress indicated just how active government had become. The Thirty-Seventh and Thirty-Eighth Congresses, of 1861 to 1863 and 1863 to 1865, passed, respectively, 428 and 411 bills. The previous record was the Twenty-Seventh Congress, of 1841 to 1843, which passed 201 bills. Meanwhile the federal budget skyrocketed from $78 million in 1860 to $1.1 billion in 1865, with the amount of nonmilitary spending more than tripling, from $49 million to $161 million. Congress got so much done because the Republicans enjoyed huge majorities in the Senate and House throughout the war.[11]

Among Washington's most daunting challenges was somehow finding enough money to both pay for the war and develop the economy.[12] As with other wars, the politicians paid for it largely by borrowing most of the money from future generations. As a result, the national debt soared from $64.8 million, or $2.06 per capita, in 1860 to $2.8 billion, or $75.42 per capita, in 1866.[13]

Plenty of "money" was available to borrow. The trouble was that much of it was of dubious value. Although the American gold dollar existed, it accounted for only a tiny fraction of business. Virtually all "money" that circulated was issued by over sixteen hundred banks, among which many were get-rich-quick, fly-by-night operations. By 1861 there were more than twelve thousand types of banknotes circulating.[14]

So Washington faced the conundrum of borrowing worthless script from unscrupulous lenders or paying sky-high interest rates for hard coin from prudent lenders. This hodgepodge financial "system" did not just confound the federal government, it was a deadweight on America's economic development. The difficulty in finding enough sound currency to borrow at reasonable rates to pay its bills forced the Treasury Department to suspend specie, or hard coin, payments on December 30, 1861. This in turn forced banks to suspend their own payments and sharply raise interest rates. The United States teetered on the brink of a financial panic or collapse that would implode the economy.

Lincoln conceived a means of averting economic catastrophe that would cripple the war effort. He wielded "military necessity" to demolish the existing inefficient, wasteful, underperforming system and replaced it with something much better. He had Treasury Secretary Salmon

Chase forge a series of policies with congressional leaders. The first decisive step came on February 25, 1862, when Congress passed the Legal Tender Act, which empowered Washington to issue $150 million in paper money, or "greenbacks," backed solely with the promise to repay them at face value. Greenbacks could be used by anyone for any type of business transaction except two—only gold would pay for import duties or interest on bonds. Later Congress authorized the issuance of another $300 million greenbacks, bringing $450 million into circulation. Yet all these greenbacks paid for only a sliver of the government's spending.

Congress established America's first income tax on August 5, 1861. The initial tax was light, a mere 3 percent on annual incomes over $800. An Internal Revenue Bureau was set up within the Treasury Department to administer the tax but lacked the means to assess let alone collect what people owed. Not surprisingly the take was modest. This forced Congress to enact a far more sweeping tax bill eleven months later. The Internal Revenue Act that Lincoln signed on July 1, 1862, had three provisions. The tax floor dropped to those annually making $600 a year; the rate was 3 percent on incomes from $600 to $10,000 and 5 percent above $10,000. An inheritance tax affected any estates worth more than $1,000. An excise tax was imposed on all business transactions worth more than $600. Finally, Washington tried to curtail state bank notes and raise revenue by imposing a 10 percent tax on any exchange of them. This last measure was perhaps the most powerful means of reforming the financial system, as it increasingly forced the purveyors and peddlers of dubious paper "money" certificates to close up shop.

There was another source of revenue. For Hamiltonians, tariffs had two virtues—they supplied government with money and protected American industries from voracious foreign rivals. Lincoln insisted that nurturing a steadily widening spectrum of industries was the best way to develop American wealth and power. "Give us a protective tariff," he once said, "and we will have the greatest country on earth."[15] The trouble was that tariff policy was set through an ideological and political tug-of-war rather than a careful analysis of just what level of protection each industry needed in order to at once promote protection, innovation, and competition. Tariffs rose and fell sharply depending on who held power in the White House and Congress. Lincoln and other progressives hoped to provide crucial government revenues and industry protection with the Morrill Tariff Act of February 1862 that steadily raised average import duties until they peaked at 47 percent in 1869. The tariffs were a great success. They not only amassed desperately needed revenues but let American industries flourish.

With tax and tariff receipts covering only about 10 percent of government spending, Washington had to borrow most of the rest. It did so by selling bonds. Treasury Secretary Chase inaugurated the practice whereby individuals as well as institutions could buy bonds.

Lincoln failed to establish one key institution of the Hamiltonian agenda. Slavery was hardly the only controversial issue that passionately split Americans. Throughout the early republic, a fierce political and ideological tug-of-war raged over whether America should have a national bank. Alexander Hamilton and his followers championed such a bank while first Thomas Jefferson and his followers and later Andrew Jackson and his followers harshly condemned such an institution. Hamiltonians prevailed with the First Bank of the United States from 1791 to 1811 and the Second Bank of the United States from 1816 to 1836, but Jeffersonians killed the first and Jacksonians the second.

The historic record is clear on whether a national bank is an asset or liability for America. The economy flourished when the bank existed and suffered roller-coaster speculative booms and busts when it was abolished. The reason was that the bank regulated the money supply by easing credit when the economy faltered and by tightening credit when speculators began pushing up prices. Both banks were partnerships between the federal government and private investors, with the ratio of shares one to five between them. Since the second bank's demise, the United States had suffered prolonged depressions following the panics or financial collapses of 1837 and 1857. The economy was struggling out of the latest depression when the Civil War erupted.

Despite history's illumination of how well America's economy did with a national bank and how poorly without one, proposals for a third U.S. bank died in Senate and House committees. The executioners were ideological and interest groups. Jeffersonians and Jacksonians opposed the institution on principle, while state-chartered banks opposed it because many of them would go bankrupt with a U.S. bank's tighter regulations and credit.

Nonetheless, the American people eventually received the next best alternative. Lincoln acted decisively on his belief that "no duty is more imperative on . . . Government than the duty it owes the people of furnishing them a sound and uniform currency."[16] He had Treasury Secretary Chase work closely with congressional leaders to devise and pass the National Banking Act, which he signed into law on February 25, 1863. The bill empowered the Treasury Department to issue charters to banks that held U.S. bonds equal to one-third of their financial holdings, in return for which they could issue banknotes up to 90 percent of the value of those bonds. At first few banks sought that arrangement. It was far more profitable to print "money" by handing out banknotes to all takers. It was not until 1865, after Congress passed a law imposing a 10 percent tax on state banknotes, that most banks joined the system. This eventually forced most of the bad money from circulation.

Thomas Jefferson famously wrote that "those who labour in the earth are the chosen people of God."[17] It was easy for Jefferson to idealize farming since he had several hundred slaves doing it for him. Abraham Lincoln held no such sentiments. He grew up farming and hated everything about it. And because of this he sought to alleviate the difficulties in the lives of farmers through policies that made it easier and cheaper for them to obtain new land and that promoted scientific farming practices that increased crop yields, reduced labor, and thus expanded wealth.

Lincoln intended to initiate an agrarian revolution through two laws. The Homestead Act that Congress passed and he signed into law on May 20, 1862, granted each settler 160 acres of public land after he or she registered and worked it for five years. Over the next three years, twenty-five thousand pioneers laid claim to three million acres. While the Homestead Act expanded the amount of land farmed, the Morrill Act that Lincoln signed into law on July 2, 1862, attempted to expand the productivity of farmland. The Department of Agriculture was established to develop the rural economy by encouraging farmers to adopt cutting-edge techniques and technologies that expanded crop and livestock yields and to send their children to state colleges funded by public land sales.

Although Lincoln may not have shared Jefferson's enthusiasm for farming, he was just as powerful an advocate for education. In his first public address as a young aspiring politician in 1832, he explained, "Upon the subject of education, not presuming to dictate any plan or system respecting it, I can only say that I view it as the most important subject which we as a people can be engaged in." He aspired "that every man may receive at least a moderate education."[18]

Three decades later Lincoln derived enormous satisfaction from signing into law the Morrill Land Grant College Act of July 1, 1862. The Morrill Act provided money to found "agricultural and mechanical" colleges in each state. Eventually sixty-nine "land grant" colleges were established. The result was to accelerate the nation's transition from subsistence to market farming, as scientific methods led to greater productivity with better harvests and herds. The Morrill Act also helped inspire an education revolution as the public share of education funding soared in volume and proportion. Public school spending tripled from $19.9 million, or 57 percent of $34.7 million in total spending among the states for education, in 1860 to $61.7 million, or 65 percent of $95.4 million, in 1870 as states with existing school systems expanded them and other states established them.[19] The Hamiltonian idea that government should help nurture the nation's intellectual development also inspired Lincoln and Congress to create the National Academy of Sciences in 1863.

"Military necessity" justified one key element of the Hamiltonian agenda. The Pacific Railway Act, which Lincoln signed on July 1, 1862, massively subsidized the expansion of railroads across the continent by eventually giving railroad companies 225 million acres of public lands. The initial grant was sixty-four hundred acres for each mile constructed, but the amount was soon doubled. In addition, the government gave railroad companies low-interest loans of $16,000 a mile on flat lands and $48,000 a mile in the mountains. The railroad and homestead acts complemented each other. The railroads conveyed and supplied settlers, who in turn provided passengers and markets for goods born by the railroads.

As the initial transcontinental railroad's terminals, Lincoln designated Sacramento, California, and Omaha, Nebraska. While no one seriously disputed those obvious choices, Congress did override his selection of a five foot width for the railroad gauge, the size used in California and most of the South, which was incompatible with the four foot, eight and a half inch width used across the North. The reason for Lincoln's preference is unclear, but it might have been a conciliatory gesture to the rebels. Congress ensured that the North's standard prevailed.

Inventions and inventers fascinated Lincoln. In 1849 he registered a patent for a device that lifted steamboats over shallow water.[20] As president he tested all of the prototypes for firearms whose adoption the military was considering. The seven-shot Spencer carbine and rifle especially impressed him, and he ordered the Ordnance Bureau to equip the army with them. Politics prevailed. The Springfield Company, which manufactured the army's standard rifle, protested and asserted all methods fair and foul to stall this transition. Although the infantry was denied the Spencer repeater rifles, the cavalry did get its hands on the carbine version.[21]

After that whirlwind of revolutionary initiatives, Lincoln had one last Hamiltonian step to make, this of little substance but richly symbolic. While all Americans enjoy the national holiday of Thanksgiving, few know who designated it. The popular view is that Thanksgiving has been around ever since the Pilgrims. Actually it was the earlier colony of Jamestown that first set aside a day for prayer and reflection. It was Lincoln who, on October 3, 1863, designated the third Thursday of every November for Americans to share that experience that helps define them as one people.[22]

10

Turning Points

Must I shoot a simple-minded soldier boy who deserts while I must
not touch a hair of a wily agitator who induces him to desert?
ABRAHAM LINCOLN

The Father of Waters again flows unvexed to the sea.
ABRAHAM LINCOLN

The Republican Party took a shellacking in the midterm elections of
November 1862. The two biggest reasons were Lincoln's Emancipation
Proclamation and growing opposition to the stalemated and ever-blood-
ier war. Democrats recaptured the statehouses of Ohio, Indiana, and
Illinois, won the governorships of Pennsylvania, New Jersey, and New
York, and ate away at Republican majorities in Minnesota, Wisconsin,
and Michigan. New York governor Horatio Seymour was an especially
fierce and unrelenting critic of the Lincoln administration as he nurtured his own presidential ambitions. Nonetheless, among the nineteen
free states, the Republicans retained control of sixteen governorships
and sixteen legislatures as well as both houses of Congress.[1]

The Emancipation Proclamation had a liberating effect on the president. In late fall Lincoln purged three armies of inept leaders. First
he replaced Don Buell with William Rosecrans, then Benjamin Butler with Nathaniel Banks. He saved the worst for last. No general was

guilty of more egregious crimes of near-traitorous dereliction of duty than George McClellan. The president prudently waited until after the November elections to fire McClellan, a Democratic Party hero. Had Lincoln martyred that paper tiger on the election's eve, the Democratic turnout would have swelled and Republican losses would have been greater. He removed the single worst obstacle to an American victory in the war on November 7. McClellan's adoring fans were not the only ones who mourned his forced early retirement. The news saddened Confederates as well. Robert E. Lee spoke for his compatriots by face-tiously remarking that "I hate to see McClellan go. He and I had grown to understand each other so well."[2]

Yet, having cleared that military deadwood, Lincoln still faced a dilemma. He explained that "I certainly have been dissatisfied with the slowness of Buell and McClellan, but before I relieved them I had great fears I should not find successors to them who would do better; and I am sorry to add that I have seen little since to relieve those fears."[3] Most of his new crop of army generals would realize those fears.

The worst was Ambrose Burnside, who replaced McClellan as the Army of the Potomac's commander. The first impression of Burnside, however, was positive, as Lincoln and others contrasted his energy, cheerfulness, and initiative with his predecessor's whining, arrogance, and sloth. Burnside launched his army against Lee's. Outnumbered two to one, Lee withdrew across northern Virginia until he reached Fredericksburg, south of the Rappahannock River, in early December. There he deployed his 75,000 troops along a low ridge overlooking the town and the river beyond. Burnside encamped his 110,000 troops just beyond cannon shot north of the Rappahannock.

Lincoln devised a strategy for Burnside to implement. He explained that "I wish the enemy to be prevented from falling back, accumulating strength as he goes, into his entrenchments at Richmond." To this end, Burnside was to split his army into three to circle, trap, and destroy Lee's army. One part would remain before Fredericksburg and distract Lee. The bulk of the Union troops would march up the river to the closest ford, cross over, and attack the enemy's left flank. Meanwhile the rest of Burnside's army would embark on transports on the Potomac and steam up the Rappahannock and Pamunkey Rivers before disembark-ing to cut off the rebel retreat.[4]

Once again tragedy resulted from a general's failure to follow the president's latest brilliant plan. Burnside ordered a frontal assault on Fredericksburg on December 13. The Union army crossed the river on pontoon bridges and valiantly marched straight against the rebel positions. By the day's end, the Union suffered 12,653 casualties to the Confederacy's 5,309. Those stunning losses were soon compounded by two battles in the west, one a victory and the other a defeat, along with an aborted campaign.

Lincoln had sent Gen. William Rosecrans, who now led the forty-two-thousand-man Army of the Cumberland that was camped around Nashville, several orders to march against Gen. Braxton Bragg, who commanded the thirty-four-thousand-man Army of Tennessee, just twenty miles south at Murfreesboro. Rosecrans finally complied. The battle of Murfreesboro, or Stone's River, that began early on December 30 and raged for three days was the war's bloodiest in the ratio of casualties to combatants, with the Federals suffering losses of 12,906 and the Confederates 11,739, or one in four and one in three, respectively. Bragg finally withdrew his battered army southeast toward Chattanooga. Rosecrans did not pursue.

Meanwhile General Grant implemented his own plan for overrunning Mississippi. He would lead most of his army due south to take Jackson, the state's capital, while General Sherman took his corps down the Mississippi River and captured Vicksburg. The two wings would then link up and march toward Montgomery and Mobile, Alabama. Grant led his troops southward, set up a supply base at Holy Springs, and reached Oxford by early December. The rebel forces withdrew slowly before Grant's juggernaut. Raids by brilliant cavalry commanders like generals Bedford Forrest and John Hunt Morgan slowed Grant's advance and diminished his army by attacking his supply lines. The worst blow came on December 20, when Gen. Earl Van Dorn and thirty-five hundred cavalry captured and destroyed Grant's key supply depot at Holy Springs. This forced Grant to withdraw all the way back to Corinth.

Sherman launched his offensive in late December, when he disembarked his thirty thousand troops at Chickasaw Bluffs overlooking the Yazoo River near its confluence with the Mississippi River just above Vicksburg. He ordered his army to attack on December 29. The result resembled Fredericksburg on a smaller scale as Union troops valiantly struggled up the bluff against entrenched rebels who slaughtered them, inflicting 1,776 casualties while losing only 207 men. Sherman partly redeemed himself when he packed his army aboard transports and steamed fifty miles up the Arkansas River to capture Fort Hindman and its 5,000 defenders at a loss of 1,061 casualties. He then withdrew his army to Memphis.

The year opened with a victory when an expedition captured Galveston on January 1, 1863, but soon morphed into the latest humiliating defeat. A well-coordinated rebel counterattack of gunboats drove off the Union flotilla while troops forced the garrison to surrender.

Shortly after the slaughter at Fredericksburg, Lincoln replaced Burnside with Joseph Hooker. The Army of the Potomac's latest commander inspired two nicknames, "Fighting Joe" for himself and "hookers" for the prostitutes whose services he was alleged to enjoy. With his boisterous, backslapping animal spirits, he was a popular choice with his troops. He boosted morale and his own popularity by improving the men's rations, getting them six months of back pay owed them, granting generous leaves, cleaning up the camps and hospitals, and issuing corps badges to nurture pride. As a result desertion and sickness rates plummeted. President Lincoln further swelled the ranks after March 10 by promising amnesty for any deserters who returned after April 1. Thousands of those absent without leave sheepishly rejoined their regiments. By spring there was ample truth in Hooker's boast that "I have never known men to change from a condition of lowest depression to that of a healthy fighting state in so short a time."[5]

Of course, an army with high morale is not an end in itself but merely a means. In reply to Lincoln's queries about his intentions, Hooker assured the president that once he led his men into the field he would destroy Lee once and for all. The general's bravado may have inspired his troops but it worried the president. "That is the most depressing thing about Hooker," the president confided. "It seems to me that he is overconfident."[6]

This was not Lincoln's only worry. The power and adulation went to Hooker's head. Rumors swirled that Hooker and others discussed overthrowing the government and forming a dictatorship. Yet Lincoln was so desperate for a general who was determined to win that he did not automatically open an investigation and fire Hooker or anyone else guilty of such treasonous remarks. Instead he offered a strange and dangerous incentive to Hooker that mercifully did not come back to haunt him and the nation: "I have heard . . . of your recently saying that both the army and the government need a dictator. Of course it was not for this but in spite of it that I have given you the command. Only those generals who gain successes can set up dictators. What I now ask of you is military success, and I will risk the dictatorship."[7]

Lincoln urged Hooker to adopt the same plan that he had failed to inspire Burnside to follow, a turning movement around Lee's western flank. To his relief, Hooker adopted this strategy, although the general did not credit its creator. In late April Hooker stole a march on Lee by marching seventy thousand troops up the Rappahannock River and crossing over at several fords. Then, inexplicably, rather than drive his corps against the rebels at Fredericksburg and pin them against the forty thousand troops he left there, he called a halt around a village named Chancellorsville.

Upon learning of Hooker's position, Lee devised a bold plan. Leaving ten thousand men at Fredericksburg, he marched fifteen thousand straight at Hooker and sent Thomas Jackson and his thirty-thousand-man corps on a seventeen-mile trek around the Union's right flank. The battle of Chancellorsville raged from May 1 to 4. Hooker finally withdrew his army back across the Rappahannock after suffering seventeen thousand casualties to Lee's thirteen thousand; tragically for the rebel cause, Jackson was among those mortally wounded.

Hooker was the latest Army of the Potomac commander to violate the most basic principles of war, principles that the nation's commander in chief understood and continually encouraged his generals to uphold. After having gained a march on the enemy, Hooker rested his troops rather than pushing them forward to assault the enemy's rear. Once attacked, Hooker failed to commit all his forces to the fight—two of the army's seven corps did not fire a shot in the entire battle. Then Hooker ordered a retreat even though his troops had fought the enemy to a standstill.

The question arose over what to do if Lee tried to sidestep Hooker westward, then circle to cut off the Army of the Potomac from Washington. Hooker promised to lead his troops against Lee's rear. Lincoln instantly saw the folly in that and revealed what a clearheaded strategist he had become when he offered Hooker elementary but profound pieces of advice. First, he warned that "in case you find Lee coming to the north of the Rappahannock, I would by no means cross to the south of it. . . . I would not take any risk of being entangled on the river like an ox jumped half over a fence and liable to be torn by dogs from the rear without a fair chance to gore one way or kick the other. If Lee would come to my side of the river, I would keep on the same side, and fight him or act on the defense according" to "my estimate of his strength relative to my own." He then explained that "Lee's Army, and not Richmond, is your true objective point. If he comes toward the Upper Potomac, follow on his flank, and on the inside track, shortening your lines, whilst he lengthens his. Fight him when the opportunity offers." As reports indicated that Lee's army was strung out across northern Virginia, Lincoln fired off a curt message: "The animal must be very slim somewhere. Could you not break him?" He also offered the sound tactical advice that "in your next fight, put in all your men."[8]

Lee, typically, did not rest on his laurels. Once again he led his army to another invasion of the North, to scour the landscape of desperately needed provisions and to prowl for a knockout blow against the Army of the Potomac. He screened his advance with Gen. J.E.B. Stuart and his cavalry. When Hooker sent his own cavalry across the Rappahannock to find Lee, it collided with Stuart at Brandy Station on June 9. The result was the war's largest cavalry battle and the first hard evidence through rebel prisoners of Lee's plan. Hooker marched his army north on a parallel route through northern Virginia, then Maryland, and finally Pennsylvania but refused the president's repeated entreaties to drive straight at Lee and defeat him. Lincoln replaced Hooker with Gen. George Gordon Meade, a corps commander, on June 28.

The battle of Gettysburg opened on July 1, when a division of rebel troops approached this strategic crossroads where a dozen roads intersected. The town's only defenders were Union cavalry that slowly gave way before the Confederate advance. Each side galloped off couriers to their respective commanders with word of the battle. Lee and Meade ordered their armies to converge on Gettysburg, with the Confederates marching from the west and north and the Federals from the south and east. Meade aligned his troops in a fishhook position along a low ridge with hills at each end.

Although outmanned by ninety thousand to seventy thousand troops, Lee typically took the initiative. Over the next three days, he launched a series of attacks to break the enemy line. He lacked two vital elements that might have brought him victory—Jackson was dead and Stuart was racing in a wide circle around the Union army. Without Stuart's cavalry as scouts, Lee had little idea of the enemy's exact numbers and deployment. Without Jackson, he lacked the general best able to quick-march his corps around the enemy, then launch a devastating assault. Instead the rebel attacks were late, uncoordinated, and ill chosen. The battle's climax came with a charge of fourteen thousand led by Gen. George Pickett against the Union army's center on the afternoon of July 3. The Union troops repelled the assault, killing, wounding, or capturing half of the attackers. As the survivors streamed back, Lee rode among them and apologized for his folly. That night Lee ordered his army to withdraw on the long road to Virginia and relative safety.

In all, Gettysburg cost the Confederates 28,063 casualties and the Union 23,049. Yet the rebels were lucky to get away with just those devastating losses. The Fourth of July brought a deluge so severe that it turned the roads into quagmires and swelled the Potomac to flood level; a Union cavalry raid had earlier destroyed the pontoon bridges linking Lee's army with Virginia. Once again the Army of Virginia was stranded north of the Potomac River after losing a battle to an enemy with overwhelming strength. And once again a Union general had Lee on the ropes and refused to administer the coup de grace that would have sharply shortened the war and its destruction.

If Meade did not pursue Lee as soon as the skies cleared and roads dried, he did inform his troops that he would eventually get around to it. In one of the war's great understatements he admitted, "Our task is not yet accomplished, and the commanding general looks to the army for greater efforts to drive from our soil every vestige of the presence of the invader." This provoked a perplexed remark from Lincoln to his secretary John Hay: "This is a dreadful reminiscence of McClellan. . . . Will our Generals never get that idea out of their heads? The whole country is our soil."[9] Eventually Meade began a timid advance but ignored a series of ever-curter orders from Lincoln via Halleck to attack the enemy.[10] Lee was finally able to get his army across the swollen Potomac over a rickety bridge hastily built at Williamsport on July 14.

Lincoln despaired when he got that news. He wrote Meade lauding his "magnificent success" at Gettysburg but castigated him for failing to "appreciate the magnitude of the misfortune involved in Lee's escape. He was within your easy grasp and to have closed upon him would, in connection with our other late successes, have ended the war. As it is the war will be prolonged indefinitely. . . . Your golden opportunity is gone, and I am distressed immeasurably because of it."[11] But in the end Lincoln did not send this letter. He reasoned that Meade had commanded the army for only four days before the titanic three-day battle erupted and left him exhausted, stunned, and uncertain over what to do.

Instead Lincoln had Halleck inform Meade of his displeasure. When Meade offered to resign, Lincoln refused to accept.[12] Yet Meade did little more than slowly follow Lee at a great distance into Virginia, where each army largely resumed its lines north and south of the Rappahannock River. The next great battle in the east would not occur until ten months after Gettysburg.

Lincoln's key strategy west of the Appalachians in early 1863 was to capture Port Hudson and Vicksburg, the last two strongholds, 240 miles apart on the Mississippi River. Ulysses Grant led seventy thousand troops downriver from Memphis to Vicksburg, while Nathaniel Banks brought his twenty thousand troops upriver from Baton Rouge to Port Hudson. Grant's mission was by far the more daunting.

Vicksburg was located on bluffs above a horseshoe bend in the Mississippi River that for scores of miles up- and downstream was lined by virtually impenetrable swamps and shallow serpentine bayous. The rebels had ringed the town with entrenchments, forts, and batteries of heavy cannons. Sherman had failed in an attack on Chickasaw Bluffs northeast of Vicksburg the previous December. Gen. John Pemberton commanded thirty thousand rebel troops in and around Vicksburg, while Gen. Joe Johnston eventually massed another thirty thousand at Jackson, fifty miles east.

Grant intended to get his army and flotilla of gunboats and transports below Vicksburg. He first tried to do so by putting most of his men to work digging a canal across a loop in the Mississippi River. As the weeks turned to months, Grant's enemies claimed that he was an inept drunkard who should be replaced. Lincoln paid the critics little heed, retorting that "I have had stronger influence brought against

Grant . . . than for any other object. . . . If I had done as my Washington friends, who fight battles with their tongues instead of swords far from the enemy, demanded of me, Grant . . . would never have been heard from again."[13] One reason for the president's confidence was that he had War Secretary Stanton send Charles Dana, a trusted aide, to Grant's headquarters to determine whether the rumors were true. Under cover of investigating the paymaster service, Dana observed Grant for weeks and had nothing but praise for him.[14]

Lincoln and Halleck, however, did encourage Grant to change his objective. Once he got his army and flotilla below Vicksburg, they wanted him to unite with Banks and take Port Hudson. For both strategic and political reasons, Grant ignored these wishes. Each general's army was powerful enough to take his respective objective independent of the other. Combining their forces against Port Hudson was not just unnecessary, it would let Pemberton mass more troops and supplies for Vicksburg's defense. Besides, Banks was a professional politician rather than soldier and owed his command to connections. Grant was determined to not to subject himself to Banks's seniority and proven incompetence.

By early April Grant abandoned the canal effort as impossible with the primitive technology then available. Instead he marched his army west of the Mississippi as Commodore David Porter steamed parts of his flotilla past Vicksburg during several dark nights. Although most of the vessels slipped past, rebel gunners were able to sink two transports and six barges carrying vital supplies. On April 27 the army and fleet reunited at a town, appropriately named Hard Times, on the river's west bank twenty-two miles downriver of Vicksburg.

Grant crossed his troops over the river to Bruinsburg, Mississippi, on May 1, then quick-marched them to Port Gibson, where they routed the defenders. Rather than head north to Vicksburg, he led his troops northeast to Jackson, Mississippi's capital, where he intended to cut off Vicksburg and destroy a rebel army massing there led by Gen. Joe Johnston. William Sherman's corps spearheaded the army's advance and scattered a rebel force at Raymond on May 12. There Grant split his forces. Sherman marched on to Jackson, routed Johnston's troops on May 14, and captured vast amounts of supplies. After having his troops tear up miles of train tracks heading north, east, and south, he led them back to the main army. Meanwhile Grant led the corps of John McClernand and James McPherson west toward Pemberton, who had deployed twenty thousand troops along a ridgeline called Champion Hill midway between Jackson and Vicksburg. Grant tried a double envelopment with his twenty-nine thousand troops by sending each corps around an enemy flank. Had McClernand displayed the same drive and tactical skill as McPherson, they might have destroyed the rebel army. Instead, while McPherson's troops crushed the enemy left, McClernand's corps was mostly still on the march. This let Pemberton extract most of his men and retreat, having suffered 3,840 casualties to the Union's 2,441. Grant raced his troops after the rebels and caught up the next day at Big Black River. Once again the Union troops routed the defenders, inflicting 1,750 casualties while losing only 200 of their own. Pemberton led his men back into the safety of Vicksburg's ring of trenches and forts, studded with hundreds of cannons.

Grant had conceived and implemented an astonishing campaign— in seventeen days, his army marched 180 miles, captured and burned Jackson, routed the enemy in five battles, inflicted seventy-two hundred casualties while losing forty-three hundred, and now massed around Vicksburg. With soaring adulation Lincoln read the military and newspaper accounts of Grant's campaign and remarked that whether or not Grant took Vicksburg, "his campaign . . . is one of the most brilliant in the world."[15]

After most of his army reached Vicksburg's outskirts on May 19, Grant ordered an attack. In doing so, he gambled that the rebels were too demoralized from their string of defeats and long retreat to put up much of a fight. He was wrong. The defenders repelled that attack and another two days later. Grant had entrenching equipment and 220 cannons brought up for a prolonged siege.

The symbolism was as rich as the substance when Pemberton surrendered 29,396 troops and 172 cannons on the Fourth of July. Lincoln lauded Grant for his victory while admitting his own weakness. Having wanted Grant to join Banks at Port Hudson, he "feared it was a mistake" when Grant headed eastward toward Jackson. "I now wish to make the personal acknowledgement that you were right and I was wrong."[16] It is through such gestures that a leader nurtures the esteem, confidence, and above all, unrelenting efforts of those below him.

In contrast to Grant's dazzling, elaborate Vicksburg campaign, Banks's effort against Port Hudson was straightforward and methodical. He faced no large rebel forces hovering in the region so he could simply steam up the Mississippi River to just beyond cannon shot of Port Hudson and its seven thousand defenders, disembark his twenty thousand troops, envelop the defenses, and batter and starve the enemy into surrender. The siege was among the first in which black troops proved that they could fight just as valiantly as white troops. The surrender of Port Hudson, the rebels' last stronghold on the Mississippi River, on July 8 inspired one of Lincoln's most evocative remarks: "The Father of Waters again flows unvexed to the sea."[17]

Grant sought to follow up Vicksburg by marching southeast to capture Montgomery and Mobile, Alabama. Lincoln and Halleck rejected that plan, but not on its impeccable strategic merits. They had succumbed to political pressure for a campaign up the Red River into northwestern Louisiana and northeastern Texas. While moving in this direction made no strategic sense, it served New England textile manufacturers whose factories were idled for want of cotton. Grant was ordered to transfer several divisions to Banks, who would lead the venture. But Banks was incapable of readying his army for this campaign until the following year and after finally launching it typically made a mess of it.

For nearly all of 1863's first half, Gen. William Rosecrans had sat tight at his Nashville headquarters and ignored all instructions to march against Gen. Braxton Bragg's army. His only act was to launch a raid led by Col. Abel Streight to tear up stretches of the railroad linking Chattanooga and Atlanta in April 1863. In what may have been a first for such a large-scale operation, the colonel and his 1,466 men were mounted on mules. The reasoning was that mules could endure over greater distances with less fodder than horses. The downside was that they were slower and bulkier. Learning of the raid, Bragg dispatched Gen. Bedford Forrest in pursuit. Forrest and his six hundred hardened troopers caught up to Streight and his men on May 3. Being outnumbered more than two to one, Forrest knew he would probably lose a direct fight with the Yankees. So under a truce flag he sent Streight a letter demanding surrender "to stop the further and useless effusion of blood." Meanwhile he had his men ride two horse artillery pieces through a clearing, then circle back through the woods to pass in sight again. When Streight expressed his astonishment that he had counted fifteen guns so far and wondered how many more were in reserve, Forrest laconically replied, "I reckon that's all that has kept up." Streight promptly surrendered.[18]

It was not until June 23 that Rosecrans finally hooked his sixty thousand troops toward the rear of Bragg's forty thousand troops. The result was a nearly bloodless campaign as Bragg withdrew all the way to Chattanooga. On July 7 Stanton fired off a message to Rosecrans informing him of the victories at Gettysburg and Vicksburg, then insisted, "You and your noble army now have the chance to give the finishing blow to the rebellion. Will you neglect the chance?" The rebuke upset Rosecrans, who retorted, "You do not appear to observe the fact that this noble army has driven the rebels from Middle Tennessee. . . . I beg in behalf of this army that the War Department may not overlook so great an event because it is not written in showers of blood."[19]

Once again Lincoln had to explain to a general that his objective was not to occupy territory but to destroy the enemy. When Rosecrans complained that he lacked enough provisions to move, Lincoln replied, "Do you not consume supplies as fast as you get them forward?"[20] This shamed Rosecrans into his campaign's second phase. He sent his army south of the Tennessee River downstream of Chattanooga. Meanwhile Gen. Ambrose Burnside led twenty-four thousand troops against ten thousand rebels holding Knoxville. Both Confederate forces withdrew. During September's first week, Burnside and Rosecrans led their armies, respectively, into Knoxville and Chattanooga. Virtually all of Tennessee was now in Union hands.

Rosecrans then received his latest entreaties from the White House to seek out and destroy Bragg's army. In mid-September Rosecrans led his army south into north Georgia. Bragg's army now outnumbered Rosecrans by seventy thousand to sixty thousand, thanks to the arrival of Gen. James Longstreet's twenty-thousand-man corps by train all the way from Virginia. Bragg unleashed his army against Rosecrans at Chickamauga Creek on September 19. The Union troops held the line until nightfall, then withdrew the next day to Chattanooga. Only the unyielding defense of Gen. George Thomas's corps prevented the retreat from turning into a rout. In all the Union suffered 16,170 casualties to the Confederacy's 18,450.

Bragg followed up his victory by besieging Rosecrans in Chattanooga. He was able to do so because Rosecrans neglected to occupy let alone fortify two crucial heights overlooking the city, Lookout Mountain to the southwest and Missionary Ridge stretching from the south to the northeast. Bragg deployed most of his army on those heights just two miles from the city. He also sent troops west to block the train line and main road that ran south of the Tennessee River and erected batteries along the riverbanks. Finally, he dispatched Longstreet and his corps to drive Burnside from Knoxville. Although Burnside held Knoxville, Rosecrans was nearly forced to surrender Chattanooga, where the troops were malnourished on half rations while starvation killed ten thousand draft animals and cavalry horses The men were too weak to fight and the surviving animals too weak to pull a wagon or mount a man.

Lincoln responded decisively to the crisis. He transferred Gen. Joseph Hooker's corps from the Army of the Potomac to Chattanooga to join Gen. William Sherman's corps that he had ordered to join Rosecrans even before news of Chickamauga. In late October he replaced Rosecrans with Thomas. Finally, he ordered Ulysses Grant to unify the Departments of the Ohio, Tennessee, and Cumberland into the Department of the Mississippi and take charge at Chattanooga.

Upon reaching Chattanooga on October 23, Grant first secured supply lines to the city. He cleared enemy forces along the routes and got provisions and fresh troops to Chattanooga by steamboat, wagon, and eventually train. By late November he had massed enough troops and supplies to take the offensive. He devised a double envelopment whereby Sherman attacked the rebel right flank on Missionary Ridge and Hooker the left on Lookout Mountain. On November 24 Hooker's men captured Lookout Mountain with only five hundred casualties, but the rebels repulsed Sherman's attack. The following day Grant ordered Hooker and Thomas to clear enemy troops from the foot of Missionary Ridge, while Sherman renewed his attack on the rebel right. The Confederates once again blunted Sherman's attack. Hooker's men routed the rebels at the ridge's west end. In vengeance for Chickamauga, Thomas's troops not only captured the foot of the ridge but, without orders, struggled up the steep slope after the fleeing Confederates. The defenders on top did not fire for fear of hitting their own men, then skedaddled with them down the far slope. By late afternoon Thomas's troops triumphantly planted their American and regimental flags along the summit. In the battle of Chattanooga, the Federals suffered 5,824 casualties while inflicting 6,667 and capturing forty cannons. Grant did not stop there but pursued the enemy for several days down to Ringgold, in north Georgia.[21]

The news of great victories arriving from the west during 1863's summer and autumn contrasted with the stalemate in the east. The two enemy armies had settled into positions in northern Virginia. Meade was content to sit tight. Lee typically sought a victory. In October he arched his army around Meade's and tried to cut his supply line to Washington. The campaign ended when federal troops repelled an attack by A. P. Hill's corps at Bristoe Station, five miles south of Manassas, on October 14. The following month Lincoln finally roused Meade from his lethargy. Emulating his adversary, Meade stole a march on Lee and led his army across the Rapidan River toward the enemy's supply line. Lee raced troops to head him off. The rebels reached and fortified Mine's Run. Meade prudently chose not to attack and instead withdrew his army to his former position.

The string of resounding military victories did not mask the worsening fatigue and outright opposition to the war on the home front. This was partly due to the war's soaring costs in blood and treasure for two years with no end in sight. But atop this, military necessity forced Lincoln and Congress to do something that exacerbated the opposition.

Solely volunteers filled Union ranks until after the Enrollment Act passed on March 3, 1863.[22] The law empowered the War Department's Provost Marshal's Bureau to organize and head a system whereby all able-bodied men from age twenty to forty-five had to register and were liable to be drafted. Each congressional district had a provost whose duty was to collect the names of all eligible men and draw them by lottery until a quota was filled. Men could avoid being drafted by finding a substitute or paying a $300 fine.

Varying proportions of people resented and resisted the draft everywhere, nowhere more than in New York City. Two groups—free blacks and Irish Catholics—competed for low-skill and low-wage jobs at the bottom of the socioeconomic hierarchy and were largely despised by the classes above them. Blacks and Irish were also political rivals. Although blacks could not vote let alone run for office, they naturally favored the Republican Party, split between those who opposed slavery's extension and those who championed its abolition. Nearly all Irish Catholics backed the Democratic Party, split between those favoring southern independence and those favoring reunification without emancipation. The Irish were and blacks were not eligible for the draft. Most Irish hated the notion of fighting for the emancipation of a different race of people who drove down wages and stole their jobs.

Violence had erupted between the two groups numerous times, most seriously when Irish rioted against blacks who took over stevedore jobs in June 1863. Hatreds were still white-hot when the provost scheduled a draft lottery for July 11. The city was stripped of its regular and militia regiments, which had been hurried off to help repel the Confederate invasion of Pennsylvania. The first day's round of picks was met with sullen fatalism. But then the men retired to their pubs and with each round of drinks more heatedly called for resisting the draft. Riots erupted the next day and persisted for four days until troops that had been rushed to the city finally reasserted control. In all, 119 people were killed; 73 soldiers, 105 police, and 128 civilians were injured; and $3 million worth of property was destroyed. Of the 443 people arrested, 221 were soon released without charges, 10 were later let go, 74 were indicted but never brought to trial, and 14 acquitted; of the 40 people convicted, 27 received plea bargains and were released and only 14 served any prison time, the longest term of which was three years for a Virginian who provoked a mob to burn a draft lottery office. In all, the rioters and murderers got off lightly.[23]

Those riots deeply aggrieved the president. He deplored the loss of innocent lives and condemned those who committed the mayhem and murder. Yet he understood the rage of the workers who feared losing their jobs to blacks or their lives on distant battlefields. In a letter he eventually deemed politically imprudent to send, he tried to convince Democratic Party leaders just why a draft was a military necessity. Men volunteered for military service from a range of motives, including "patriotism, political bias, ambition, personal courage, love of adventure, want of employment, convenience." Unfortunately, after more than two devastating years of war, these motives among physically fit young men had sharply diminished. Thus military necessity demanded and the Constitution empowered the government to institute a draft to fill the widening gap between the army's growing needs and its diminishing volunteers.[24]

"Copperhead" was the derogatory label for Peace Democrats. A copperhead was a venomous northern snake whose coloring blended in with the forest floor and whose bite could be deadly. Copperheads, the political variant, infested the southern half of Ohio, Indiana, and Illinois because southerners had largely settled this region and remained culturally and economically tied to their ancestral slave states. Copperheads were not confined to the western states. Some big-city Democratic mayors back east were just as vociferous in expressing similar sentiments, most notoriously Fernando Wood of New York, who organized what he called a "Monster Peace Convention" that attracted thirty thousand demonstrators on June 3, 1863. In the North the abolition of slavery most threatened laborers who feared that liberated blacks would take their jobs by accepting much lower wages.

While many of those who supported the war smeared Copperheads as traitors, most Peace Democrats simply wanted to end the fighting by giving in to rebel demands. Nonetheless, secret groups did exist, like the Knights of the Golden Circle, Sons of Liberty, and Order of American Knights, that were dedicated to undermining the Union and aiding the Confederacy. Hundreds of rebel agents infiltrated the United States to gather intelligence, foment dissent, and instigate riots and sabotage. At times the line between pacific and traitorous beliefs and groups was hazy. Gen. Ambrose Burnside, the Department of the Ohio's commander in 1863, was determined to cut through that haze. On April 13 he issued General Order Number 13, warning that anyone who committed treasonous speech or acts would be subject to arrest and prosecution.[25]

Depending on one's point of view, the most renowned Peace Democrat or most reviled Copperhead was Clement L. Vallandigham, an Ohio congressman. Secretly he was the Sons of Liberty's "Grand Commander."[26] Publicly, he mercilessly attacked Lincoln's handling of the war and called for foreign intervention to impose a peace. On May 1 he made an especially incendiary speech that urged mass resistance against the war, including draft evasion and desertion. Burnside had the congressman arrested on May 5. A military tribunal convicted Vallandigham of treason and sentenced him to prison for the war's duration. This provoked a chorus of protests from both Peace Democratic and Radical Republican leaders and newspapers. These usually fiercely opposed groups united in condemning the administration for violating Vallandigham's rights of freedom of speech and habeas corpus.

Lincoln found a way to finesse their arguments. On May 25 he had Union cavalry escort Vallandigham under a flag of truce to the rebel lines near Murfreesboro, Tennessee, an act that at once freed the agitator while making the point that he was a traitor. In a letter to the *New York Tribune*, Lincoln explained that he exiled Vallandigham "because he was damaging the army, upon the existence and vigor of which the life of the nation depends." He tried to evoke public empathy with a haunting question: "Must I shoot a simple-minded soldier boy who deserts while I must not touch a hair of a wily agitator who induces him to desert?"[27] The Loyal Publication Society, affiliated with the Republican Party, published and distributed half a million copies of that letter as a pamphlet that perhaps as many as ten million people may have read.[28]

The sky over Gettysburg was crystal blue and the bright sun soon drove off the morning chill on November 19, 1863. The air, however, reeked with the stench of thousands of often half-buried, rotting corpses of men and horses. Scattered in the fields surrounding the town were clusters of hogs, vultures, and bluebottle flies feeding off any exposed flesh.

Toward noon four military bands played martial songs and led a procession that included the president, a group of dignitaries, and many of Gettysburg's twenty-five hundred people from the main square along the road to the cemetery on the eastern hill. Upon reaching the cemetery's heart, Lincoln and the other dignitaries took their seats atop a platform flanked by the bands and the crowd massed in front. A minister opened the ceremony with a prayer. The marine band played a dirge. Edward Everett, the keynote speaker, stepped behind the podium. Everett was popularly known as the nation's finest orator. Whether or not that was true, he certainly did not want for words—his speech lasted for two hours as the crowd thinned. After he finally sat down, a glee club sang a poem composed for the occasion.

Finally the president rose, briefly scanned the audience, and spoke a mere two and a half minutes before sitting down.[29] Observers differed sharply over whether the crowd's applause was polite or enthusiastic. What is unquestionable is that Abraham Lincoln distilled into a mere 272 words the essence of the ideals upon which America was founded and one day might realize, and he did so with a haunting eloquence that will forever be revered. He structured his speech like a classic Greek funeral oration in the manner of Pericles, first commemorating the dead, then explaining the larger meaning of their passing.

Lincoln began by reminding his listeners that a mere "four score and seven years" separated them from when "our fathers brought forth on this continent a new nation conceived in liberty and dedicated to the proposition that all men were created equal. Now we are engaged in a great civil war, testing whether that nation or any nation so conceived and so dedicated can long endure." They had gathered to consecrate a military cemetery for the dead of Gettysburg, "who gave their lives that that nation might live." He then called for "the living" to dedicate themselves "to the unfinished work which they who fought here so nobly advanced." He ended his talk by calling on the American people to "resolve that these dead shall not have died in vain—that this nation, under God, shall have a new birth of freedom—and that the government of the people, by the people, for the people, shall not perish from the earth."[30]

II

Total War

The war . . . must go on till the last man of this generation
falls in his tracks . . . unless you acknowledge our right to self-
government. We are not fighting for slavery. We are fighting
for independence—and that or extermination we will have.

JEFFERSON DAVIS

We are not only fighting hostile armies, but a hostile people,
and must make [them] . . . feel the hard hand of war.

WILLIAM SHERMAN

Eat out Virginia clear and clean . . . so that crows flying over
it . . . will have to carry their provender with them.

ULYSSES GRANT

Those not skinning can hold a leg.

ABRAHAM LINCOLN

Total war is a strategy whereby one mobilizes all the essential hard-
and soft-power resources of one's side to devastate one's enemy. Gen.
William Sherman explained how to do that: "We must keep the war
South until they are not only ruined and exhausted, but humbled in
pride and spirit."[1] The related industrial, transportation, and commu-

nications revolutions made total war possible. The government could mass, equip, transport, and coordinate the strategies of vast armies that ruthlessly and systematically demolished the enemy's physical and psychological capacity to resist.

It took a year or so for Lincoln and ever more of his generals to recognize that only total war could end the rebellion.[2] For Gen. Ulysses Grant, Shiloh was when "I gave up all idea of saving the Union except by complete conquest." Until then,

> I as well as thousands of other citizens, believed that the rebellion . . . would collapse suddenly and soon, if a decisive battle could be gained against any of its armies. . . . Up to that time it had been the policy of our army . . . to protect the property of the citizens whose property was invaded, without regard to their sentiments, either Union or Secession. After this . . . I regarded it as humane to both sides to protect the person of those found in their homes, but to consume everything that could be used to support or supply armies. . . . Supplies within reach of Confederate armies I regards as much contraband as arms or ordnance stores. Their destruction was accomplished without bloodshed and tended to the same result as the destruction of armies. . . . This policy I believe exercised a material influential in hastening the end.[3]

No one wielded total war more thoroughly than Sherman. He explained that "we are not only fighting hostile armies, but a hostile people, and must make [them] . . . feel the hard hand of war."[4] When Gen. John Bell Hood and Atlanta's government protested Sherman's order to burn Atlanta, Sherman replied, "You cannot qualify war in harsher terms than I will. War is cruelty and you cannot refine it, and those who brought war into our country deserve all the curses and maledictions a people can pour out."[5] In his infamous "march to the sea," Sherman vowed to "make Georgia howl." He was true to his word. Along the way his troops "confiscated 6,871 mules and horses, 13,294 head of cattle, 10.4 million pounds of grain, and 10.7 million pounds of fodder" from Georgia. His men were just as rapacious as they marched through South and North Carolina, where they took "at least 7 million pounds of foodstuffs, 11.6 million pounds of corn, 83 million pounds of fodder, and 11,825 horses and mules."[6] Atop that they burned or destroyed anything of military value, including factories, warehouses, and railroads. Sherman explained to Grant that what he was doing "may not be war, but rather statesmanship."[7]

President Lincoln struggled with just how far to carry "total war."[8] He knew that the United States could crush the Confederacy only by destroying its material and psychological means to resist, including freeing the slaves who upheld the rebel armies and economy. Yet a dilemma haunted him—the hard measures necessary to win the war might jeopardize the peace. For instance, liberating the slaves clearly undermined the rebel war effort while sowing hatreds among southerners that might take generations to overcome. Somehow the government had to inspire the rebel people to abandon slavocracy and become loyal American citizens "dedicated to the proposition that all men are created equal." And this demanded a sensitivity and benevolence anathema to total war. While Lincoln mostly gave free rein to Grant and Sherman, he cautioned lesser generals. For instance, he wrote Gen. William Rosecrans that "I wish you to do nothing merely for revenge, but that what you may do, shall be solely done with reference to the security of the future."[9]

If total war was to be unleashed on the South, Lincoln knew just who was best capable of directing it. He issued an order to Grant on March 3, 1864, to journey to Washington, where he would take command of the entire American army and receive the rank of lieutenant general; Gen. Henry Halleck would act as the army's chief of staff and Lincoln's closest military advisor in Washington. Among the reasons why Lincoln worked so well with Grant was that the general was as humble and uncaring of appearances as the president. Lincoln could breathe easily with Grant after suffering the pomposity of McClellan and all too many other generals whose egos bloated with their rank.

Accompanied only by his son, Grant reached Washington on March 8, 1864, and tried to check into the Willard Hotel. The manager took one look at his rumpled uniform with no clear indication of his rank and haughtily declared that he had only a small room left. Grant nodded and signed the register. The sight of the signature jolted the manager, who apologized effusively and ordered a bellboy to convey the guests to the hotel's finest suite. The next day, before a crowd of dignitaries at the White House, Lincoln presented Grant with his lieutenant general's commission. In his remarks, the president explained that Grant would be the first general since George Washington to bear that rank. Grant was always bashful and tongue-tied when he had to speak publicly and was especially overwhelmed at receiving such an honor. Fortunately the president was sensitive to Grant's affliction and earlier had helped him prepare a short acceptance speech that he read.[10]

Grant got to work early the following morning, March 10, by sending orders to all field generals and the heads of all seventeen military departments, with combined forces of 530,000 troops, to attack the closest rebel forces as soon as possible. He hoped to crush the Confederacy by launching simultaneous offensives by all available forces. Of course, he recognized that two armies, Meade's Army of the Potomac against Lee's army in Virginia and Sherman's Army of the Tennessee against Johnston's army in northern Georgia, were central to that strategy's success, while other forces played supporting roles. Lincoln graphically summed up this plan: "Those not skinning can hold a leg."[11] Nonetheless, Lincoln and Halleck altered Grant's plan in two crucial and ultimately tragic ways that prolonged the war.

Grant had called for Gen. Benjamin Butler at Norfolk to crowd his Army of the James on transports, steam around to the federal enclave at New Bern, North Carolina, then march inland to Raleigh and cut the railroad that led north to Richmond. With that railroad severed, Richmond would have to rely solely on the railroad that ran through the western Carolinas to Lynchburg, then eastward to Richmond. Grant intended to cut that link with an army led by Gen. Franz Sigel marching up the Shenandoah Valley, then over to Lynchburg, a campaign that would take longer to realize and face more perils along the way than the one against Raleigh. Nonetheless, with both railroads in Union hands, Lee's Army of Northern Virginia would be starved of supplies. Acting on Halleck's advice, Lincoln prevailed on Grant to launch Butler's army against Richmond instead.

That would have been the superior strategy had a skilled, decisive general led the campaign—as Grant attacked Lee from the north, the Army of the James could have captured Richmond from the south. This decisive blow combined with Sherman's against Atlanta might have ended the war. Instead, rather than drive relentlessly against Richmond, Butler let Pierre Beauregard's five thousand troops defeat his thirty-thousand-man Army of the James on May 16 at Drewry's Bluff, just eight miles short of the rebel capital, then seal it off with entrenchments inside Bermuda Hundred, a loop of the James River. Skilled Confederate generalship also routed the Union drive up the Shenandoah Valley. With just five thousand troops, Gen. John Breckinridge routed Sigel's sixty-five hundred at New Market on May 15. Sigel did not halt his retreat until he reached his supply base at Winchester.

Another element of Grant's strategy for 1864 was an Army of the Gulf campaign, led by Gen. Nathaniel Banks, that captured Mobile, then marched northeast across Alabama toward Atlanta, where it would join Sherman. In one of his few strategic mistakes, Lincoln instead launched Banks and his army up the Red River. The president justified this campaign on political, economic, and diplomatic grounds. The Red River slants across Louisiana from the northwest to join the Mississippi River about two-thirds of the way down the state. Ascending the Red River would bring Louisiana's cotton-growing hinterland under Union control all the way to Shreveport, a back door to northeastern Texas. The campaign's most enthusiastic backers were northeastern textile factory owners who envisioned the tens of thousands of cotton bales that they could haul off and transform into millions of yards of cloth. Lincoln emphasized bringing a progressive government to most of Louisiana to serve as a reconstruction model for other rebel states. These political and economic rationales were as clear as the diplomatic angle was murky. Lincoln eventually hoped to use Shreveport as a staging area to invade Texas. To those who argued that Texas had no strategic worth, Lincoln replied that one day massing an American army on the Rio Grande would intimidate France's Emperor Napoleon III, who in 1862 had dispatched an army to conquer Mexico and install a puppet emperor, Maximilian I. If that was Lincoln's intent, he was literally going about it the wrong way; Shreveport is a long way from the Rio Grande.

In the end, Banks failed to win any of these objectives. With less than half the number of men, Gen. Richard Taylor's Confederates defeated the Federals at Mansfield, forty miles short of Shreveport, on April 8. Low water stranded the Union fleet of transports and gunboats as they withdrew back down the Red River. They evaded capture only when Col. Joseph Bailey damned the river to raise the water level, then exploded

the dam so that the flotilla could race downstream on the surging current to safety. Grant then replaced the utterly hapless but politically
powerful Banks with Gen. Edward Canby and assigned him the task
of organizing a thrust against Mobile. That campaign eventually would
take place, but only nearly a year later in the war's closing days.[12]

Although Meade officially headed the Army of the Potomac, Grant
was actually in charge. He established his headquarters beside Meade's
and used that general simply as a conduit for his plans. He organized
the 120,000-man Army of the Potomac into three infantry corps; Philip
Sheridan led the cavalry corps. Gen. Ambrose Burnside commanded a
fifteen-thousand-man corps encamped around Warrenton in northern
Virginia guarding the approach to Washington.

Grant launched his campaign on May 5 by marching his army
into the Wilderness region a dozen miles west of Fredericksburg. Lee
rapidly converged sixty-five thousand troops to block that advance.
The result was a vicious two-day battle that ended in a bloody stalemate. Rather than withdraw his army to safety, Grant sidestepped Lee
southeastward and raced his troops to the enemy's rear, while sending
Sheridan and his cavalry toward Richmond to sever the supply line.
On May 11 Gen. J. E. B. Stuart led his cavalry against Sheridan's at
Yellow Tavern and repelled them; Stuart died in the fighting. Meanwhile Lee again blocked Grant's advance, this time at Spotsylvania.
What ensued was another bloodbath from May 9 to 17. Grant barely
gave his men time to rest before he marched them farther south, but
the rebels blocked them at North Anna from May 23 to 26. Grant
tried his campaign's fourth turning but Lee once again nosed ahead
at Cold Harbor, where his men strengthened existing fortifications.
Grant launched his army against the rebel lines on June 2, and in two
days of fighting suffered twelve thousand casualties to the enemy's
twenty-five hundred. He later admitted that ordering these attacks
was his worst mistake of the war.[13]

Within a month the Union army had suffered 39,259 casualties while
inflicting 25,000 on the Confederates.[14] Ever more politicians and newspaper editors attacked Grant as a "butcher" and called for his dismissal.
Grant's defiant reply was, "I propose to fight it out on this line if it takes
all summer."[15] Lincoln fully supported Grant's strategy: "I have seen
your dispatch expressing your unwillingness to break your hold where

you are. Neither am I willing. Hold on with a bull-dog grip, and chew and choke as much as possible."[16]

Grant tried to crack the stalemate in mid-June with yet another flanking movement, this time one that marched the army to the James River, where it crossed a twenty-one-hundred-foot pontoon bridge, the largest ever constructed, on June 14. He sent his advanced troops racing toward Petersburg, a critical railroad junction twenty miles south of Richmond. Tragically, rebel troops got there just in time and repelled the initial attack. This won Lee time to transfer most of his army there by railroad and dig an increasingly elaborate system of trenches that began east of Petersburg on the Appomattox River, then curled south around the city. As Grant brought up more troops and extended his line westward, Lee stretched his own men thinner in his own parallel line.

Haunted by what came to be called the "Cold Harbor syndrome," Grant swore off any more frontal assaults unless there was an excellent chance of success. For the indefinite future the only apparent strategy was literally and figuratively to dig in for a prolonged siege. Then Grant was presented a scheme that just might break the stalemate.

The colonel of the Forty-Eighth Pennsylvania, whose ranks were filled with coal miners, overheard a private remark that "we could blow that damn fort out of existence if we could run a mine shaft under it." He hurried with the idea to his brigade's general, who led him to the division general, and so on up the hierarchy to the commanding general himself, who approved. It took nearly a month for the miners to burrow a 511-foot-long shaft ending with a 40 foot cross-shaft that they packed with gunpowder barrels. Meanwhile a division of black troops was trained to spearhead the attack through the gap blown in the enemy line. Tragically, General Burnside, the corps commander, doubted the black troops' fighting abilities and on the attack's eve substituted an inexperienced division of white troops. On July 30 the mine was detonated in a deafening roar that blew the rebel fort apart and left behind a smoldering hole 170 feet long, 60 feet wide, and 30 feet deep. The Union troops rushed forward but charged into the crater rather than surging around either side and then fanning out to roll up the rebel lines. The result was the latest debacle. Rebel troops rushed to the brink and fired at will on the trapped soldiers below, killing, wounding, or capturing four thousand men while routing the rest. Grant described the battle of the Crater as "the saddest affair I have witnessed in the war. Such an opportunity for carrying fortifications I . . . do not expect again to have." And so the siege dragged on for month after month.[17]

Sherman, meanwhile, launched his own one-hundred-thousand-man army south against Johnston's sixty thousand rebel troops on May 7. Like Grant, he tried to sidestep the enemy and get to their rear, but Johnston always managed to get wind of the movement and race his own army to block Sherman's advance. Small battles were fought at Dalton on May 7, Resaca on May 14 and 15, Cassville on May 19, and New Hope Church from May 23 to 28. All along Sherman spared his men and ordered attacks only if they appeared to have a reasonable chance of success. Within four weeks his army had marched eighty miles and was within twenty miles of Atlanta. But Johnston had fortified a string of hills centered on Kennesaw Mountain so Sherman called a halt to rest his men and bring up supplies. Nearly a month later, on June 27, Sherman opened his campaign's second phase with an assault on Kennesaw Mountain. When the rebels drove back his men, Sherman sent them on yet another wide turning movement that finally forced Johnston to withdraw into Atlanta's ring of defenses on July 9.

Sherman's juggernaut was now within sight of Atlanta's church spires. Over the previous two months Johnston had proved himself a worthy opponent; although his army was outgunned nearly two to one, he checked every Union advance and slowly withdrew, trading space for time. The campaign had cost the Federals and Confederates seventeen thousand and fourteen thousand respective casualties, a fraction of the bloodbath between Grant and Lee in Virginia. Sherman admitted that he felt lucky beating "Johnston, for he had the most exalted reputation with our old army as a strategist."[18]

Yet President Jefferson Davis did not appreciate Johnston's Fabian strategy and replaced him on July 17 with John Bell Hood, renowned for his reckless courage and aggression. Lee's description of Hood was apt: "All lion, none of the fox."[19] The result was a disaster for the rebel cause. Hood immediately launched a series of attacks on Sherman's forces stretching around Atlanta, at Peachtree Creek on July 20, at various points on July 22, and at Ezra Church on July 28. These battles cost the Federals about six thousand men to the Confederates' fifteen thousand. For the next month Hood hunkered down with his troops in the city's ring of entrenchments while Sherman steadily tightened his grip.

By late August 1864 the Union siege of Atlanta had been dragging on for nearly a month when Sherman conceived a strategy to flush Hood into the open. On August 30 the Federal troops abruptly abandoned their trenches, but rather than withdraw north, Sherman led them south to capture the railroad juncture of Jonesborough, Atlanta's umbilical supply line. Hood abandoned Atlanta on September 1 and Sherman led his army triumphantly into the city the next day. The news of Atlanta's fall inspired jubilation in the North and provoked despair in the South.

A blockade of southern ports was among the many interrelated actions that contributed to the American victory. This mission was anything but easy. The navy somehow had to seal off thirty-five thousand miles of coastline that included ten major ports and 180 bays, inlets, and river mouths perfect for smuggling. To this end, Navy Secretary Gideon Welles expanded the navy from 76 ships manned by seven thousand sailors when he took office to 671 ships and fifty-one thousand sailors when the war ended. Usually 150 ships in a dozen flotillas were on blockade patrol at any one time, while the rest were refitting in safe harbors. All these vessels weekly consumed five thousand tons of coal.[20]

The rebel coast was split into four regions, two along the Atlantic Ocean and two along the Gulf of Mexico, with each headed by an admiral. The naval blockade steadily tightened to painful if not crippling levels. Even at its height, the blockade was hardly foolproof. Of the war's eight thousand smuggling voyages, perhaps as many as five of six ships slipped past, with the ratio dropping as the number of Union ships and ports in Union hands increased; in 1861 nine of ten got through compared to one of two in 1865. During these four years, the rebels smuggled out half a million cotton bales and smuggled in a million pairs of shoes, half a million rifles, a thousand tons of gunpowder, and several hundred cannons.[21]

If these figures appear to discredit the blockade, one must question how the war would have ended had the attempt never been made. The rebels could have imported all the military supplies that they needed. They would not have had to divert tens of thousands of troops to coastal or inland defense. They would have evaded the hyperinflation that rendered their currency worthless, with a Confederate dollar worth a penny by the war's end.

The navy plugged a large hole in the blockade on August 5, 1864, when Adm. David Farragut led four monitors and fourteen wooden ships through a barrage of cannon fire from three forts and floating mines guarding Mobile Bay's entrance. A mine blew up and sank the lead monitor. When an officer called for turning back, Farragut uttered his immortal reply: "Damn the torpedoes, full speed ahead!"[22] Over the next three weeks, combined operations of the navy and army captured each fort, although the expedition lacked enough troops and supplies to take Mobile, thirty miles north.

The American enclaves carved out along the rebel coast might have served as bases for raids or even campaigns into the interior. Instead operations were usually confined to aiding the blockade. The few times that local commanders tried something more ambitious they met with failure. The worst defeat was Gen. Truman Seymour's five-thousand-man expedition from Jacksonville. Seymour's mission was to march west and capture Tallahassee, Florida's capital. A rebel army of equal numbers led by Joseph Finnegan routed the invaders at the battle of Olustee on February 20, 1864, inflicting casualties of 203 killed, 1,152 wounded, and 506 captured, while losing 93 killed and 841 wounded.[23]

The blockade hurt not only the South but also Britain, at least initially. Indeed, the Confederacy actually boycotted any cotton exports to Britain, ideally to pressure Whitehall into an alliance. This gamble failed to pay off literally and figuratively. In 1862 the British imported only 3 percent of the amount of southern cotton that they had imported the previous year. The loss of the South's cotton and markets threw a quarter million Britons out of work and put half a million on relief. But rather than aid the Confederacy, the British swiftly adapted by importing cotton from Egypt and India. Textile production rose and unemployment fell. By 1863 the crisis was over.[24]

Indirectly Britain did give some limited aid to the rebels. British shipyards built three Confederate warships, of which the most notable was the css *Alabama* that destroyed 250 American ships valued at $15.5 million. Charles Francis Adams, America's minister to Britain, warned Foreign Secretary Russell that if two more warships that were currently being built were delivered to the rebels, "This is war." Russell conceded. Tension eased when the USS *Kearsage* sank the *Alabama* in June 1864.

The British and French took advantage of the Civil War to assert their interests in America's backyard. Mexico typically owed enormous sums of money to foreign creditors and refused to pay. In 1861 Britain, France, and Spain launched a joint expedition that occupied Veracruz and refused to leave until the Mexicans paid up. Britain and Spain withdrew their contingents in 1862 after cutting a deal with the Mexicans for partial repayment. The French insisted on full repayment. When the Mexicans stonewalled, Napoleon III used this as an excuse to send a thirty-five-thousand-man army all the way to Mexico City. The French deposed the Mexican government and installed their emperor's distant cousin in the presidential palace, where he reigned as Emperor Maximilian I. Troops were dispatched to secure other key regions and cities, including Matamoros, at the Rio Grande mouth just across from Brownsville, Texas.

Straightjacketed by the Civil War, the Lincoln administration could do nothing but protest France's conquest of Mexico. Eventually Lincoln reasoned that if Union troops overran Texas, they would at once weaken the Confederacy and pressure the French in Mexico. Virtually all of Lincoln's decisions during the war were strategically sound except the expeditions he ordered directly or indirectly against Texas. The state was a strategic sideshow and the more forces that he committed to there, the fewer troops, transport, munitions, and provisions that were available at crucial fronts. As if this were not bad enough, nearly all of the Texas expeditions suffered humiliating defeats, including Gen. William Franklin's up the Sabine River in 1863 and Gen. Nathaniel Banks's up the Red River in 1864. Although Banks did succeed in capturing Brownsville at the mouth of the Rio Grande in September 1863, the rebels thwarted his attempts to seize other Texas ports.

Black troops were yet another critical element of waging total war against the Confederacy. As with so many other controversial issues, Lincoln developed this policy through a series of palatable political steps.[25] He initiated the policy on August 25, 1862, when he authorized War Secretary Stanton to set up the Bureau of Colored Troops in his department and recruit the first five-thousand-man brigade. The outpouring of black volunteers caused Stanton to authorize more regiments. By the war's end, 186,017 blacks had served in the army, or one in ten of all troops, and about 10,000 in the navy.[26]

Lincoln's decision to raise black regiments hardly met with universal approval in the North. The president's biggest worry was the effect on army officers and soldiers who angrily insisted that they fought to restore the United States, not to liberate slaves. To this, Lincoln made a typically pointed and wise response:

> You say you will not fight to free Negroes. Some of them seem willing to fight for you; but no matter. Fight you, then, exclusively to save the Union. I issued the proclamation on purpose to aid you in saving the Union. . . . I thought that in your struggle for the Union, to whatever extent the Negroes should cease helping the enemy, to that extent it weakened the enemy in his resistance to you. Do you think differently? I thought that whatever Negroes can be got to do as soldiers leaves just so much less for white soldiers to do in saving the Union.

He warned that opposing black troops could have unfortunate future consequences: "There will be some black men who remember that, with silent tongue and clenched teeth and steady eye and poised bayonet, they have helped mankind on to this great consummation while, I fear, there will be some white ones unable to forget that with malignant heart and deceitful speech, they have strove to hinder it."[27]

The question inevitably arose over what those blacks were fighting for. Was it simply slavery's abolition or something more? What rights, if any, would emancipated blacks enjoy? To those who would deny freedom or any other benefits to black soldiers, Lincoln countered that "Negroes, like other people, act upon motives. Why should they do anything for us if we will do nothing for them? If they stake their lives for us they must be prompted by the strongest motive, even the promise of freedom. And the promise, being made, must be kept."[28] To renege on this promise would devastate the Union's war effort: "All recruiting of colored men would instantly cease, and all colored men in our service would instantly desert us. And rightfully, too. Why should they give their lives for us, with full notice of our purpose to betray them? . . . I should be damned in time and eternity for so doing. The world shall know that I will keep my faith to friends and enemies, come what may."[29] Lincoln eventually called for more than just freedom for black soldiers. He advocated that soldiers and "intelligent blacks" should enjoy the right to vote.

Most whites believed that blacks could never match them in courage, skills, and discipline. Black troops disproved that in every battle they fought, starting with an attack on the rebel lines at Port Hudson on May 27, 1863. Nonetheless, at first black privates got only ten dollars a month, compared to thirteen dollars for white privates.

This discrimination led to the first meeting between Frederick Douglass and Abraham Lincoln on August 10, 1863. After listening carefully to Douglass's argument that black and white troops should be paid the same and that black officers should command black troops, Lincoln promised that the discrimination would one day end and asked for patience until then. He sent Douglass to make his case to War Secretary Stanton.[30] Blacks began receiving the same pay as whites from June 1864, although African Americans did not begin to receive officer commissions until after the war.

Black troops faced the possibility of being murdered or enslaved if they were captured. Confederate officials openly declared their intention to commit these crimes to deter the Union from using black troops. The rebel Congress decreed that officers of black regiments would "if captured be put to the death or otherwise punished." Blacks themselves would be treated according to the laws of the state in which they were captured; in all states that meant they could be flogged and reenslaved and in some that they could be executed. Regardless, blacks would not be considered prisoners of war subject to fair treatment and exchange. This was the official policy. Many rebel civilian and military leaders angrily declared no quarter for any black regiments. As for "white officers serving with negro troops," Confederate secretary of war James Seddon asserted that "we ought never to be inconvenienced by such prisoners."[31]

Upon learning of those threats, Lincoln proclaimed on July 30, 1863, that "for every soldier of the United States killed in violation of the laws of war, a rebel soldier shall be executed; and for every one enslaved by the enemy, . . . a rebel soldier shall be placed at hard labor on the public works. . . . If the enemy shall sell or enslave anyone because of his color, the offense shall be punished by retaliation upon the enemy's prisoners."[32]

Lincoln's evocation of a biblical eye for an eye justice was straightforward enough and ideally would deter future Confederate war crimes. Unfortunately, passion rather than reason drives most people, especially in wartime. Lincoln's policy did not deter rebel troops from venting their murderous hatreds. In early 1864 alone, Confederates massacred black troops who surrendered at Olustee, Florida; Fort Pillow, Tennessee; Poison Springs, Arkansas; and Plymouth, North Carolina.

Lincoln convened his cabinet to debate whether to fulfill his pledge to retaliate for such crimes, and if so, how. He admitted that his warning had been a bluff: "The difficulty is not in stating the principle, but in practically applying it." As a humanitarian and an American committed to upholding the Constitution, the idea of placing innocent prisoners picked at random before firing squads sickened him. He insisted that "blood cannot restore blood, and government should not act for revenge." Lincoln instructed Secretary of War Stanton to write President Davis that the U.S. government condemned the massacres and warn that an equivalent number of rebel soldiers "shall be treated other than according to the laws of war" if Davis did not renounce future such massacres by July 1, 1864. Should Davis not comply, what then? Lincoln and his cabinet agreed that military tribunals would try any captured suspects charged with committing war crimes. The United States also would end any prisoner exchanges unless the rebel government agreed that it would treat blacks equally with whites. Meanwhile Davis called Lincoln's bluff; he and his cabinet angrily rejected any notion of equality.[33]

Lee suggested a prisoner exchange to Grant in early October 1864. Grant agreed, provided that black troops would be released with white troops. Lee curtly replied that "negroes belonging to our citizens are not considered subjects of exchange and were not included in my proposition." Grant expressed his regret at that policy, noting that the American government "is bound to secure to all persons received into her armies the rights due to soldiers."[34] And there the possibility died of releasing thousands of prisoners from wretched conditions that emaciated all and killed many.

Crushing the Confederacy posed a terrible legal and moral dilemma for Lincoln.[35] Should a president violate the Constitution in order to

save it? Or, as he rhetorically put it, "Must a government, of necessity, be too strong for the liberties of its own people or too weak to
maintain its own existence?"[36] He argued that the Constitution fully
empowered him to do what was necessary to preserve it: "Certain proceedings are constitutional when, in cases of rebellion or invasion, the
public safety requires them, which would not be constitutional when,
in the absence of rebellion or invasion, the public safety does not
require them."[37] He insisted that "as commander-in-chief of the army
and navy in time of war . . . I have a right to take any measure which
may best subdue the enemy." What's more, as president "I may in an
emergency do things on military grounds that cannot be done constitutionally by Congress."[38] He typically bolstered his legal case with
moral arguments: "Was it possible to lose the nation and yet preserve
the Constitution? By general law life and limb must be protected, yet
often a limb must be amputated to save a life; but a life is never wisely
given to save a limb." In other words, "Was it possible to lose the
nation, and yet preserve the Constitution?"[39] Indeed, he anticipated a
time when "I shall be blamed for having made too few arrests rather
than too many."[40] Yet, having asserted all that, he acknowledged limits to a president's wartime powers: "Nothing justifies the suspending
of the civil by the military authority but military necessity, and of the
existence of that necessity the military commander, and not a popular
vote, is to decide."[41]

Citing military necessity, Lincoln suspended habeas corpus in parts
of the country on April 19, 1861, August 8 and September 24, 1862, and
September 15, 1863, and later restored it after law and order again prevailed. Congressional majorities approved these acts. John Sherman, an
Ohio senator and William Tecumseh's brother, captured the prevailing
sentiment: "I approve of the action of the President. . . . He did precisely what I would have done if I had been in his place—no more, no
less, but I cannot . . . declare that what he did do was . . . strictly legal,
and in consonance with the . . . constitution."[42]

The Supreme Court concurred. In the *Prize* case of 1863, the justices
ruled by five to four that Lincoln's actions from April 15 to July 4, 1861,
when Congress was out of session, were constitutional. While reaffirm-
ing that only Congress can start a war, the majority argued that a president can certainly fight a war started by others: "Whether the President

in fulfilling his duties as Commander in Chief in suppressing an insurrection has met with such armed hostile resistance and a civil war is a
question to be settled by him."[43]

The justices offered a more nuanced view in their 1866 *Ex Parte Milligan* decision. The case involved Lambdin Milligan, an Indiana civilian who was convicted of treason by a military tribunal in 1864. The
majority overruled Milligan's conviction on the grounds that "martial
law can never exist when the courts are open, and in the proper and
unobstructed exercise of their jurisdiction." Thus Milligan should have
been tried in an existing civilian court rather than a military court. The
justices also pointed out that the power to suspend habeas corpus is
given to Congress, not the president. They concluded that, "as necessity creates the rule, so it limits its duration."[44] So even where extraordinary circumstances render civilian courts abeyant, the civilian law
must be reintroduced as soon as the emergency ends.

Just how many civilians were arrested under the Lincoln administration's suspension of habeas corpus? Historian Mark Neely found at least
866 arrests from the war's beginning until February 15, 1862, and "the
lowest estimate is 13,535 arrests" from then to the war's end. That works
out to 1 arrest for every 1,563 northerners. Neely notes that February 15
marked the date when authority for the arrests shifted from the State
Department to the War Department. The army conducted 4,271 trials,
of which 1,940, or 45.4 percent, took place in the Border States, 1,339,
or 31.4 percent, in occupied regions of the eleven rebel states, and 212,
or 5.0 percent, in the northern states.[45] How much these arrests, trials,
convictions, and prison terms actually suppressed or deterred enemy
subversion or outright rebellion is impossible to say.

History is replete with instances of individuals emerging from relative obscurity to shift its course. This happened in November 1862,
when Dr. Francis Lieber, a law professor, proposed to Gen. Henry Halleck that the government "issue a set of rules and definitions . . . for
. . . the Law and usages of War," to be drafted by a three-man committee of experts.[46] Halleck shared the idea with Lincoln, who enthusiastically approved and appointed Lieber to chair the committee. Lieber
was eminently qualified for the task. He was born in Prussia and as
a young man fought in the army against Napoleon, then later in the
Greek war of independence. He fled to exile in the United States in 1827

after a government crackdown on liberal activists like himself. In New York City he studied and from 1857 taught law at Columbia College.

Lincoln approved what became known as the Lieber Code and issued it on April 24, 1863. The Lieber Code significantly developed international law related to war. It became the foundation for the 1868 St. Petersburg Declaration, the 1874 Brussels Declaration, and the Hague Regulations on the Laws and Customs of War on Land of 1899 and 1907.

"Military necessity" is the Lieber Code's core principle. Soldiers from the highest general to the lowest private can only commit acts "that are indispensable for securing the ends of war." Lincoln himself typically expressed this concept with succinct eloquence: "The true rule for the military is to seize such property as is needed for Military uses and reasons, and leave the rest alone." This would rule out the gratuitous or vengeful destruction or confiscation of property and infliction of suffering on soldiers and civilians alike.[47]

And what should happen to those who violate the law? The question of how to treat war criminals can be problematic under any circumstances, especially when fighting against peoples who lack a formal legal code, let alone being acquainted with the international law of war. One way is to assert the universally understood principle of "an eye for an eye." However, this "solution" can be troubling for people living in a liberal democracy and committed to upholding the rule of law upon which it is grounded.

A president literally has the power of life and death in his hands, and not just in wartime. The power to pardon is also the power to condemn. Every president receives pleas from those convicted for crimes. During the Civil War, the official number of Union soldiers executed was 272, among whom 141 were deserters and 22 were rapists. That number would have been far higher had not Lincoln carefully reviewed at least 661 cases and issued 570 pardons or reduced sentences. The exact figure may never be known, as the records are incomplete. His most far-reaching act of clemency was to issue on March 10, 1863, a general amnesty for all deserters who returned to their regiments by April 1. Although Lincoln's mercy is legendary, his search for justice was even more powerful. Among one batch of fifty-nine convictions of officers in late 1863, he actually imposed tougher penalties on fourteen.[48]

Women played a low-profile but important part in the Union cause. Over two hundred thousand women volunteered to act as nurses, raise money, or produce items needed by the troops. The Sanitary Commission, led by Clara Barton and Dorothea Dix, was the most important institution that cared for the sick and wounded. Of the twenty thousand women who served as nurses, three thousand were army nurses. Thousands of other women worked elsewhere in the federal bureaucracy, mostly in clerical positions. Over one hundred thousand women filled positions in the private sector, usually in a post traditionally occupied by a man. The proportion of factory jobs held by women rose from one-quarter to one-third during the war.[49]

Meanwhile the First Lady persisted in stirring up gossip and controversy. Mary Lincoln provoked the latest criticism when she invited her sister Emilie Todd Helm to live in the White House after Emilie's husband, Confederate general Benjamin Helm, was killed in battle. Gen. Dan Sickles spoke for countless appalled Americans when he advised Lincoln not to "have that rebel in your house." That prompted a steely reply from Lincoln: "General Sickles, my wife and I are in the habit of choosing our own guests. We do not need from our friends either advice or assistance in the matter."[50]

More than protecting his home's privacy inspired Lincoln's response. Emilie's cheerful presence steadily pulled Mary from the deep depression that she had suffered since Tad died. Eventually Mary shed her mourning clothes and expressed ever more the vivacious side of her nature. That in turn alleviated some of the crushing emotional burdens that her husband was forced to carry.

Lincoln received a stunning message from Horace Greeley, the *New York Tribune*'s editor, on July 7. A southern peace delegation was on the Canadian side of Niagara Falls and was interested in talks. The envoys included former Mississippi congressman Jacob Thompson, former senator Clement Clay, and University of Virginia professor James Holcombe. The president shared the news with his cabinet and they discussed the legal question of whether talking with the rebels constituted recognizing their government. Lincoln finally decided to send Greeley and his secretary John Hay to the envoys and determine whether they had official credentials from Jefferson Davis. If the envoys were legitimate, Hay would hand them a letter from Lincoln in which he wrote that he would consider "any proposition which embraces the restoration of peace, the integrity of the whole Union, and the abandonment of slavery."[51] If the envoys accepted those preconditions then Hay and Greeley were to conduct them to Washington to write up a peace treaty.

In handling the envoys that way Lincoln once again displayed his profound understanding of power. He had two interests that might either clash with or complement each other depending on how he asserted them. He genuinely wanted peace on the terms that he presented. He also needed to win reelection and his party had to retain its congressional majorities. Ever more people were sick of the war and would welcome any excuse to end it as soon as possible. The rebel peace envoys offered just such a chance. If Lincoln dismissed the opportunity, he would push countless voters into Democratic Party ranks. Yet peace at any price was unacceptable. So he offered terms that he knew the rebels would reject, and in doing so he heaped upon the Confederacy the terrible onus of carrying on the war. Lincoln compounded this stigma by publicly releasing a recent declaration made by Davis to two northern journalists who visited the Confederate White House: "The war . . . must go on till the last man of this generation falls in his tracks . . . unless you acknowledge our right to self-government. We are not fighting for slavery. We are fighting for independence—and that or extermination we will have."[52]

During most of the war, the question of how to win the war naturally superseded that of how to win the peace. Yet political leaders, most prominently the president, increasingly recognized that winning the war and winning the peace were inseparable. Reconstruction was the term for winning the peace. Just what reconstruction meant and how it would be implemented were disputed. Lincoln continually sought to forge a coalition among three fiercely opposed factions. Liberal or Radical Republicans championed reunification along with immediate abolition and racial equality. Conservative Republicans favored reunification, future abolition, and racial inequality. War Democrats favored reunification and opposed abolition for the slave states and racial equality in the free states.[53]

And after a policy was hammered out, what then? If it took years to win a military victory, it might well take decades or even generations to transform millions of hearts and minds from defending to abhorring slavery. Just how would that be done?

To answer this question, Lincoln carefully followed developments in the occupied rebel territories to determine what worked and what failed.[54] He then formulated a blueprint for reconstruction that he presented to Congress on December 8, 1863. The United States would welcome back into the Union any state in which 10 percent of the number of those qualified to vote in 1860 signed loyalty oaths and agreed to submit to the federal government and abolish slavery. Pardons would be denied only to high-ranking rebel officials, officers who resigned from the U.S. army to fight for the rebel cause, and those who abused black soldiers and their white officers. With that formula, he hoped to swiftly entice Louisiana back into the United States as a model for other rebel states.[55]

Typically, this proposal was blasted by Radical Republicans for not going far enough and by Peace Democrats for going too far. Liberals insisted that not only should slavery be abolished but blacks should enjoy equal rights with whites. Conservatives condemned any notion of granting blacks equal rights. Both attacked the 10 percent voter threshold level as undemocratic.

As usual Lincoln was many moves ahead of everyone else. Liberals and conservatives alike were blind to the reality that over the long term the 10 percent threshold would result in far more progressive governments than if the 50 percent threshold suggested as an alternative prevailed. Lincoln reckoned that at least one of ten men in each rebel state must be secretly loyal to the United States and represent the most liberal minds. Encouraging them to come forward under the protection of the American army would bring each state's most progressive men to power and thus accelerate the liberal democratic revolutions that Lincoln hoped to instigate. This in turn would encourage conservatives to proclaim loyalty to the United States, if only to block or dilute progressive reforms. The result would eventually be the restoration of democracy, but on a broad and liberal rather than narrow, conservative, elitist foundation.

Benjamin Wade and Henry Davis sponsored a reconstruction bill that raised the statehood threshold to 50 percent of registered voters in 1860, who had to sign a loyalty oath. Obviously this standard would take much longer to reach and those who declared allegiance to the United States would be of far more questionable loyalty than at Lincoln's 10 percent level. The Wade-Davis Bill passed by seventy-three to fifty-nine in the House and by eighteen to fourteen in the Senate on July 2, 1864.

Lincoln pocket vetoed the bill. When asked why, he explained that the bill would overturn reconstruction governments in Louisiana, Tennessee, and Arkansas that were formed by 10 percent of the electorate. He hinted that he might sign a bill that exempted those states from the 50 percent rule.[56]

This act provoked the wrath of the bill's Radical authors. On August 5 the *New York Tribune* published their Wade-Davis Manifesto, which condemned the president for vetoing their bill. Although the president remained publicly mute to their protest, he privately expressed his sorrow: "To be wounded in the house of one's friends is perhaps the most grievous affliction that can befall a man."[57]

Meanwhile the war voraciously devoured ever more blood and treasure, with the Union suffering as many pyrrhic victories and outright defeats as decisive triumphs. After Sigel's rout at New Market in May, Grant replaced him with Gen. David Hunter as the Shenandoah Valley's army commander. While Hunter was a more skilled general, he was ultimately no more successful. His orders were the same as those of his predecessor. He was to march his fifteen-thousand-man army up the valley, cross the Blue Ridge Mountains to Charlottesville, then head south and capture Lynchburg, thus severing that rail link with Richmond. Like Sigel, he lacked enough troops to accomplish this mission. Rebel raider John Mosby and his men ranged across Hunter's lengthening supply line, attacking isolated wagon trains and garrisons. Although Hunter had to hive off more troops to protect his supply line, he did reach Lynchburg's outskirts on June 17. Facing him in entrenchments surrounding the town was Gen. Jubal Early with ten thousand troops. Short of men and munitions, Hunter chose to withdraw.

Early hounded Hunter's retreat all the way back to the Shenandoah Valley, then down it. As Hunter withdrew to Winchester, Early veered east, crossed the Potomac River on July 6, routed a Union force at a Monocracy River ford on July 9, and approached Fort Stevens, which defended Washington's northwest side, on July 11. Lincoln took his duty as commander in chief literally when he rode out to Fort Stevens. Atop the parapet, he peered curiously at the rebels as bullets whizzed past such a conspicuous target. This so appalled Oliver Wendell Holmes, then a captain and decades later a Supreme Court justice, that he reputedly yelled to Lincoln, "Get down, you fool!" The president obeyed.[58]

Early finally withdrew his army, but not before his men looted and burned scores of surrounding houses, including that of Postmaster General Montgomery Blair.[59] He then led his men across Maryland, along the way levying ransoms of $20,000 on Hagerstown and $200,000 on Frederick. On July 30 he and his footsore men reached Chambersburg, Pennsylvania, which he ordered burned on July 30 after its leading citizens were unable to pay a ransom of $100,000 in gold or $500,000 in greenbacks. He justified the devastation and robbery as retaliation for similar acts committed by the Yankees. By early August his army was back in the Shenandoah Valley.

Among the reasons why Union armies suffered repeated and humiliating defeats in the Shenandoah Valley and surrounding regions was that no one general commanded all the others. After three years of war, Lincoln finally established unity of command on July 31 by combining all forces in the region into the Middle Military Division. Even better, he acted on Grant's advice to name Gen. Philip Sheridan to head the Army of the Shenandoah.[60]

Meanwhile Lincoln sought to stifle the ever-escalating cycle of vengeful destruction. He asked Grant to ask General Lee "for a mutual discontinuance of house-burning and other destruction of private property."[61] Although Lee was sympathetic, he declined a formal agreement. This prompted Grant to order Sheridan to wage total war: "Eat out Virginia clear and clean . . . so that crows flying over it . . . will have to carry their provender with them."[62]

Sheridan launched his thirty-seven thousand troops at Early's fifteen thousand outside of Winchester on September 19 and routed them. Early rallied his troops twenty miles south at Fisher Hill, where Sheridan again scattered them on September 22. Early withdrew his army's remnants far up the valley to the gap leading over to Charlottesville and there slowly replenished his ranks and supplies. Sheridan dispersed his brigades through the Shenandoah Valley to systematically destroy what was Virginia's breadbasket.

Early, having received reinforcements, advanced down the valley and launched a surprise attack on Sheridan's army at Cedar Creek on October 19. Sheridan himself was fifteen miles north at Winchester, where he heard the distant thunder of cannon firing. He immediately mounted his horse and galloped to his men. After capturing thirteen hundred Federals and eighteen cannons and routing the rest of Sheridan's army, the famished rebels scattered through the Union camp to devour its provisions. Sheridan rallied his retreating regiments and led them back toward Cedar Creek. He launched a counterattack in late afternoon that pulverized Early's army, taking one thousand prisoners and twenty-three cannons and retaking the eighteen cannons earlier lost.

The last rebel invasion of Missouri opened in early September 1864, when Gen. Sterling Price led twelve thousand troops into the state. After capturing Springfield, his army headed toward St. Louis. About halfway between these cities were one thousand Federals manning a fort at Pilot Knob. Rather than bypass this stronghold, Price ordered an attack. Union rifles and cannons firing grapeshot and canister killed or wounded more than fifteen hundred rebels. With his force sharply diminished, Price gave up his dream of capturing St. Louis and instead veered northwest toward Jefferson City. The Union had turned that town into a stronghold ringed by five forts. This time Price prudently sidestepped and pushed on toward Kansas City. Along the way his ranks swelled with recruits and bushwhacker bands led by "Bloody Bill" Anderson and William Quantrill, with Jesse and Frank James among the murderous followers. Gen. Samuel Curtis commanded the twenty thousand Union troops defending Kansas City. The armies fought at Westport, a half-dozen miles south of the city, on October 23. The Federals repulsed a Confederate attack, then counterattacked and routed them. Pursued relentlessly by Union forces, Price and his thirty-five hundred remaining troops did not reach relative safety until they crossed to the Arkansas River's south bank on December 15.

The president had not only a war but an election to win.[63] Indeed, the two were inseparable. The Republicans held what they called their National Union convention at Baltimore on June 7 and 8. Lincoln did not attend. He won on the first ballot with 506 of 528 votes cast, with 22 of the dissidents going to Grant. But having made their point, the dissidents threw their votes to Lincoln in a show of unanimity. Lincoln sent word of his grateful acceptance. He tapped Andrew Johnson to replace Hannibal Hamlin as his vice president. This choice made perfect political sense at the time but would have disastrous consequences that no one could have then foreseen. As Tennessee's governor, Johnson very effectively implemented Lincoln's reconstruction plan. After becoming president, Johnson would swiftly transform himself from a moderate progressive into a reactionary conservative.

The votes for Grant deeply embarrassed and angered him. When he first learned that some Republicans favored him over the president, Grant declared, "They can't compel me to do that!" and insisted that it was "as important for the cause that [Lincoln] should be elected as that the army should be successful in the field."[64] Grant was a loyal soldier, not a politician. Yet one day he would take the presidential oath.

Despite the seeming unanimity at the convention, the Republican Party was split. John Frémont broke away to run as the hastily formed Radical Democracy Party's candidate. Then, on August 28, twenty-five prominent liberal Republicans met in the home of New York mayor George Opdyke. Among them were Senators Benjamin Wade and Henry Davis, Massachusetts governor John Andrew, and Horace Greeley, Parke Gordon, Theodore Tilton, and George Wilkes, the respective editors of the *Tribune, Evening Post, Independent,* and *Spirit of the Times.* They debated whether they should break with the Republican Party and call their own convention to nominate a candidate for president, with Treasury Secretary Salmon Chase their favorite.

The Democrats did not convene until August 30. Shortly after gathering at Chicago, they enthusiastically chose George McClellan as their presidential candidate and George Peddleton of Ohio, who was closely aligned with the Copperhead Clement Vallandigham, as his running mate. McClellan promised that if elected he would immediately call an armistice and negotiate for reunion without emancipation. The Democrats colored this message with vicious racism and fear-mongering that smeared Republicans as championing equality and miscegenation between blacks and whites.

Lincoln was deeply pessimistic about the upcoming election. "You think I don't know I am going to be beaten?" he admitted.[65] On August 23 he gathered his cabinet and asked them to sign, sight unseen, what he would later reveal as an explosive statement: "This morning . . . it seems exceedingly probable that this Administration will not be re-elected. Then it will be my duty to so co-operate with the President elect as to save the Union between the election and the inauguration; as he will have secured his election on such ground that he cannot possibly save it afterwards."[66] He likely asked for this blind signing from fear that if the text leaked to the press, the revelation of Lincoln's defeatism might be another reason to vote against him. Then again, this dire warning of the results of voting for McClellan might spur some fence-sitters to Lincoln's side. In the end, the incident provides insights into Lincoln's complex, seething mind.

From this nadir, Lincoln's reelection prospects enjoyed a series of significant boosts. The first came on September 3, when Gen. William Sherman telegraphed Lincoln that his army had captured Atlanta. Then, on September 22, Senator Zachariah Chandler of Michigan talked Frémont into abandoning his presidential bid in exchange for a promise to find him a new field command. Finally, Lincoln pacified Chase by offering to name him the Supreme Court's chief justice after Roger Taney died on October 12; Chase gratefully accepted.

When the votes were tallied on November 8, Lincoln won by a landslide, taking twenty-three states and 212 electoral votes to McClellan's four states and 21 electoral votes and 2,203,831 to 1,797,019 votes. Perhaps the most gratifying aspect of those results to Lincoln was that he won the votes of 119,754 soldiers, or 78 percent of the total, while McClellan got only 34,291.[67] The Republican Party won just as decisively, outnumbering Democrats by 149 to 42 in the House and by 42 to 10 in the Senate. Tragically, Lincoln would have little time to make the most of that overwhelming political power.[68]

12

With Malice toward None

> With malice toward none; with charity toward all; with
> firmness in the right, as God gives us to see the right, let us
> strive on to finish the work we are in; to bind up the nation's
> wounds . . . to do all which may achieve and cherish a just
> and a lasting speech among ourselves and with all nations.
>
> ABRAHAM LINCOLN

> Thank God that I lived to see this. It seems to me
> that I have been dreaming a horrid dream for four
> years, and now the nightmare is gone.
>
> ABRAHAM LINCOLN

> We are all Americans.
>
> ELY PARKER

Abraham Lincoln enjoyed the powerful mandate of an overwhelming election victory for himself and his party. In his annual December address to Congress, he called on the American people to devote
themselves to resolving the conflict that "can only be tried by war and
decided by victory . . . on the part of those who began it."[1] News from
distant fronts in late 1864 and early 1865 stirred hopes that victory might
well be within grasp.

In Atlanta, Gen. William Sherman faced the dilemma of strategic consumption. Vast amounts of manpower were deployed either protecting or moving supplies to his army. Gen. John Bell Hood's rebel army remained just beyond reach, while smaller forces raided Sherman's supply line. Sherman eventually devised a bold and ruthless strategy to resolve that dilemma. On November 15 he ordered the city's evacuation, then had Atlanta burned to the ground. Splitting his army in two, he sent Gen. George Thomas with 60,000 troops back to Nashville, while he led 62,000 troops southeast toward Savannah, 285 miles away. His corps marched along parallel routes with the front varying from twenty to sixty miles wide. With no significant rebel forces in his way, Sherman's strategic object was "to make Georgia howl" and destroy the state's capacity to supply the rebel war effort. In cutting their communications and living off the land, Sherman and his men disappeared into a void from which only wild rumors emerged. The army's fate would remain unknown for the next month until, on December 22, Sherman famously sent word to President Lincoln that "I beg to present you, as a Christmas gift, the city of Savannah, with 150 heavy guns and 25,000 bales of cotton."[2]

To this Lincoln expressed his "many, many thanks . . . to your whole army, officers, and men." Then he went deeper, revealing more of himself. He admitted that he "was anxious, if not fearful" when Sherman cut loose his army from the railroad umbilical cord of supplies and telegraph lines of communications but conceded that the general "was the better judge. . . . Now the undertaking being a success, the honor is all yours. . . . But what next? I suppose it will be safer if I leave Gen. Grant and yourself to decide."[3]

General Hood, meanwhile, did not pursue Sherman but instead invaded central Tennessee. Thomas had divided his army between thirty thousand troops under his own command at Nashville and thirty thousand under Gen. John Schofield at Pulaski, nearly a hundred miles south. Hood hoped to cut off and destroy Schofield's army with his forty thousand men, then march against Thomas. Schofield withdrew but Hood caught up with him at Franklin, fifteen miles south of Nashville, and attacked on November 30. The Federal troops killed or wounded 6,252 rebels while suffering 2,326 casualties. That night Schofield withdrew his army within Nashville's ring of defenses. Although outnumbered by almost two to one, Hood followed and opened a siege of Nashville. Learning of this disparity, Grant fired off one telegram after another to Thomas, urging him to attack. Yet for two weeks Thomas did nothing, until December 15, when he launched his army against Hood's. The battle raged all that day and through the next. When the guns finally fell silent, Hood and his remaining 15,000 men were hurrying south, having lost 1,500 killed and 4,500 captured to Thomas's 3,061 casualties. A vigorous commander like Grant, Sherman, or Sheridan would have ruthlessly pursued until he wiped out that entire demoralized horde depleted of provisions and munitions. But Thomas rested on his victory's laurels and let the rebels get away.[4]

The blockade's last large, gaping hole was the Cape Fear River leading to Wilmington, North Carolina. Fort Fisher guarded the Cape Fear River mouth. The expedition launched in December 1864 to capture Fort Fisher and Wilmington could not have had a more capable naval commander—Adm. David Porter—and a more inept army commander—Gen. Benjamin Butler. Butler concocted the scheme of packing an old vessel with 215 tons of gunpowder and detonating it near the fort. Neither the explosion nor the naval bombardment that followed severely damaged the fort. Butler gave up and ordered the flotilla to sail back north. Grant used this failure as an excuse to finally rid the war effort of Butler, replacing him with Gen. Alfred Terry. On January 13, 1865, as Porter's warships bombarded the fort, Terry led eight thousand troops packed in longboats from the transports to the neck of the peninsula leading to Fort Fisher. Two days later Terry ordered a massive assault that captured the fort.

Sherman began his march from Savannah through the Carolinas on February 1. He led most of his sixty thousand troops straight to Columbia while detaching a force to take Charleston. As his troops neared Columbia on February 17, the Confederates burned or blew up anything of military value; the fires spread and destroyed most of South Carolina's capital. Fortunately, the rebels spared the beautiful city of Charleston when they fled on February 18. The United States won a vital symbolic victory the following day when American troops marched unopposed into the Confederacy's epicenter of secessionism and slavocracy. By mid-March Sherman's army was advancing through the center of North Carolina. The only significant battle came at Bentonville, where the Union army repelled an attack by Gen. Joe Johnston's troops on March 18 and routed them in a counterattack three days later. Then Sherman's soldiers resumed their steamroller advance, steadily backing the twenty thousand remnants of Johnston's army toward Virginia, where Lee's thinning gray lines manned the entrenchments ringing Petersburg and Richmond.

Lincoln used his reelection as an excuse to shake up his circle of advisors. He replaced Edward Bates with James Speed, the brother of his old friend Joshua, as attorney general; John Usher with Senator James Harlan of Iowa, as Interior Department secretary; Montgomery Blair with William Dennison as postmaster general; and William Fessenden with Hugh McCulloch as treasury secretary. His two secretaries were exhausted from their labors. Lincoln rewarded John Nicolay and John Hay by sending them to Paris as the consul and secretary, respectively, of America's legation. Noah Brooks, a brilliant correspondent for the *Sacramento Union*, agreed to take their place. The only familiar faces were those of William Seward, Edwin Stanton, and Gideon Welles as the respective state, war, and navy secretaries.

Although it could not be foreseen at the time, Lincoln's most notable change was to replace Hannibal Hamlin with Andrew Johnson. Like many vice presidential picks, Johnson seemed to make solid political sense at the time. He had an impressive resume, having served in the House of Representatives from 1843 to 1853, as Tennessee's governor from 1853 to 1857, and as a U.S. senator from 1857 to March 1862. He was from mountainous east Tennessee, where slaves were few and Unionist sentiments were strong. He was the only southern senator who remained loyal after his state seceded. He supported abolition and the recruitment of black regiments. Although he owned five slaves, he voluntarily freed them in August 1863. In return for all this, Lincoln rewarded him by naming him Tennessee's military governor in March 1862. As a southerner and Democrat loyal to the United States, Johnson appeared to be symbolically a perfect national unity running mate for Lincoln in 1864.

At times private American citizens have conducted their own, unauthorized, diplomacy in hopes of resolving deadlocked international conflicts. These efforts have generally provoked far more resentment than gratitude from the White House. The freelancers tend to thicken rather than cut through thorny diplomatic problems. This happened in January 1865, when Francis Blair, a prominent Maryland Republican, journeyed to Richmond to meet with his old friend Jefferson Davis. He proposed that the two sides resolve their differences by uniting to drive the French from Mexico. Although Davis was cool to this idea, he sent Blair back to Washington with a letter promising to appoint a commission "to secure peace to the two countries." Lincoln returned Blair to Richmond with the message that he hoped to secure the southern "people to the people of our one common country."[5] He did so assuming that would end the initiative.

Instead, Davis named three envoys, Confederate vice president Alexander Stephens, Assistant Secretary of War John Campbell, and Virginia senator Robert Hunter, and informed Grant of his intention to send them across the lines at Petersburg. Grant talked the envoys into deleting any reference to separate countries in their instructions. He then hosted them at his headquarters.

Lincoln and Seward embarked on the presidential steamboat *River Queen* for the voyage from Washington to Hampton Roads. The rebel envoys were ushered aboard the *River Queen* on February 3. The meeting started out genially enough, as Lincoln was delighted to see Stephens, an old friend and respected colleague from his congressional stint from 1847 to 1849. During the subsequent talks, Lincoln insisted that peace was possible only after the Confederacy unconditionally surrendered, the nation was reunited, and slavery was abolished. Until then the American government and people would relentlessly war against the rebels. Yet he made a huge concession when he suggested leaving slavery's abolition in the hands of the courts and state governments rather than Congress. He hinted that if the rebel states rejoined the nation they could vote against the ratification of the Thirteenth Amendment abolishing slavery. But the rebel envoys spurned this stunning idea and instead insisted on independence. They parted without an agreement.

Upon returning to Washington, Lincoln drew up a proposal whereby Congress would appropriate $400 million to buy the freedom of slaves from their masters. Half the money would be paid on April 1 if the rebels accepted peace, with the rest paid on July 1 if the Thirteenth

Amendment was ratified. But the cabinet rejected his proposal when they reviewed it on February 5. The war would be won on the battlefield rather than at the negotiation table.

As for the Thirteenth Amendment that abolished slavery, it was slowly lumbering along the path to ratification. Liberals had introduced the amendment in June 1864. Although the Senate vote surpassed the two-thirds approval requirement, the House killed it when sixty-six Democrats voted against it, while all ninety-three Republicans and two liberal Democrats voted for it. In his December 1864 address, Lincoln urged Congress to pass the Thirteenth Amendment. The House approved slavery's abolition on January 31, 1865, with 119 for and 56 against, just two more votes than the required two-thirds majority; 102 Republicans and 17 Democrats voted for the amendment, while 8 Democrats abstained. With enormous satisfaction and relief, the president signed the Thirteenth Amendment the same day. This was just the first crucial step. Three of four states had to approve that amendment before it became part of the law of the land. Sadly, Lincoln would not live to see that happen.

The inaugural day procedure was for the vice president to take the oath and make a speech before a select group of dignitaries within the Capitol, followed by the president's oath and speech outside before the fifty thousand spectators that had gathered. Andrew Johnson made a very poor first impression that proved to be a harbinger of the trials to come. He was still shaky from surviving a bout with typhoid fever and sought to drown with whiskey his nervousness at making his speech. The result was a rambling, barely coherent discourse on democracy and his own humble origins. As Johnson babbled on, Lincoln was observed to have "closed his eyes and seemed to retire into himself as though beset by melancholy reflection." After Johnson finally finished, Lincoln whispered to the parade marshal not to "let Johnson speak outside."[6]

Lincoln's second inaugural address was the shortest and among the most eloquent in American history: "Fondly we do hope—fervently we do pray—that this mighty scourge of war may speedily pass away. Yet if God wills that it continue, until all the wealth piled up by the bondman's two hundred and fifty years of unrequited toil shall be sunk, and until every drop of blood drawn with the lash shall be paid by another drawn by the sword, as was said three thousand years ago, so still it must be said, 'the judgments of the Lord, are true and righteous altogether.'" He then sought to comfort those families that had paid the highest sacrifice in the struggle: "I pray that our Heavenly Father may assuage the anguish of your bereavements and leave you only the cherished memory of the loved and lost, and the solemn pride that must be yours, to have laid so costly a sacrifice on the altar of freedom." He ended with beautifully haunting lines: "With malice toward none; with charity toward all; with firmness in the right, as God gives us to see the right, let us strive on to finish the work we are in; to bind up the nation's wounds . . . to do all which may achieve and cherish a just and a lasting speech among ourselves and with all nations."[7]

Among the barrage of unrelenting criticisms that Abraham and Mary Lincoln endured was the charge that their oldest son, Robert, was a "shirker." Rather than serve in the army he was safely ensconced at Harvard University and, after graduating in 1864, was just as safe in the White House as he prepared to return to Harvard to study law. Mary was adamant that she not lose a third son and refused Robert's plea that he enlist. With the war's end near, Lincoln sought a safe but honorable post for Robert at the front. He asked Grant as a friend whether he could give his son a nominal rank and duty in his headquarters. Grant was happy to comply. He commissioned Robert a captain and assigned him to his staff.

Lincoln himself joined the army for a jubilant ten days that began on March 28, in a war council with Grant and Sherman aboard the *River Queen* at City Point. They discussed how best to end the war and then begin to win the peace. Lincoln explained his desire to "get the deluded men of the rebel armies disarmed and back to their home." Once there "they won't take up arms again. . . . I want submission and no more bloodshed. . . . I want no one punished; treat them liberally all around. We want those people to return to their allegiance to the Union and submit to the laws."[8]

Although Grant's army outgunned Lee's by 120,000 to 55,000 troops, the trenches magnified the rebel army's strength manyfold. The only sure way to crush the enemy was to sidestep and cut off the last two rail links that fed them supplies. On March 29 Grant sent Sheridan with his cavalry and an infantry corps due west toward Five Forks. When Lee learned that Sheridan's men had taken that strategic junction, he had no choice but to abandon Petersburg and Richmond and march his army westward as swiftly as possible in hopes of eventually veering south and joining Johnston. President Davis ordered Richmond burned, then fled with his high-ranking officials and family. On April 2 Grant sent more of his army westward while he ordered the rest to charge the rebel lines at Petersburg. The Union assault swept away the handful of soldiers that Lee had left behind.

Lincoln and Grant triumphantly toured Petersburg the next day. The president was even more exhilarated when, on April 4, accompanied by a small escort and surrounded by a growing crowd of worshipful African Americans, he strolled through Richmond. "Thank God that I lived to see this," he suddenly exclaimed. "It seems to me that I have been dreaming a horrid dream for four years, and now the nightmare is gone."[9]

On parallel roads the enemy armies raced each other westward, with Grant ordering probes and attacks northward. The key battle came at Saylor's Creek on April 6, when Union troops cut off and captured a quarter of the rebel army. The race ended on April 7, when Sheridan's corps got ahead and blocked the rebel retreat at Appomattox Court House. Grant sent a letter to Lee calling on him to surrender. Lee replied the next day by asking for terms. They agreed to meet the following day.

The war's two greatest generals shook hands at Wilber McLean's house in Appomattox on the afternoon of April 9. The contrast between the men was striking. Lee was immaculately dressed in his gray uniform and stood ramrod stiff his full six-foot height. Grant, typically, was rumpled and mud-spattered; with his tendency to slouch, he appeared even shorter than his five foot, seven inches. Only one aide accompanied Lee to share the ignominy of surrender. Grant brought his entire staff and Sheridan, although he entered the McLean parlor with only a secretary.

Grant tried to ease Lee's tormented feelings by reminiscing about their shared Mexican War experiences. Indeed, he grew so animated that Lee had to remind him just why they had gathered. Grant apologized. They sat down beside a small, round table and Grant scribbled out a surrender document. The terms were generous. The rebels were paroled and could simply go home. Those who owned horses could keep them. Officers could retain their swords and sidearms. Lee expressed his gratitude. Each signed the document.

Afterward, Grant introduced Sheridan and his staff to Lee. When he got to Ely Parker, a Seneca Indian, Lee remarked, "I am glad to see one real American here." To this Parker offered the appropriate and hopeful reply, "We are all Americans here."[10]

The generals strolled outside together. Lee mentioned that his twenty-five thousand remaining men were starving. Grant immediately ordered three days of rations sent to the Confederate camp. Then each mounted, saluted, wheeled, and rode back to his headquarters.

Abraham Lincoln made the last speech of his life on April 11. Having won universal abolition with a series of small steps, he sought to do the same for black civil rights. In doing so, he tried to straddle the gap between liberals and conservatives and gradually, gently, reasonably pull the latter toward the former. Racial equality was an end so distant that it was beyond the political horizon. Yet as for the right to vote, he "would myself prefer that it were now conferred on the very intelligent and on those who serve our cause as soldiers."[11]

This was the first time that Lincoln publicly declared his support for black suffrage. Had he lived out the full four years of his second term, he would have undoubtedly returned to the notion of racial equality, each time suggesting a few more steps that he believed would pull conservatives toward liberals, who ideally wanted immediate and genuine equality.

The notion of equal rights between blacks and whites doubtless angered many people in the crowd, none more than John Wilkes Booth. For months Booth had plotted with a small group over ways to either kidnap or kill the president. He now made up his mind which method to take.[12]

Lincoln met with his cabinet and General Grant on April 14. Stanton noted that he had never seen Lincoln "grander, graver, more thoroughly up to the occasion." Seward recalled that everyone present "expressed kindly feelings toward the vanquished" and had a "hearty desire to restore peace . . . with as little harm as possible to the feelings or the property of the inhabitants." The key question was just how to reform and reunite the rebel states. "We can't undertake to run state governments in all these southern states," Lincoln concluded. "Their people must do that—although I reckon that at first some of them may do it badly."[13]

The president assigned each department an appropriate role in overseeing each state's rehabilitation, with war providing security, treasury collecting and disbursing revenues, justice upholding the laws, interior disposing of public lands, and the postmaster general reestablishing the post offices and mail routes.

Lincoln ended the meeting cheerfully by predicting that they would soon receive good news. His expectation came from a recurring dream that had most recently visited him the previous night and always preceded a great victory. In the dream he was in "some singular indescribable vessel . . . moving with great rapidity towards an indefinite shore."[14] That night the president and his wife attended the play *Our American Cousin* at Ford's Theater.

3

Reconstruction, 1865–1876

13

Revolution

The right of revolution is never a legal right. . . . At most it is
but a moral right, when exercised for a morally justifiable
cause. When exercised without such a cause, revolution is
no right, but simply a wicked exercise of physical power.

ABRAHAM LINCOLN

The whole fabric of southern society must be changed. . . . Without
this, this Government can never be as it has been, a true republic.

THADDEUS STEVENS

This is a country for white men, and by God, as long as I
am President, it shall be a government for white men.

ANDREW JOHNSON

Do you inquire why, holding these views . . . I accept
so imperfect a proposition? I answer, because I
live among men and not among angels.

THADDEUS STEVENS

After Appomattox, American armies swiftly mopped up the last rebel
forces. With twenty thousand men, Gen. Joe Johnston surrendered
the largest surviving Confederate army to Gen. William Sherman at
Durham, North Carolina, on April 26. The war effectively ended on

May 10, when Union cavalry captured Jefferson Davis and his entourage at Irwinsville, Georgia, even though the Confederate government never signed an official surrender document with the United States.

Although ultimately the sheer weight of Union arms crushed the outgunned rebels, the American victory was as much a triumph of economic as military power. Economically the Civil War invigorated the North and devastated the South. During the 1860s the North's economy swelled by 50 percent and the South's shriveled by 60 percent. In all, the North's share of the U.S. economy soared from 70 percent to 88 percent, while the South's shrank from 30 percent to 12 percent. Per capita income among southerners dropped from two-thirds to two-fifths that of northerners. Every southern state was bankrupt. In all, the war destroyed about two-thirds of the South's wealth.[1]

Finally, there was ideological triumph of Americanism itself. Gen. Ulysses Grant, along with countless other northerners, saw a southern victory beyond its military and economic devastation: "There was no time during the rebellion when I did not think . . . that the South was more to be benefited by its defeat than the North. The latter had the people, the institutions, and the territory to make a great and prosperous nation. The former was burdened with an institution abhorrent to all civilized people not brought up under it, and one which degraded labor, kept it in ignorance, and enervated the governing class. . . . The war was expensive to the South as well as to the North, both in blood and treasure, but it was worth the cost."[2]

The people of Washington City celebrated the war's end by cheering the largest parade of raw military power in the nation's history. It took two eight-hour days for two hundred thousand victorious troops to march down Pennsylvania Avenue from the Capitol to the White House, with Gen. Gordon Meade's Army of the Potomac passing on May 23 and Gen. William Sherman's Army of the Tennessee the next day. In the reviewing stand scores of prominent people joined President Andrew Johnson and Gen. Ulysses Grant to watch the astonishing procession.

The more thoughtful among Americans pondered the costs of victory. The rebellion was crushed and the nation was reunited at the official toll of 617,528 lives, of which the Union lost 364,511 and the Confederacy 253,017; the actual number of soldiers and civilians who died was

Table 1. Federal spending and debt (in millions of dollars)

	FEDERAL BUDGET	DEFENSE BUDGET	NONDEFENSE BUDGET	% DEVOTED TO DEFENSE	BUDGET DEBT	NATIONAL DEBT
1860	$78.0	$29.0	$49.0	37%	$13.4	$64.8
1861	$80.2	$36.4	$43.8	45%	$30.3	$90.6
1862	$485.9	$437.9	$48.0	90%	$425.6	$524.0
1863	$726.1	$663.6	$62.5	91%	$602.0	$1,119.8
1864	$878.0	$781.5	$96.5	89%	$600.9	$1,815.8
1865	$1,331.3	$1,170.3	$161.0	88%	$963.0	$2,680.7
1866	$536.2	$343.4	$192.8	64%	-$36.3	$2,773.2

Source: Rick Beard and Richard Rabinowitz, "The Legacy of the Civil War," in National Park Service, *The Civil War: 150 Years*, table 1, http://www.nps.gov/features/waso/cw150th/reflections /legacy/page2.html.

recently estimated to have surpassed 750,000. Another one million men from both sides were wounded, with hundreds of thousands crippled physically and emotionally. As in all wars up to the twentieth century, germs were deadlier than bullets—among official Union soldier deaths, battle killed 110,070 and disease 249,498, or together one in six of the 2,213,363 men who served in the Union army. The Confederate losses were even more horrendous. Of the million southerners who fought for the rebel cause, one-quarter died and another quarter were wounded.[3]

The North's military, economic, and ideological triumph was as dearly bought in treasure as in blood. The cumulative military, nonmilitary, and total federal budgets from 1861 to 1865 were $3.1 billion, $411.8 million, and $3.5 billion, respectively. Americans were no more eager to pay for the Civil War as they fought it than other generations were for their respective wars. For every six dollars of expenses, they paid off one dollar with existing revenues and borrowed the other five dollars from future generations. As a result, the national debt skyrocketed from $90.6 million in 1861 to $2.7 billion in 1865.

With the war over, Washington rapidly demobilized the army and navy. The army numbered over a million men on May 1, 1865, but fell to 152,000 by New Year's 1866 and 38,000 by December 1866. The army was split between regiments occupying the South and the West. The defense budget plummeted by nearly three-quarters, from $1.17 billion in 1865 to $343 million in 1866. Meanwhile nondefense spending rose from $161 million to $192 million as the nation's interests shifted from destroying to reconstructing the South.

While everyone agreed on the vital need for Reconstruction, there were sharp differences over what it meant and how to do it.[4] For virtually all northern and most southern whites, the challenge was primarily emotional. Hundreds of thousands of households had to adjust to the terrible loss of loved ones who were either killed or whose bodies or minds were shattered during the war. Reconstruction for countless southerners was quite literal—it meant rebuilding all that the war had destroyed, including not just the ruined houses, barns, warehouses, courthouses, mills, bridges, railroads, factories, and plantations but an entire economy and society. It took the South a decade or so to restore most of what had been physically destroyed and more than a century to catch up economically with the northern states.

Radical Republicans had more in mind for the vanquished South than emancipating slaves and pardoning rebels in return for loyalty oaths.[5] Only a sweeping political, economic, and social revolution could justify the loss of 750,000 lives and billions of dollars of wealth. Abolition was merely the first stage toward the realization of American ideals for all Americans. Senator Charles Sumner of Massachusetts explained that "we must insist upon Equal Rights as the condition of the new order of things." Representative Thaddeus Stevens of Pennsylvania insisted that "the whole fabric of southern society must be changed. . . . How can republican institutions . . . exist in a mingled community of nabobs and serfs?" Representative George Julian of Indiana contrasted his vision for the South's future with its sordid past: "Instead of large estates, widely scattered settlements, wasteful agriculture, popular ignorance, social degradation, the decline of manufacturers, contempt for honest labor, and a pampered oligarchy, you want small farms, thrifty tillage, free schools, social independence, flourishing manufactures and the arts, respect for honest labor, and equality of political rights."[6] In other words, Radical Republicans sought to remake the South in the image of the North.

To impose this revolution, the Radicals legally armed themselves with the Constitution, especially Article IV, Section 4: "The United States shall guarantee to every State in this Union a Republican form of Government." Politically, they enjoyed majorities in both houses of Congress and coordinated their policies and bills through the Joint

Committee on Reconstruction. Yet they faced overwhelming economic, political, social, and cultural forces that ultimately either gutted or stunted nearly all their efforts.

Abolition resolved a massive human rights problem that had festered for centuries, but it created two new overwhelming problems: where and how would four million freed slaves live?[7] Virtually all were trapped in a vicious cycle of being penniless, landless, and illiterate. If they stayed with their masters they would be little better off than when they were chattel. In effect, they would have simply exchanged slavery for serfdom, while remaining mired in poverty and exploitation. But what was the alternative?

Plenty of land was certainly available. Many slaveholders abandoned their plantations after their slaves either fled or became unmanageable. Other estates went on the auction block because the owners were bankrupt or failed to pay their taxes. Radical Republicans argued that the crisis of black landlessness could be resolved simply by confiscating the property of their former masters and dividing it equally among them. Powerful political forces prevented this from being implemented on a scale large enough even to begin to resolve the problem of black landlessness.

During the war a few enterprising commanders tried various land and wage programs that alleviated conditions in their respective regions. The largest effort was in Louisiana. In 1862 Gen. Benjamin Butler enacted a contract system between former plantation masters and slaves whereby the former guaranteed the latter fixed amounts of wages, food, clothing, and housing in return for fixed work hours. His successor, Gen. Nathaniel Banks, established a uniform rate of three dollars a month or the equal division of 5 percent of the plantation's earnings for set work hours and the inability of blacks to leave without the owner's permission. The system peaked with fifty thousand laborers on fifteen hundred plantations.[8]

Gen. Ulysses Grant initiated a similar program in the region occupied by his troops. In November 1862 he assigned Gen. Lorenzo Thomas to enact this policy. Thomas gave black men in refugee camps a choice among signing up as a soldier, military laborer, or plantation worker. Army privates got ten dollars a month; laborers for the military or private sector earned seven dollars if they were male and five dollars if they were female. President Lincoln was so impressed with the program that, in 1863, he asked Treasury Secretary Salmon Chase to take over and expand it to all Union-occupied rebel territory. Chase briefly considered raising wages and directly administering plantations leased from owners, but a lack of money, skilled administrators, and above all, potential profits killed that plan.

Humanitarians criticized these programs for perpetuating the subjection of blacks rather than liberating them. They argued that true freedom could come only when blacks had their own farms and businesses. A general soon provided them with a working model with which to realize this goal.

Gen. William Sherman met with twenty local black leaders at Savannah on January 12, 1865, and asked them how the government could best help their people. Their primary request was for land of their own. This inspired Sherman's famous "forty acres and a mule" policy. In the Sea Islands off the Georgia and South Carolina coasts most owners had fled their plantations. In Field Order Number Fifteen, Sherman had those lands confiscated and redistributed to the blacks who lived there. He envisioned each family owning a forty-acre plot in a zone extending from the coast thirty miles inland.

Inspired by Sherman's policy, Radical Republicans passed the Freedmen's Bureau Act that established the Bureau of Refugees, Freedmen, and Abandoned Lands on March 3, 1865. The Freedmen's Bureau was empowered to break up any abandoned or confiscated lands into forty-acre tracts and give them away to black men. The bureau had a lot of land to give away—850,000 acres in 1865. For Radical Republicans this was not enough. Thaddeus Stevens proposed confiscating an additional 394 million acres owned by the South's landowners, arguing that it would be "far easier to exile 70,000 proud, bloated, and defiant rebels than to expatriate 4,000,000 laborers . . . even if the owner was willing to sell at the postwar depressed price."[9]

The man Lincoln picked to head the Freedmen's Bureau could not have been a better choice. Gen. Oliver Otis Howard was a courageous and skilled general who lost an arm at Fair Oaks and eventually rose to command a corps in the Army of the Potomac.[10] He was an outstanding administrator and humanitarian. Howard University would be named for him. Under Howard's leadership, the Freedmen's Bureau expanded its duties from resettling blacks on land of their own to providing desperately needed food, jobs, skills, schools, health care, and civil rights.

The Freedmen's Bureau's greatest short-term success was to avert mass starvation. During the war tens of thousands of slaves escaped from their plantations. As word of the rebel surrender spread, tens of thousands more blacks left their masters to search for freedom. The result was a massive refugee problem whereby countless blacks lived a hand-to-mouth existence in shantytowns on the fringes of cities or army camps. Malnutrition was pervasive but mass starvation loomed with the second refugee wave at the war's end. In just fifteen months after the war, the bureau handed out thirteen million rations, each of which included enough cornmeal, wheat flour, and sugar to feed one person for a week.[11]

Education was perhaps the Freedmen's Bureau's most notable long-term success. Every southern state except Tennessee outlawed schooling for blacks. Despite this law, some masters taught their slaves or slaves secretly taught themselves. At the time of emancipation nine of ten blacks could not read or write. Efforts by blacks to organize schools were hampered by a lack of qualified teachers and money. By 1869 the bureau had established a system of three thousand lower schools with ten thousand teachers and 150,000 students as well as founded the colleges of Atlanta, Fisk, Hampton, Alcorn, and Tugaloo.[12] Booker T. Washington graduated from Hampton College and went on to achieve renown as an educator and scientist.

Education was not just a federal government effort. Liberal church and humanitarian groups also contributed. The most famous was Gideon's Band, or the Gideonites, composed of young graduates of Harvard, Yale, and other elite universities who devoted a year or so to living in the South and teaching blacks how to read, write, and do sums. They tended to be highly idealistic, with a vision of black people and southern whites shaped by *Uncle Tom's Cabin*. Not surprisingly, southern whites feared and hated them and did what they could to drive them away.

The efforts of the Freedmen's Bureau and liberal groups to promote education were more symbolic than substantive. The pilot schools that they established pointed the way to a better future but usually died after they left. Only state governments had the power to devise and fund school systems that embraced all children and other needy people. During the postwar decades, one southern state after another did erect the bare bones of a system. The trouble, then as now, was the American practice of decentralized education whereby local tax receipts finance local schools. This practice was as disastrous in the South as elsewhere. Schools were segregated by class and race. The wealthier the district, the more likely its schools got first-rate teachers, administrators, buildings, and textbooks, and the poorer the district, the more likely essential elements of education were wanting. Black schools tended to be as poverty-stricken as their surrounding neighborhoods. Thus did public school systems reinforce rather than diminish the South's racist and feudalistic economic, social, and political hierarchy. By 1880 seven of ten southern blacks remained illiterate.[13]

The Radical Republicans' clear vision and political heft were not powerful enough to realize their liberal political and economic revolution. White supremacists in each southern state fought and eventually beat them every step of the way. But until March 4, 1869, their most formidable foe was in the White House.

Andrew Johnson was sworn in as the president of the United States on April 15, 1865, shortly after Abraham Lincoln died. Historians generally rate him among the very worst presidents.[14] Solid reasons ground that damning assessment. From virtually his first days in power, he asserted increasingly conservative policies that provoked more Republicans to despise, resist, and finally, impeach him. In short, Andrew Johnson failed utterly at the art of power. General Sherman observed, "He attempts to govern after he has lost the means to govern. He is like a General fighting without an army."[15]

What explains Johnson's transformation from a centrist into an increasingly hardened conservative? Perhaps most important were the demons lurking in his psyche. He was notorious for being stubborn, short-tempered, and intolerant. Although he was a politician, he lacked such fundamental skills as the ability to forge relationships and cut deals. Like Lincoln, he was born into poverty and rose steadily in wealth, status, and power largely by his own efforts. Yet, unlike Lincoln, as Johnson struggled to be a "self-made man," he was inspired by Andrew Jackson and the Democrats rather than Henry Clay and the Whigs. He lacked Lincoln's deep intellect and morality. He felt cowed rather than inspired around people of greater learning and erudition in Washington and elsewhere. He bristled at the southern planter elite and later at the northern New England elite who looked down on him as a nouveau riche hillbilly. He especially hated northern liberals, who tended to be far more nimble of mind and tongue than himself. As president he longed to assert control but liberals stole the show.

The result was a vicious circle whereby the more he reacted against Radical Republicans, the more openly they displayed their contempt for him. Symbolically this culminated with a White House visit by Senator Charles Sumner, who hoped to strike a deal. Johnson angrily rejected Sumner's arguments and showed him to the door. Outside Sumner put on his top hat and discovered that Johnson had used it as a spittoon![16]

Johnson was a racist to the very core of his being. He not only held slaves most of his life but believed that ideally the practice should be universal: "I wish to God every head of a family in the United States had one [slave] to take the drudgery and menial service off the family." Even after he grudgingly accepted abolition's inevitability during the Civil War, he insisted that "freedom simply meant liberty to work and enjoy the products of their labor and that was all there was of it." Any notion of equal rights enraged him: "This is a country for white men, and by God, as long as I am President, it shall be a government for white men." Yet he did support a limited franchise for blacks, a position between liberals who advocated complete and equal suffrage for all males and conservatives who would deny any black the right to vote. He explained his view to William Sharkey, whom he had named Mississippi's governor: "If you could extend the elective franchise to all persons of color who can read the Constitution . . . and write their names, and . . . who own real estate valued at least two hundred and fifty dollars, and pay taxes therein, you would completely disarm the adversary [liberal Republicans], and set an example the other states will follow."[17]

The first clash between Johnson and Republicans was over personnel rather than policy. Determined to pack his administration with loyalists, he initiated sweeping firings and hirings. Yet this attempt to assert and swell his power backfired. The loss of a job converted many a moderate Republican into a liberal determined to resist Johnson by whatever possible means. Johnson's purge inspired Congress eventually to pass the 1867 Tenure of Office Act that forbade the dismissal of any federal official unless the Senate had approved his successor.

Johnson's most controversial acts directly attacked Radical Republican policies. On May 29, 1865, he issued a proclamation promising a blanket amnesty, pardon, and return of all property except slaves to nearly anyone with less than $20,000 of assessed wealth who took an ironclad oath to the United States and its Constitution; those with more than $20,000, along with former federal officers and officials who turned traitor and prominent rebel officers and officials, had to apply for amnesty. In practice, Johnson assured that virtually any applications were rubber stamped. Johnson's policy of forgiveness was a stunning political and moral flip-flop. After Lincoln's assassination, he had angrily asserted that "treason must be made odious. . . . Traitors must be punished and impoverished . . . their social power destroyed."[18]

In the end, although by definition any U.S. citizen who either fires on the American flag or orders others to do so is a traitor, only three rebel leaders were deprived of their liberty, or in one case his life, for their treason. President Jefferson Davis was imprisoned without trial for two years. Vice President Alexander Stephens served just a few weeks before he was released. Henry Wirz, the notorious commandant of the Andersonville prisoner-of-war camp where thirteen thousand of the forty-five thousand inmates died from disease and starvation, was found guilty of war crimes by a military tribunal and executed. Another fifteen thousand or so southerners with more than $20,000 of assessed wealth were initially deprived of their rights to vote or run for public office, but they swiftly regained these rights after applying to the federal government.

To his credit, Johnson did try to take his arguments to "the people." In August 1865 he launched a speaking tour of the northern states to justify his policies and ask folks to vote for candidates who upheld his views. Yet if his intent was constructive, his performance was dismal. When a heckler in a Cleveland audience interrupted his speech with the cry, "Hang Jeff Davis," Johnson replied, "Why not hang Thad Stevens and Wendell Phillips?"[19]

Johnson abruptly ended the Freedmen Bureau's land redistribution policy in September 1865 by issuing a directive restoring confiscated lands to former owners who took the ironclad oath. Over forty thousand blacks had actually taken title when Johnson killed the policy and had government officials expel them from their new homes. After liberal Republicans drew up and passed the Freedmen's Bureau bill that renewed for two years the institution and its policies, Johnson vetoed it on February 19, 1866.

After mustering two-thirds majorities that overrode the veto, Republicans passed the 1866 Southern Homestead Act, which allocated three million acres of public lands in the South for blacks and loyal whites if claims were filed before 1867 and extended landownership to unmarried black women. When Johnson vetoed the bill, Republicans promptly overrode the veto. The good intentions behind this bill collided with the realities of what was actually being given away. Public lands in the South were mostly swamps or tangled forests, hardly fit for viable farms or comfortable lives. Only four thousand black families acquired land under the bill, mostly in Florida. How many of those homesteads survived, let alone flourished, is unknown.

No matter where they lived, nearly all rural blacks remained trapped in poverty's vicious cycle. Without the low-interest loans available to most whites, they could not buy the land, seed, equipment, draft animals, and other essentials needed to establish a viable farm. Instead they had no choice but to become dependent on loan sharks to borrow money for all their needs at predatory prices. Thus for generations they remained debt-ridden and poverty-stricken peasants rather than becoming middle-class farmers. Sharecropping was pervasive and entrenched across the South for more than a century. Generally the tenant gave away two-thirds of his crop if he borrowed money and merely half if he did not. Yet there was some limited progress. From 1860 to 1900 landownership among blacks rose from less than 1 percent to 20 percent, while illiteracy diminished among blacks from about nine of ten to about one of two.[20]

Poverty, debt, and malnutrition afflicted not just blacks but many rural whites. The value of the average southern farm plummeted from $22,819 to $2,340 from 1860 to 1870, with much of this loss caused by the elimination of $3 billion worth of slave property. Farm production fell steadily after the war as blacks cut back their work hours. The result was less food at higher costs. In contrast, the bottom fell out of cotton prices, which, before the war, were the road to riches for plantation owners. Supply and demand explains why. When the Civil War erupted, southern cotton accounted for two-thirds of global supply. The rebel leaders tried to capitalize on this dependence. The Confederate president, cabinet, and congress agreed to withhold the 1861 cotton harvest to provoke a British economic crisis, then British intervention on the South's side. The crisis came, the British did not. Instead Britain and other cotton consumers looked for alternatives. Within a few years, textile factories spun cotton grown in India, Egypt, and elsewhere. After the war, southern cotton planters tried to recapture their former markets. The result was a global cotton glut whereby prices plummeted as growers tried to undercut each other.[21]

Radical Republicans sought to liberate blacks politically as well as economically. In early 1866 they introduced a civil rights bill that passed the House by 33 to 12 on February 2 and the Senate by 111 to 38 on March 12. This law was a major step toward upholding the liberal democratic ideals upon which America's independence as a nation and system of government were justified. It defined a citizen as anyone other than an Indian born or naturalized in the United States. It granted to all citizens equal rights for making contracts, bringing lawsuits, and enjoying protection for one's person and property. Finally, it empowered the federal government to prosecute those who violated any citizen's rights. Yet there was a glaring omission. Nowhere did the bill mention the right to vote.

Nonetheless, this bill was too radical for conservatives, including President Johnson, who vetoed it on March 27, 1866. He justified doing so by insisting that the bill was unconstitutional, violated "states' rights," would make blacks lazy and dependent on the government, and would encourage mingling between the races. The veto at once enraged and inspired liberals. First they overrode the veto with votes of 35 to 19 in the Senate and 126 to 47 in the House. Then they sought to solidify the law with a constitutional amendment.

In contrast to the Thirteenth Amendment's short and simple language abolishing slavery, the Fourteenth Amendment contained five sections of related rights asserted in ponderous legalese. Section 1 granted citizenship to all people (except Indians) born in the United States or to naturalized immigrants, forbade any state from depriving any citizen of his or her privileges or immunities, and guaranteed equal protection and due process to uphold the life, liberty, and property of any person. Section 2 apportioned congressional seats according to the total of all people (except Indians) in a state and thus eliminated the notorious previous constitutional tenet that counted a slave as three-fifths of a person. A state's representation in Congress could be reduced if it denied the right to vote to any male twenty-one years of age or older except for unpardoned rebels or criminals. Section 3 denied any federal elected or appointed office to anyone who had previously taken an oath to the United States and violated it as a rebel or given aid and comfort to America's enemies. It empowered Congress to override this rule by two-thirds votes of both houses. Section 4 guaranteed the payment of America's national debt but forbade Washington or any state government from servicing the rebel government's debt. Finally, Section 5 empowered Congress to enforce the amendment with appropriate laws.

While liberal and moderate Republicans agreed on all these tenets, they differed over whether to include voting among the rights of citizenship. The omission proved to be a huge loophole that let racists in the states use various devices to deny suffrage to blacks. Although moderate Republicans insisted on the language that excluded voting in order to entice Democrat votes, not a single Democrat in Congress voted for the amendment. In the end, liberals held their noses and voted for the diluted amendment as a far lesser evil than having no civil rights at all. Thaddeus Stevens explained that reasoning, "Do you inquire why, holding these views . . . I accept so imperfect a proposition? I answer, because I live among men and not among angels."[22]

Despite the compromises, the Fourteen Amendment was revolutionary. It overturned the Supreme Court's 1833 *Barrow v. Baltimore* ruling that required only Washington and not the states to uphold the Bill of Rights and the 1858 Dred Scott decision that denied citizenship to blacks. For these and other reasons conservatives did all that they could to kill it. They nearly succeeded. Initially ten former rebel states rejected the amendment; only Tennessee voted in favor. For the time being this effectively shelved the Fourteenth Amendment.

Meanwhile President Johnson fought the Radical Republicans on every issue. In 1866 he abolished the military commissions that the Freedmen's Bureau used to protect black civil rights. This forced blacks to appeal to southern judicial systems dominated by conservatives who either denied them standing or dismissed their cases. Then, in January 1867, he vetoed yet another liberal bill, this one granting blacks the right to vote in the District of Columbia. Liberals overrode this veto and vetoes on two more laws in 1867, the Habeas Corpus Act, which made it easier for citizens to appeal to federal courts, and the Peonage Act, which outlawed forced labor to pay off debts. Johnson was hardly the only critic of those bills; he simply represented the prevailing conservative view. Yet liberals could be just as blistering by arguing that these bills were toothless expressions of principles that would never work in practice unless backed by federal authority.

The conservative obstructionism by Johnson and the former rebel states inspired Radical Republicans to devise a blueprint for the South's transformation from slavocracy to democracy. They had the power to enact their blueprint, since they emerged from the November 1866 election with veto-proof congressional majorities of 128 to 33 in the House and 61 to 11 in the Senate. Congress passed reconstruction acts on March 6, March 23, and July 19, 1867, with each new one remedying the defects or bolstering the powers of the preceding. The first, known as the Military Reconstruction Act, split the eleven former rebel states among five military districts with each under martial law. A state could revert to equal status within the United States only after fulfilling two requirements. First, it had to write, ratify by a majority of registered voters, and enact a constitution that guaranteed equal protection, due process, and universal manhood suffrage for all white and black men. Second, it had to vote for ratification of the Fourteenth Amendment. The United States deployed twenty thousand troops to help enforce that act. Federal civilian or military officials were empowered to remove any state officials or persecute anyone who denied the civil rights of any citizen. Johnson vetoed each act and Congress overrode each veto. This allowed the Fourteenth Amendment to join the Constitution on July 9, 1868.

Passing progressive laws and constitutional amendments was tough enough. Realizing the letter and spirit of these measures was nearly impossible. For newly liberated blacks, the political marketplace was as alien as the economic marketplace. Yet blacks had enormous potential political power. They outnumbered whites in South Carolina, Mississippi, and Louisiana and made up sizable minorities elsewhere. Regardless of what share of a population they held, it was in black interests everywhere to forge an alliance with whatever liberal or moderate whites could be found.

Across the South progressive whites were either a minority or a nullity. To varying degrees, every southern state was split between low country and up country. Slavery's viability as an economic and thus political and social system diminished as the land's altitude and tilt increased and its fertility decreased. Slavery flourished in the flat, rich soils of the tidewater region, less so in the piedmont, and was a curiosity in any state's mountainous region. The zealotry of secessionists naturally varied with slavery's prevalence. Across the South, Unionists dominated local politics in northern Alabama and Georgia; western Virginia, North Carolina, and South Carolina; Arkansas's Ozarks; and Texas's Hill Country. Unionists tended to be Republicans and thus natural allies for blacks.[23]

Three institutions helped prepare blacks for the rights and duties of citizenship. Wherever they existed, black churches became bastions for addressing political problems and developing civic skills among their members. The trouble was that at first there were so few of them. Southern whites had mostly discouraged and often repressed black churches during slavocracy. Churches proliferated after abolition. The army was the best training ground for black leaders. Despite racial double standards for promotion, the army was largely a progressive institution. Military life instilled pride, discipline, and hope for nearly all and a platform for upward economic and political mobility for some. The historian Eric Foner found veterans among "forty-one delegates to state constitutional conventions, sixty-four legislators, three lieutenant governors, and four congressman."[24] Finally, the Freedmen's Bureau set up Union Leagues of literate blacks, church leaders, and former soldiers. Liberal Republicans and northern black leaders journeyed south and founded radical associations that mobilized southern blacks to assert their political rights, especially equal protection and suffrage.

Blacks increasingly began to organize themselves politically. As early as 1862, a group in New Orleans founded the newspaper *L'Union* with first a French, then a bilingual edition that addressed the array of problems facing free and still-enslaved blacks. *L'Union*'s success inspired another group to begin publishing the *Tribune* in 1864. Under Jean Houzeau's expert editing, the *Tribune* became renowned not just for championing humanitarian causes but also for its literary style. Houzeau and a group of other black leaders founded the Equal Rights League to fight discrimination against blacks in suffrage and streetcars. In May 1864 a group in Beaufort, South Carolina, elected and sent sixteen delegates to the Republican Party convention. The first recorded elections in which blacks voted in the South occurred at Mitchelville, on one of South Carolina's Sea Islands, and Amelia Island, Florida, in 1865.

The result across the South was token political progress. A two-party system between conservative Democrats and liberal Republicans briefly flared in the southern states during Reconstruction, then died as white supremacists retook power. In all, 2 blacks, both from Mississippi, served in the U.S. Senate and 15 blacks won seats in the House of Representatives, while 633 blacks served as state legislators. Most southern whites did everything possible to stunt black political power, and they largely succeeded. Black voting turnouts peaked in the 1872 election. The number of black federal or state elected or appointed officials nosedived after 1876, when the last federal troops and officials were withdrawn.[25]

Liberal Republicans could thwart President Johnson's obstructionism in only two ways—they could override and impeach. They mustered enough votes to enact bills over most of his vetoes. Meanwhile they searched for an excuse to impeach him. In the impeachment process, the House of Representatives acts like a grand jury and the Senate like a jury. Johnson's enemies first tried with a vote on December 5, 1867, but the list of impeachment charges was so flimsy that only 57 congressmen supported it while 108 voted against it. Then, a few months later, Johnson gave his enemies the excuse to rally a majority against him.[26]

Johnson's character clearly harbored an aggressive and self-destructive dimension. He loved to goad his ever-lengthening list of enemies despite, or more likely because of, their power to retaliate. He knew that his enemies would pounce after he dismissed Secretary of War Edwin Stanton on February 21, 1868, but he defiantly did so anyway. In firing Stanton, he at once got rid of a hated cabinet member and challenged a hated law. Eleven months earlier, in March 1867, he had vetoed on constitutional grounds the Tenure of Office Act that forbade a president from firing a federal appointee until the Senate confirmed his successor. Congress overrode his veto. When the House of Representative voted 128 to 47 for eleven articles of impeachment against Johnson on February 24, 1868, nine were related to his firing of Stanton. The charges then went to the Senate for the actual trial. He was acquitted in three separate votes in which each resulted in thirty-five senators voting for and nineteen against conviction, one shy of the required two-thirds majority. The first vote was on May 16 and the second and third votes on May 19, 1868.

Johnson was not humbled by the impeachment charges or by winning acquittal by only one vote. He continued to speak out angrily against the Radical Republican agenda and on December 25, 1868, gave the former rebel leaders the Christmas gift of their lives when he granted them unconditional amnesty. Each was now free to resume all the rights of citizenship.

Four days after the Senate acquitted the president by a single vote, the Republican Party convention opened in Chicago on May 20. The next day the delegates unanimously acclaimed Ulysses Grant their presidential nominee. Upon accepting the nomination, Grant endorsed the party's platform and ended his speech by simply declaring, "Let us have peace."[27]

The Democrats took a lot longer to forge a consensus behind a candidate. It was not until the twenty-first ballot that two-thirds of the delegates endorsed for president Horatio Seymour, then New York's governor and formerly New York City's mayor during the draft riots that he was partly responsible for provoking.

Grant crushed Seymour by winning 214 to 80 electoral votes, twenty-six to eight states, and 52 percent of the popular vote. He had never before held elected office and was the youngest man yet to be elected president. This was either irrelevant or advantageous in his supporters' minds. After all, Grant was the general whose strategy had ultimately destroyed the Confederacy. They hoped that he would bring the same relentless vigor to restoring the nation.

14

Night Riders and Black Codes

There will be some black men who remember that, with silent tongue
and clenched teeth and steady eye and poised bayonet, they have
helped mankind on to this great consummation while, I fear, there
will be some white ones unable to forget that with malignant
heart and deceitful speech, they have strove to hinder it.

ABRAHAM LINCOLN

Slavery is dead. The negro is not, there is the misfortune.

CINCINNATI ENQUIRER

The slave went free; stood a brief moment in the
sun, then moved back again toward slavery.

W. E. B. DUBOIS

Bitter animosities disrupted the protocol of Ulysses Grant's presidential
inauguration. En route to the Capitol, Grant's carriage stopped briefly
before the White House. Johnson sent word that he was too busy to
attend the ceremony. This actually relieved Grant, who loathed Johnson. Yet the incident gave his administration a sour start. In his address,
Grant reassured Americans that "I shall on all subjects have a policy
to recommend, but none to enforce against the will of the people."[1]

The polices that Grant recommended over the next eight years were shaped by diametrically opposed ideologies. Conservatives cheered Grant's policies that bolstered the power of the corporate business world. Yet ethically Grant was a genuine liberal. He promoted civil rights for blacks, a just peace for Indians, free public secular education for all children, the strict separation of church and state, and the taxing of church property. He boldly called on the American people to uphold their nation's ideals of "free thought, free speech, a free press, pure morals unfettered by religious sentiments, and of equal rights and privileges to all men, irrespective of nationality, color, or religion."[2] In 1871 he established the Civil Service Commission to transform federal officials from creatures of political patronage into professionals.

Four powerful related forces prevented Grant from realizing his progressive agenda. Conservatives in Congress and the Supreme Court eventually gutted all of his proposed reforms. Allied with these conservative politicians were increasingly powerful business corporations. From the beginning his administration harbored people who betrayed the trust of the president and the nation. Finally, there were the flaws in Grant's own character—he was too unquestioningly loyal to his friends and family, too fawning before powerful business magnates, and too easily susceptible to the get-rich-quick schemes of shysters.

The Senate approved most of Grant's initial cabinet picks, including John Schofield as secretary of war, Ebenezer Hoar as attorney general, Jacob Cox as interior secretary, Adolph Borie as navy secretary, and John Cresswell as postmaster general. For various political reasons, the senators turned down Elihu Washburne and Alexander Stewart as the respective secretaries of state and treasury, although they did eventually approve Hamilton Fish and George Boutwell for these posts. Ely Parker, a Seneca, became the Indian affairs commissioner. Grant tapped Orville Babcock, Horace Porter, and Frederick Dent, a brother-in-law, to be his secretaries. Only Fish stayed with Grant throughout his eight years in the White House, while twenty-three men served as other department secretaries. Each resignation had its own unique reasons, but many left either under the stench of scandal or after accepting a golden parachute from one of the corporations that their department was supposedly overseeing.

Meanwhile liberal attempts to impose a sweeping political, economic, social, and cultural revolution on the South never took root.[3] The progressives overreached and thus provoked the racist counterrevolution that they hoped to forestall. Southerners hated the "Yankees" who arrived in their midst to enact reforms or make money. They dismissed them all as "carpetbaggers" and condemned all southerners who worked with them as "scalawags" or "white negroes."

Southern conservatives were dead set to undermine and eventually crush the liberal revolution imposed upon them. Increasingly systematic and violent terror was the key means whereby they did so. Mobs rampaged against "uppity" blacks in the cities, while night riders bullied and murdered blacks in the countryside. Terrorist groups like the Ku Klux Klan, White Camellias, Red Shirts, and White League became the Democratic Party's military wing. Conservatives understood how to manipulate the minds of blacks. For instance, the Klan wore white robes both to assert their racial supremacy and to terrorize superstitious blacks who believed that they were the ghosts of Confederate soldiers. Those who fought to turn back the clock called themselves "redeemers" who sought the "redemption" or restoration of their political, economic, and social rule. They eventually succeeded in retaking power.[4]

White supremacist violence during Reconstruction was nothing new. It differed only in scale from that of the antebellum era. Across the South, violence was a time-honored means whereby conservatives retained their dominance. Masters not only whipped defiant slaves mercilessly, they could literally get away with murder. Militia patrolled the roads at night to intimidate slaves against leaving their quarters. After the war, southerners simply resumed their old habits. They justified their terrorism as self-defense.

Southern whites everywhere felt ever more besieged, especially in the cities. The war was over, their cause had lost, and they were overrun by Yankee troops, bureaucrats, businessmen, do-gooders, and thousands of blacks scrounging for food, shelter, and jobs. Prices and crime rates soared. Atop all that, the Yankees imposed measures of "Negro Rule" that "Africanized" the South politically, economically, and culturally. Desperate whites looked for any excuse to reassert their control.

The first mass violence erupted in Memphis in May 1866, when forty-six blacks and two whites died. The death toll—thirty-four blacks and three whites—was only slightly less horrific in New Orleans in July 1866. Of the latter bloodbath, Gen. Phil Sheridan reported that "it was no riot, it was an absolute massacre by the police without the shadow of a necessity."[5] The worst mass murder of all took place in Colfax, Louisiana, in April 1873, when whites slaughtered perhaps 280 blacks. In New Orleans in September 1874, thirty-five hundred White Leaguers routed black militia and white police in the battle of Liberty Place and captured the city hall, statehouse, and arsenal. They relinquished these positions and dispersed only when President Grant ordered federal troops to retake the city. All four massacres came from white mobs reacting to Reconstruction policies by venting rage on blacks and white officials.

While white supremacist mobs in cities and towns inflicted the worst massacres on blacks, night riders in the countryside murdered far more. Conservatives did not just target politicians but cross-haired officials, relief workers, ministers, teachers, and businessmen as well. Indeed, they considered as fair game anyone who helped alleviate the plight of blacks and tried to fulfill America's ideals. Black political leaders were prime targets. One of ten black delegates who attended the state constitutional conventions of 1867 and 1868 was a victim of white supremacist violence. The White League murdered six Republican officials in Red River Parish, Louisiana, in August 1874, just months before that year's election. In all, white supremacists shot, hanged, burned, or tortured to death over a thousand blacks and a score of whites from 1865 to 1868 alone. During those three years in Texas, whites murdered 372 blacks while blacks murdered 10 whites.[6] These statistics reveal numbers, not motives. Just how many were politically driven will never be known. One thing is certain. The intimidation or outright murder of "uppity" blacks was the most effective means whereby conservatives eventually regained power.

For years, Washington did nothing to quell the worsening terrorism. Instead the federal government unwittingly encouraged the violence by steadily reducing the number of troops deployed across the South and stationing many regiments far from where the worst crimes took place. The demobilization was rapid, with the number of occupation troops plummeting from 1 million in April 1865 to 152,000 by December 1865 and a mere 6,000 by December 1871. The latter number remained fairly constant until the newly elected president Rutherford Hayes ordered them withdrawn within days after entering the White House in March 1877. Yet federal policies were legally hamstrung by the constitutional constraint that made law and order a state rather than federal duty.

Liberal governors like Robert Scott of South Carolina, Powell Clayton of Arkansas, and Edmund Davis of Texas eventually suppressed the Klan and other terrorist groups. They did so by declaring martial law, organizing blacks into militia companies, forming state police forces, planting informers in hate group ranks, and making mass arrests. In Texas alone, officials rounded up six thousand Klan suspects. Although few terrorists were prosecuted, most groups decided to disperse and lay low.[7]

This strategy did not work everywhere. North Carolina governor William Holden tried it but backed off when conservatives mobilized opposition in the state assembly and newspapers. Democrats won back control of North Carolina in the 1870 election. This same year for similar reasons conservatives recaptured the governments of Alabama and Georgia.

The worsening violence, demise of liberalism, and reassertion of conservative rule across the South finally provoked a reaction among liberal and conservative Republicans alike. General Sherman expressed the consensus that "I am willing to . . . again appeal to the power of the nation to crush, as we have done before, this organized civil war."[8] But Washington lacked the full legal authority to do so.

With the Fifteenth Amendment, liberals sought to cut the Gordian knot of nefarious southern techniques to disenfranchise blacks. The wording was straightforward: "Section 1. The right of citizens of the United States to vote shall not be denied or abridged by the United States or by any State on account of race, color, or previous condition of servitude. Section 2. The Congress shall have the power to enforce this article by appropriate legislation." Two-thirds majorities in Congress approved the Fifteenth Amendment on February 26, 1869, and three-fourths of the states ratified it by March 30, 1870. But, as always, enforcement was immeasurably more difficult than passage.

President Grant sought new powers to counter the white supremacist terrorism spreading across the South. On May 31, 1870, he signed the Enforcement Act, the first of three versions that empowered the federal government to crack down on certain categories of crime, including terrorism and civil rights violations. Thereafter Washington could intervene through the federal court system if state and local officials failed to uphold the law. The headquarters for this war against racism and terrorism was the newly established Department of Justice, headed by the attorney general and including an Office of Solicitor General.

Armed with the power not just to issue indictments but to declare a state of insurrection in a county or an entire state and to suspend habeas corpus, the Justice Department issued over three thousand indictments in 1871, with six hundred ending in convictions. This broke the power of the Ku Klux Klan and other terrorist groups.[9]

This victory, however, was fleeting. Tragically, Washington intervened too late. The Confederacy was not the era's only "lost cause." Reconstruction lasted just a few years before white supremacists killed it. While the Justice Department could defeat terrorist groups, it could not transform the white supremacist culture that nourished them. The federal government simply lacked enough courts, prosecutors, officials, and troops to begin to confront the South's pervasive racism and violence. Atop this, conservatives steadily retook governor's mansions, statehouses, city halls, and state and local courts and did all they could to thwart federal initiatives. They did so largely by stuffing ballot boxes and beating or murdering liberals.

Then, while they could not restore slavery, they could nullify the liberal reforms, impose an apartheid system, and solidify their rule by gerrymandering electoral districts to render their power impregnable. Ironically, slavery's abolition actually helped boost conservative rule. After the 1870 census, the South got more congressional representatives because each black was counted as one person rather than three-fifths of a person.

Faced with constant harassment and violence, progressive politicians and social workers increasingly gave up and left. Northern humanitarian groups cut their losses. The turning point came in 1874, when the New England Freedmen's Aid Society disbanded itself and the American Missionary Association stopped sending liberal ministers to the South. The same year, Democrats recaptured Congress and reversed or ended virtually all Reconstruction programs. This conservative counterrevolution was perhaps best symbolized when Congress rescinded the 1866 Southern Homestead Act and opened southern public lands to railroad, lumber, and mining corporations.

With liberals rousted, one by one the southern states enacted black codes that curtailed both civil and labor rights. Laws made it all but impossible for blacks to vote, usually by imposing literacy and tax requirements. Laws forced blacks to sign work contracts binding them to white employers, and they could be jailed and fined up to $500 if they broke their contract or worked for someone else. Laws forbade blacks from migrating to cities and confined those already living there to certain "colored" districts. Laws either segregated or outright barred blacks from schools, transportation, lodging, restaurants, hospitals, parks, and orphanages. Laws forbade marriage between blacks and whites. Laws either forbade blacks from owning firearms or limited the number and type. Laws barred blacks from juries. Laws let banks discriminate against giving loans to blacks. Laws let officials issue business licenses to blacks that effectively limited them to certain occupations in certain districts. The result of this conservative counterrevolution was to lock most southern blacks into peonage, debt, illiteracy, poverty, and humiliation. W. E. B. Dubois captured the essence of what happened: "The slave went free; stood a brief moment in the sun, then moved back again toward slavery."[10]

Reconstruction was not confined to the South. Most northerners were just as racist. The *Cincinnati Enquirer* bluntly expressed the feelings of countless whites when an editorial declared, "Slavery is dead. The negro is not, there is the misfortune."[11] Before the Fifteenth Amendment was ratified only eight northern states permitted blacks to vote and nearly all discriminated against blacks in other ways. Although one by one the northeastern states abolished slavery after the United States won independence, most of them, along with new northern states that forbade slavery, enacted black codes that, to varying degrees, imposed limits on blacks for lodging, transport, schooling, dining, marriage, property ownership, employment, service on juries or in the military, voting, and running for public office, to cite the more prominent. The North's antebellum black codes inspired the South to emulate them after the war.

The 1866 Civil Rights Law forced northern and southern states alike to rewrite their constitutions and legal systems. Northern states largely complied while southern states resisted. Thereafter northern blacks could vote, serve on juries, and testify against whites; relatively few southern blacks enjoyed those fundamental rights. Yet social and economic racism across the North remained pervasive. City and state ordinances continued to limit where blacks could live, work, go to school, dine, and lodge and whom they could marry.

President Grant unwittingly aided the conservative counterrevolution by his Supreme Court. appointments. In doing so he reversed a shift from conservatism to liberalism that began after President Lincoln appointed progressive Salmon Chase to replace slavocrat Roger Taney as the chief justice in 1864. Chase's court issued two notable liberal decisions. In the 1866 *Ex Parte Milligan* decision the Supreme Court ruled that military courts could not replace civilian courts as long as civilian courts continued to operate. In the 1869 *Texas v. White* decision a majority upheld the constitutionality of Washington's reconstruction policies and asserted that the Constitution had established "an indestructible Union, composed of indestructible States," and thus there was no legal foundation for secession and the governments of those states that had seceded were illegal. Under the "Guarantee Clause," Congress was empowered to restore "republican" forms of government to the rebel states.

Grant was torn between a genuine liberal belief in justice and opportunity for all and a conservative Social Darwinian belief that might makes right. The conservative side of his nature was ascendant when he appointed four corporate lawyers as justices, including Morton Waite as the chief justice after Salmon Chase died on May 7, 1873. The result was a nearly unbroken succession of decisions that bolstered the power of corporations' and states' rights over civil rights and the public good.[12]

The Slaughterhouse Cases of 1873 were the first major Supreme Court rulings against the federal government's ability to promote republican governments and civil rights in the states. The plaintiffs were white butchers in Louisiana who challenged a monopoly granted by Republican Party officeholders to a slaughtering company partly owned by blacks. They argued that the monopoly violated their Fourteenth Amendment due process right. In a five to four decision, the Supreme Court rejected the butchers' suit with the dubious claim that the Fourteenth Amendment distinguished state and national citizenship.

The Supreme Court hammered two of the last nails into Reconstruction's coffin with key decisions in 1876. In *United States v. Reese* the justices struck down the 1870 Enforcement Act that empowered the federal government to uphold civil rights in the states. In *United States v. Cruikshank* they ruled that solely the states and not the federal government nor individuals were required and empowered to uphold the Fourteenth and Fifteenth Amendments. The *Cruikshank* decision was especially egregious because it threw out the convictions of three men found guilty of participating in the Colfax, Louisiana, massacre of 280 blacks by a white mob.

Yet this same year the Supreme Court bucked its own conservative trend and issued two surprisingly progressive decisions that bolstered Hamiltonism. Indeed, the nation's first treasury secretary could have ghostwritten Chief Justice Waite's key argument in *Munn v. Illinois*: "When private property is devoted to a public use, it is subject to public regulation." In *Welton v. Missouri* a majority ruled that "interstate commerce shall be free and untrammeled," thus overturning a Missouri law that violated this constitutional principle.

White supremacism was hardly the only problem afflicting the United States during the Reconstruction era. Corruption is endemic in American politics. It does, however, vary in scale and brazenness from one era to the next. Corruption soared with the industrial revolution as corporate leaders diverted portions of their soaring fortunes to buy off politicians and bureaucrats. The subsequent favors helped concentrate the profits from economic growth in fewer hands as increasingly larger corporations asserted monopolies or oligopolies over more industries. The result was what Mark Twain dubbed the Gilded Age, characterized by the elite's accumulation of unprecedented wealth while the middle class and poor got poorer. The power of the "robber barons" to corrupt politicians steadily morphed the Republican Party from liberalism and populism into conservatism and corporatism. Plutocracy or government of the rich, by the rich, and for the rich trumped Lincoln's championing of American democracy of the people, by the people, and for the people.[13]

At the federal level, the potential for corruption expanded with the size of the government's budget and the number of government personnel. The more complex a department's budget, the more opportunities for officials to engage in creative bookkeeping to reward supplicants for kickbacks. Presidents could potentially fill as many as a hundred thousand federal government positions. This is a lot of political payback.

Ulysses S. Grant presided over one of the more corrupt administrations in America history. High-ranking officials forced to resign under corruption charges included George Robeson, the navy secretary; William Belknap, the war secretary; George Williams, the attorney general; Columbus Delano, the interior secretary; and William Richardson and George Williams, successive assistant treasury secretaries. Congressional investigations forced their resignations. While Grant himself was not venal, he turned a blind eye and deaf ear to the blatant pillaging of public resources for private gain not just by many of his subordinates but by family members including his brother-in law John Dent, his brother Orville, and his wife, Julia. When allegations arose against any of them, Grant reacted with angry denials and defenses of the accused. With time, confronted by overwhelming evidence of guilt, he realized that some members of his inner circle had hoodwinked him as well as the nation. He felt deep sorrow at being betrayed by those whom he trusted. In his last speech to Congress, in December 1876, he admitted, "Failures have been made resulting from errors of judgment, but not of intent."[14]

What explains such behavior, which was at best neglectful and at worst devious? Grant's biographers describe him as naïve, trusting, loyal to his friends, and admiring of those who acquired great wealth. Grant himself had failed at every business he ever started and was deeply grateful to the friends who helped him out when he was struggling. All this is clear enough, but Grant's character harbored dimensions that may never be completely understood. William Sherman was Grant's friend for many years but ultimately concluded, "He is a mystery to me and I believe a mystery to himself."[15]

The Gold Ring was the first scandal to rock Grant's White House. Jay Gould and Jim Fisk were Wall Street speculators who concocted a plot to corner the gold market. To aid their scheme, they enlisted Grant's secretary Horace Porter and brother-in-law Abel Corbin by entangling them in webs of kickbacks, conflicts of interest, and insider trading. Through Corbin, Gould won what he believed was Grant's acquiescence to push gold prices ever higher. By September 23, 1869, Gould and Fisk had bought up over $100 million in gold that was selling for $160 an ounce. They hoped to dump their horde when the price reached $200. Had they succeeded, they would have made a killing and sparked a financial meltdown that would have thrown the economy into a deep and prolonged depression.

Fortunately, Treasury Secretary Boutwell got wind of the machinations and, with Grant's approval, sold off $5 million of gold. Within a few days, the price of an ounce dropped to $130. This broke the Gold Ring and other speculators who had been selling on margin. While the selloff produced a short recession, it avoided a catastrophe had prices plummeted from $200. The federal government's decisive intervention was a first in American economic history.

The Grant White House was also darkened by a scandal that actually began when Andrew Johnson was president. The Union Pacific Railroad Company's directors registered a dummy corporation named Credit Mobilier in Pennsylvania. Credit Mobilier's purpose was to act as a conduit for bribes to congressmen in the form of huge wads of cash, stocks, and, for the most cooperative, seats on the board of directors. Credit Mobilier's point man in Congress was Representative Oakes Ames of Massachusetts. Not everyone he approached was venal. A few were so appalled by such blatant corruption that in 1873 they succeeded in forming House and Senate committees to investigate. The committees found plenty of circumstantial evidence to implicate numerous senators and representatives but only enough hard evidence to punish three people: the House censored Ames and James Brooke of New York, who was a Union Pacific director, while the Senate expelled James Patterson of New Hampshire.

The Whiskey Ring was a group who developed a system of kickbacks to convince tax collectors to turn a blind eye to liquor sales. During 1874 and 1875 alone, the Whiskey Ring cost the federal treasury $4 million in revenues. Treasury Secretary Benjamin Bristol spearheaded the investigation. Orville Babcock, Grant's personal secretary, was indicted on corruption charges in St. Louis. The jury acquitted Babcock after listening to the president's three-hour testimony on his behalf; apparently Grant's presence so awed the jurors that they ignored a mountain of evidence of Babcock's guilt.

The Indian Ring developed a system whereby speculators bought Indian trading post concessions from high-ranking officials. In 1876 Secretary of War William Belknap was accused of pocketing $25,000 for the Fort Sill concession. Although the House Judiciary Committee voted to impeach him, he was eventually acquitted.

These scandals came to light because one of Grant's department secretaries was determined to eliminate corruption from all ranks of government. From his appointment in June 1874, Treasury Secretary Benjamin Bristow and his staff launched an anticorruption crusade that eventually purged nearly eight hundred lower-ranking officials on various charges. Liberals sought not just to purge but to transform the system. To this end they worked to reform the civil service from a patronage into a professional system with increased government efficiency and reduced corruption.[16]

Corruption was hardly confined to the White House or Washington. Big cities were the tar babies of American politics. Competing for urban votes inevitably meant taking and making payoffs. To facilitate these ends and means Democrats constructed vast big-city political machines, with "Boss" William Tweed's New York operation the most inspiring or notorious, depending on one's values. Tweed's most vital allies were the financial giants Jay Gould and Jim Fisk. So how could Republicans curry favor when they were outgunned locally? To compete, Republicans had to outbid Democrats. If Democrats emphasized a grassroots organization that mobilized the lower class, Republicans increasingly courted the socioeconomic pinnacle—financiers, railroaders, and manufacturers.[17]

The Civil War had a revolutionary impact on how most Americans saw the world. Before 1861 nearly all Americans, northerners and southerners alike, viewed abolitionism as a radical notion. By the Civil War's end, this once-radical notion had become mainstream, accepted by most northerners moralistically and most southerners fatalistically. However, other views still struck most Americans as radical, most notably equal rights not just for blacks, but for women and workers as well.[18]

The women's rights movement emerged from the 1848 Seneca Falls Convention but never attracted a large following and receded during the Civil War, when its leaders agreed to resume their pre-1848 emphasis on abolition over feminism. In 1863 Susan B. Anthony and Elizabeth Stanton established the National Women's Loyal League to mobilize support behind the Thirteenth Amendment that ended slavery. Women who worked in the abolition movement gained vital skills, confidence, and connections. With the crusade to abolish slavery won, some activists retired, others sought other worthy causes to champion. For most the choice was obvious. Having won freedom for slaves, they now worked toward winning equal rights for women.

To this end, Stanton and Anthony founded the National Woman Suffrage Association. The drive for female suffrage scored two victories when the territories of Wyoming and Utah granted women the right to vote in 1869. The motivations, however, were practical rather than principled. With only one female for every seven males, Wyoming men hoped to entice single women to their realm with the promise of equality. The vote for women in Utah let Mormon males retain their political majority, since many of them had two or more wives. Elsewhere sexism remained as entrenched as racism, delaying female suffrage until 1920.[19]

The temperance movement was a channel through which women could assert their latent political power indirectly. Women at once advocated traditional family and Christian values along with their political rights by condemning alcoholism and saloons for impoverishing and breaking up families and communities. Activists formed the Women's Christian Temperance Union in 1874. By showing their ability to mobilize and rationally take a stand on an issue, these women refuted arguments that they were too emotional and flighty to vote, let alone run for office.[20]

In sheer numbers, the labor movement far surpassed the suffrage movement. Workers increasingly tried to organize themselves and win shorter workdays, more pay, and better conditions. Charles Dana, a liberal Massachusetts Republican, popularized the eight-hour workday movement. With wartime restrictions over, workers began to back their demands with strikes. The largest came in 1867, with a general strike in Chicago. This was surpassed in 1872, when as many as one hundred thousand workers shut down New York City. All along conservatives condemned the labor movement as socialist or communist assaults on private property and free enterprise. They killed any attempts at establishing federal jobs, relief programs, or regulation of wages, workplace safety, and railroad-carrying costs. As with women's rights, the struggle for workers' rights was launched during the Age of Lincoln but took generations to achieve.

The Civil War had a revolutionary impact on the national economy.[21] The North's economy swelled steadily as the South's withered. The transition from a war to a peace economy was remarkably swift and painless. From 1865 to 1873 America's industrial output soared by 75 percent, with nearly all this in the North. Around thirty-five thousand miles of new train tracks were laid, mostly across the northern and western states. Three million immigrants set foot in the United States, again virtually all in the North.

Congress accelerated this uneven regional growth with laws and policies. Of $104 million in federal funds dispensed for internal improvements from 1865 to 1873, the South received a mere $4.4 million.[22] The West was the primary benefit of the Mineral Acts of 1866, 1869, and 1873 that gave away public land, eventually amounting to millions of acres, to mining companies that staked and developed claims. The West again largely benefited from the Railroad Act of 1862, whereby Washington handed out over 125 million acres to railroad companies from then to 1872 alone, and eventually 223 million acres. Federal subsidies to the railroads varied from $16,000 to $48,000 per mile, depending on the difficulty of construction. This policy symbolically culminated on May 10, 1869, when a golden spike was driven into the last rail of the transcontinental railroad at Promontory Point, Utah, joining the Central Pacific tracks laid from San Francisco and those of the Union Pacific from Omaha. Railroad subsidies, however, like corporate welfare for other powerful industries, have persisted ever since.[23]

The first bill that Grant signed into law was the Act to Strengthen Public Credit on March 18, 1869. The law promised holders of bonds and greenbacks that Washington would redeem those notes with "gold or its equivalent." The bill realized its desired effect to cut inflation and boost confidence. Gold prices dropped along with other prices as the government bought more bonds and greenbacks.

The Supreme Court briefly undercut the administration's economic policies when it ruled unconstitutional the Legal Tender Act by a vote of four to three on February 7, 1870. The ruling disrupted financial markets, as greenback holders feared that their investments were worthless. Treasury Secretary Hoar appeared before the Supreme Court on March 31, 1870, and asked the justices to reevaluate their decision. They complied and issued a five to four decision on March 31, 1871, that reversed their previous decision.

The 1873 panic was triggered in September when Jay Cooke and Company, a key pillar of the financial system, imploded after failing to sell millions of dollars' worth of Northern Pacific Railroad bonds to service its vast debt. This set off a wave of bankruptcies through a financial system in which everyone was in debt to everyone else. The New

York Stock Exchange tried to stem the collapse by suspending trading for ten days after September 20, but the plummet resumed with the reopening of the exchange.

The result was a devastating depression. From 1873 through 1876, 21,559 businesses worth $668,742,000 declared bankruptcy. Average daily wages plummeted from $5.50 to $3.50. Perhaps as many as one in five workers was either jobless or underemployed. Railroads, the economy's literal and figurative engine, took a severe beating, with 89 of 364 companies going belly up. The economy gradually revived after 1876.[24]

In this Darwinian market age, the federal government lacked the power to contain the collapse and conservatives fought attempts by progressives to give Washington such powers. On April 14, 1874, seven months after the 1873 panic began, Congress passed a bill that would have released $100 million of government reserves into the economy to reinflate it, but Grant succumbed to conservative pressure to veto the bill. He did, however, resist conservative calls to sharply cut back government spending, which would have exacerbated the depression. All along he sought a middle ground between economic progressives and conservatives. To that end, he signed on January 14, 1875, the Resumption Act whereby on January 1, 1879, Washington resumed specie payments for its debts that were suspended early in the Civil War.

The depression drastically affected the labor movement. Initially laborers set aside their eight-hour workday vision to demand either jobs or public relief for the homeless and hungry. The "work or bread" movement peaked with the Tompkins Square riot in New York in January 1874, when police broke up a crowd of seven thousand protestors. This prompted Samuel Gompers, who headed the American Federation of Labor (AFL), to narrow the goals of the movement from broader social issues to specific issues of wages, hours, and safety. At one point, when asked just what the AFL wanted, Gompers famously answered "more." Workers on railroads and in western mines struck for higher pay in 1874, and those in the textile and coal mining industries in 1875. The collapse of food prices prompted hard-pressed midwestern farmers to organize the Grange movement, which advocated the regulation of railroad carrying costs and price supports for crops. The Grange movement peaked in 1876, with over eight hundred thousand members in fourteen thousand locals.[25]

The ultimate nightmare for capitalists were the Molly Maguires, Pennsylvania coal miners so incensed at abysmal pay and conditions that they terrorized business owners. In May 1876 twenty went on trial for a variety of charges, including arson and murder. All twenty were found guilty and condemned to death by hanging.

Reconstruction faded away amid these other national issues, crises, and movements. The Civil Rights Act of 1875 was Reconstruction's last legal hurrah. The law prohibited racial discrimination in public areas but provided Congress no powers to enforce it. White southern congressmen ensured that the law was toothless.

What southern conservatives failed to win with armies, they won with terrorists. During Reconstruction mobs and night riders murdered thousands of blacks and scores of whites who sought racial equality. For years President Grant and liberal Republicans tried to crush these terrorist movements, but they eventually gave up. American troops, officials, and aid workers were withdrawn. White supremacists ruled the South for another century and remain a powerful political force to this day.

All that remained of Reconstruction were unenforceable constitutional amendments and civil rights laws that granted liberty and equality to all Americans, black and white. Southerners did all they could to render this legal framework "dead letters on the statute book."[26] In each state, conservatives gutted the legal system with black codes that deprived blacks of civil rights and condemned them to separate and grossly unequal public facilities like schools, transportation, lodging, restaurants, and even drinking fountains. In the countryside, feudalism replaced slavery; while blacks were theoretically free and could earn their own income, most remained chained to the land as poverty-stricken sharecroppers who gave up much of their crops and deepened their debts to rich landlords. Given all this, some historians have questioned Reconstruction's significance. C. Vann Woodward pointed out "how essentially nonrevolutionary and conservative Reconstruction was."[27]

In assessing why Reconstruction failed, President Grant concluded that "the wisest thing would have been to have continued . . . military rule. That would have enabled the Southern people to pull themselves together and repair material losses. Military rule would have been just to all: the negro who wanted freedom, the white man who wanted protection, the Northern man who wanted Union."[28]

But even this would have been inadequate. What was needed was a cultural revolution and that was impossible. The South has always been and likely always will be dominated by one ideology—conservatism. At different times different parties have served as conservatism's vehicles—Jefferson's Republican Party from the 1790s through the 1820s, Jackson's Democratic Party from the 1820s to the 1932 election, and Reagan's Republican Party from the 1980s through today and for the indefinite future.

This legacy causes most analysts to agree with Eric Foner, the era's most prolific historian: "What remains certain is that Reconstruction failed and that for blacks its failure was a disaster whose magnitude cannot be obscured by the genuine accomplishments that did endure. For the nation as a whole, the collapse of Reconstruction was a tragedy that deeply affected the course of future development."[29]

15

Frontiers

Can not the Indian be made a useful and productive
member of society? If the effort is made in good faith,
we will stand better before the civilized nations of the
earth and our own consciences for having made it.

ULYSSES S. GRANT

This is a measure which is inspired by corporate greed and
natural selfishness against national pride and beauty.

SAMUEL COX

If they are hungry, let them eat grass.

ANDREW MYRICK

Call me Ishmael.

HERMAN MELVILLE

Nations, like people, define themselves by what they do and why they
do it. This is what makes each nation, like each individual, unique. Of
all the metaphors attached to the American experience, perhaps none
is more appropriate than *frontier*. The word first evokes the nation's
expansion across the continent and beyond, a process characterized
by the displacement, destruction, and death inflicted on the original

inhabitants, the hardscrabble lives of most subsequent settlers, the vast riches reaped by the lucky enterprising or privileged few, and the justification of it all through the ideology of Manifest Destiny.[1]

Even after the United States expanded across the continent, many powerful citizens and corporations were not content to accept the Pacific Ocean as America's final frontier; they wielded the ideology of Manifest Destiny to seek lands, markets, and influence in increasingly distant regions of the world. The United States began to become a global imperial power during the Age of Lincoln, wielding gunboat diplomacy to force open Japan, buying Alaska from the Russians, squaring off with France over its puppet regime in Mexico, and meddling in the affairs of such faraway island nations as Hawaii, the Dominican Republic, and Cuba, among others. The American frontier was increasingly anywhere around the globe where the Stars and Stripes fluttered or a deal was cut.

A second meaning of *frontier* became increasingly evident during the nineteenth century and helped make sense of the first. Ever more Americans journeyed deeper within themselves to explore their own creative frontiers through writing, painting, and other arts. In doing so they better defined who they were along with the nation that created them. But in all of this exploration and development of frontiers during the Age of Lincoln, the establishment of the world's first national park in 1872 arguably had the most revolutionary impact of all.

Imperialism is the conquest and exploitation of one people and their territory by another. By this definition America was imperialist from its inception when, in May 1607, a hundred or so Englishmen disembarked on foreign soil and began clearing land for a settlement they called Jamestown. British imperialism in America was a joint venture of the government and private companies. Enterprises received charters to establish colonies in demarcated parts of America; when they failed, the government took over and directly ruled the colony. Some imperialist groups had ambitions as broad as the continent. The Crown granted charters to several companies entitling them to strips of land stretching from the Atlantic Ocean westward all the way to the Pacific Ocean. Yet, however indomitable Britain's empire may have appeared on a map, the monarchy's grip over thirteen of its American colonies was insidiously eaten away as each generation of colonial inhabitants became less British and more American.

The U.S. government formally inherited this imperial role when it declared independence from Britain in July 1776. Like its predecessor, American imperialism was a partnership whereby the government promoted and protected private companies that invaded and exploited designated lands and in the process killed or drove off whatever Indians were living there. No grand strategy guided American imperialism any more than it had British imperialism. The United States spread across the continent as different administrations took advantage of opportunities that arose to acquire new territory from the nation's neighbors, either by diplomacy or by war followed by diplomacy. Each acquisition involved a two-step diplomatic process. The first was with whichever country had legal title to the land, whether it was Britain, Spain, France, or Mexico. The second was with whatever Indian tribes actually lived there, a process that took decades and even generations depending on the territory's size, the accessibility of its resources to exploitation, and the resistance of its inhabitants.

In this imperial process, the American president inherited from the British king the title of "Great Father" to the tribes. In Indian eyes this role demanded that the president be generous and just to his "red children." Although most presidents took this moral and legal role seriously rather than approaching it cynically, they had to contend constantly with political forces beyond their control.

Powerful interest groups sought to enrich themselves by seizing and exploiting Indian lands. They expected and demanded that not just the president but Congress and the courts collaborate with them to do whatever it took to realize their ambitions. These groups either pressured Washington to war against and take the land of tribes with valuable resources, or they bribed officials to violate federal laws, regulations, and policies so that they could wring more profits from their existing access.

Although the details differed from one tribe to the next, American imperialism toward the Indians followed a distinct pattern. The influx of Americans onto a tribe's land violated existing treaties and eventually provoked war. The U.S. Army inevitably won the war. The federal government then imposed a treaty whereby the defeated tribes ceded land in return for a "guaranteed" territory, usually farther west, a pile of goods upon signing the treaty, and annual receipt of goods thereafter. Then, sooner or later, greed-driven Americans would begin violating the new Indian territory, thus igniting the same vicious cycle of invasion, war, and dispossession.

When peace prevailed it was anything but just. Indian policy enriched contractors and agents at the expense of the tribes. For every four dollars in the federal budget for Indian affairs, corruption stole and inefficiency squandered three dollars; only one dollar actually reached the Indians and it was often all but worthless. Tribes bitterly complained that their annuities consisted of spoiled or scanty food, rotten blankets, sickly livestock, and broken promises. As if this were not bad enough, ethnic cleansing became increasingly important to Indian policy as agents and missionaries tried to convert Indians into farmers, Christians, and second-class Americans. Genocide, however, was never a federal government policy. No administration ever sought to exterminate any one tribe, let alone all Indians.[2]

Although American imperialism west of the Mississippi River began with the 1803 Louisiana Purchase, it did not peak until the Age of Lincoln. Before then the federal government supported private interest groups by negotiating access treaties with tribes, issuing trade licenses, and dispatching several exploring expeditions across swaths of the West. During the 1830s President Jackson forced the eastern tribes to sign treaties that took their land and forced them west along a Trail of Tears to settle in allotments between the Red and Platte Rivers. From 1803 to 1854 the army fought only one Indian war west of the Mississippi River, in 1823 against the Arikaras after they attacked a trapping party encamped beside their villages on the Missouri River.[3]

The first major assertion of American power did not come until 1846, when President Polk forced Britain to cede Oregon Territory south of the forty-ninth parallel and began a war with Mexico that led to the conquest of California and New Mexico. These huge acquisitions provoked a policy debate. The president and a congressional majority understood that Washington's institutions had failed adequately to manage the existing lands west of the Mississippi River and were incapable of governing all this new territory, especially the populous Mexican settlements with their alien culture.

To remedy this, they established the Interior Department and transferred the War Department's Indian Bureau to it in 1849. Forts were erected along trails leading to the west coast, up the Missouri River, on the Texas frontier, and in New Mexico and California. Congress divided then subdivided the West based on white settlement. After five thousand or more Americans settled in a region, Washington organized it into a territory with an appointed governor and three judges; when the population surpassed sixty thousand, the people could apply for statehood. The Interior Department drew its own lines across the map that encompassed groups of tribes; designated an Indian superintendency for each; appointed superintendents and agents and awarded contracts to companies to supply annuities; and eventually negotiated a treaty or more with each tribe on issues of war, peace, trade, and land. The most ambitious effort was the 1851 Fort Laramie council, when Indian commissioners signed treaties with most of the northern plains tribes, including the Sioux, Cheyennes, Arapahos, Crows, Gros Ventres, Assiniboines, Mandans, and Arikaras. A similar set of treaties was signed with the southern plains tribes the Comanches, Kiowas, and Apaches at Fort Bent on the Santa Fe Trail in 1853. These agreements designated tribal regions and sought to keep the peace among the tribes as well as between them and the Americans.

Violence erupted despite these efforts. In August 1854 a war broke out with the Brule band of Sioux after an emigrant complained to Fort Laramie's commander that an Indian had killed and butchered his stray cow. Lt. John Grattan marched with thirty men to the nearby village, demanded compensation, and after Chief Conquering Bear dismissed the notion, ordered his men to open fire. Although the initial volley killed Conquering Bear, the enraged Brules slaughtered Grattan and all but one of his men, then packed up and fled northward. The army was so thinly spread across the West that a retaliatory expedition was not organized until 1855. Col. William Harney and his six hundred dragoons and infantry finally reached and attacked the Brules at Ash Hollow in western Nebraska in September. The troops killed eighty-five Brules and captured seventy women and children while losing four killed, seven wounded, and one missing. Harney sent the captives with an escort to Fort Kearney as he marched northward after the hundred or so Brules who escaped. In October the expedition reached Fort Pierre on the Missouri River without having found any Indians along the way. In March 1856 Harney signed a treaty with the Brules and several other Sioux bands whereby the chiefs agreed to a system in which a head chief would be responsible for any violence or theft by any village member.

War after war followed, some with as trivial a cause as the Brule war, others with far more at stake, like gold in the Black Hills. The army fought the Jicarilla Apaches and Utes in 1854; the Mescalero Apaches in 1855; the Yakamas in 1855 and 1856; the Cayuses, Walla Wallas, Pelouses, and Umatillas in 1856 and 1857; the Cheyennes in 1856; the Comanches and Kiowas from 1857 through 1859; the Chiricahua Apaches from 1857 to 1860; the Mohaves from 1858 to 1859; the Navajos from 1858 to 1861; the Mescalero Apaches from 1861 to 1864; the Gila Apaches from 1861 to 1865; the Dakota Sioux from 1862 to 1864; the Shoshones, Bannocks, Utes, and Gosiutes from 1862 to 1863; the Navajos from 1863 to 1865; the Cheyennes and Oglala Sioux from 1863 to 1865; the Comanches from 1864 to 1865; the Yanktonais, Santee, and Teton Sioux in 1865; the Oglala, Brule, Hunkpapa, Sans Arc, Miniconjou, Blackfoot, and Two Kettle Sioux, Cheyennes, and Arapahos from 1865 to 1868; the Cheyennes, Comanches, and Kiowas from 1867 to 1868; the Mescalero and Gila River Apaches from 1867 to 1869; the Paiutes from 1866 to 1869; the Piegan Blackfeet from 1869 to 1870; the Modocs from 1872 to 1873; the Chiricahua, Warm Spring, Mimbre, and Mogollon Apaches from 1872 to 1873; the Comanches, Cheyennes, and Kiowas from 1874 to 1875; and finally, the Hunkpapa, Brule, Two Kettle, Sans Arc, Blackfoot, and Miniconjou Sioux, Cheyennes and Arapahos from 1876 to 1877. This was hardly the end of the bloodshed. Most Indians died during the 1850s, when gangs of armed civilian men, at times backed by the army, slaughtered thousands among the largely peaceful tribes of California and Oregon west of the Sierras and Cascade Mountains to steal their land, in retaliation for usually minor crimes, or just for sadistic pleasure.[4]

These wars shared characteristics across the different regions where the army operated and the different tribes that the army fought. Virtually all soldiers, especially West Point graduates and Mexican or Civil War veterans, found Indian warfare frustrating. All the tribes fought hit-and-run guerrilla wars against the Americans. Man for man, Indian warriors surpassed the soldiers in endurance, courage, stealth, riding, and shooting. Their villages were mobile and nearly impossible to catch up to as they hurried across the West's vast plains, deserts, or mountains.

At the rare times when an army column actually found a village, it was as likely to be peaceful as hostile. Despite the uncertainty, commanders often ordered an attack without bothering to determine the band's status. The most important reason was that surprise reduced one's own casualties and inflicted more on the enemy, while forcing the survivors to abandon their lodges and thus their ability to sustain themselves. But at times commanders and troops alike vented an explosive mix of racism and rage against known peaceful Indians and slaughtered women and children along with the men. Of the half-dozen massacres of peaceful villages, the most notorious was the murder of a hundred or more of Black Kettle's Cheyenne band at Sand Creek by Col. John Chivington and his Colorado volunteers in December 1864. For practical as well as moral reasons, the federal government disavowed these deliberate massacres.

How can a war be won against such an elusive foe? Generals like William Sherman and Phil Sheridan concluded that they could defeat the Indians only with the same total war strategy that had crushed the Confederacy. This meant destroying the hostile bands' ability to sustain themselves. Converging columns that kept Indians on the run prevented them from harvesting, hunting, or stealing food. The best season for pursuit was winter, when food and fuel were most scarce. To increase the army's mobility, supplies were packed on mules instead of in wagons. To increase the ability to find hostile bands, as many friendly Indians as possible were recruited as scouts. This strategy resulted in far more bands eventually giving up to avoid starvation than because of lost battles.

The dependence of the plains Indians on buffalo for their livelihoods made them especially vulnerable to Washington's total war and ethnic cleansing policies. Interior Secretary Columbus Delano candidly explained how in January 1874 testimony before the House Military Affairs Committee: "The buffalo are disappearing rapidly. . . . I regard the destruction of such game as Indians subsist upon as facilitating the policy of the Government, of destroying their hunting habits, coercing them on reservations, and compelling them to begin to adopt the habits of civilization." Before the same committee, Gen. William Sher-

man noted that the decimation of the buffalo was doing "more to settle the vexed Indian question than the entire regular Army has done in
the last thirty years."[5]

Although Abraham Lincoln genuinely sympathized with the Indians'
plight, he had little time to devote to Indian policy during his presidency. On March 27, 1863, in a meeting with fifteen plains chiefs at the
White House, he at once apologized for and asked for understanding
of the times when American officials or citizens violated treaties: "It is
the object of this government to be on terms of peace with you, and
try to observe them; and if our children should behave badly, and violate their treaties, it is against our wish." Most likely with a wry smile
as he imagined his own rambunctious offspring, he said, "You know it
is not always possible for any father to have his children do precisely
as he wishes them to do." To their request for "advice about their life
in this country," he offered an answer that they likely found at once
frustrating and refreshingly honest: "I really am not capable of advising you whether, in the providence of the great spirit, who is the father
of us all, it is best for you to maintain the habits and customs of your
race or adopt a new mode of life."[6]

Lincoln was especially sensitive to the dilemmas of Indian policy.
Just the previous year, one of the bloodiest Indian wars had erupted,
followed by the largest mass execution in American history, and as
president Lincoln made critical choices about who among the Indians
convicted of murder and rape would live or die.[7]

The chiefs of the Dakota Sioux had succumbed to pressure in 1851
to sign a treaty whereby they gave up twenty-four million acres of land
and their nomadic way of life to live in two narrow reservations along
the Minnesota River; the federal government promised to turn them
into farmers and annually give them money and food. Few Dakotas
adapted to the plow and by the summer of 1862 corruption, cheating,
and incompetence by the Indian Bureau and its contractors brought
them to starvation's brink. The annuities of food and money were late
and deficient. When Indians protested, a storekeeper named Andrew
Myrick quipped, "If they are hungry, let them eat grass."[8] Four desperate and enraged Sioux men murdered a white farm family that refused
to share their food with them, then admitted to the tribal council what
they had done. A majority of warriors called for an uprising that caught

the whites by surprise. The Indians struck on August 18 and over the next couple of weeks slaughtered over four hundred men, women, and children and captured hundreds more; some of the women were raped. Among those killed was Myrick; his body was found mutilated and his mouth stuffed with grass.

Gen. John Pope received orders to crush the Dakota Sioux. He expressed the collective outrage and demand for vengeance: "The horrible massacres of women and children and the outrageous abuse of female prisoners . . . call for punishment beyond human power to inflict. There will be no peace in this region by virtue of treaties and Indian faith. It is my purpose . . . to utterly exterminate the Sioux if I have the power to do so. . . . Destroy everything belonging to them and force them out to the plain. . . . They are to be treated as maniacs or wild beasts, and by no means as people with whom treaties or compromises can be made."[9]

Pope partly fulfilled his vision. Within a month the army had forced most Dakota bands to surrender and hand over any warriors who had participated in the uprising. This relatively easy victory came because the Indians ran out of ammunition and food and had no place to go for more. Under a treaty signed in 1863, the Dakotas surrendered all their land in Minnesota for land farther west, along the Missouri River in the Dakotas.

Meanwhile a five-man military commission tried those suspected of committing crimes during the uprising. The result was the most notorious example of "victor's justice" in American history.[10] The presiding judge was Henry Sibley, Minnesota's governor and a man who had enriched himself in part by skimming a fortune from contracts to supply provisions to the Dakotas. Transcripts of the proceedings reveal that most of the court's sentences were not grounded on hard evidence. Those who admitted to having participated in an attack were treated as having admitted to committing a crime. The commission tried 392 prisoners, sentenced 307 to death on charges of murder and rape, imposed 16 prison terms for lesser crimes, and released the rest.

President Abraham Lincoln was stunned by the verdicts. He had two legal experts spend weeks carefully examining the transcripts. Acting on their advice, he wielded his pardon power to either reduce or dismiss the sentences of 264 of those condemned to death. The announcement of his decision provoked a chorus of criticism, not just from Minnesotans and others in frontier states but from across the country. Although he did not publicly reply to his critics, he did unleash a pointed rejoinder to a remark that the Republicans might win more votes in the next election had more Indians been hanged: "I could not afford to hang men for votes."[11] This grim reply reveals Lincoln's paramount commitment to the rule of law. Nonetheless, the largest mass execution in American history took place at Mankato, Minnesota, on December 26, 1862, when trap doors dropped beneath thirty-eight men with nooses tightened around their necks.

Of the seven presidents during the Age of Lincoln, only Ulysses Grant expended ample time and thought on Indian policy and sought genuine reforms grounded on humanitarianism, efficiency, and justice. He did so because he sympathized with the Indians' plight and deplored past federal policies of conquest. In his first address to Congress, he condemned the "wars of extermination" against hostile tribes as "demoralizing and wicked. Our superiority should make us lenient toward the Indian."[12] In his second inaugural address, he issued this challenge to the nation: "Can not the Indian be made a useful and productive member of society? If the effort is made in good faith, we will stand better before the civilized nations of the earth and our own consciences for having made it."[13]

Grant acted on his principles. His first step was to free Indian policy from the corruption and incompetence of those who implemented it. To oversee his Peace Policy, he appointed a board of commissioners of ten prominent humanitarians, mostly Quakers. On May 27 he met with that board, along with Interior Secretary Jacob Cox and Indian Affairs Commissioner Ely Parker, himself a Seneca, at the White House. After explaining his policy, he empowered those men to reform the system through investigating, hiring, and firing, backed, if need be, by Justice Department subpoenas and prosecutions.[14]

Grant's Peace Policy was innovative in its quest to purge corruption from Indian policy and to uphold existing treaties. Unfortunately, Grant's efforts failed. Allegations of a corrupt "Indian Ring" forced the resignations of Interior Secretary Cox in 1870 and Indian Affairs Commissioner Parker in 1871, although a congressional investigation later exonerated Parker. This scandal was hardly the only failing of Grant's policy. He also unwittingly set in motion a conflict that would explode into the bloodiest Indian war west of the Mississippi River.

With the Civil War over, the nation's diplomatic, military, and business elite could once again devote themselves to expanding American wealth and power around the world. During the Johnson administration, Secretary of State William Seward and Senate Foreign Relations Chair Charles Sumner worked together to devise policies to protect or enhance specific national interests overseas.[15]

The most pressing problem was how to get a French army and regime out of Mexico. In 1861 France, along with Britain and Spain, had sent troops to Mexico to force its government to resume its debt payments. After the Mexicans did so, the British and Spanish withdrew their contingents. French emperor Napoleon III, however, took advantage of the civil wars raging in both Mexico and the United States to send an army to the capital and install in power his distant cousin Archduke Ferdinand Maximilian as his puppet emperor. Until 1865 concerned Americans could only glare angrily at such blatant French imperialism just beyond their southern border. Now, with the Confederacy destroyed and a million troops in its army, the United States could act. President Johnson sent fifty-two thousand troops to the Rio Grande and military aid to Benito Juarez, the rightful president, who held out with an army in northern Mexico. Over time, Mexican troops and guerrillas won back more of their country. In 1867 Napoleon III finally cut his losses and ordered his troops back to France. Shorn of this support, Emperor Maximilian's government collapsed and he was executed.

While Secretary of State Seward played a secondary role in these events, he was crucial in forging a deal that greatly enhanced American power. On April 9, 1867, he signed a treaty whereby the United States purchased Alaska from Russia for $7.2 million. The Senate ratified the treaty despite criticism of it as "Seward's folly" and "Seward's icebox." For the first time the United States had taken land beyond its immediate territory.

Later that year Seward signed a treaty whereby the United States would pay Denmark $7.5 million for its Virgin Islands territory of St. Thomas and St. John in the Caribbean. The timing could not have been worse. A hurricane and tidal wave wrecked those islands, while President Johnson faced impeachment charges. Seward tabled the treaty until a more opportune political moment arose to present it to the Senate for ratification. The result was a very long wait. The United States eventually acquired part of the Virgin Islands, but not until 1917.

Upon becoming president in March 1869, Ulysses Grant continued the policy of acquiring available foreign lands with economic and strategic importance. Yet this policy conflicted with his own principle: "I do not believe that the Creator ever placed the different races on this earth with a view of having the strong exert all his energies in exterminating the weak."[16]

Hamilton Fish, Grant's secretary of state, proved to be as able as Seward.[17] He was the quintessential northeastern elitist, with old-money ancestry, an Ivy League degree, and the experience of a Grand Tour of Europe, and atop that he was fluent in four languages. To foreign policy he brought intelligence, knowledge, sophistication, and a clear view of just what American national interests were and how best to realize them. Although Grant and Fish could not have differed more in their respective backgrounds, they worked well together. Fish was Grant's only department chief to keep his job all eight years.

Cuba was the Grant administration's first foreign policy challenge. Cuban nationalists revolted against Spanish rule in 1868 and their exile groups in the United States lobbied for American intervention on their behalf. They backed their appeals to America's moral and economic interests in a free Cuba by distributing to influential politicians, financiers, and newspaper editors millions of dollars of Cuban bonds that could be redeemed only by a sovereign Cuban government. This had the desired effect of provoking a national debate over whether Washington should support the rebellion.

The United States clearly had economic and humanitarian interests in an independent Cuba. Exporters and investors sought to end Spanish rule in order to gain access to Cuba's markets, while liberals envisioned the liberation of half a million slaves. In reply, realists urged restraint, pointing out that the rebels had no government, army to speak of, or large following and thus had little chance of success. The United States would have to defeat Spain in war and drive its forces from Cuba, at a high cost in American lives and money. And if Cuba were free, what then? Many prominent voices argued that Cubans were no fitter to rule themselves than other Latin Americans, whose wars of independence earlier that century had resulted not in democracy and development but in a political seesaw of despotism and anarchy amid worsening poverty.[18]

The political balance leaned toward intervention. On April 29, 1869, a majority in the House of Representatives voted for a resolution to support the rebels and President Grant if he called for intervention. The Grand Army of the Republic, a veterans' organization, declared its willingness to fight for Cuban freedom.

Like the nation, Grant's cabinet split over what to do. War Secretary John Rawlins, Treasury Secretary George Boutwell, Attorney General Ebenezer Hoar, Interior Secretary Jacob Cox, and Postmaster General John Creswell called for intervention; Secretary of State Hamilton Fish and Navy Secretary Adolph Borie argued that asserting military power would harm rather than enhance American interests. Grant himself was divided; he sympathized with the rebels but questioned whether their cause was worth the vast human and financial cost of winning their liberation. A pecuniary interest appears to have fixed the position of at least one of those secretaries; Rawlins, who died later that year, was discovered to have received $28,000 in Cuban bonds.

Grant embraced Fish's arguments that Spain's corrupt, inept, and brutal rule would eventually collapse beneath its own dead weight, and then Americans would be welcomed to assist in Cuba's political and economic development. The United States could accelerate this process by offering to help negotiate an armistice between Spain and the rebels, then pay off Madrid to relinquish its colony. Upon receiving this offer in July, Spain's government debated its merits until October, when it finally rejected the proposal and instead exerted more resources to crush the rebellion. This rejection might have provoked the Grant White House and Congress to intervene had their attention not shifted to another troubled country in the Caribbean basin.[19]

The Dominican Republic had been independent since 1821, but increasing numbers of its people recognized that sovereignty was anything but a panacea for their nation's worsening array of political, economic, and social problems. The country had dissolved into anarchy and various rebel groups threatened to topple the government. To save themselves, the elite clinging to the shards of power took a desperate option—they called for annexation by the United States. By a vote of

63 to 110 in January 1869, the House of Representatives rejected a resolution that would have accepted the plea.[20]

Upon entering the White House two months later, Grant was eager to grasp that opportunity. His primary motives were strategic and racial rather than economic or humanitarian. Located on the Dominican Republic's northeastern coast, Samana Bay was among the world's best anchorages, and Grant sought the American navy's exclusive control of it, fearing that if the United States did not take it, another great power would. But he also valued the island as a place where black Americans could emigrate and thus dilute racial tensions within the United States.

Grant had his secretary, Orville Babcock, negotiate a treaty of annexation with the Dominican government. Babcock signed a treaty on November 29, 1869, whereby the United States took the Dominican Republic in exchange for assuming its debt of $1.5 million, and it leased Samana Bay for a $150,000 annual payment. Upon receiving this treaty on January 2, 1870, Grant promptly walked it over to the nearby home of Charles Sumner, who chaired the Senate Foreign Relations Committee. Although the two men despised each other, they kept up a public decorum. Sumner, who was presiding over a dinner party, extended the platitude that he backed his administration. Grant left, believing that Sumner intended to work for the treaty's approval. Instead, on March 15, 1870, the Senate committee rejected the treaty by a five to two vote. Sumner and other opponents cited the financial and political costs of trying to integrate such an alien culture and economy into the United States.

Grant was stunned. He vowed not only to get his treaty approved but to punish Sumner for his betrayal. He succeeded in one of these goals. He devoted most of his State of the Union address in December 1870 to arguments for annexation. He advanced the treaty a step and got even with Sumner when, in March 1871, the Republican caucus voted twenty-six to twenty-one to eject Sumner from the Senate Foreign Relations Committee. In April 1870 a commission reported that annexation was in American interests, given the Dominican Republic's fertile soil, Samana Bay's strategic importance, and the people's overwhelming desire to become part of the United States. In May the Committee on Foreign Relations voted to submit the treaty to the Senate. Yet, despite winning this string of minor victories, Grant lost his campaign. On

June 30, 1871, the Senate rejected the treaty by a twenty-eight to twenty-eight vote, far short of the required two-thirds majority.

One foreign policy success of the Grant administration was finally to resolve the issue of British aid to rebel commerce raiders during the Civil War. Charles Sumner reignited this issue during a Senate speech in April 1869, when he asserted that Britain's policy had cost the United States $2 billion and that America should take Canada as compensation. War hawks loudly echoed the call.

These belligerent demands promptly got the attention of policy makers on both side of the Atlantic. Prime Minister William Gladstone called for mutual concessions on not just the claims case but other festering issues, including the San Juan Islands boundary, trade, fisheries, and access to Great Lakes canals. President Grant agreed. A joint commission was set up in Washington in February 1871.

The result was the Treaty of Washington, signed on May 8, 1871, whereby the Americans and British agreed to split the difference on the boundary, trade, and fisheries issues, open the Great Lakes canals to both nationalities, and submit the claims cases to a binding five-person arbitration committee to be established in Geneva, Switzerland. The Senate approved the treaty by fifty to twelve on May 24. The arbitration committee ruled in December 1872 that Britain owed the United States an indemnity of $15.5 million for damages inflicted by rebel raiders.[21]

A crisis erupted in 1873 that brought the United States and Spain to war's brink over Cuba. The Spanish navy intercepted a ship carrying volunteers, arms, and munitions for the Cuban rebels. Several Americans were among the fifty-three men that Spanish authorities ordered shot for piracy. Secretary of State Fish demanded an apology and indemnity. The Spaniards faced a tough choice. Defending their pride and right of self-defense would likely lead to war with the United States. If that happened, Spain would lose both the war and Cuba. This catastrophe could be averted if they swallowed their pride and right. Madrid eventually agreed to extend an apology and pay an $80,000 indemnity to the United States.

Fish's last important assertion of American interests was a treaty in 1875 whereby the United States asserted a protectorate over the Hawaiian Islands. That treaty recognized a power relationship that had developed over decades. The first American vessels had dropped anchor in that kingdom, then known as the Sandwich Islands, as early as the 1790s, to buy sandalwood and replenish food and water in their circuit through the global trade network. Over time more Americans stayed to invest in sugarcane plantations, cattle ranches, and other enterprises. As the American community's economic power grew, it increasingly intervened blatantly in Hawaiian politics. As early as 1842, President Tyler publicly declared that America's economic and strategic interests in Hawaii had reached the point where they were worth fighting for against any foreign nation that threatened them. Subsequent presidents upheld the Tyler Doctrine whenever complaints reached Washington of British or French meddling in Hawaiian affairs. Despite these interests and policies, the Senate failed to ratify the treaty. It would be nearly another quarter century until, in 1898, the United States finally annexed Hawaii.

America as a distinct culture began to evolve from the first settlements in the early seventeenth century. With time more Americans creatively expressed themselves and, in doing so, their culture, and these expressions became more refined and profound. Cultural icons that reflected the American experience proliferated.

The first great wave of American art emerged during the late 1820s, with writers and painters inspired by the philosophy of transcendentalism, the belief that humanity and nature are inseparable and divine. The synergy between painters and writers was best portrayed by Asher Durand's 1849 painting *Kindred Spirits*, which showed the poet William Cullen Bryant and the painter Thomas Cole reveling in a sublime wilderness setting.

The expression of transcendentalism through painting was initiated with Cole's first landscapes in 1825. He and other landscape painters were called the Hudson River school, as that region inspired many of their greatest works, while seascape painters were known as luminists. Although Cole passed away in 1848, a growing fraternity of painters like Durand, Jasper Cropsey, Sanford Gifford, John Kensett, Robert Salmon, Fitz Hugh Lane, Martin Heade, Worthington Wittredge, George Inness, and most vividly of all, Frederick Church, continued to create magnificent landscapes and seascapes inspired by transcendentalist ideals.

Outstanding painters in other genres emerged during the mid-nineteenth century. George Caleb Bingham depicted the tumultuous, practical, land-hungry, money-making, power-seeking world of Jacksonian democracy at odds with transcendentalism through such paintings as *Fur Traders Descending the Missouri* (1845), *Daniel Boone Escorting Settlers through the Cumberland Gap* (1852), *The County Election* (1852), *Canvassing for a Vote* (1852), *Stump Speaking* (1854), *Verdict of the People* (1854), and *The Jolly Flatboatmen* (1857). Although Henry Inman and William Sidney Mount were actually more skilled artists who painted more intimate scenes of rural life, perhaps only Mount's *Eel Spearing at Setauket* (1845) nears the iconic status of Bingham's half-dozen best-known paintings.

The Far West was a subject for many artists, although together they neither constituted a school nor were explicitly inspired by transcendentalism. Alfred Jacob Miller and George Catlin journeyed with trading expeditions to the Great Plains and Rocky Mountains during the 1830s and realistically captured the heyday of the mountain man era. During the 1840s and 1850s a more refined group of artists, including Charles Wimar, John Stanley, William Ranney, Seth Eastman, Arthur Tait, and most powerfully, Charles Deas, made their own western excursions and memorable paintings. The two finest painters of Far West scenes were Albert Bierstadt and Thomas Moran, who joined army exploring expeditions in 1858 and 1871, respectively, then returned to New York City to convert scores of sketches into magnificent paintings. Of all the works created by these artists, the most iconic ones of America's westward movement are Miller's *Trapper's Bride* (1845), Deas's *Long Jakes* (1844) and *Death Struggle* (1845), Ranney's *Advice on the Prairie* (1853), and Bierstadt's *Emigrants Crossing the Plains* (1867). As for American icons, Emmanuel Leutze painted two of the most popular, *Washington Crossing the Delaware* (1851) and his 1861 mural for the Capitol, *Westward the Course of Empire Takes Its Way*.

The Civil War became a watershed in painting, along with so much else in American life. Three great artists—James Whistler, Thomas Eakins, and Winslow Homer—emerged during the 1860s and reached heights of skill and style during the 1870s. Whistler was the most innovative; his *The White Girl* (1862), *Arrangement in Grey and Black* (1871), better known as *Whistler's Mother*, and *Nocturne in Blue and Gold* (1875) anticipated impressionism and pointed the way to abstract expressionism. Stylistically Eakins went in the opposite direction. His early paintings, like *Max Schmitt in a Single Scull* (1871) and *Sailboats Racing on the Delaware* (1874), verged on impressionism, but from his *The Gross Clinic* (1875), he switched to a hard-edged realism. No painter better depicted the Civil War and its aftermath than Homer, especially his *Veteran in a New Field* (1865) and *Prisoners from the Front* (1866). But during the 1870s he turned to creating landscapes and seascapes like *Snap the Whip* (1872) and *Breezing Up* (1876) with haunting psychological dimensions that exuded exhilaration at the brink of danger.

Photography as an art came of age during the Civil War. No one was more prolific or skilled than Mathew Brady, whose hundreds of photographs explored virtually every aspect of the war. Alexander Gardner and Timothy O'Sullivan worked with Brady and captured their own haunting images. After the war O'Sullivan, along with William Henry Jackson, Carleton Watkins, and A. J. Russell, found a new monumental and epic subject to photograph—the West. Of the hundreds of photographs these men produced, the two most iconic of the Civil War and Far West, respectively, were Brady's *Rebel Prisoners at Gettysburg* (1863) and Russell's *Driving of the Golden Stake* (1869).

During the mid-nineteenth century, America produced as fascinating an array of writers as it did painters. No writer more powerfully affected the Age of Lincoln than Harriet Beecher Stowe, although her impact was much greater on public opinion than on literature. Washington Irving and Nathaniel Hawthorne were still writing, although their best works were behind them. Americans enjoyed a vivid firsthand account of the frontier through Francis Parkman's *The Oregon Trail* (1849).

This age's greatest writer was Herman Melville. In his earlier novels he obeyed the adage to write about what one knows; his experiences during several years at sea inspired *Typee*, (1846), *Omoo* (1847), *Redburn* (1849), *Mardi* (1849), *White-Jacket* (1850), and above all, *Moby-Dick; or, The Whale* (1851). Later he explored the complexities of urban life and the human psyche through *Pierre* (1852) and *The Confidence-Man* (1857). *Moby-Dick* is certainly the greatest American novel of the nineteenth century and arguably the greatest of all time. Like all brilliant works of art, the novel has multiple levels. On the surface, *Moby-Dick* is a vividly written adventure story. Yet beneath this swirl various interpretations of a tapestry of symbols that Melville has woven. Most analysts agree that the whaling ship the *Pequod* and its thirty-four sailors represent America and its thirty-four states. The book appeared in 1851, the year after John Calhoun died. Some believe that Calhoun's humorless, obsessed character inspired Captain Ahab and that Moby Dick symbolized the abolitionist movement that Ahab sailed the world's oceans to seek and destroy, eventually ending up provoking it to destroy himself.[22]

Samuel Clemens, better known by his pen name Mark Twain, did not achieve fame as a novelist until the very end of the Age of Lincoln, when, in 1876, *The Adventures of Tom Sawyer* appeared and soon became America's most beloved work of fiction. He had spent the dozen previous years honing his writing skills, mostly as a journalist and humorist. His first book, *Innocents Abroad* (1869), lampoons the misadventures of himself and other Americans journeying through Europe and the Holy Land. *Roughing It* (1872) is a hilarious account of his attempts to seek his fortune out West, especially in California's mining camps. *The Gilded Age: A Tale of Today* (1874), which he cowrote with his friend Charles Warner, labels and exposes the excesses and absurdities of an America whose economic, political, and social systems were increasingly dominated by huge corporations and the greed-driven millionaires they spawned. Only the blackest humor kept Mark Twain from despair. Rather than watch helplessly, he offered a running satirical commentary on the nation's excesses and follies. His greatest work, *The Adventures of Huckleberry Finn*, would not appear until 1883.[23]

Poetry flourished during the Age of Lincoln. Walt Whitman was clearly the titan; his poems soared in style and sensuality far beyond those of John Greenleaf Whittier, William Cullen Bryant, Henry Wadsworth Longfellow, James Russell Lowell, and Oliver Wendell Holmes, whose works few people read today. Whitman's *Leaves of Grass* first appeared with only 12 poems in 1855, but he added more with each edition until there were 389 poems in the ninth edition of 1892. During much of the Civil War he lived in Washington and served as a nurse, often behind the Army of the Potomac's front lines. These experiences inspired a group of poems published as *Drum-Taps* in 1865. After the war he increasingly expressed himself though essays in various journals and magazines; he published many them in *Specimen Days* (1882). Throughout his writings he celebrated individuality, freethinking, self-expression, Abraham Lincoln, and America in all its diversity, achievements, and potential.[24]

During the Age of Lincoln, a chasm emerged and widened between the nation's intellectual and political elite. This was a disturbing but inevitable departure from the nation's heritage. The American Revolution was led by a distinct and well-established elite who were at once wealthy, highly educated, and deeply involved in politics, of whom Benjamin Franklin, Thomas Jefferson, Alexander Hamilton, John Adams, and John Jay were the greatest. The economic, political, and cultural domination of this elite and its descendants persisted for several generations. Their power, however, was steadily diluted as more states entered the United States and sent to Congress more "self-made men," who were born poor but through hard work and good luck joined the elite. Their wealth often poorly hid a lack of education. Andrew Jackson personified the transformation of America's political culture when he was elected president in 1828.

An intellectual class autonomous from politics emerged during the 1840s. It had two epicenters. Harvard University's Saturday Club included such luminaries as Ralph Waldo Emerson, Nathaniel Hawthorne, Henry Wadsworth Longfellow, James Russell Lowell, and Richard Henry Dana. Emerson also presided over a smaller circle twenty miles west at Concord, which included Henry David Thoreau, Margaret Fuller, and Bronson Alcott. Most of these intellectuals shared a background of being raised in middle- or upper-class New England homes and educated at the best universities. Their experiences shaped a broad outlook that lacked a name but philosophically mingled the values of Hamiltonianism, Unitarianism, transcendentalism, and abolitionism, with the blend varying with each thinker.

A new generation of cutting-edge thinkers emerged after the Civil War, exemplified by Harvard's Metaphysical Club that Oliver Wendell Holmes, William James, Charles Pierce, and John Dewey, among others, founded in 1872. Their outlook was grounded in science, skepticism, and pragmatism and inspired by Charles Darwin, in contrast to the romanticism of Emerson's generation of thinkers. Metaphysical Club adherents sought to live by hard reason rather than transcendent feelings. Their most profound work and influence, however, did not appear until long after the Age of Lincoln had ended.[25]

Emerson continued to reign as America's leading intellectual until at least 1872, when his health and intellect began noticeably to decline.

During the Age of Lincoln, his writings and addresses expounded less transcendentalism's lofty sentiments and more the principles and policies that could help America fulfill its founding ideals. He was a Radical Republican who insisted on the emancipation and integration of blacks within American civilization.[26]

The invention of mass steam presses drastically slashed the cost of books, journals, magazines, and newspapers. Literacy, meanwhile, soared, mostly across the North from east to west as one state after another established public school systems. The result was the mass production of things to read for a mass market of readers. Politically the most important publications were *Harper's Weekly*, the *Nation*, the *Atlantic Monthly*, the *National Quarterly Review*, the *Saturday Evening Post*, and *Publishers' Weekly*. Such brilliant editors as George Curtis, Edwin Godwin, and William Dean Howells employed outstanding journalists to explore the nation's most pressing issues. The book industry experienced a revolutionary advance in 1876, when Lakeside Library of Chicago began publishing each week a new title priced at a mere ten cents.

It was during the Age of Lincoln that two of America's most recognizable cultural types became popular, Horatio Alger and the Western Hero. Horatio Alger, the son of a Unitarian minister, was a graduate of Harvard Divinity School whose piety and morality were challenged by a sojourn in Paris. He returned to New York to write a series of novels in which poor boys became rich men through hard work, cleverness, and entrepreneurship. The Western Hero had a more varied literary background. In his Leatherstocking novels, James Fenimore Cooper established the Western Hero as a solitary, brave, and good-hearted survivalist. Starting in the 1860s, dime novels by Frederick Whittaker, Edward Ellis, and Edward Judson, whose pen name was Ned Buntline, popularized frontiersmen like Kit Carson, Wild Bill Hickok, and "Buffalo Bill" Cody.

The relationship between real life and popular fiction reached an intriguing crossroads in 1850, when Kit Carson led a pursuit to rescue Anna White, whom the Jicarilla Apaches had captured. It did not have a happy ending. As Carson and his men approached the Apache camp, the raiders murdered White and fled. Among the loot retrieved was Charles Averill's best-selling pulp novel *Kit Carson: The Price of the Gold Hunters*, whose climatic scene involved the hero rescuing a beautiful woman from Indian savages. Carson imagined White reading the novel during her captivity and praying for just such a rescue for herself. But the gap between the uplifting myth and the tragic reality overwhelmed Carson. When someone offered him a copy of the novel, Carson demanded that he "burn the damn thing." For centuries, most Americans have obscured the complex and often disturbing realities of their history behind a tapestry of idyllic self-images.[27]

As an art form, American theater would not come of age until the rise of the great playwrights of the twentieth century. As a popular entertainment, however, theater flourished during the nineteenth century. Like tens of thousands of other Americans, Abraham Lincoln loved attending the theater, although virtually all the plays were penned by British playwrights. A distinct form of American entertainment emerged with the minstrel shows of song, dance, and buffoonery by white men in blackface. These shows helped make Stephen Foster America's first great songwriter with such works as "My Old Kentucky Home," "Sewanee River," and "Oh! Susannah." P. T. Barnum was the first great mass-entertainment promoter, with extravaganzas that were part circus, part freak show. "Buffalo Bill" Cody capitalized on his fame as a dime-novel hero to launch his Wild West show during the late 1860s. From this mass-entertainment industry was born American "celebrity culture" in which people were famous largely for being famous. The Buffalo Bills of the world became caricatures of their own genuine deeds when myths submerged reality.

Vulgarity was not confined to showmen like Buffalo Bill Cody or P. T. Barnum. As the rich and middle class made more money, they found more garish ways to display it, especially in their homes. Gone were the elegance and simplicity of the late colonial and early republic eras. Now the prevailing decorating taste favored excessive ornamentation, colors, and clutter for furniture, wallpaper, carpets, draperies, and knickknacks.

To their credit, ever more well-to-do Americans sought self-improvement. In 1874 the Chautauqua Institute was founded to satisfy this craving by offering lectures and classes. This popularized the American notion of continuous education that had originated with Benjamin Franklin over a century earlier.

Art and politics converged at only one significant point during the Age of Lincoln, but the impact was revolutionary. President Grant signed on March 1, 1872, a bill that created Yellowstone National Park, the world's first such institution. This act led eventually to a radical transformation in how most Americans see their natural and historical heritage, and thus themselves. The idea was born in an army exploring expedition to the Yellowstone region in 1870. The area's natural wonders so dazzled some participants that they vowed to get the region preserved for all Americans forever rather than allow it to be privatized, divvied up, exploited, and, inevitably, ruined. After returning east, Nathaniel Langford promoted this vision by lobbying key congressional leaders and writing two articles for *Scribners' Monthly*. Congress authorized a second expedition the following year, this one accompanied by the geologist Ferdinand Hayden, the painter Thomas Moran, and the photographer William Henry Jackson. Hayden's subsequent report, with Moran's sketches and Jackson's photographs, helped convince congressional majorities to vote for making Yellowstone a national park.

The debate, however, created a bitter national cleavage between preservationists and developers, or conservationists and conservatives, that has persisted ever since. Representative Lewis Payson of Illinois, a major financial beneficiary of the railroad and mining corporation that wanted to exploit Yellowstone, vividly expressed the enduring conservative mentality: "I cannot understand the sentiment which favors the retention of a few buffaloes to the development of mining interests amounting to millions of dollars." To this Representative William McAdoo of New Jersey offered the classic environmentalist reply that "the inspiring sights and mysteries of nature . . . elevate mankind and bring it to closer communion with omniscience" and thus "should be preserved on this, if for no other ground." He challenged his colleagues to choose preserving "the beautiful and sublime" over "heartless mammon and the greed of capital." When a motion was made to amend the bill to let a railroad run through Yellowstone, Representative Samuel Cox of New York retorted, "This is a measure which is inspired by corporate greed and natural selfishness against national pride and beauty."[28]

16

Eighteen Seventy-Six

When private property is devoted to the public use, it is subject to public regulation.

MUNN V. ILLINOIS

Our present civil system, born of General Jackson and the Democratic Party, is so idiotic, so contemptible, so grotesque that it would make the very savages of Dahomey jeer and the very gods of solemnity laugh.

MARK TWAIN

The result will be that the Southern people will practically treat the constitutional amendments as nullities and the colored man's fate will be worse than when he was in slavery.

RUTHERFORD HAYES

Americans celebrated their nation's one hundredth birthday in 1876. The highlight was the Philadelphia Centennial International Exposition that opened on May 10, ran until November, and was attended by as many as one in five, or eight million, Americans. The exposition was America's first world's fair and the planet's fourth, following those in Paris, Vienna, and London. In holding their own, Americans proudly proclaimed to the rest of humanity that their nation had come of age.

The centennial exposition was a Hamiltonian production. Although Philadelphia's city fathers conceived the project, they could not raise enough public or private money to pay for it. Washington came to the rescue in January 1876, when Congress, in near-party-line votes of Republicans for and Democrats against, passed a bill that appropriated $1.5 million for the exposition. This crucial financial contribution let President Grant proclaim the exposition a world's fair and invite all countries to contribute pavilions and visitors.

The site was Fairmount Park, west of the Schuylkill River. Of Fairmount Park's 3,160 acres, 450 were fenced off for the exposition. Within those grounds, two hundred buildings covering forty-eight acres were erected, of which the most prominent were the Machine Hall, Agricultural Hall, Government Building, Women's Pavilion, and pavilions for each of the thirty-four states and such foreign countries as Britain, France, Russia, Austria, Japan, China, and Brazil. The most popular pavilion was Machine Hall with its huge steam engines, rows of inventions, and electric light illumination. Perhaps the most fascinating invention displayed was the telephone; most people just could not comprehend how one's voice could be conveyed through a wire and emerge audibly at the other end.

The United States had come a long way over the preceding century. The population was now forty-four million, tenfold greater than the four million when Americans declared independence. America's frontiers had expanded in a series of huge acquisitions south to the Gulf of Mexico, west to the Pacific Ocean, and then leapfrogged north across Canada to embrace Alaska. The economy had been transformed from an agrarian nation of farmers and slaves into an industrial, commercial, corporate, and financial powerhouse poised to surpass Britain as the world's greatest.

Yet, tragically, a century after winning their war for independence, Americans were fighting their latest war and they appeared to be losing. Just two days after celebrating their nation's hundredth birthday, Americans were stunned to learn that on June 26 the Lakota Sioux and their Cheyenne and Arapaho allies wiped out Lt. Col. George Custer and 262 of his troops at the battle of the Big Horn. This devastating defeat thickened the pall cast earlier by word that the Indians had defeated Gen. George Crook and his army at the battle of the Rosebud on June

17. With the spoils of these two victories, the hostile bands scattered. Columns of troops hunted fruitlessly for them the rest of that year and well into the next.

Like virtually every Indian war, greed ultimately caused the Great Sioux War of 1876 and 1877.[1] The federal commissioners who negotiated the 1868 Treaty of Fort Laramie sought to forge a lasting peace with all the northern plains Indians. Each tribe was allocated a reservation, promised annual annuities for sustenance, and assigned an agent to ensure that all went well. The Black Hills were in the heart of the territory designated for the six Lakota Sioux bands. This Sioux title to land that they worshipped as sacred would be fleeting.

The Northern Pacific Railway Company hoped to build a transcontinental railroad that partly ran westward through the reservations of the Sioux and numerous other tribes. In 1873 the company pressured the Grant administration into launching an expedition that surveyed the route. Col. David Stanley, with Custer second in command, led the column of fifteen hundred troops, four hundred civilians, and 275 wagons that invaded the region during the summer. In the face of such overwhelming power, the Sioux under the leadership of Hunkpapa chief Sitting Bull and Oglala chief Crazy Horse could at best only skirmish with isolated detachments. Rumor reached the expedition that gold glittered in the streams of the Black Hills, south of their route. In 1874 Custer was assigned to lead an expedition to determine the rumor's veracity. The word that Custer's column had indeed found gold provoked a rush into the Black Hills in 1875. The 1868 treaty committed the United States to protect the Indians from any invasions of their territory. As with previous presidents and scores of other treaties, Grant succumbed to pressure to ignore the law. The White House's failure to prevent the horde of prospectors, merchants, prostitutes, and outlaws from overrunning the Black Hills provoked war with the Sioux.

Gen. William Sherman devised a strategy intended to crush the Sioux and their allies in 1876. Three columns with a combined force of over five thousand cavalry and infantry would converge on the hostile Indians: General Crook's from Fort Laramie to the south; Gen. Alfred Terry's, with Custer second in command, from Fort Abraham Lincoln to the east; and finally, Col. John Gibbon's from Fort Ellis to the west. The plan made perfect sense on paper but failed in the field. Under the brilliant leadership of Sitting Bull and Crazy Horse, the Indians took advantage of their central position to concentrate their warriors on first defeating Crook on the Rosebud River, then wiping out Custer and a third of his Seventh Cavalry along the Little Big Horn River, and finally evading Gibbon and other pursuing army columns.

Eventually the United States won that war as it had nearly every Indian war in its history. One by one the bands surrendered to the overwhelming power that the army massed against them. The last holdout was Sitting Bull and his Hunkpapa band, who fled to safety in Canada; he led the remnants of his people back to the reservation in 1881. But in 1876 most Americans could only mourn the "Custer massacre"; few sympathized with the Indians or regretted that imperialism and treaty breaking called into question the nation's highest ideals.

Although the Republican Party was only twenty-two years old in 1876, it was undergoing a profound ideological transformation from liberalism to conservatism as policies increasingly promoted big business and finance rather than the common working man and civil rights. Unfairly or not, liberals condemned President Grant as leading and personifying this transformation. Grant had mulled a third term but decided against it after an embarrassing resolution passed the House of Representatives in December 1875; liberal Republicans joined the majority Democrats to vote 234 to 18 that Grant's reelection would be "unwise, unpatriotic, and fraught with peril to our institutions."[2] The liberal Republican rebellion against conservatives peaked with a convention led by Carl Schurz, Charles Francis Adams, William Cullen Bryant, and Frederick Law Olmsted at New York on May 15. They agreed not to break away and form a third party but instead vowed to work within the Republican Party to pressure it to live up to the progressive ideals upon which it was founded. They would lose this crusade.

The Republican Party convention opened at Cincinnati on June 14. Corruption accusations tainted the front-runners, senators Roscoe Conklin and James Blaine. The delegates eventually turned to squeaky-clean candidate Rutherford Hayes, Ohio's governor, who won on the seventh ballot by 384 votes to Blaine's 351. Hayes was a good choice, having risen to the rank of general during the Civil War and afterward returned home to champion reform, first as a congressman, then as governor.

The Democratic Party also picked a reform candidate after it convened at St. Louis on June 27. Samuel Tilden, New York's governor,
won unanimously on the second ballot. Tilden was acclaimed by progressives for breaking up Boss Tweed's political machine in New York
City. He declared that "centralism in government and corruption in
administration are the twin evils of our times. They threaten with swift
destruction civil liberty and the whole fabric of our times."[3]

Unfortunately, the presence of two progressives battling for the presidency did not prevent the 1876 election from becoming notorious as
the second most disputed in American history.[4] There were widespread
stories of ballot box stuffing in northern cities and across swaths of the
South. Conservative southerners asserted the full repertoire of means
to intimidate blacks from voting. Nowhere was this more blatant than
in South Carolina, where white supremacist Martin Gary popularized
a "Plan of Campaign" for the election whereby each white man would
"control the vote of at least one negro by intimidation, purchase, keeping him away or as each individual may determine," since blacks "can
only be influenced by their fears."[5] The result of such tactics was to
intimidate perhaps as many as 250,000 black voters from participating
in southern polls.[6]

When the votes were tallied after the November 7 election, Tilden
led with three hundred thousand more popular votes and a total of 184
electoral votes, 1 vote short of victory, to Hayes's 166 electoral votes.
Republicans and Democrats disputed the election results in three states—
Florida, Louisiana, and South Carolina. Election commissions in these
states had conflicting Republican and Democratic counts.

To resolve the impasse, Congress passed a bill that Grant signed into
law on January 29, 1877. The Electoral Commission Act established a
fifteen-member commission composed of five senators, five representatives, and five Supreme Court justices to determine who won the
deadlocked election. With Republicans holding eight and Democrats
seven of the seats, the Electoral Commission accepted the Republican
counts in the three states and thus threw the election to Hayes by 185
to 184 electoral votes. The House of Representatives certified this result.

Before this decision, Hayes assumed that he would be found the loser
and despaired that a Democratic president would turn a blind eye to
whatever southern conservatives did, with catastrophic results. He con-

fided to his diary that "I do care for the poor colored men of the south. . . . The result will be that the Southern people will practically treat the constitutional amendments as nullities and the colored man's fate will be worse than when he was in slavery."[7] Yet as president, Hayes followed exactly the same policy. He did so because of an understanding reached between the party leaders whereby the Democrats would accept Hayes if he ended Reconstruction. A Kansas Republican leader captured his party's new outlook: "I think the policy of the new administration will be to conciliate the white men of the South. Carpetbaggers to the rear, and niggers take care of themselves."[8]

After being inaugurated on March 4, 1877, President Hayes's first act was to order all federal troops withdrawn from the southern states. Actually the "Bargain of 1877" was not much of a concession. As a means of imposing liberal democracy and civil rights on the South, Reconstruction had died years earlier, killed off by the white supremacist counterrevolution spearheaded by terrorism. Pulling out the handful of remaining federal troops and officials from the South was no more than a symbolic gesture. Henry Adams, a black Louisiana politician, explained that by then the "whole South—every state in the South had got in the hands of the very men that held us as slaves."[9] In all, the South might have lost the Civil War, but it won Reconstruction.

17

Legacy

Fellow citizens, we cannot escape history. . . . The dogmas
of the quiet past are inadequate to the stormy present.

ABRAHAM LINCOLN

It became necessary for me to choose whether . . . I should let the
government fall into ruin, or whether, availing myself of the broader
powers conferred by the Constitution I would make an effort to
save it with all its blessings for the present age and posterity.

ABRAHAM LINCOLN

I claim not to have controlled events, but confess plainly that
events have controlled me. Now at the end of three years
struggle the nation's condition is not what either party or
any man devised or expected. God alone can claim it.

ABRAHAM LINCOLN

There was a right side and a wrong side in the late war, which
no sentiment ought to cause us to forget, and while today
we should have malice toward none, and charity toward all,
it is no part of our duty to confound right with wrong.

FREDERICK DOUGLASS

Why will men believe a lie, an absurd lie, that could not [be] imposed upon a child, and cling to it and repeat it in defiance of all evidence to the contrary?

ORVILLE BROWNING

He now belongs to the ages.

EDWIN STANTON

During the Age of Lincoln, those with national power wielded it to protect or enhance American interests as they interpreted them across a spectrum of issues. No American interest was more vital than defeating the rebellion of the slave states and reunifying the nation.

So how did the North win?[1] Of the array of explanations, Abraham Lincoln's leadership was by far the most important. It was his brilliant leadership that mobilized enough vital hard- and soft-power resources for the United States to crush the Confederacy. Ulysses Grant's praise was unequivocal: "I have no doubt that Lincoln will be the conspicuous figure of the war. He was incontestably the greatest man I ever knew."[2]

This was not at all evident when the war broke out. In comparing the resumes of the enemy presidents, Jefferson Davis's was as impressive as Abraham Lincoln's was skimpy. Davis was a West Point graduate and Mexican War veteran; Lincoln was a militia captain for three months and never saw action. Davis served as the secretary of war and ran his Mississippi plantation; Lincoln never administered anything other than his law partnership. Davis was a two-term U.S. senator; Lincoln's congressional experience was confined to a term in the House of Representatives. Yet resumes can be deceptive.

Despite these glaring differences, Lincoln proved to be by far the greater leader.[3] In some ways he benefited from his own inexperience. He was not bound by standard procedures and lacked the skills that might have tempted him to micromanage. Instead he continually thought and acted outside bureaucratic and political boxes.

Lincoln at once relished and reviled his role as commander in chief. He once asked a friend visiting him in the White House, "Doesn't it strike you as queer that I, who couldn't cut the head off of a chicken and who was sick at the sight of blood, should be cast into the middle of a great war with blood flowing all about me?"[4] He grew steadily into his duties.[5] At first he tended to yield too much to the experts. Lacking any significant military experience of his own, he felt genuine respect toward and perhaps was awed by those who had not only made the military their careers but had fought valiantly in many a battle. When the Committee on the Conduct of the War expressed its astonishment that the president did not know the army commander's plans, Lincoln replied that he "did not think he had any right to know, but that, as he was not a military man, it was his duty to defer to General McClellan."[6] With no firm hand at the tiller during the first year of war, the armies tended to march or camp largely clueless of each other's directions or locations. The Union was in desperate need of a grand strategy.

Lincoln eventually firmly grasped the military tiller. Typically, he alleviated his ignorance through study. He borrowed from the Library of Congress *The Elements of Military Art and Science*, written by Henry Halleck, whom he later tapped to be the commanding general. His secretaries John Hay and John Nicolay recalled that he "gave himself night and day to the study of the military situation. He read a large number of works on strategy. He pored over the reports from the various departments and districts of the field of war. He held long conferences with imminent generals and admirals, and astonished them by the extent of his special knowledge and keen intelligence of his questions."[7]

With time Lincoln became an accomplished military strategist, superior to most of his generals. He grasped the war's essence and what was necessary to win it. He succinctly explained to Gen. Henry Halleck his "general idea of this war," which was "that we have the greater numbers and the enemy has the greater facility of concentrating forces upon points of collision; that we must fail unless we can find some way of making our advantage an overmatch for his; and that his can only be done by menacing him with superior forces at different points at the same time, so that we can safely attack, one, or both if he makes no change, and that if he weakens one to strengthen the other, forbear to attack the strengthened one, but seize and hold the weakened one, gaining so much."[8]

Unlike many panicky generals, politicians, newspaper editors, and average Americans, Lincoln saw Confederate invasions of the North more as opportunities than threats. The rebel armies faced the same dilemma as their foes—ever-longer umbilical cords stretching back to supply sources. This gave a vigorous commander the chance to sidestep the invaders, sever their lifeline, and fight on ground of his choosing the hastily withdrawing enemy army. The trouble for Lincoln was finding generals who shared his strategic vision. Historian James McPherson noted that time after time timid Union generals let defeated foes escape, as in "Jackson's Shenandoah campaign in spring of 1862; Lee's invasion of Maryland in September 1862; Bragg's and Kirby Smith's simultaneous invasion of Kentucky [in fall 1862]; Lee's invasion of Pennsylvania in June 1863; and Jubal Early's raid to the suburbs of Washington in July 1864."[9]

Among Lincoln's worst frustrations was getting generals to grasp and assert the essential strategy for winning the war:

> To avoid misunderstanding, let me say that to attempt to fight the enemy slowly back to his entrenchments at Richmond, and then to capture him, is an idea I have been trying to repudiate for quite a year. . . . My last attempt upon Richmond was to get McClellan, when he was nearer there than the enemy was, to run in ahead of him. Since then I have constantly desired the Army of the Potomac to make Lee's army, and not Richmond, its objective point. If our army cannot fall upon the enemy and hurt him where he is, it is plain to me it can gain nothing by attempting to follow him over a succession of entrenched lines into a fortified city.[10]

Of course, this was the strategy by which Gen. Ulysses Grant eventually won the war in Virginia. Destroying Lee's army and capturing Richmond came to be inseparable. Lee was able to block Grant's attempts to sidestep him and blunt his subsequent attacks all the way back to the entrenchments of Petersburg and Richmond. It did not have to come to that. Had Grant commanded the Army of the Potomac at Antietam or Gettysburg, he would have destroyed Lee's army, whose retreat each time was blocked by the rain-swollen Potomac River.

Victory depended on sound campaign strategies and battlefield tactics backed by a ruthless killer instinct. Lincoln did not find generals with such skills and instincts until 1864, with Grant commanding in the east and Sherman in the west. Until then generals like McClellan, Halleck, Buell, Rosecrans, and Meade actually tried to avoid a decisive victory. Halleck, whose *Elements of Military Art and Science* was a key textbook at West Point, believed that battles were only a last resort.

McClellan and Meade fought reluctantly at Antietam and Gettysburg, respectively, then failed to follow up their tactical victories and destroy Lee's army when they had the chance. Buell explained that the "object is not to fight a great battle but by demonstrations and maneuvering to prevent the enemy from concentrating his forces."[11]

These attitudes disgusted generals like Ulysses Grant and William Sherman, the North's greatest generals.[12] Indeed, of the many reasons why the United States won the Civil War when and how it did, the leadership of these two men was the most essential after Lincoln's. Grant was stunned by the belief that "the mere occupation of places was to close the war while large and effective rebel armies existed."[13] For him and his like-minded brothers in arms, the whole point of war was to destroy the enemy as swiftly and decisively as possible. Ideally this meant destroying enemy armies. If this was not possible, it meant destroying the enemy's economic and psychological means of waging war.

There was a curious symmetry when comparing the truly outstanding generals of both sides, with Ulysses S. Grant, William Tecumseh Sherman, and Phil Sheridan balanced by Robert E. Lee, Thomas "Stonewall" Jackson, and Bedford Forest. What they shared was a killer instinct for destroying the enemy and the skills for doing so.

It is often said that generals are made, not born. Of the war's six greatest generals, only Forrest did not attend the West Point military academy. This may have been to his advantage. West Point transformed young men into educated, professional soldiers. The emphasis, however, was on discipline, conformity, and engineering skills rather than the practice of war. The academy's approach to war was a methodical, chess-like, eighteenth-century approach that emphasized taking strategic cities rather than fighting decisive battles that destroyed enemy armies.

West Point graduates supplied officers to both armies with a rough ratio of two Union to one Confederate. But the rebels' military leadership was boosted by the eight military schools located across the South, with the Virginia Military Institute at Lexington and the Citadel at Charleston the most famous. The Virginia Military Institute supplied one of three officers in Virginia regiments, while 1,781 of its 1,902 graduates fought for the Confederacy.[14]

Professional officers filled less than half the posts of either army. Volunteer regiments elected their officers. As for generals, of the 583 that

Lincoln commissioned, two-thirds had some military experience and many others were promoted because of the courage and skills they displayed in the war.[15] Yet being a veteran or West Point graduate was no guarantee against ineptness, as George McClellan, Don Buell, Ambrose Burnside, and Joe Hooker amply proved. McClellan and Buell were timid, indecisive leaders who together may have delayed the rebel defeat by a year or more. Burnside and Hooker were aggressive but also murderously inept. Lincoln based his promotions on the candidate's performance. The trouble was that a man might be proficient at one level of command and disastrous at the next. Or luck and overwhelming forces rather than leadership may have helped him win a battle or two. As if trying to figure out which professional officers were fit for high command was not challenging enough, Lincoln was pressured to commission some generals because of their political power. Not surprisingly, many prominent politicians who wrangled generalships made a mess of things, with Benjamin Butler, Dan Sickles, Nathaniel Banks, and John McClernand among the more egregious examples. Nonetheless, here again inexperience did not necessarily always end in disaster—John Logan was a first-rate general.

The industrial revolution's factories, railroads, steamboats, and telegraphs also revolutionized warfare. Northern and southern leaders made the most of mass production, rapid transportation, and near-instantaneous communications. Industrialization favored the strategic offensive and the tactical defense.[16]

The South had several crucial advantages that initially offset much of the hard power that the North amassed. First, strategically the southerners were fighting on the defensive. They could more easily take advantage of interior lines to transfer troops, provisions, munitions, and ordnance from one front to another. They could chose and fortify sites that Union armies would have to either assault, besiege, or bypass at their peril. Magnifying this strategic advantage was the South's vast land area of 750,000 square miles. Somehow Union armies had to invade and either secure or devastate the South's key regions. The North faced the "strategic consumption dilemma," whereby the farther an army advanced, the more troops it had to detach to guard lengthening and vulnerable supply lines. As rebel armies withdrew, they got closer to their own supplies and absorbed garrisons along the way. For the war's first three years, this dilemma diluted much of the North's manpower and logistical advantage.

War and supply are inseparable. Logistics may not determine strategy but certainly limits its possibilities. Logistics is all about getting enough essential resources for war to those who fight it. For the industrialized North, producing enough bullets and beans was not difficult. Getting all that to the front, however, was a Herculean, and at times Sisyphean, labor. Railroads, steamboats, and wagons were all vital links in the transportation system. Each had its own vulnerabilities. Raiders could tear up train tracks. Fortifications, obstructions, and low water could halt steamboats. Sooner or later all the provisions and munitions conveyed by trains or boats were unloaded and transferred to wagons.

Wagons drawn by draft animals posed their own problems. Hours each day were consumed feeding and watering and hitching and unhitching the beasts. Horses, mules, and oxen differ in how much energy they can exert each day to pull their wagons, and that of course varies with the weight of the load, grade of the road, and miles of journey. Generally a draft animal pulling a full load can go only two-thirds as far as a man marching with a full pack, including the eating, sleeping, resting, and preparation times for each. Forage was the biggest drawback to draft animals and cavalry mounts. Even during the lush summer months, animals will soon eat and trample grassy fields into muddy or dusty earth; the more grazing animals, the quicker the destruction. Winter magnifies the forage problem. Enough hay and oats must be harvested across the country in the preceding late summer, stored, then shipped for half the year to the mouths of hundreds of thousands of draft animals and cavalry horses.

A terrible legacy haunted the North and South alike. Tactics and technology are inseparable, with the latter determining the former. During the Civil War there was a huge disconnect in the minds of most professional officers between their previous training and experiences and the current conflict. An entire generation of West Point graduates had studied Napoleon's campaigns, then fought in the Mexican War. What they learned was to maneuver, pin down the enemy, then crush them with massive attacks. This formula's first two elements were and remain essential to victory. Technology, however, rendered the third element obsolete. The brilliant victories of Napoleon and Winfield Scott were won in an age of inaccurate, short-range muskets; massed troops could smash through an enemy's line, often not so much because of the musket fire but as the defenders fled before the glint of massed bayonets rushing toward them. The Civil War was fought with rifles with accurate killing ranges of several hundred yards, which thus made any assault all but suicidal. The advantage shifted to defenders, especially if they leveled their rifles at the enemy from behind a breastwork or within a trench. During the war, defenders defeated seven of eight attacks.

Tragically, the older mindset trapped most officers despite the repeated, blood-soaked lessons of failed attacks. Usually in the heat of battle but sometimes from cold miscalculation, a general ordered a massed charge that experience should have warned would have only one result—mass slaughter. Even the two greatest respective generals of the North and South were responsible for such debacles—Grant at Spotsylvania and Cold Harbor, and Lee at Malvern Hill and Cemetery Ridge. This was partly because frontal assaults occasionally worked, as did Grant's at Missionary Ridge or Lee's at Gaines's Mill and Chancellorsville.

The U.S. Navy made two vital contributions to the American victory by blockading rebel ports and conveying armies down rebel rivers.[17] These strategies were essential parts of the strategy known as the Anaconda Plan, devised by Gen. Winfield Scott in the war's first month.

Navy Secretary Gideon Welles brilliantly implemented the blockade.[18] By one count, the U.S. Navy captured 1,149 and burned 355 enemy merchant vessels for a total of 1,504. Impressive as this seems, perhaps ten times more ships slipped through the blockade. At Wilmington, for instance, of 2,054 attempts to run the blockade during the Civil War, 1,735, or 84 percent, succeeded. Nonetheless, the blockade steadily cut off more crucial imports like munitions, rifles, cannons, and machinery and prevented crucial exports like cotton to pay for all this.[19]

More important for the South's conquest than the blockade was the navy's domination of the South's navigable rivers. With flotillas of transports protected by iron-clad gunboats developed by the brilliant engineer James Eads, Union forces could move swiftly and mostly safely deep into enemy territory via the Mississippi, Cumberland, Tennessee, James, and Red Rivers. At a certain point, of course, armies had to disembark to march and fight. But the strategic attrition of forces hived off to protect the supply lines of river-borne armies was a fraction of those supplied by railroads; the more river miles an army wove into its supply line, the fewer troops were needed to protect it. In contrast, the longer a supply line ran along railroads, the more troops it consumed for its protection and the more vulnerable it was to disruption.

The Union equaled or exceeded the Confederacy in every element of the art of war except three—large-scale raids, cavalry commanders, and guerrillas. During the war, rebel infantry generals like Kirby Smith and Earl Van Dorn and cavalry generals like Nathan Bedford Forrest, J. E. B. Stuart, John Hunt Morgan, Joe Wheeler, Wade Hampton, and John Mosby conducted devastating raids deep into the enemy's rear. Of these generals Forrest was by far the greatest because he was just as deft in commanding large bodies of infantry as he was cavalry and he excelled at both strategy and tactics.

The rifle eliminated the crucial role that cavalry could play on battlefields during earlier eras of warfare. Volleys of massed rifle fire could decimate a cavalry charge hundreds of yards away. Each side understood this and kept their horsemen on the periphery of any large-scale battle. It was the Confederates, however, who initially understood the vital strategic role that cavalry could play. Thousands of horsemen riding fast and far could raid behind enemy lines to destroy railroad tracks, wagon trains, and supply depots. The most devastating raids brought Union offensives to a dead halt, like Buell's into eastern Tennessee, Grant's into northern Mississippi, and Banks's into northwestern Louisiana. It took years for the North to narrow the gap with the South's initial vast advantage in cavalry commanders. Eventually Phil Sheridan proved to be nearly as able and bold a general as Forrest, while Benjamin Grierson, George Armstrong Custer, and Wesley Merritt were excellent cavalry commanders.

Guerrilla tactics were exclusively a Confederate way of war because nearly all of the war was fought in the South. Guerrillas lived behind enemy lines, often hiding in plain sight wearing civilian clothes and performing civilian tasks. They anxiously awaited word from their leaders to gather for raids in which they usually masked themselves by night and at times by wearing blue uniforms. They would strike to destroy lives and supplies, then disperse to their homes or hidden camps. Sherman vividly described guerrilla warfare as a situation in which "armies pass across . . . the land, the war closes in behind and leaves the same enemy behind," where "every house is a nest of secret, bitter enemies."[20] The Confederacy made guerrilla warfare an official part of its grand strategy with its Partisan Ranger Act of June 28, 1862, which empowered the government to issue commissions to guerrilla leaders and integrate them within the Confederate command structure.

Terrorism is the threat or use of destruction of the lives and property of noncombatants. This definition might appear easy enough to apply to history. The trouble in doing so is that politics and prejudices often distort the application. As the saying goes, one man's terrorist is another's freedom fighter. Through most northern eyes, terrorism was exclusively a rebel strategy, most notoriously wielded by such cold-blooded murderers as "Bloody Bill" Anderson, William Quantrill, and Jesse James, who usually wore no uniforms and took no prisoners. Confederate terrorism provoked more terrorism. In Missouri, Union general Clinton Fisk explained the pathology: "There is scarcely a citizen in the county but wants to kill someone of his neighbors for fear that said neighbor may kill him."[21] The worst Confederate atrocity was the murder of 181 unarmed men and boys and the looting and burning of Lawrence, Kansas, on August 23, 1863.

The American government faced similar political, strategic, and moral dilemmas in combating Confederate guerrillas as it has in more recent wars. Guerrillas hide among either a sympathetic or an intimidated population. How does the army find and destroy them without destroying the lives and property of the broader population in which they shelter, and thus provoking more people to join their ranks? The obvious strategy is to separate the guerrillas from the people. To this end, Gen. Henry Halleck issued two orders in March 1862. The first required all civilians to take an oath of allegiance to the United States. The second warned that "every man who enlists in a . . . guerrilla band . . . will not, if captured, be treated as ordinary prisoners of war, but will be hung as robbers and murderers." Attorney General Edward Bates followed up Halleck's decree by announcing that any guerrillas captured without uniforms would be summarily shot.[22] On August 25, 1863, Gen. Thomas Ewing, who commanded a military district headquartered in Kansas City, tried to suppress guerrillas by ordering all civilians to evacuate their homes in three adjacent counties. Just how much such measures reduced or multiplied the guerrilla ranks is impossible to determine.

To most southern eyes the deliberate destruction of homes, barns, fields, livestock, and railroads by Sherman's army in Georgia and the Carolinas or Sheridan's army in the Shenandoah Valley constituted terrorism. Those who wage or think about total war would reply that destroying the enemy's capacity to fight is justified not only on practical but on ethical grounds. The more devastating the destruction, the sooner the enemy surrenders, and this saves lives, treasure, and property over the long run.

An obviously essential element of war is mobilizing enough people and things both at and behind the lines to win. The North surpassed the South by virtually every measure of hard power. First of all, the U.S. federal government was up and running, while the Confederates had to build and finance a government from nothing. With a population of 22,338,989, the North had twice as many people as the South's 9,103,332, of whom 5,449,462 were whites, 3,521,110 were slaves, and 132,760 were free blacks. The North had a five to two advantage in men eligible for military service. Although the Confederacy mobilized enough troops to stave off defeat for four years, it suffered an irremediable deficiency in a key element of power—the U.S. Navy numbered eighty-two warships when the war began; the South would have to build a navy from scratch. The North's economic lead was even more formidable, with 110,000 factories employing 1.1 million workers compared to the South's 18,000 factories employing 110,000 workers. Many factors explain this gap, but Yankee ingenuity in innovation and enterprise was critical—New Englanders accounted for 93 percent of the patents registered from 1790 to 1860. The North's 21,973 miles of railroad were more than twice the extent of the South's 9,283 miles. There were eight hundred thousand draft animals in the North and only three hundred thousand in the South. As for financial power, the North accounted for 79 percent of the nation's financial markets and 88 percent of the circulating money. The United States gained as well as lost states during the Civil War. Kansas was admitted on January 29, 1861, West Virginia on July 23, 1863, and Nevada on October 31, 1864. Each of these states supplied both troops to the Union and votes mostly to Republicans.[23]

Soft power animates hard power. Morale is a key element of soft power. Of the many forces that shape morale, perhaps the most vital is the belief that one's cause is just and thus worth the greatest sacrifices. The "rally around the war flag effect" that initially brings a nation together after the first shots are fired will sooner or later dissipate. Crucial to the art of power in war is sustaining the initial burst of patriotism, especially if the toll of death and defeat soars. Lincoln understood that and did what he could to mobilize and sustain the North's spirits. Ideally this was as much a bottom-up as a top-down process.[24]

Eventually the Union army raised 2,213,363 troops, of whom nine of ten were volunteers.[25] In the first year, most men joined motivated solely by patriotism. With time the evident horrors of war, with lengthening casualty lists and countless amputees returning from the front, dulled the ardor of ever more men, forcing federal and state governments to offer a more prosaic reason to join the ranks than mere love of country. State enlistment bonuses ranged from $600 to $1,000. In October 1863 Washington offered a $300 bonus.

Unfortunately, the substitution fees and volunteer bonuses encouraged countless acts of "bounty jumping," or joining and pocketing the money, deserting, joining a different regiment and pocketing more money, deserting, and so on. Regardless of whether they enlisted once or more times, obviously the temptation to take the money grew the poorer one was. Of the two million men who served in the Union army and navy, half a million, or one in four, were immigrants. This is hardly surprising considering that many immigrants were young, single men who stepped ashore friendless and all but penniless.

As genuine enlistments dwindled, Washington had no choice but to institute a draft. Congress passed and Lincoln signed the Militia Law on July 17, 1862. This law rendered all able-bodied men from eighteen to forty-five years of age liable for federal service of nine months. Each state had to supply a quota of troops proportional to its population. On August 4, 1862, Lincoln issued just such a call and by the year's end was able to raise eighty-eight thousand nine-month militia atop the three hundred thousand three-year volunteers he had earlier called for. But nine-month draftees were of little military use. They were no sooner mustered, equipped, trained, and dispatched to distant fronts than their enlistments expired and they dispersed to their homes. To remedy this deficiency, Lincoln got Congress to pass the Enrollment Act of March 6, 1863. The bill required all able-bodied men from twenty to forty-five years of age to register for the draft; those drafted had to either serve or find a substitute.

In all, the government issued four drafts between March 1863 and the war's end. Two men dodged the draft for every man who ended up serving. Of 776,000 who received notice, 161,000 went into hiding, 315,000 got doctors to certify that they were ineligible, and 87,000 paid the $300 fine. Of the 170,000 men who joined the ranks, only 50,000 were actually draftees, while 120,000 were substitutes found by those whose names were called.[26]

If patriotism, duty, and money explain why men served either willingly or fatalistically, those who dodged the draft did so for more diverse reasons. Most naturally feared being killed or maimed. Many had no desire to kill or maim others. Some sympathized with the South. Some opposed the idea of fighting for abolition. Some were genuine pacifists. Some insisted that the poor were fighting for the interests of the rich and that this was wrong. Some asserted two or more of these reasons.

Whether a man volunteered or was drafted, he most likely shared a similar background with most other men in the ranks. As with all wars, the complaint that the Civil War was "a rich man's war, poor man's fight" is irrefutable. A U.S. Sanitary Commission survey found that 47.5 percent of all soldiers were farmers and farm laborers, 25.1 percent were skilled laborers, and 15.9 percent were unskilled laborers, while only 5.1 percent were clerks or businessmen and 3.2 percent were professionals; 3.2 percent were of miscellaneous or unknown background.[27]

Every strategic question is also a moral question. For instance, the Union faced a dilemma over what to do about prisoners of war. Feeding and guarding them was expensive; paroling them was deadly if they broke their promise and rejoined the rebel ranks. The dangers of a parole policy became evident within months after July 1863, when Grant and Banks took the oath from, respectively, thirty thousand rebels at Vicksburg and seven thousand at Port Hudson. Rather than go and stay home until they were officially exchanged, many reenlisted. Grant ended up recapturing at Chattanooga some of those who violated their oath. A formal exchange was just as problematic. Grant pointed out that the Union's better-treated rebel captives would be released "hale, hearty, and well-fed" and thus able to "become active soldiers against us at once," while Union troops freed from dismal conditions in southern camps would be "half-starved, sick, and emaciated" and thus be unable to fight again. Actually the death rates for prisoners were similar, with 30,128, or 15.5 percent, of 194,743 Union troops dying in southern camps, and 25,976, or 12.1 percent, of 214,865 rebels dying in northern camps.[28]

Slavery was the only clear Confederate hard-power advantage. Slaves sowed and reaped crops, hauled supplies, and built fortifications. Lincoln eventually devised a strategy that depleted this advantage and transformed it into a source of Union power. But in doing so he faced a dilemma.

Throughout much of the war, Lincoln faced the problem of how to motivate enough men to abandon their homes and livelihoods to go to war. Reunifying the nation was the first cause that inspired hundreds of thousands of men to enlist. But enthusiasm for the Union waned steadily as the war stalemated and the death toll soared. So the president took a gamble and insisted that the emancipation of slaves was crucial to winning reunification—promising not to return slaves who escaped their rebel masters would steadily drain a vital source of Confederate power. Although he cited military necessity rather than morality to justify his Emancipation Proclamation, he privately reveled in inflicting a blow against an institution that he had always detested. Lincoln not only liberated the slaves, he opened the American army to enlistment by all able-bodied black men.[29]

This forced the South to face a strategic and moral dilemma, perhaps best articulated in January 1865 by Gen. Robert E. Lee: "We must decide whether slavery shall be extinguished by our enemies and the slaves be used against us, or use them ourselves at the risk of the effects which may be produced upon our social institutions. My opinion is that we should employ them without delay."[30] In practice this meant enlisting blacks in return for granting them freedom. While southern leaders discussed this possibility in the war's last desperate months, they ultimately rejected the idea, along with all other forms of emancipation. South Carolina fire-eater Robert Barnwell Rhett explained that "slavery and independence must stand together. . . . To abandon our most essential institution is to abandon . . . that very thing for which we began the fight."[31]

An ideology can be a source of power by unifying and mobilizing a population. Myths are often vital elements of an ideology. During the Civil War, rebel soldiers insisted that they fought for states' rights rather than slavery. In reality, slavery was the only real "right" that was at stake in that war. And, with murderous irony, with only one in four southerners actually a slaveholder, the other three were fighting for the slaveholder's way of life rather than their own, usually hardscrabble, lives. But the power of the ideology of slavocracy overwhelmed such realities in the minds of most southerners.

Another southern myth was their belief in the superiority of their fighting skills. Most southerners cheered the bombardment and capture of Fort Sumter even though they knew it would likely lead to civil war. They had overwhelming faith in their ability to whip the Yankees. In this they emphasized the importance of soft-power assets like leadership, morale, and fighting skills over hard-power resources like population, factories, railroads, and ships.

It may seem extraordinary to well-informed people that a century and a half after the Civil War ended, some people still dispute its cause. For the vast majority of professional and amateur historians alike the truth is a no-brainer. Had slavery not existed, the southern states would have had absolutely no reason to secede, let alone war against the United States.[32]

Yet from the firing on Fort Sumter through today, there have been those, a few even armed with doctorates in history, who reject this view. Contrary to the statements of the South's leaders, neo-Confederates assert that the war was not over slavery but over states' rights. While this belief is grounded in mythology rather than history, it remains popular across the South and beyond. It may be easily refuted intellectually but not emotionally.[33]

States' rights is the belief that the United States is not a sovereign nation but simply an association of sovereign states. States' rights, however, was an excuse and not a reason why eventually eleven southern states committed treason by seceding from and warring against the United States. Southern leaders asserted states' rights to justify whatever measures they took to defend slavery. Had slavery not existed, the belief in and assertion of states' rights would have been moot.

An ideology can be a source of weakness as well as strength. The South's states' rights doctrine was ultimately self-defeating. Slavocrats waved this banner to justify secession from and war against the United States. Yet their Confederacy was just that—an alliance of states in which each claimed sovereignty. The resulting disunity prevented the South from mobilizing all its potential power as each state jealously horded its financial, human, and natural resources. The United States suffered the same debilitating weaknesses during the Revolutionary War when a confederacy of thirteen sovereign states revolted against the British Empire.

Reflecting and shaping the states' rights ideology is the American tendency to want something for nothing. Southerners wanted independence but did not want to be taxed to pay for it. So instead the Confederacy borrowed and printed money. The inevitable result by the Civil War's end was that a Confederate dollar was worth about as much as a Continental dollar, which Congress mass printed during America's war for independence.

Rebel apologists cite the tariff as an issue that deeply split the industrializing North from the agrarian South; northern manufacturers lobbied for protective tariffs on cheaper-priced, better-made foreign—mostly British—imports. They then point out that a civil war nearly erupted during the Nullification Crisis of 1833, when South Carolina nullified or declared that it would no longer recognize or permit federal officials to collect the tariff in its territory.[34] In reality the northern and southern economies complemented rather than conflicted with each other. This bond was most powerful between northern textile factories and southern cotton plantations. As for tariffs, disputes over the rates peaked in 1833 and steadily declined in importance over the next three decades.

The economic problems that slaveholders and other southerners faced were largely self-inflicted. Slavocracy blinded adherents to the economic sacrifice most southerners made to uphold their way of life. Slavery depressed wages for free laborers. The hatred of the tariff along with all taxes was self-defeating. Although a low or no tariff keeps import prices low, it also leaves the federal government with fewer resources with which to subsidize infrastructure like railroads, canals, and roads, which promote the creation and distribution of more wealth over the long term. Yet slavocrats opposed federal policies that developed infrastructure because tariffs and taxes were needed to pay for them.

In reality, all American consumers of foreign goods would have loved to pay lower prices by reducing or eliminating the tariff. Yet most northerners accepted the tariff not just because it provided vital revenues but also because it nurtured industries that strengthened the nation. Most southerners grudgingly accepted the tariff for revenues but hated it for any protection that it might render American factories.

The disdain for northern manufacturing went beyond whatever impact buying higher-priced goods made in America had on southerners' pocketbooks. Slavocrats wanted to believe that northern workers were far worse off than the blacks laboring in their fields. This belief was easily refuted by asking, as Lincoln did, how many northern factory workers escaped their plight by volunteering to become slaves for southern planters.

The southern fear that northern politicians sought to abolish slavery was pathological—all evidence revealed that it was simply unfounded. Lincoln and most other Republicans continually tried to reassure slavocrats that, while they hated slavery, they accepted the reality that the Constitution protected it and they had no desire to change that. They merely wanted to prevent slavery's spread to the new western territories. Yet ironically, by acting on their paranoia and rebelling, southerners forced President Lincoln and America eventually to fulfill their prophecy.

Alas, most of those who so zealously advocated states' rights for themselves were quick to deny it for others. Slavocrats scored a major victory in 1850 by enacting the Fugitive Slave Act that forced people in free states to assist masters and their posses in recapturing escaped slaves. Those who refused to cooperate could be fined up to $1,000. Those who helped escaped slaves could be sentenced to prison.

In reality, slavery not only overshadowed all other issues as the nation's most divisive issue but ultimately was the only issue that prompted the slave states to rebel and attack the United States. Frederick Douglass offered timeless words of moral clarity for the Age of Lincoln's core issue: "There was a right side and a wrong side in the late war, which no sentiment ought to cause us to forget, and while today we should have malice toward none, and charity toward all, it is no part of our duty to confound right with wrong."[35]

Revolutions involve rapid, systematic change. By this definition, the United States did indeed experience a revolution during the Civil War and Reconstruction. Abraham Lincoln spearheaded this revolution through his policies that crushed the rebellion, ended slavery, imposed the Hamiltonian agenda, and initiated the transformation of the southern states into liberal democracies in which blacks had civil rights and, eventually, into a region in which the notion of "American" would be an increasingly important part of its identity. Not all parts of any revolution move at the same pace. The first three parts of Lincoln's revolution took years to accomplish; it took more than a century for the South, along with other racist parts of America, to realize the liberal democratic ideals upon which the United States was founded.

Lincoln himself believed in evolution rather than revolution, in compromise rather than unilateralism, in due legal and political processes rather than brute force, and above all in the Declaration of Independence's values and the Constitution's institutions. He continually sought to be a moderate voice and bridge between extremes. Nonetheless, he recognized that the forces he was unleashing were indeed revolutionary All along he was guided by the understanding that "the right of revolution is never a legal right. . . . At most it is but a moral right, when exercised for a morally justifiable cause. When exercised without such a cause, revolution is no right, but simply a wicked exercise of physical power."[36]

Slavery's abolition was truly revolutionary in itself. Yet how significant was a revolution that converted four million slaves mostly into four million serfs? Nearly all blacks remained mired in poverty as their status changed from slave to sharecropper. Abolition clearly was just the first step. The legal, political, and cultural struggle to transform the figurative fate of all black Americans from, in William Lloyd Garrison's words, "the auction block to the ballot box," would be just as challenging, bitterly fought, and even more prolonged.[37] Racism remained embedded in American life, North and South, East and West. The black codes imposed by white supremacists straightjacketed the ability of African Americans to advance economically or politically.

A second phase of Reconstruction began seventy years after the first phase ended. It took two decades of hard struggle by blacks and liberal whites in the 1950s and 1960s before the legal promises of the 1860s were fulfilled with the 1964 Civil Rights Act and 1965 Voting Rights Act. As for economic equality between the races, even today average black income is only about three-quarters that of whites and Asians and lags behind that of Hispanics. The election of the first black president in 2008 and his reelection in 2012 surely reveal how far the nation has come, but these events tend to obscure all the blood, sweat, and tears shed during the intervening decades, especially the first century.

The Emancipation Proclamation and the Thirteenth Amendment were the first two decisive national legal strides along the long, arduous, often violent road of liberating African Americans and integrating them into the nation's political, economic, and social mainstream. Lincoln's role was critical in pushing these measures through the political system. These stunning achievements reflected his mastery of the art of power. All along he struggled to bridge liberals and conservatives, restraining the former from surging so far ahead that they provoked a political backlash and urging on the reluctant latter to catch up. In wielding the art of power, knowing when to act is as critical as knowing how to act. When Senator Charles Sumner demanded why Lincoln did not announce the Emancipation Proclamation on July 4, 1862, he replied, "I would do it if I were not afraid that half the officers would fling down their arms and three more states would rise."[38] Yet another critical element of the art of power is a leader's ability to convince others that by following him they serve themselves. Lincoln's struggle to get most congressmen and citizens to back emancipation boiled down to a slogan as pithy as it was appealing: "In giving freedom to the slave, we assure freedom to the free."[39]

The North experienced an ideological conversion. Before the Civil War most northerners were indifferent or fatalistic toward slavery. The Republican Party's leaders repeatedly tried to reassure southerners that they had no intention of challenging slavery in the states where it existed but sought only to limit its spread to new territories. The South's rebellion and attack on Fort Sumter inspired a tidal wave of American nationalism across the North. Hundreds of thousands of men joined the army to reunify the nation; relatively few fought with the hope that victory might lead to slavery's abolition. But, largely through Lincoln's leadership, over the next four years the American cause was transformed from solely reunification to reunification and abolition.[40]

During his decades in public life, Lincoln's views on race evolved with his views on all other vital issues. He went from solely opposing slavery's extension to supporting its total abolition, from advocating compensating owners and colonizing blacks overseas to seeking no compensation or colonization and limited suffrage for literate blacks and soldiers. Had he lived another decade he would have sooner rather than later embraced the liberal Republican insistence on equal rights for all. But when he died, his view of most black Americans was certainly racist not just by today's standards but by those of the Radicals of his own time. Yet, while he was darkly pessimistic about whether genuine racial equality was possible or even desirable, he extolled the merits of educated black men.

Abraham Lincoln was the first president to invite black men to the White House for talks or festivities. Frederick Douglass recalled their first meeting. As he was ushered in to see the president, he was surprised that Lincoln bore

> no vain pomp and ceremony about him. I was never more quickly or more completely put at ease in the presence of a great man. . . . Long lines of care were already deeply written on Mr. Lincoln's brow, and his strong face, full of earnestness, lighted up as soon as my name was mentioned. As I approached and was introduced to him he arose and extended his hand and bade me welcome. . . . Proceeding to tell him who I was and what I was doing, he promptly but kindly stopped me, saying, "I know who you are, Mr. Douglass; Mr. Seward has told me all about you. Sit down, I am glad to see you."

Douglass was moved that Lincoln "treated me as a man; he did not let me feel for a moment that there was any difference in the color of our skins."[41]

Nonetheless, Douglass's feelings about Abraham Lincoln and his legacy were decidedly mixed. Eleven years after he last spoke with Lincoln, he did not mince his words in a speech dedicating the Freedmen's Memorial Monument in Washington City on April 14, 1876. He declared that Lincoln "was preeminently the white man's president" and that "we [blacks] are at best only his step-children." Yet he was more judicious in assessing Lincoln's priorities and thus his policies: "Had he put the abolition of slavery before the salvation of the Union, he would have inevitably driven from him a powerful class of the Americans and rendered resistance to rebellion impossible. Viewed from the genuine abolition ground, Mr. Lincoln seemed tardy, cold, dull, and indifferent; but measuring him by the sentiment of his country, a sentiment that he was bound as a statesman to consult, he was swift, zealous, radical, and determined."[42]

America's revolution during the Age of Lincoln went far beyond racial issues. Lincoln inaugurated a profound cultural revolution in how Americans saw themselves. Across the entire country the United States was increasingly referred to using "is" rather than "are," thus denoting the transformation of many identities into one.[43] President Grant noted that progress in a September 1875 speech, then peered into the future: "If we are to have another contest in the near future of our national existence, I predict that the dividing line will not be Mason and Dixon, but between patriotism and intelligence on the one side, and superstition, ambition, and ignorance on the other."[44]

The Civil War shifted the regional and ideological balance of political power within the United States decisively from South to North. During the seventy-two years from 1789 to 1861, southern slaveholders served as president for forty-nine years, as twenty-three of thirty-six Speakers of the House of Representatives, as twenty-four of thirty-six presidents pro tem of the Senate, and as twenty of thirty-five Supreme Court justices. During the next fifty years, there were no southern House Speakers or Senate presidents, while only five of twenty-six Supreme Court justices were Democrats.[45]

Another vital dimension of Lincoln's revolution was the role of government in the nation's development. The Republicans capitalized on their domination of the White House and Congress by establishing in law and policy the entire Hamiltonian agenda of developing America by investing in railroads, canals, ports, and roads; solidifying the financial sector through policies that encouraged productive investments and curbed speculation; supporting manufacturing with protective tariffs; building a transcontinental railroad through land giveaways; and expanding minds through public education and the National Academy of Sciences. This agenda's philosophical foundation was the idea that a muscular, problem-solving federal government working with the private sector could expand the economy far more swiftly and profoundly than if the Darwinian market was left to itself.

If Hamiltonianism had a flaw, it was conceptual. There was an intellectual contradiction in the version of Hamiltonianism developed by Henry Clay and implemented by Abraham Lincoln. Clay coined the term "self-made man" and upheld himself as its personification. This notion appeals to anyone who has risen in wealth and status seemingly by his or her own efforts. Indeed, it is among American culture's core values, celebrated as "individualism" by Benjamin Franklin a century earlier and as "rugged individualism" by Theodore Roosevelt later in the nineteenth century. Yet in the same breath, Hamiltonians expounded the value of the public and private sectors working together to develop the economy and thus create more opportunities for more individuals to realize their unique potentials and dreams. How "self-made" is anyone in such a nation?

During the Age of Lincoln, the United States finally shed the tar baby of slavery only to entangle itself in as sticky a tar baby of monopoly and oligopoly capitalism. Mark Twain called this system of massive corporations and corruption the Gilded Age. In a speech before Republican Party leaders in Hartford, Connecticut, Twain bleakly noted, "Our present civil system, born of General Jackson and the Democratic Party, is so idiotic, so contemptible, so grotesque that it would make the very savages of Dahomey jeer and the very gods of solemnity laugh."[46] It would be another generation before progressives led by Theodore Roosevelt developed and asserted a new version of Hamiltonianism designed to break up the cartels, conserve the nation's natural resources, and impose health, safety, and sanitation standards.

One dimension of power where Abraham Lincoln played a secondary role was in advancing American imperialism. There President Polk surpassed all others with his acquisition of Oregon, California, and New Mexico and with international recognition of the earlier annexation of Texas. Outstanding secretaries of state like Daniel Webster, William Seward, and Hamilton Fish made their own contributions by upholding the Monroe Doctrine in the Western Hemisphere and the Tyler Doctrine in regard to Hawaii.

There is a symbiotic relationship between wealth and power, with each asserted to bolster the other. During the Age of Lincoln, the United States increasingly wielded military power to protect or enhance its swelling economic interests in the Caribbean Basin and Central America and across the Pacific Basin. Washington's most spectacular and far-reaching act was to force Japan to abandon isolationism and join the global system. In doing so the United States came of age as a global power. Yet a dilemma haunted this transformation. As with domestic policy, interest groups became increasingly powerful in shaping American foreign policy. Symbolically the flag followed profits and the pulpit, best represented by the Chamber of Commerce and the Board of Commissioners for Foreign Missions.

The Lincoln revolution failed to dent one enduring, dark dimension of American culture. Most Americans tend to prefer mythology to history.[47] It is certainly a lot less demanding. Mythology is all about good versus evil whereby larger-than-life heroes take center stage to battle against and eventually vanquish larger-than-life villains. History reveals that even the most prominent individuals, groups, and nations are beset by overwhelming political, economic, social, psychological, and cultural forces that they can barely understand let alone control. Few people appreciated this more than Abraham Lincoln, who confessed that he had not led but had been led by history. Rather than let this awareness intimidate him as it does most folks, Lincoln was inspired to understand the history in which he was entangled, hoping that he might find some wiggle room in which to progress.

P. T. Barnum, who originated the practices of modern marketing, succinctly explained why most Americans tend to prefer mythology to history: "There is a sucker born every minute." Although the reasons are obviously more complex than this, Barnum was on to something. There is a very human inclination to blindly believe rather than critically think, to follow a strong leader who is wrong than a weak leader who is right. Lincoln's good friend Senator Orville Browning of Illinois captured that common human flaw: "Why will men believe a lie, an absurd lie, that could not [be] imposed upon a child, and cling to it and repeat it in defiance of all evidence to the contrary?"[48]

Doing so, of course, can lead to disaster. Mythology is a double-edged sword. It is at once a source of unity and of delusion for those who believe it. Demagogues can wield mythology to whip a population into a frenzy against contrived "enemies," foreign and domestic. Related to the power of myth is the power of projection onto hated others the unresolved inner pathologies of one's self or group.

The South personified these pathologies during the Age of Lincoln. Southerners spun a mythology in which slavocracy was the most exalted human invention while they projected onto abolitionists such characteristics as being cruel, avaricious, dangerous, and treasonous. After Abraham Lincoln won the presidency in November 1860, slavocrats in eventually eleven southern states acted on the delusion that the Republican Party sought to destroy their key institution and thus they had no choice but to rebel from and war against the United States. In doing so, southerners accelerated slavery's demise by generations.

There is strange twist in the psyches of many, perhaps most, people—the more illogical their excuses for believing or doing something, the more fervently they insist that they are right. In war, as a nation's losses in people, property, and treasure mount, the tendency increases for leaders and followers to insist that even more sacrifices be made so that the previous sacrifices were not in vain.

Which brings us to the Confederate cause. During the nearly nine decades following America's declaration of independence, slavery was the nation's core toxic issue that infected virtually all others. Economic, moral, and thus political disputes over slavery led to crises in 1820, 1837, 1845, 1850, and 1854 that skilled statesmen eventually finessed with compromises. The crisis over slavery in 1860, however, was so severe that it overwhelmed all voices of reason and resulted in secession, rebellion, and war. While the Civil War had many causes, one, slavery, caused all the others. Had slavery never existed the rebel states would have had no cause to quit, let alone fight, the United States.[49]

In 1860 America's economy, and thus its social and moral system, was schizophrenic. A nation's power is no greater than its unity. With the United States half slave and half free, it was split into two nations rather than one. The concept of America as a nation weakened as southern identity and belief in states' rights grew.[50] Free labor and capital markets prevailed across the North but overlapped with slavery and feudalism across the South. In 1860 one of five people living in the southern states was black, and virtually all blacks, or four million people, were slaves. Meanwhile four of ten southern whites were so poor that they did not own the land that they farmed. The white middle class of shopkeepers, blacksmiths, and wheelwrights was limited in numbers and income. For southerners slavery was the surest route to wealth, power, and prestige.

The average slaveholder held $25,000 of assessed wealth, fourteen times more than the average of $1,800 for farmers without slaves.[51]

Slavery hurt nearly everyone except those who actually owned and exploited the slaves. How can white laborers compete with slaves performing the same labor in the next field or workshop? Nonetheless, while poor white southerners may have complained about being in a "rich man's war, poor man's fight," most of them fought heroically all the same. In doing so, they fought for abstract notions of "honor" and "states' rights" against their own hard economic interests.

Slavocrats provoked first secession, then an increasingly devastating war with the United States. The slavocrat promise that the South would swiftly triumph in a glorious victory quickly proved chimerical. Yet the rebels fought on for four blood-soaked years, all along clinging to the Orwellian delusion that they were defending states' rights rather than slavery. This belief was at once a strength and a weakness—it mobilized the population for war and worsened their destruction and eventual defeat. The South's ideology of slavocracy was not a source of power but of self-inflicted, devastating wounds. And this presents a vital insight into the art of power—the ultimate source of power is a devotion to understanding and advancing one's interests in the world as it is rather than how one might like it to be.

The Declaration of Independence is said to express "the American mind." This, of course, is only partly true. The text pronounced a set of ideals that progressive Americans have struggled to realize ever since. It represents how Americans would like to see themselves much more than how they really are. The Declaration of Independence's ideals guided Abraham Lincoln throughout his life. No one from 1848 to 1876 did more to advance the nation's ability to live up to the ideals upon which it is founded.

Upon meditating on the dead body of the man he had served for four years and came to deeply admire, Secretary of War Edwin Stanton remarked, "Now he belongs to the ages."[52] And so does the America that Abraham Lincoln so decisively shaped.

ABBREVIATIONS

Grant Memoirs	Ulysses S. Grant. *The Personal Memoirs of Ulysses S. Grant*. Princeton NJ: Collectors Reprints, 1998.
Lincoln Works	Roy P. Basler et al., eds. *The Collected Works of Abraham Lincoln*. 9 vols. New Brunswick NJ: Rutgers University Press, 1853–55.
Lincoln Writings	Allan Nevins, ed. *The Life and Writings of Abraham Lincoln*. New York: Modern Library, 2000.
Official Records	*War of the Rebellion: A Compilation of the Official Records of the Union and Confederate Armies*. 70 vols. Washington DC: Government Printing Office, 1880–1901.

NOTES

INTRODUCTION

1. William Nester, *The Revolutionary Years, 1775–1789: The Art of American Power during the Early Republic* (Washington DC: Potomac Books, 2011); William Nester, *The Hamiltonian Vision, 1789–1800: The Art of American Power during the Early Republic* (Washington DC: Potomac Books, 2012); William Nester, *The Jeffersonian Vision, 1801–1815: The Art of American Power during the Early Republic* (Washington DC: Potomac Books, 2012); William Nester, *The Age of Jackson and the Art of American Power, 1815–1848* (Washington DC: Potomac Books, 2013).

2. The thousands of books and articles on Abraham Lincoln could fill a small library. For overviews of the literature, see Richard Booker, *Abraham Lincoln in Periodical Literature, 1860–1940* (Chicago: Falwey Brost, 1941); Jay Monaghan, *Lincoln Bibliography, 1839–1939*, 2 vols. (Springfield: Illinois State Historical Library, 1943); Paul M. Angle, *A Shelf of Lincoln Books: A Critical Selective Bibliography of Lincolniana* (New Brunswick NJ: Rutgers University Press, 1946); Benjamin P. Thomas, *Portrait for Posterity: Lincoln and His Biographers* (New Brunswick NJ: Rutgers University Press, 1947); Don Fehrenbacher, *The Changing Image of Lincoln in American Historiography* (New York: Oxford University Press, 1968); Merrill D. Peterson, *Lincoln in American Memory* (New York: Oxford University Press, 1994); John Channing Briggs, *Lincoln's Speeches Reconsidered* (Baltimore: Johns Hopkins University Press, 2005).

For the most extensive studies by those who knew him, see William H. Herndon and Jesse W. Weik, *Herndon's Lincoln: The True Story of a Great Life*, 3 vols. (Chicago:

Belford, Clarke, 1889); John G. Nicolay and John Hay, *Abraham Lincoln: A History*, 10 vols. (New York: Century, 1890).

For the best one-volume histories, see Benjamin P. Thomas, *Abraham Lincoln: A Biography* (New York: Alfred A. Knopf, 1952); Reinhard H. Luthin, *The Real Abraham Lincoln* (Englewood Cliffs NJ: Prentice Hall, 1960); Stephen Oates, *With Malice toward None: The Life of Abraham Lincoln* (New York: Harper and Row, 1977); David Herbert Donald, *Lincoln* (New York: Simon and Schuster, 1995).

For the best books on his presidency, see Mark F. Neely, *The Last Best Hope of Earth: Abraham Lincoln and the Promise of America* (Cambridge MA: Harvard University Press, 1993); Philip Shaw Paludan, *The Presidency of Abraham Lincoln* (Lawrence: University Press of Kansas,1994); William Lee Miller, *President Lincoln: The Duty of a Statesman* (New York: Alfred A. Knopf, 2008).

3. Sun Tzu, *The Art of War* (New York: Basic Books, 1994).

4. Abraham Lincoln to Albert Hodges, April 4, 1864, *Lincoln Works*, 7:281–82.

5. Abraham Lincoln to Reverdy Johnson, July 26, 1862, *Lincoln Works*, 5:342–43.

6. Herndon and Weik, *Herndon's Lincoln*, 2:334.

7. Notes for Speeches, August 21, 1858, *Lincoln Works*, 2:552.

8. Abraham Lincoln to H. L. Pierce, April 6, 1859, *Lincoln Writings*, 540.

9. Abraham Lincoln to Isaac Schermerhorn, September 12, 1864, *Lincoln Works*, 8:1.

10. "Mediation on the Divine Will," September 30, 1862, *Lincoln Writings*, 728.

11. Tyler Dennett, ed., *Lincoln and the Civil War in the Letters and Diaries of John Hay* (New York: Dodd, Mead, 1939), 19; "A House Divided," June 16, 1858, *Lincoln Works*, 2:461–62.

12. Gabor S. Boritt, *Lincoln and the Economics of the American Dream* (Memphis: Memphis State University Press, 1978), 159, 190.

13. For other books that wholly or partly explore that era, see William R. Brock, *Conflict and Transformation: The United States, 1844–1877* (New York: Penguin, 1973); Richard H. Sewell, *A House Divided: Sectionalism and the Civil War, 1848–1865* (Baltimore: Johns Hopkins University Press, 1988); William L. Barney, *Battleground for the Union: The Era of the Civil War and Reconstruction, 1848–1877* (Englewood Cliffs NJ: Prentice Hall, 1990).

14. Nester, *Age of Jackson*.

15. Mark W. Summers, *The Plundering Generation: Corruption and the Crisis of the Union, 1849–1861* (New York: Oxford University Press, 1987).

16. Address at Cooper Institute, February 27, 1858, *Lincoln Writings*, 591.

1. EIGHTEEN FORTY-EIGHT

1. Chaplain W. Morrison, *Democratic Politics and Sectionalism: The Wilmot Proviso Controversy* (Chapel Hill: University of North Carolina Press, 1967).

2. Gabor S. Boritt, "Lincoln's Opposition to the Mexican War," *Journal of the Illinois State Historical Society* 67 (February 1974): 79–100; Mark E. Neeley, "War and Partisanship: What Lincoln Learned from James K. Polk" *Journal of the Illinois State*

Historical Society 74, no. 3 (Autumn 1981): 199–216; Mark E. Neeley, "Lincoln and the Mexican War: An Argument by Analogy," *Civil War History* 24 (March 1979): 5–23.

3. House of Representatives Speech, January 12, 1848, *Lincoln Works*, 1:431–42.

4. Resolution in the United States House of Representatives, December 22, 1847, *Lincoln Writings*, 297–99.

5. Robert W. Merry, *A Country of Vast Designs: James K. Polk, the Mexican War, and the Conquest of the American Continent* (New York: Simon and Schuster, 2009), 341–42.

6. Herndon's letter is not preserved but its content can be surmised by Lincoln's reply; Abraham Lincoln to William Herndon, February 15, 1848, *Lincoln Writings*, 299–300.

7. House of Representatives Speech, January 12, 1848, *Lincoln Writings*, 306.

8. *Grant Memoirs*, 24–25, 18.

9. *Grant Memoirs*, 25.

10. Albert K. Weinberg, *Manifest Destiny: A Study of Nationalist Expansion in American History* (Chicago: Quadrangle Press, 1963); Frederick Merk, *Manifest Destiny and the Mission in American History* (New York: Alfred A. Knopf, 1963); Reginald Horsman, *Race and Manifest Destiny: The Origins of American Racial Anglo-Saxonism* (Cambridge MA: Harvard University Press, 1981); Thomas Hietala, *Manifest Destiny: Anxious Aggrandizement in Late Jacksonian America* (Ithaca NY: Cornell University Press, 1985); Amy Greenberg, *Manifest Manhood and the Antebellum American Empire* (New York: Cambridge University Press, 2005).

11. Samuel Flagg Bemis, *John Quincy Adams and the Union* (Westport CT: Greenwood Press, 1980), 536.

12. Richard Griswold del Castillo, *The Treaty of Guadeloupe Hidalgo* (Norman: University of Oklahoma Press, 1990).

13. Michael A. Morrison, *Slavery and the American West: The Eclipse of Manifest Destiny* (Chapel Hill: University of North Carolina Press, 1999).

14. Rodman Paul and Elliott West, *Mining Frontiers of the Far West* (Albuquerque: University of New Mexico Press, 2001), 13; Brian Roberts, *American Alchemy: The California Gold Rush and Middle-Class Culture* (Chapel Hill: University of North Carolina Press, 2000); Susan Johnson, *Roaring Camp: The Social World of the California Gold Rush* (New York: W. W. Norton, 2001); Kenneth Owen, *Riches for All: The California Gold Rush and the World* (Lincoln: University of Nebraska Press, 2002).

15. John D. Unruh, *The Plains Across: The Overland Emigrants and the Trans-Mississippi West, 1840–1860* (Urbana: University of Illinois Press, 1978); Michael Tate, *Indians and Emigrants: Encounters on the Overland Trails* (Norman: University of Oklahoma Press, 2006).

16. Charles Dickens, *American Notes for General Circulation* (New York: Penguin, 1985), 164.

17. *Historical Statistics of the United States, 1789–1845* (Washington DC: Government Printing Office, 1949), 32; David M. Potter, *The Impending Crisis, 1848–1861* (New York: Harper and Row, 1976), 11, 12.

18. Joseph Ferrie, *Yankees Now: Immigrants in the Antebellum United States* (New York: Oxford University Press, 1999).

19. Ellen C. Dubois, *Feminism and Suffrage: The Emergence of an Independent Women's Movement in America, 1848–1869* (Ithaca NY: Cornell University Press, 1978); Blanche Hersh, *The Slavery of Sex: Feminist-Abolitionists in America* (Urbana: University of Illinois Press, 1978); Jean Fagan Yellin and John C. Van Horne, eds., *The Abolitionist Sisterhood: Women's Political Culture in Antebellum America* (Ithaca NY: Cornell University Press, 1994); Sylvia Hoffert, *When Hens Crow: The Woman's Rights Movement in Antebellum America* (Bloomington: University of Indiana Press, 1995); Margaret McFadden, *Golden Cables of Sympathy: Transatlantic Sources of Nineteenth-Century Feminism* (Lexington: University of Press Kentucky, 1999); Barbara Cutter, *Domestic Devils, Battlefield Angels: The Radicalization of American Womanhood, 1830–1865* (DeKalb: Northern Illinois University Press, 2003); Judith Wellman, *The Road to Seneca Falls* (Urbana: University of Illinois Press, 2004).

20. Sally Gregory Miller, *Seneca Falls and the Origins of the Women's Rights Movement* (New York: Oxford University Press, 2008), 93–94.

21. For the election, see Joseph G. Rayback, *Free Soil: The Election of 1848* (Lexington: University Press of Kentucky, 1978). For the Democratic Party, see Yonatan Eyal, *The Young America Movement and the Transformation of the Democratic Party, 1828–1861* (New York: Cambridge University Press, 2007). For the Whig Party, see Thomas Brown, *Politics and Statesmanship: Essays on the American Whig Party* (New York: Columbia University Press, 1985); Daniel Walker Howe, *The Political Culture of the American Whigs* (Chicago: University of Chicago Press, 1988); Michael F. Holt, *The Rise and Fall of the American Whig Party: Jacksonian Politics and the Onset of the Civil War* (New York: Oxford University Press, 2003).

22. Speech, November 13, 1847, in *The Papers of Henry Clay*, ed. James F. Hopkins, 10 vols. (Lexington: University Press of Kentucky, 1959–92), 10:361–77.

23. Frederick J. Blue, *The Free Soilers: Third Party Politics, 1848–1854* (Urbana: University of Illinois Press, 1973); Jonathan Halperin Earle, *Jacksonian Antislavery and the Politics of Free Soil, 1824–1854* (Chapel Hill: University of North Carolina Press, 2004).

24. Kwame Anthony Appiah, introduction to Frederick Douglass and Harriet Jacobs, *"Narrative of the Life of Frederick Douglass, an American Slave" and "Incidents in the Life of a Slave Girl"* (New York: Modern Library, 2004).

2. YOUNG LINCOLN

1. John Scripps to William Herndon, June 24, 1865, in *Herndon's Informants: Letters, Interviews, and Statements about Abraham Lincoln*, ed. Douglas L. Wilson and Rodney O. Davis (Urbana: University of Illinois Press, 1998), 57. For the most detailed book on Lincoln's younger years, see Albert J. Beveridge, *Abraham Lincoln,*

1809–1858, 2 vols. (Boston: Houghton Mifflin, 1928). For the best book on his psychological development, see Michael Burlingame, *The Inner World of Abraham Lincoln* (Urbana: University of Illinois Press, 1994).

2. Abraham Lincoln to John Johnston, January 13, 1851, *Lincoln Works*, 2:96–97.

3. Abraham Lincoln to Andrew Johnston, April 18, 1846, *Lincoln Writings*, 287–88.

4. Abraham Lincoln to Albert Hodges, April 4,1864, *Lincoln Writings*, 807.

5. For the best book on this period of his life, see Benjamin P. Thomas, *Lincoln's New Salem* (New York: Alfred A. Knopf, 1954).

6. Wilson and Davis, *Herndon's Informants*, 372–73. See Harry E. Pratt, "Lincoln in the Black Hawk War," *Bulletin of the Abraham Lincoln Association* 54 (December 1938): 2–13.

7. Lincoln's First Public Address, March 9, 1832, *Lincoln Writings*, 221–24.

8. For the best books on Lincoln as a lawyer, see Albert A. Woldman, *Lawyer Lincoln* (Boston: Houghton Mifflin,1936); John J. Duff, *A. Lincoln: Prairie Lawyer* (Urbana: University of Illinois Press, 1960); John P. Frank, *Lincoln as a Lawyer* (Urbana: University of Illinois Press, 1961).

9. For the best book on this period of his life, see Paul Simon, *Lincoln's Preparations for Greatness: The Illinois Legislative Years* (Urbana: University of Illinois Press, 1971).

10. Resolutions by the General Assembly of the State of Illinois, Note 2 of Protest in Illinois Legislature on Slavery, March 3, 1837, *Lincoln Works*, 1:75.

11. First Debate, Ottawa, August 21, 1858, *Lincoln Works*, 3:29.

12. Eulogy on Henry Clay, July 6, 1852, *Lincoln Works*, 2:126.

13. Daniel Walker Howe, "Why Lincoln Was a Whig," *Journal of the Abraham Lincoln Association* 16, no. 1 (Winter 1995): 27–38. For Clay's most comprehensive biography, see Robert V. Remini, *Henry Clay: Statesman for the Union* (New York: W. W. Norton, 1991).

14. Eulogy on Henry Clay, July 6, 1852, *Lincoln Works*, 2:126; Gabor S. Boritt, *Lincoln and the Economics of the American Dream* (Memphis: Memphis State University Press, 1978); William Nester, *The Hamiltonian Vision, 1789–1800: The Art of American Power during the Early Republic* (Washington DC: Potomac Books, 2012).

15. For the best book on the Springfield years, see Paul M. Angle, *"Here I Have Lived": A History of Lincoln's Springfield, 1821–1865* (New Brunswick NJ: Rutgers University Press, 1950).

16. William H. Herndon and Jesse W. Weik, *Herndon's Lincoln*, ed. Douglas L. Wilson and Rodney O. Davis (Urbana: University of Illinois Press, 2006). See also Wilson and Davis, *Herndon's Informants*.

17. Notes for a Law Lecture, July 1, 1850, *Lincoln Writings*, 329.

18. Thomas F. Schwartz, "The Springfield Lyceum and Lincoln's 1838 Speech," *Illinois Historical Journal* 83 (1990): 45–49. For leading works on Lincoln's political

philosophy, see James G. Randall, *Lincoln the Liberal Statesman* (New York: Dodd, Mead, 1947); Richard Current, ed., *The Political Thought of Abraham Lincoln* (Indianapolis: Bobbs-Merrill, 1967); John Thomas, ed., *Abraham Lincoln and the American Political Tradition* (Amherst: University of Massachusetts Press, 1986).

19. "The Perpetuation of Our Political Institutions," January 27, 1838, *Lincoln Works*, 1:108–15.

20. Abraham Lincoln to James Shields, September 17, 1842; Memorandum of Instructions to E. H. Merryman, Lincoln's Second in the Lincoln-Shields Duel, September 19, 1842; Abraham Lincoln to Joshua Speed, October 4, 1842, *Lincoln Writings*, 273–74, 274–75, 276–77.

21. David Herbert Donald, *Lincoln* (New York: Simon and Schuster, 1995), 68.

22. Abraham Lincoln to Mary Owens, May 7, 1837, *Lincoln Writings*, 228–29.

23. Doris Kearns Goodwin, *Team of Rivals: The Political Genius of Abraham Lincoln* (New York: Simon and Schuster, 2006), 93.

24. Announcement of Political Views, June 13, 1836, *Lincoln Works*, 1:48.

25. Isaac Cogdal interview, in Wilson and Davis, *Herndon's Informants*, 440.

26. Abraham Lincoln to Mary Owens, May 7, August 16, 1837, *Lincoln Writings*, 228–29, 230–31.

27. Abraham Lincoln to Mrs. Orville Browning, April 1, 1838, *Lincoln Works*, 1:118–19.

28. For the best books on his marriage, see Ruth Painter Randall, *Mary Lincoln: Biography of a Marriage* (Boston: Little, Brown, 1953); Ruth Painter Randall, *The Courtship of Mr. Lincoln* (Boston: Little, Brown, 1957); Jean H. Baker, *Mary Todd Lincoln: A Biography* (New York: W. W. Norton, 1987).

29. Donald, *Lincoln*, 85.

30. William H. Herndon and Jesse W. Weik, *Herndon's Lincoln: The True Story of a Great Life*, 3 vols. (Chicago: Belford, Clarke, 1889), 2:213.

31. Abraham Lincoln to John Stuart, January 23, 1841; Abraham Lincoln to Joshua Speed, January 3, February 3, 13, 25 (two letters), March 27, July 4, 1842, *Lincoln Writings*, 247, 255–57, 257–59, 267–69, 270–71, 271–73.

32. Abraham Lincoln to Samuel Marshall, November 11, 1842, *Lincoln Works*, 1:305.

33. Donald W. Riddle, *Lincoln Runs for Congress* (New Brunswick NJ: Rutgers University Press, 1948); Paul Findley, *A. Lincoln: The Crucible of Congress* (New York: Crown, 1979).

34. Handbill Replying to Charges of Infidelity, July 3, 1846, *Lincoln Writings*, 1:382–84.

35. Carl Schurz, *The Reminiscences of Carl Schurz*, 3 vols. (New York: McClure, 1907).

36. Herndon and Weik, *Herndon's Lincoln* (1889), 3:586.

37. Beveridge, *Abraham Lincoln*, 2:359.

38. For psychological studies of Lincoln, see Richard Current, *The Lincoln That Nobody Knows* (New York: Hill and Wang, 1958); George B. Forgie, *Patricide in the House Divided: A Psychological Interpretation of Lincoln and His Age* (New York: W. W. Norton, 1979); Michael Paul Rogin, "The King's Two Bodies: Abraham Lincoln, Richard Nixon, and Presidential Self-Sacrifice," *Massachusetts Review* 20 (Autumn 1979): 553–73; Dwight G. Anderson, *Abraham Lincoln: The Quest for Immortality* (New York: Alfred A. Knopf, 1982); George M. Frederickson, "Lincoln and His Legend," *New York Review of Books*, July 15, 1982, 13–16; Charles B. Strozier, *Lincoln's Quest for Union: Public and Private Meanings* (New York: Basic Books, 1982); Richard N. Current, "Lincoln after 175 Years: The Myth of the Jealous Son," *Papers of the Abraham Lincoln Association* 6 (1984): 15–24; James Chowning Davis, "Lincoln: The Saint and the Man," *Presidential Studies Quarterly* 17 (Winter 1987): 25–35; Gabor S. Boritt, *The Historian's Lincoln: Pseudohistory, Psychohistory, and History* (Urbana: University of Illinois Press, 1988); Burlingame, *Inner World of Abraham Lincoln*; Allen C. Guelzo, "Abraham Lincoln and the Doctrine of Necessity," *Journal of the Abraham Lincoln Association* 18, no. 1 (Winter 1997): 57–81; Gabor Boritt, ed., *The Lincoln Enigma: The Changing Faces of an American Icon* (New York: Oxford University Press, 2001).

39. Speech at Springfield, Illinois, June 16, 1858, *Lincoln Writings*, 429.

40. Allen T. Rice, ed., *Reminiscences of Abraham Lincoln by Distinguished Men of His Time* (New York: North American Publishing, 1886), 575–76.

41. Abraham Lincoln to Mary Lincoln, April 16, June 12, 1848, *Lincoln Writings*, 313, 315.

42. Abraham Lincoln to Mary Speed, September 27, 1841, *Lincoln Works*, 1:261.

43. William J. Wolf, *The Almost Chosen People: A Study of the Religion of Abraham Lincoln* (Garden City NY: Doubleday, 1959); Hans Morgenthau and David Hein, eds., *Essays on Lincoln's Faith and Politics* (Lanham MD: University Press of America, 1983).

44. Goodwin, *Team of Rivals*, 56.

45. Farewell Address at Springfield, February 11, 1861, *Lincoln Works*, 4:190.

46. Noyes Miner, "Personal Recollections of Abraham Lincoln," 46–48, quoted in Richard Carwardine, "Lincoln, Evangelical Religion, and American Political Culture in the Era of the Civil War," *Journal of the Abraham Lincoln Association* 18, no. 1 (Winter 1997): 51.

47. Handbill Replying to Charges of Infidelity, July 3, 1846, *Lincoln Writings*, 1:382–84.

48. Abraham Lincoln to Oliver Morton, February 11, 1861, *Lincoln Works*, 4:194.

49. Abraham Lincoln to Albert Hodges, April 4, 1864, *Lincoln Works*, 7:282.

50. Abraham Lincoln to William Herndon, July 10, June 22, 1848, *Lincoln Writings*, 320, 316. For a critical account of Lincoln as a self-made man, see the chapter "Abraham Lincoln and the Self-Made Myth" in Richard Hofstadter, *The American Political Tradition and the Men Who Made It* (New York: Vintage, 1989), 119–74.

51. Herndon and Weik, *Herndon's Lincoln* (1889), 2:306.

52. Handbill Replying to Charges of Infidelity, July 31, 1846, *Lincoln Works*, 1:382.

53. Lincoln's First Public Address, March 9, 1832, *Lincoln Writings*, 224.

3. UNCLE TOM'S CABIN

1. Forrest Wilson, *Crusader in Crinoline: The Life of Harriet Beecher Stowe* (Philadelphia: J. B. Lippincott, 1941), 484–85. See also Harriet Beecher Stowe, *Uncle Tom's Cabin, an Annotated Edition*, ed. Philip Van Doren Stern (New York: P. S. Erikson, 1964).

2. Joan D. Hedrick, *Harriet Beecher Stowe: A Life* (New York: Oxford University Press, 1994), 211–15; Harriet Beecher Stowe, *Uncle Tom's Cabin: A Norton Critical Edition*, ed. Elizabeth Ammons (New York: W. W. Norton, 1994).

3. Ira Berlin, *Many Thousands Gone: The First Two Centuries of Slavery in America* (Cambridge MA: Harvard University Press, 1998); Don E. Fehrenbacher, *The Slaveholding Republic: An Account of the United States Government's Relation to Slavery* (New York: Oxford University Press, 2001); James Oliver Horton and Lois E. Horton, *Slavery and the Making of America* (New York: Oxford University Press, 2005).

4. Thomas Jefferson, *Notes on the State of Virginia*, ed. William Peden (Chapel Hill: University of North Carolina Press, 1955), 162, 138.

5. Alexander Keysar, *The Right to Vote: The Contested History of Democracy in the United States* (New York: Basic Books, 2000), 336–41.

6. Aileen S. Kraditor, *Means and Ends in American Abolitionism: Garrison and His Critics on Strategy and Tactics, 1834–1850* (New York: Pantheon Books, 1969); Gerald Sorin, *Abolitionism: A New Perspective* (New York: Praeger, 1972); Lewis Perry, *Radical Abolitionism: Anarchy and the Government of God in Antislavery Thought* (Ithaca NY: Cornell University Press, 1973); Ronald Walters, *The Antislavery Appeal: American Abolitionism after 1830* (Baltimore MD: Johns Hopkins University Press, 1976); James Bremer Steward, *Holy Warriors: The Abolitionists and American Slavery* (New York: Hill and Wang, 1976); Richard Sewell, *Ballots for Freedom: Antislavery Politics in the United States, 1837–1860* (New York: Oxford University Press, 1976); William Wiecek, *The Sources of Antislavery Constitutionalism, 1760–1848* (Ithaca NY: Cornell University Press, 1977); John R. McKivigan, *The War against Proslavery Religion: Abolitionism and the Northern Churches* (Ithaca NY: Cornell University Press, 1984); Edward Magdol, *The Antislavery Rank and File: A Social Profile of the Abolitionists' Constituency* (Westport CT: Greenwood Press, 1986); Jean Fagan Yellin and John C. Van Horne, eds., *The Abolitionist Sisterhood: Women's Political Culture in Antebellum America* (Ithaca NY: Cornell University Press, 1994); Stanley Harrold, *The Abolitionists and the South, 1831–1861* (Lexington: University Press of Kentucky, 1995); Julie Roy Jeffrey, *The Great Silent Army of Abolitionism: Ordinary Women in the Antislavery Movement* (Chapel Hill: University of North Carolina Press, 1998); John Stauffer, *The Black Hearts of Men: Radical Abolitionists and the Transformation of Race* (Cambridge MA: Harvard University Press, 2002); Richard Newman, *The Transformation of*

American Abolitionism: Fighting Slavery in the Early Republic (Chapel Hill: University of North Carolina Press, 2002); Michael D. Pierson, *Free Hearts, Free Homes: Gender and American Antislavery Politics* (Chapel Hill: University of North Carolina Press, 2003); Eric Burin, *Slavery and the Peculiar Institution: A History of the American Colonization Society* (Gainesville: University Press of Florida, 2005); Timothy Patrick McCarthy and John Stauffer, eds., *Prophets of Protest: Reconsidering the History of American Abolitionism* (New York: New Press, 2006).

7. Henry Mayer, *All on Fire: William Lloyd Garrison and the Abolition of Slavery* (New York: St. Martin's Press, 1998).

8. William Lloyd Garrison, *Selections from the Writings and Speeches of William Lloyd Garrison* (New York: New American, 1964), 110.

9. Louis Filler, *The Crusade against Slavery, 1820–1860* (New York: Harper and Brothers, 1960), 18.

10. Patrick Rael, *Black Identity and Black Protest in the Antebellum North* (Chapel Hill: University of North Carolina Press, 2002).

11. Frederick Douglass, *Narrative of the Life of Frederick Douglass: An American Slave, Written by Himself,* ed. David W. Blight (Boston: Bedford/St. Martin's Press, 2003); Philip Foner, ed., *Frederick Douglass on Slavery and the Civil War: Selections from His Writings* (Mineola NY: Dover, 2003); Eric Foner, *Frederick Douglass: A Biography* (New York: Citadel Press, 1964); Waldo E. Martin, *The Mind of Frederick Douglass* (Chapel Hill: University of North Carolina Press, 1984); William S. McFeely, *Frederick Douglass* (New York: W. W. Norton, 1991).

12. David Grimsted, *American Mobbing, 1828–1861: Toward Civil War* (New York: Oxford University Press, 1998); John McKivigan and Stanley Harrold, eds., *Antislavery Violence: Sectional, Racial, and Cultural Conflict in Antebellum America* (Knoxville: University of Tennessee Press, 1999).

13. Avery O. Craven, *The Growth of Southern Nationalism, 1848–1861* (Baton Rouge: Louisiana State University Press, 1953); William R. Taylor, *Cavalier and Yankee: The Old South and American National Character* (New York: G. Braziller, 1957); Ronald T. Takaki, *A Pro-slavery Crusade: The Agitation to Reopen the African Slave Trade* (New York: Free Press, 1971); John McCardell, *The Idea of a Southern Nation: Southern Nationalists and Southern Nationalism, 1830–1860* (New York: W. W. Norton, 1979); Drew Gilpin Faust, ed., *The Ideology of Slavery: Pro-slavery Thought in the Antebellum South, 1830–1860* (Baton Rouge: Louisiana State University Press, 1981); Larry E. Tise, *Proslavery: A History of the Defense of Slavery in America, 1701–1840* (Athens: University of Georgia Press, 1987); Eric Walther, *The Fire-Eaters* (Baton Rouge: Louisiana State University Press, 1992); Elizabeth Moss, *Domestic Novelists in the Old South: Defenders of Southern Culture* (Baton Rouge: Louisiana State University Press, 1992); Mitchell Snay, *The Gospel of Disunion: Religion and Separatism in the Antebellum South* (New York: Cambridge University Press, 1993); Leonard L. Richards, *The Slave Power: The Free North and Southern Domination, 1780–1860*

(Baton Rouge: Louisiana State University Press, 2000); William C. Davis, *Rhett: The Turbulent Life and Times of a Fire-Eater* (Columbia: University of South Carolina Press, 2001); Paul Finkelman, *Defending Slavery: Proslavery Thought in the Old South* (Boston: Bedford/St. Martin's Press, 2003); Lorman A. Ratner and Dwight L. Teeter, *Fanatics and Fire-Eaters: Newspapers and the Coming of the Civil War* (Champaign: University of Illinois Press, 2003); Michael O'Brien, *Conjectures of Order: Intellectual Life and the American South, 1810–1860*, 2 vols. (Chapel Hill: University of North Carolina Press, 2004); Adam L. Tate, *Conservatism and Southern Intellectuals, 1789– 1861: Liberty, Tradition, and the Good Society* (Columbia: University of South Carolina Press, 2005); Elizabeth Fox-Genovese and Eugene D. Genovese, *The Mind of the Master Class: History and Faith in the Southern Slaveholders' Worldview* (New York: Cambridge University Press, 2005).

14. Cohens v. Virginia, 6 Wheat. 264 at 413–14 (1821).

15. Elizabeth R. Varon, *Disunion!: The Coming of the American Civil War, 1789– 1859* (Chapel Hill: University of North Carolina Press, 2008), 82.

16. Calhoun and Yancey quotes from James M. McPherson, *Abraham Lincoln and the Second American Revolution* (New York: Oxford University Press, 1991), 50; Harvey Wish, *George Fitzhugh, Propagandist of the Old South* (Baton Rouge: Louisiana State University Press, 1943).

17. James Oakes, *The Ruling Race: A History of American Slaveholders* (New York: W. W. Norton, 1982), 141.

18. Bertram Wyatt-Brown, *Southern Honor: Ethics and Behavior in the Old South* (New York: Oxford University Press, 1982).

19. Harvey Wish, ed., *Ante-Bellum: The Writings of George Fitzhugh and Hinton Rowan Helper on Slavery* (New York: Capricorn, 1960); Davis, *Rhett*.

20. David M. Potter, *The Impending Crisis, 1848–1861* (New York: Harper and Row, 1976), 124.

21. Eric Foner, *Free Soil, Free Labor, Free Men: The Ideology of the Republican Party before the Civil War* (New York: Oxford University Press, 1995), 72.

22. James L. Huston, *Calculating the Value of the Union: Slavery, Property Rights, and the Economic Origins of the Civil War* (Chapel Hill: University of North Carolina Press, 2003).

23. For the best books on all or part of this thirteen-year period, see Allan Nevins, *Ordeal of the Union: Fruits of Manifest Destiny, 1847–1852* (New York: Charles Scribners' Sons, 1947); Allen Nevins, *Ordeal of the Union: A House Dividing, 1852–1857* (New York: Charles Scribners' Sons, 1947); Russell Welter, *The Mind of America, 1820–1860* (New York: Columbia University Press, 1975); Potter, *Impending Crisis*; Michael F. Holt, *The Political Crisis of the 1850s* (New York: John Wiley and Sons, 1978; repr., New York: W. W. Norton, 1983); Mark W. Summers, *The Plundering Generation: Corruption and the Crisis of the Union, 1849–1861* (New York: Oxford University Press, 1987); Richard H. Sewell, *A House Divided: Sectionalism*

and the Civil War, 1848–1865 (Baltimore: Johns Hopkins University Press, 1988); William W. Freehling, *The Road to Disunion: Secessionists at Bay, 1776–1854* (New York: Oxford University Press, 1991); Michael F. Holt, *Political Parties and American Political Development from the Age of Jackson to the Age of Lincoln* (Baton Rouge: Louisiana State University Press, 1992); David Ericson, *The Shaping of American Liberalism: The Debates over Ratification, Nullification, and Slavery* (Chicago: University of Chicago Press, 1990); Eric H. Walther, *The Shattering of the Union: America in the 1850s* (Wilmington DE: Scholarly Resources, 2004); Bruce Levine, *Half Slave and Half Free: The Roots of Civil War* (New York: Hill and Wang, 2005); William W. Freehling, *The Road to Disunion: Secessionists Triumphant* (New York: Oxford University Press, 2008).

24. Jack K. Bauer, *Zachary Taylor: Soldier, Planter, Statesman of the Old Southwest* (Baton Rouge: Louisiana State University Press, 1993); Elbert B. Smith, *The Presidencies of Zachary Taylor and Millard Fillmore* (Lawrence: University Press of Kansas, 1988).

25. Benson Lee Grayson, *The Unknown President: The Administration of Millard Fillmore* (Latham MD: University Press of America, 1981).

26. David Herbert Donald, *Lincoln* (New York: Simon and Schuster, 1995), 135.

27. Congressional Resolution, January 10, 1849, *Lincoln Works*, 2:20–22.

28. Congressional Resolution, January 10, 1849, *Lincoln Works*, 2:20–22.

29. Merrill D. Peterson, *The Great Triumvirate: Webster, Clay, and Calhoun* (New York: Oxford University Press, 1987), 449–76; Mark J. Stegmaier, *Texas, New Mexico, and the Compromise of 1850: Boundary Dispute and Section Crisis* (Kent OH: Kent State University Press, 1996); John C. Waugh, *On the Brink of Civil War: The Compromise of 1850 and How It Changed the Course of American History* (Wilmington DE: Scholarly Resources, 2003).

30. Potter, *Impending Crisis*, 128.

31. Stanley W. Campbell, *The Slave Catchers: Enforcement of the Fugitive Slave Law of 1850–1860* (Chapel Hill: University of North Carolina Press, 1970), 207.

32. Larry Gara, *The Liberty Line: The Legend of the Underground Railroad* (Lexington: University Press of Kentucky, 1961). For an overview on estimates, see Potter, *Impending Crisis*, 135–37.

33. Don E. Fehrenbacher, *Prelude to Greatness: Lincoln in the 1850s* (Stanford CA: Stanford University Press, 1962).

34. Michael Burlingame, *The Inner World of Abraham Lincoln* (Urbana: University of Illinois Press, 1994), 57–72.

35. David Herbert Donald, *Lincoln* (New York: Simon and Schuster, 1995), 159–60.

36. Donald, *Lincoln*, 160.

37. Abraham Lincoln to Williamson Durley, October 3, 1845, *Lincoln Writings*, 284–85.

38. Abraham Lincoln to Williamson Durley, October 3, 1845, *Lincoln Writings*, 285–86.

39. Jean H. Baker, *Affairs of Party: The Political Culture of Northern Democrats in the Mid-nineteenth Century* (Ithaca NY: Cornell University Press, 1983).

40. Roy F. Nichols, *Franklin Pierce: Young Hickory of the Granite Hills* (Norwalk CT: Easton Press, 1988); Larry Gara, *The Presidency of Franklin Pierce* (Lawrence: University Press of Kansas, 1991).

41. Michael F. Holt, *The Rise and Fall of the American Whig Party: Jacksonian Politics and the Onset of the Civil War* (New York: Oxford University Press, 2003).

42. Potter, *Impending Crisis*, 241–42.

43. Tyler Anbinder, *Nativism and Slavery: The Northern Know Nothings and the Politics of the 1850s* (New York: Oxford University Press, 1992); Jonathan A. Glickstein, *American Exceptionalism, American Anxiety: Wages, Competition, and Degraded Labor in the Antebellum United States* (Charlottesville: University of Virginia Press, 2002).

4. BLEEDING KANSAS

1. George Milton, *The Eve of Conflict: Stephen A. Douglas and the Needless War* (Boston: Houghton Mifflin, 1934); Robert W. Johannsen, *Stephen A Douglas* (New York: Oxford University Press, 1973); William S. McFeely, *Frederick Douglass* (New York: W. W. Norton, 1991).

2. James C. Malin, *The Nebraska Question, 1852–1854* (Lawrence: University Press of Kansas, 1953).

3. Speech at Chicago, July 10, 1858, *Lincoln Writings*, 442.

4. Speech at Peoria, Illinois, in Reply to Senator Douglas, October 16, 1854, *Lincoln Writings*, 338–85.

5. Matthew Pinsker, "Senator Abraham Lincoln," *Journal of the Abraham Lincoln Association* 14 (Summer 1993): 1–21.

6. Abraham Lincoln to E. B. Washburne, February 9, 1855, *Lincoln Writings*, 385–87.

7. James A. Rawley, *Race and Politics: "Bleeding Kansas" and the Coming of the Civil War* (Lincoln: University of Nebraska Press, 1979); Nicole Etcheson, *Bleeding Kansas: Contested Liberty in the Civil War Era* (Lawrence: University Press of Kansas, 2004).

8. Rawley, *Race and Politics*, 81.

9. Sean Wilentz, *The Rise of American Democracy: Jefferson to Lincoln* (New York: W. W. Norton, 2005), 686; David M. Potter, *The Impending Crisis, 1848–1861* (New York: Harper and Row, 1976), 200–201.

10. David Donald, *Charles Sumner and the Coming of the Civil War* (Chicago: University of Chicago Press, 1960); T. Lloyd Bentsen, *The Caning of Senator Sumner* (Belmont CA: Wadsworth/Thomas Learning, 2004).

11. William Marcy to Pierre Soulé, April 3, 1854, in *Diplomatic Correspondence of*

the United States: Inter-American Affairs, 1831–1860, ed. William R. Manning, 12 vols. (Washington DC: Government Printing Office, 1932–39), 11:175–76.

12. Don E. Fehrenbacher, *The Slaveholding Republic: An Account of the United States Government's Relation to Slavery* (New York: Oxford University Press, 2001), 129.

13. Robert E. May, *The Southern Dream of a Caribbean Empire, 1854–1861* (Baton Rouge: Louisiana State University Press, 1973); Charles H. Brown, *Agents of Manifest Destiny: The Lives and Times of the Filibusters* (Chapel Hill: University of North Carolina Press, 1980); Robert E. May, *Manifest Destiny's Underworld: Filibustering in Antebellum America* (Chapel Hill: University of North Carolina Press, 2002).

14. Albert Carr, *The World and William Walker* (New York: Harper and Row, 1963); Frederic Rosengarten, *Freebooters Must Die!: The Life and Death of William Walker* (Wayne PA: Haverford House, 1976).

15. James D. Richardson, ed., *A Compilation of the Messages and Papers of the Presidents*, 20 vols. (Washington DC: Government Printing Office, 1897–1917), 7:2731–32.

16. Robert E. May, *John A. Quitman: Old South Crusader* (Baton Rouge: Louisiana State University Press, 1985).

17. Abraham Lincoln to Joshua Speed, August 24, 1855, *Lincoln Works*, 2:323.

18. William Gienapp, *The Origins of the Republican Party* (New York: Oxford University Press, 1988); James D. Bilotta, *Race and the Republican Party, 1848–1865* (New York: Peter Lang, 1992); Eric Foner, *Free Soil, Free Labor, Free Men: The Ideology of the Republican Party before the Civil War* (New York: Oxford University Press, 1995); Robert Engs and Randall Miller, eds., *The Birth of the Grand Old Party: The Republicans' First Generation* (Philadelphia: University of Pennsylvania Press, 2002).

19. Andrew Rolle, *John Charles Frémont: Character as Destiny* (Norman: University of Oklahoma Press, 1991); John Charles Frémont, *Memoirs of My Life* (New York: Cooper Square Press, 2001).

20. Speech at Springfield, June 26,1857, *Lincoln Writings*, 422, 427.

21. James M. McPherson, *The Battle Cry of Freedom: The Civil War Era* (New York: Oxford University Press, 1988), 162.

5. DRED SCOTT AND HARPERS FERRY

1. Frederick Binder, *James Buchanan and the American Empire* (Selinsgrove PA: Susquehanna University Press, 1994); Michael J. Birkner, ed., *James Buchanan and the Political Crisis of the 1850s* (Selinsgrove PA: Susquehanna University Press, 1996); Jean H. Baker, *James Buchanan* (New York: Henry Holt, 2004).

2. Philip Klein, *President James Buchanan* (University Park: Pennsylvania State University Press, 1962); Elbert B. Smith, *The Presidency of James Buchanan* (Lawrence: University Press of Kansas, 1975).

3. Stanley Kutler, ed., *The Dred Scott Decision: Law or Politics* (Boston: Houghton Mifflin, 1967); Don E. Fehrenbacher, *The Dred Scott Case: Its Significance in American Law and Politics* (New York: Oxford University Press, 1978); Paul Finkelman, *Dred Scott v. Sandford: A Brief History with Documents* (Boston: Bedford/St. Martin's Press, 1997).

4. Dred Scott v. John F. A. Sandford, 60 U.S. (19 Howard) 399–454.

5. Speech at Springfield, Illinois, June 26, 1847, *Lincoln Works*, 2:401.

6. Speech at Springfield, Illinois, June 26, 1857, *Lincoln Works*, 2:401.

7. For the best overview, see Kenneth M. Stampp, *America in 1857: A Nation on the Brink* (New York: Oxford University Press, 1990).

8. Fawn M. Brodie, *No Man Knows My History: The Life of Joseph Smith, the Mormon Prophet* (New York: Alfred Knopf, 1945); Leonard J. Arrington and Davis Bitton, *The Mormon Experience: A History of the Latter-Day Saints* (New York: Alfred Knopf, 1979); Jan Shipps, *Mormonism: The Story of a New Religious Tradition* (Urbana: University of Illinois Press, 1985); Leonard J. Arrington, *Brigham Young: American Moses* (Urbana: University of Illinois Press, 1986).

9. Edward L. Lyman, *Political Deliverance: The Mormon Quest for Utah Statehood* (Urbana: University of Illinois Press, 1986).

10. Juanita Brooks, *The Mountain Meadows Massacre* (Stanford CA: Stanford University Press, 1950); Norman F. Furniss, *The Mormon Conflict, 1850–1859* (New Haven CT: Yale University Press, 1960); William Wise, *The Massacre at Mountain Meadows: An American Legend and a Monumental Crime* (New York: Crowell, 1976).

11. George W. Van Vleck, *The Panic of 1857* (New York: Columbia University Press, 1943); Bray Hammond, *Banks and Politics in America from the Revolution to the Civil War* (Princeton NJ: Princeton University Press, 1957); James L. Huston, *The Panic of 1857 and the Coming of the Civil War* (Baton Rouge: Louisiana State University Press, 1987).

12. John W. Forney, *Anecdotes of Public Men* (New York: Harper and Brothers, 1873), 2:179.

13. "A House Divided," June 16, 1858, *Lincoln Works*, 2:461–62.

14. Abraham Lincoln to Stephen Douglas, July 24, 29, 31, 1858, *Lincoln Writings*, 457–58, 458–60, 460.

For overviews of the struggle between Lincoln and Douglas, see Allen Nevins, *The Emergence of Lincoln: Douglas, Buchanan, and Party Chaos, 1857–1859* (New York: Charles Scribners' Sons, 1950); Roy Morris, *The Long Pursuit: Abraham Lincoln's Thirty-Year Struggle with Stephen Douglas for the Heart and Soul of America* (New York: HarperCollins, 2008).

For the debates, see Harry E. Pratt, *The Great Debates of 1858* (Springfield: Illinois State Historical Library, 1956); Robert W. Johannsen, *The Lincoln-Douglas Debates, 1858* (New York: Oxford University Press, 1965); Richard Allen Heckman, *Lincoln vs. Douglas: The Great Debates Campaign* (Washington DC: Public Affairs Press, 1967); Harry Jaffa, *The Crisis of the House Divided: An Interpretation of the Issues in the Lincoln-Douglas Debates* (Chicago: University of Chicago Press, 1982); David Zarefsky, *Lincoln, Douglas, and Slavery: In the Crucible of Public Debate* (Chicago: University of Chicago Press, 1990); Harold Holzer, ed., *The Lincoln-Douglas Debates: The First Complete, Unexpurgated Text* (New York: Harper Collins, 1993).

15. Pratt, *Great Debates of 1858*, 5.

16. Freeport Debate, August 27, 1858, *Lincoln Works*, 3:43.

17. Johannsen, *Lincoln-Douglas Debates*, 22–36.

18. George M. Frederickson, "A Man but Not a Brother: Abraham Lincoln and Racial Equality," *Journal of Southern History* 41 (February 1975): 39–58; Don E. Fehrenbacher, "Only His Stepchildren," in *Lincoln in Text and Context: Collected Essays*, ed. Don E. Fehrenbacher (Palo Alto CA: Stanford University Press, 1987), 95–112; George Stickler, *The Racial Attitudes of American Presidents from Abraham Lincoln to Theodore Roosevelt* (Garden City NY: Doubleday), 1971.

19. Speech at Springfield, July 17, 1858, *Lincoln Writings*, 456.

20. Johannsen, *Lincoln-Douglas Debates*, 256.

21. Reply at Alton, October 15,1858, *Lincoln Writings*,530.

22. Fragment on Slavery, July 1, 1854, *Lincoln Works*, 2:222–23.

23. Speech at Springfield, June 26, 1857, *Lincoln Works*, 2:405–6.

24. Michael Vorenberg, "Abraham Lincoln and the Politics of Black Colonization," *Journal of Abraham Lincoln* 14 (Summer 1993): 23–45.

25. Opening Speech at Charleston, Illinois, September 18, 1858, *Lincoln Works*, 2:404–5.

26. David Herbert Donald, *Lincoln* (New York: Simon and Schuster, 1995), 228.

27. Abraham Lincoln to Anson Henry, November 19, 1858, *Lincoln Works*, 3:339.

28. Avery O. Craven, *The Growth of Southern Nationalism, 1848–1861* (Baton Rouge: Louisiana State University Press, 1953); Ronald T. Takaki, *A Pro-slavery Crusade: The Agitation to Reopen the African Slave Trade* (New York: Free Press, 1971); John McCardell, *The Idea of a Southern Nation: Southern Nationalists and Southern Nationalism, 1830–1860* (New York: W. W. Norton, 1979); Drew Gilpin Faust, ed., *The Ideology of Slavery: Pro-slavery Thought in the Antebellum South, 1830–1860* (Baton Rouge: Louisiana State University Press, 1981); Larry E. Tise, *Proslavery: A History of the Defense of Slavery in America, 1701–1840* (Athens: University of Georgia Press, 1987); Eric Walther, *The Fire-Eaters* (Baton Rouge: Louisiana State University Press, 1992); Elizabeth Moss, *Domestic Novelists in the Old South: Defenders of Southern Culture* (Baton Rouge: Louisiana State University Press, 1992); Mitchell Snay, *The Gospel of Disunion: Religion and Separatism in the Antebellum South* (New York: Cambridge University Press, 1993); William C. Davis, *Rhett: The Turbulent Life and Times of a Fire-Eater* (Columbia: University of South Carolina Press, 2001); Paul Finkelman, *Defending Slavery: Proslavery Thought in the Old South* (Boston: Bedford/St. Martin's Press, 2003); Lorman A. Ratner and Dwight L. Teeter, *Fanatics and Fire-Eaters: Newspapers and the Coming of the Civil War* (Champaign: University of Illinois Press, 2003); Michael O'Brien, *Conjectures of Order: Intellectual Life and the American South, 1810–1860*, 2 vols. (Chapel Hill: University of North Carolina Press, 2004); Adam L. Tate, *Conservatism and Southern Intellectuals, 1789–1861: Liberty, Tradition, and the Good Society* (Columbia: University of South Carolina Press, 2005); Elizabeth Fox-Genovese and Eugene D. Genovese, *The Mind of the Master Class: History and Faith in the Southern Slaveholders' Worldview* (New York: Cambridge University Press, 2005).

29. Hinton Rowan Helper, *The Impending Crisis of the South: How to Meet It* (Cambridge MA: Harvard University Press, 1967); David Brown, *Southern Outcast: Hinton Rowan Helper and the Impending Crisis* (Baton Rouge: Louisiana State University Press, 2006).

30. Elizabeth R. Varon, *Disunion!: The Coming of the American Civil War, 1789–1859* (Chapel Hill: University of North Carolina Press, 2008), 294–95.

31. Stephen B. Oates, *To Purge This Land with Blood: A Biography of John Brown* (Amherst: University of Massachusetts Press, 1984); Benjamin Quarles, *Allies for Freedom: Blacks and John Brown* (New York: Oxford University Press,1974); Jeffrey S. Rossbach, *Ambivalent Conspirators: John Brown, the Secret Six, and a Theory of Slave Violence* (Philadelphia: University of Pennsylvania Press, 1982); John Stauffer and Zoe Trodd, eds., *Meteor of War: The John Brown Story* (Maplecrest NY: Brandywine Press, 2004); David S. Reynolds, *John Brown, Abolitionist: The Man Who Killed Slavery, Sparked the Civil War, and Seeded Civil Rights* (New York: Alfred Knopf, 2005).

32. Paul Finkelman, ed., *His Soul Goes Marching On: The Responses to John Brown and the Harpers Ferry Raid* (Charlottesville: University of Virginia Press, 1995); Peggy A. Russo and Paul Finkelman, eds., *The Terrible Swift Sword: The Legacy of John Brown* (Athens: Ohio University Press, 2005).

33. Eric Foner, *Free Soil, Free Labor, Free Men: The Ideology of the Republican Party before the Civil War* (New York: Oxford University Press, 1995), 315.

34. Speech at Leavenworth, Kansas, December 3, 1859, *Lincoln Works*, 3:496.

35. *Richmond (VA) Enquirer*, October 25, 1859.

6. THE ELECTION

1. For the following figures and descriptions, see *The United States on the Eve of the Civil War as Described by the 1860 Census* (Washington DC: U.S. Civil War Centennial Commission, 1963); *Statistical History of the United States from Colonial Times to the Present* (Stamford CT: Fairfield, 1965); George Rogers Taylor, *The Transportation Revolution, 1815–1860* (New York: Holt, Rinehart, and Winston, 1951).

2. Roger Ransom, *Conflict and Compromise: The Political Economy of Slavery, Emancipation, and the American Civil War* (New York: Cambridge University Press, 1989), 62, 76, 46.

3. Donald R. Adams, "Prices and Wages," in *The Encyclopedia of American Economic History*, ed. Glenn Porter, 3 vols. (New York: Scribner, 1980), 1:234. For the best works on these revolutions, see Douglass North, *Economic Growth in the United States, 1790–1860* (New York: W. W. Norton, 1966); Thomas Cochran, *Frontiers of Change: Early Industrialization in America* (New York: Oxford University Press, 1983); Walter Licht, *Industrializing America* (Baltimore: Johns Hopkins Press, 1995); Taylor, *Transportation Revolution*; John Stover, *American Railroads* (Chicago: University of Chicago Press, 1961); Albert Fishlow, *American Railroads and the Transformation of the Antebellum Economy* (Cambridge MA: Harvard University Press, 1965); Carter Goodrich et al., *Canals and American Economic Development* (Port Washington NY: Kennikat Press, 1972).

4. Stuart Bruchey, *Enterprise: The Dynamic Economy of a Free People* (Cambridge MA: Harvard University Press, 1990), 251.

5. Louis Hacker, Rudolf Modley, and George Taylor, *The United States: A Graphic History* (New York: Modern Age Books, 1937).

6. Bruchey, *Enterprise*, 228, 238–53; Ransom, *Conflict and Compromise*, 62, 65, 70.

7. Eric Foner, *Free Soil, Free Labor, Free Men: The Ideology of the Republican Party before the Civil War* (New York: Oxford University Press, 1995), 41, 42, 52.

8. Lincoln Family Tax Assessment, 1860, *Lincoln Works*, 3:58.

9. Abraham Lincoln to Salmon Chase, June 20, 1859, *Lincoln Writings*, 542.

10. Harold Holzer, *Lincoln at Cooper Union: The Speech That Made Abraham Lincoln President* (New York: Simon and Schuster, 2004).

11. Address at Cooper Institute, February 27, 1860, *Lincoln Writings*, 590.

12. Douglas R. Egerton, *Year of Meteors: Stephen Douglas, Abraham Lincoln, and the Election that Brought on the Civil War* (New York: Bloomsbury Press, 2010).

13. Willard King, *Lincoln's Manager: David Davis* (Cambridge MA: Harvard University Press, 1960).

14. Endorsement on Margin of *Missouri Democrat*, May 17,1860, *Lincoln Works*, 4:50.

15. W. Dean Burnham, *Presidential Ballots, 1836–1892* (Baltimore: Johns Hopkins University Press, 1955), 236–43.

16. Kenneth Stampp, *And the War Came: The North and the Secession Crisis, 1860–1861* (Chicago: University of Chicago Press, 1964); Charles B. Dew, *The Apostles of Disunion: Southern Secession Commissioners and the Causes of the Civil War* (Charlottesville: University of Virginia Press, 2002).

17. William Lee Miller, *President Lincoln: The Duty of a Statesman* (New York: Alfred A. Knopf, 2008), 10–11.

18. David M. Potter, *Lincoln and His Party in the Secession Crisis* (New Haven CT: Yale University Press, 1962).

19. Charles Francis Adams, *Address on the Life, Character, and Services of William Henry Seward* (Albany NY: Weed, Parsons, 1873), 48–49.

20. Miller, *President Lincoln*, 15.

21. William L. Barney, *Battleground for the Union: The Era of the Civil War and Reconstruction, 1848–1877* (Englewood Cliffs NJ: Prentice Hall, 1990), 116; George C. Rable, *But There Was No Peace: The Role of Violence in the Politics of Reconstruction* (Athens: University of Georgia Press,1984), 16.

22. For the best overall study of the Civil War, see James M. McPherson, *The Battle Cry of Freedom: The Civil War Era* (New York: Oxford University Press, 1988). See also James Rawley, *Turning Points of the Civil War* (Lincoln: University of Nebraska Press, 1974); Richard E. Beringer, Herman Hattaway, Archer Jones, and William N. Still, *Why the South Lost the Civil War* (Athens: University of Georgia Press, 1986); Herman Hattaway and Archer Jones, *How the North Won: A Military History of the*

Civil War (Urbana: University of Illinois Press, 1991); Archer Jones, *Civil War Command and Strategy: The Process of Victory and Defeat* (New York: Free Press, 1992); Russell F. Weigley, *A Great Civil War: A Military and Political History, 1861–1865* (Bloomington: Indiana University Press, 2000); David Williams, *A People's History of the Civil War: Struggling for the Meaning of Freedom* (New York: New Press, 2005).

7. LIMITED WAR

1. Inaugural Address, March 4,1861, *Lincoln Works*, 4:268; Thomas J. Pressly, "Bullets and Ballots: Lincoln and the 'Right of Revolution,'" *American Historical Review* 67 (April 1962): 647–62.

2. Abraham Lincoln to Lyman Trumbull, December 10, 1860, *Lincoln Works*, 4:149–50. See also Abraham Lincoln to Truman Smith, November 10, 1860; Abraham Lincoln to John Gilmer, December 15, 1860; Abraham Lincoln to Thurlow Weed, December 17, 1860, *Lincoln Writings*, 623, 627–29, 629. For analyses of the transition and early days of the Lincoln presidency, see David M. Potter, *Lincoln and His Party in the Secession Crisis* (New Haven CT: Yale University Press, 1962); Kenneth Stampp, *And the War Came: The North and the Secession Crisis* (Baton Rouge: Louisiana State University Press, 1950); Richard N. Current, *Lincoln and the First Shot* (Philadelphia: J. B. Lippincott, 1963).

3. John G. Nicolay and John Hay, *Abraham Lincoln: A History*, 10 vols. (New York: Century, 1890); Tyler Dennett, ed., *Lincoln and the Civil War in the Diaries and Letters of John Hay* (New York: Dodd, Mead, 1939).

4. Harry Carman and Reinhard Luthin, *Lincoln and the Patronage System* (New York: Columbia University Press, 1943); Paul Van Riper and Keith A. Sutherland, "The Northern Civil Service, 1861–1865," *Civil War History* 11 (December 1965): 351–69.

5. For the outstanding book on his cabinet, see Doris Kearns Goodwin, *Team of Rivals: The Political Genius of Abraham Lincoln* (New York: Simon and Schuster, 2006). See also Burton Hendrick, *Inside Lincoln's War Cabinet* (Boston: Little, Brown, 1946).

6. Glyndon Van Deuson, *William Henry Seward* (New York: Oxford University Press, 1967).

7. David Donald, ed., *Inside Lincoln's Cabinet: The Civil War Diaries of Salmon Chase* (New York: Longmans, Green, 1954); Frederick Blue, *Salmon P. Chase: A Life in Politics* (Kent OH: Kent State University Press, 1987).

8. Erwin Stanley Bradley, *Simon Cameron: Lincoln's Secretary of War* (Philadelphia: University of Pennsylvania Press, 1966).

9. Hendrick, *Inside Lincoln's War Cabinet*, 51–52.

10. William Ernest Smith, *The Francis Blair Family in Politics*, 2 vols. (New York: Macmillan, 1933), 2:90–111.

11. Marvin Cain, *Lincoln's Attorney General: Edward Bates of Missouri* (Columbia: University of Missouri Press, 1965); Howard K. Beale, ed., *The Diary of Gideon*

Welles: Secretary of the Navy under Lincoln and Johnson, 3 vols. (New York: W. W. Norton, 1960); John Niven, *Gideon Welles: Lincoln's Secretary of the Navy* (New York: Oxford University Press, 1973).

12. Farewell Address at Springfield, Illinois, February 11, 1860, *Lincoln Writings*, 635–36.

13. David Donald, *Liberty and Union* (Lexington MA: D. C. Heath, 1975), 5.

14. Speech at Independence Hall, Philadelphia, February 22, 1861, *Lincoln Writings*, 644.

15. Inaugural Address, March 4, 1861, *Lincoln Works*, 4:266.

16. Nicolay and Hay, *Abraham Lincoln*, 4:65.

17. Russell F. Weigley, *The History of the United States Army* (New York: Macmillan, 1967), 199–200.

18. Winfield Scott to Abraham Lincoln, March 9, 1861, *Lincoln Works*, 4:279–80.

19. Note to Each of the Cabinet Members Asking for Opinion on Fort Sumter, March 15, 1861, *Lincoln Works*, 4:284.

20. Winfield Scott to Simon Cameron, March 28, 1861, *Official Records*, ser. 1, vol. 4, pp. 200–201.

21. William Seward, "Some Thoughts for the Consideration of the President," April 1, 1861, *Abraham Lincoln Papers at the Library of Congress*, Manuscript Division, American Memory Project, http://memory.loc.gov/ammem/malquery.html.

22. Brooks D. Simpson, *The Reconstruction Presidents* (Lawrence: University Press of Kansas, 1998), 14; Abraham Lincoln to William Seward, April 1, 1861, *Lincoln Works*, 4:316.

23. Howard Beale, ed., *The Diary of Edward Bates* (Washington DC: Government Printing Office, 1933), 220.

24. Abraham Lincoln to Francis Pickens, April 6, 1861, *Lincoln Works*, 4:324.

25. Timothy D. Johnson, *Winfield Scott: The Quest for Military Glory* (Lawrence: University Press of Kansas, 1998); John S. D. Eisenhower, *Agent of Destiny: The Life and Times of General Winfield Scott* (Norman: University of Oklahoma Press, 1999).

26. Abraham Lincoln to the Senate and House of Representatives, May 26, 1862, *Lincoln Works*, 5:241–42.

27. William W. Freehling, *The South vs. the South: How Anti-Confederate Southerners Shaped the Course of the Civil War* (New York: Oxford University Press, 2001), 57.

28. Abraham Lincoln to Winfield Scott, April 18, 1861; Expansion of Military, May 3, 1861, *Lincoln Works*, 4:337, 353–54.

29. For the best overview, see Mark E. Neely, *The Fate of Liberty: Abraham Lincoln and Civil Liberties* (New York: Oxford University Press, 1991).

30. David Herbert Donald, *Lincoln* (New York: Simon and Schuster, 1995), 304.

31. Message to Congress, July 4, 1861, *Lincoln Works*, 4:385.

32. Message to Congress, July 4, 1861, *Lincoln Works*, 4:426–38.

33. Fred R. Shannon, *The Organization and Administration of the Union Army*, 2 vols. (Cleveland: Arthur Clark, 1928).

34. James M. McPherson, *The Battle Cry of Freedom: The Civil War Era* (New York: Oxford University Press, 1988), 326.

35. William Skelton, "Officers and Politicians: The Origins of Army Politics in the United States before the Civil War," *Armed Forces and Society* 6 (1979): 48n52, 22–28; McPherson, *Battle Cry of Freedom*, 313; Allan Nevins, *The War for the Union*, 4 vols. (New York: Charles Scribner's Sons, 1959–71), 1:108; Nicolay and Hay, *Abraham Lincoln*, 4:103–4.

36. McDowell testimony, Joint Committee on the Conduct of the War, 37th Cong., 3rd Sess., pt. 2, 35–38 (1863).

37. Unless otherwise noted, army strengths and casualties are taken from either McPherson, *Battle Cry of Freedom*, or Herman Hattaway and Archer Jones, *How the North Won: A Military History of the Civil War* (Urbana: University of Illinois Press, 1991).

38. Stephen W. Sears, *George B. McClellan: The Young Napoleon* (New York: Ticknor and Fields, 1988); Russell H. Beattie, *The Army of the Potomac: McClellan Takes Command, September 1861–February 1862* (Cambridge MA: Da Capo Press, 2004); George B. McClellan, *McClellan's Own Story* (New York: Charles L. Webster, 1887).

39. George McClellan to Mary McClellan, October 31, 1861, in *The Civil War Papers of George B. McClellan: Selected Correspondence, 1860–1865*, ed. Stephen W. Sears (New York: Ticknor and Fields, 1989), 82.

40. Michael Burlingame and John R. Turner, eds., *Inside Lincoln's White House: The Complete War Diary of John Hay* (Carbondale: Southern Illinois University Press, 1997), 30.

41. Abraham Lincoln to Orville Browning, September 22, 1861, *Lincoln Works*, 4:532.

42. McPherson, *Battle Cry of Freedom*, 284.

43. William E. Parish, *The Turbulent Partnership: Missouri and the Union, 1861–1865* (Columbia: University of Missouri Press, 1965).

44. Abraham Lincoln to John Fremont, September 2, 1862; Order to General Fremont, September 11, 1861, *Lincoln Writings*, 678–80.

45. John G. Nicolay, *The Outbreak of Rebellion* (New York: Da Capo Press,1995), 138.

46. Oliver P. Temple, *East Tennessee and the Civil War* (Freeport NY: Books for Libraries Press, 1971); James W. Patton, *Unionism and Reconstruction in Tennessee, 1860–1869* (Chapel Hill: University of North Carolina Press, 1934).

47. Burlingame and Turner, *Inside Lincoln's White House*, 32, 289.

48. Benjamin Thomas and Harold Hyman, *Stanton: The Life and Times of Lincoln's Secretary of War* (New York: Alfred A. Knopf, 1962).

49. Donald, *Lincoln*, 186; Ralph and Adeline Emerson, *Mr. and Mrs. Ralph Emerson's Personal Recollections of Abraham Lincoln* (Rockford IL: Wilson Brothers, 1909), 7.

50. Thomas and Hyman, *Stanton*, 146; A. Howard McNeely, *The War Department, 1861* (New York: Columbia University Press, 1928), 318n.

51. William Swinton, *Campaigns of the Army of the Potomac* (New York: Charles B. Richardson, 1866), 80.

52. Sears, *George B. McClellan*, 141.

53. General Order Number One, January 27, 1862, *Lincoln Works*, 5:115.

54. Ruth Painter Randall, *Mary Lincoln: Biography of a Marriage* (Boston: Little, Brown, 1953), 254–56.

55. Belle Becker Sideman and Lillian Friedman, eds., *Europe Looks at the Civil War* (New York: Orion Press, 1960).

56. Ephraim D. Adams, *Great Britain and the American Civil War*, 2 vols. (New York: Longmans, Green, 1925); D. P. Crook, *The North, the South, and the Powers, 1861–1865* (New York: John Wiley and Sons, 1974); Brian Jenkins, *Britain and the War for the Union* (Montreal: McGill University Press, 1974); Howard Jones, *Union in Peril: The Crisis over British Intervention in the Civil War* (Chapel Hill: University of North Carolina Press, 1992).

57. Revision of William Seward to Charles Francis Adams, May 21, 1861, *Lincoln Works*, 4:376–80.

58. Norman B. Ferris, *The Trent Affair: A Diplomatic Crisis* (Knoxville: University of Tennessee Press, 1977).

59. Frederick W. Seward, *Seward at Washington as Senator and Secretary of State* (New York: Derby and Miller, 1891), 25–26.

60. For the best books, see *Grant Memoirs*; William S. McFeely, *Grant: A Biography* (New York: W. W. Norton, 1981); Brooks D. Simpson, *Let Us Have Peace: Ulysses S. Grant and the Politics of War and Reconstruction, 1861–1868* (Chapel Hill: University of North Carolina Press, 1991); Brooks D. Simpson, *Ulysses S. Grant: The Triumph over Adversity, 1822–1865* (Boston: Houghton Mifflin, 2000); Jean Edward Smith, *Grant* (New York: Touchstone, 2001).

61. Smith, *Grant*, 15, 199, 200.

62. *Grant Memoirs*, 107.

63. *Grant Memoirs*, 123.

64. *Grant Memoirs*, 124–44.

65. Abraham Lincoln to Don Carlos Buell, January 9, 1862, *Lincoln Works*, 5:91.

66. James M. McPherson, *Tried by War: Abraham Lincoln as Commander in Chief* (New York: Penguin, 2008), 72; *Grant Memoirs*, 149–50.

67. William Davis, *The Duel between the First Ironclads* (Garden City NY: Doubleday, 1975).

68. T. Harry Williams, *Lincoln and His Generals* (New York: Alfred A. Knopf, 1952), 86.

69. *Grant Memoirs*, 174.

70. Abraham Lincoln to George McClellan, February 3, 1862, *Lincoln Writings*, 693–94.

71. Bruce Tap, *Over Lincoln's Shoulder: The Committee on the Conduct of the War* (Lawrence: University Press of Kansas, 1998), 113.

72. McPherson, *Tried by War*, 76.

73. For the best book on the Peninsula Campaign, see Stephen W. Sears, *To the Gates of Richmond: The Peninsula Campaign* (New York: Ticknor and Fields, 1992).

74. Joe Johnston to Robert E. Lee, April 22, 1862, *Official Records*, ser. 1, vol. 11, pt.3, pp. 455–56.

75. Abraham Lincoln to George McClellan, April 9, 1862, *Lincoln Writings*, 699–700.

76. Robert G. Tanner, *Stonewall in the Valley: Thomas J. "Stonewall" Jackson's Shenandoah Valley Campaign, Spring 1862* (Garden City NY: Doubleday, 1976).

77. Wallace Schultz and Walter N. Trenery, *Abandoned by Lincoln: A Military Biography of John Pope* (Urbana: University of Illinois Press, 1990).

78. Abraham Lincoln to George McClellan, May 25, 1862, *Lincoln Works*, 5:236.

79. George McClellan to Edwin Stanton, June 28, 1862, in Sears, *Civil War Papers of McClellan*, 322–23.

80. Stephen Ambrose, *Halleck: Lincoln's Chief of Staff* (Baton Rouge: Louisiana State University Press, 1962).

8. EMANCIPATION

1. John Hope Franklin, *The Emancipation Proclamation* (New York: Anchor Books, 1965); Lawanda Cox, *Lincoln and Black Freedom: A Study in Presidential Leadership* (Columbia: University of South Carolina Press, 1981); Allen C. Guelzo, *Lincoln's Emancipation Proclamation: The End of Slavery in America* (New York: Simon and Schuster, 2004).

2. T. Harry Williams, *Lincoln and the Radicals* (Madison: University of Wisconsin Press, 1941); James M. McPherson, *The Struggle for Equality: Abolitionists and the Negro in the Civil War and Reconstruction* (Princeton NJ: Princeton University Press, 1964); David Montgomery, *Beyond Equality: Labor and the Radical Republicans* (New York: Vintage, 1967); Hans L. Trefousse, *The Radical Republicans: Lincoln's Vanguard for Racial Justice* (New York: Alfred A. Knopf, 1969); David H. Donald, *Charles Sumner and the Rights of Man* (New York: Alfred A. Knopf,1970); Allan G. Bogue, *The Earnest Men: Republicans in the Civil War Senate* (Ithaca NY: Cornell University Press, 1981); Allan G. Bogue, *The Congressman's Civil War* (New York: Cambridge University Press, 1989).

3. Christopher Dell, *Lincoln and the War Democrats: The Grand Erosion of Conservative Tradition* (Rutherford NJ: Fairleigh Dickinson University Press, 1975); Joel Silbey, *A Respectable Minority: The Democratic Party in the Civil War Era, 1860–1868* (New York: W. W. Norton, 1977); Jean H. Baker, *Affairs of Party: The Political Culture of Northern Democrats in the Mid-nineteenth Century* (Ithaca NY: Cornell University Press, 1983).

4. Bruce Tap, *Over Lincoln's Shoulder: The Committee on the Conduct of the War* (Lawrence: University Press of Kansas, 1998).

5. *Congressional Globe*, 37th Cong., 1st Sess. 222–23 (1863).

6. Richard Sewall, *A House Divided: Sectionalism and the Civil War* (Baltimore: Johns Hopkins University Press, 1988), 161.

7. Theodore Calvin Pease and James G. Randall, eds., *The Diary of Orville Hickman Browning*, 2 vols. (Springfield: Illinois State Historical Library, 1925–33), 1:477–78.

8. Abraham Lincoln to Orville Browning, September 22, 1861; Abraham Lincoln to John Frémont, September 2, 11, 1861, *Lincoln Writings*, 681–83, 678–80.

9. Message to Congress Recommending Compensated Emancipation, March 6, 1862,; Abraham Lincoln to James McDougall, March 14, 1862, *Lincoln Writings*, 696–97, 697–98.

10. Proclamation, May 19, 1862, *Lincoln Writings*, 701–3.

11. Peyton McCrary, *Abraham Lincoln and Reconstruction: The Louisiana Experiment* (Princeton NJ: Princeton University Press, 1978); Joseph G. Dawson, *Army Generals and Reconstruction: Louisiana, 1862–1877* (Baton Rouge: Louisiana State University Press, 1982); Ted Tunnell, *Crucible of Reconstruction: Radicalism and Race in Louisiana, 1862–1867* (Baton Rouge: Louisiana State University Press, 1984).

12. Hans Trefousse, *Ben Butler: The South Called Him Beast* (New York: Twayne, 1957); Richard West, *Lincoln's Scapegoat General: A Life of Benjamin Butler* (Boston: Little, Brown, 1965).

13. James M. McPherson, *The Battle Cry of Freedom: The Civil War Era* (New York: Oxford University Press, 1988), 551–52.

14. Abraham Lincoln to a Committee of Religious Dominations, September 13, 1862, *Lincoln Works*, 5:357–63.

15. Abraham Lincoln to Black Delegation, August 14, 1862, *Lincoln Works*, 5:370–75.

16. Abraham Lincoln to Horace Greeley, August 22, 1862, *Lincoln Works*, 5:388–89.

17. Reply to a Committee of Religions Denominations, September 13, 1862, *Lincoln Writings*, 720–23.

18. Gary Vitale, "Abraham Lincoln and the Mormons: Another Legacy of Limited Freedom," *Journal of the Illinois State Historical Society* 101 (Fall–Winter 2008), 269, 260–71.

19. Abraham Lincoln to George McClellan, September 15, 1862, *Lincoln Works*, 5:425.

20. Abraham Lincoln to George McClellan, October 6, 1862, *Official Records*, ser. 1, vol. 19, pt. 1, p. 272; Abraham Lincoln to George McClellan, October 13,1862, *Lincoln Writings*, 729–30; Abraham Lincoln to George McClellan, October 23, 1862, *Lincoln Works*, 5:474; Michael Burlingame, ed., *An Oral History of Abraham Lincoln: John G. Nicolay's Interviews and Essays* (Carbondale: Southern Illinois University Press, 1996), 16.

21. Henry Halleck to Don Carlos Buell, October 19, 23, 1862, *Official Records*, ser. I, vol. 19, pt. 2, pp. 627, 638.

22. Preliminary Emancipation Proclamation, September 22, 1862; Final Emancipation Proclamation, January 1, 1863, *Lincoln Writings*, 723–26, 746–48.

23. Abraham Lincoln to Hannibal Hamlin, September 28, 1862, *Lincoln Writings*, 727.

24. Phillip Shaw Paludan, *The Presidency of Abraham Lincoln* (Lawrence: University Press of Kansas, 1994), 154–55.

25. William L. Barney, *Flawed Victory* (New York: Praeger, 1975), 130.

26. Francis Bicknell Carpenter, *Six Months at the White House* (Boston: Houghton, Mifflin, 1883), 269.

27. Annual Message to Congress, December 1, 1862, *Lincoln Works*, 5:537.

9. THE HAMILTONIAN TRIUMPH

1. Leonard Curry, *Blueprint for Modern America: Non-military Legislation of the First Civil War Congress* (Nashville: Vanderbilt University Press, 1968); Gabor S. Boritt, *Lincoln and the Economics of the American Dream* (Memphis: Memphis State University Press, 1978).

2. For the best overview, see Boritt, *Lincoln and the Economics of the American Dream.*

3. John Larson, *Internal Improvements: National Public Works and the Promise of Popular Government in the Early United States* (Chapel Hill: University of North Carolina Press, 2001).

4. Speech at New Haven, Connecticut, March 6,1860, *Lincoln Writings*, 592.

5. Speech at Columbus, Ohio, September 16, 1859, *Lincoln Writings*, 543.

6. Speech at Cincinnati, Ohio, September 17, 1859, *Lincoln Writings*, 556–57.

7. Boritt, *Lincoln and the Economics of the American Dream*, 159, 190.

8. Speech at Cincinnati, September 17, 1859, *Lincoln Writings*, 557.

9. Speech at New Haven, Connecticut, March 6, 1860, *Lincoln Writings*, 592.

10. From Notes for a Tariff Discussion, December 1, 1847, *Lincoln Writings*, 296–97.

11. Phillip Shaw Paludan, *The Presidency of Abraham Lincoln* (Lawrence: University Press of Kansas, 1994), 108–9.

12. Irwin Unger, *The Greenback Era: A Social and Political History of American Finance* (Princeton NJ: Princeton University Press, 1964); Bray Hammond, *Sovereignty and an Empty Purse: Banks and Politics in the Civil War* (Princeton NJ: Princeton University Press, 1970).

13. Unger, *Greenback Era*, 16–17.

14. Unger, *Greenback Era*, 17.

15. Boritt, *Lincoln and the Economics of the American Dream*, 103.

16. Boritt, *Lincoln and the Economics of the American Dream*, 67.

17. Thomas Jefferson, *Notes on the State of Virginia*, ed. William Peden (Chapel Hill: University of North Carolina Press, 1955), 164–65.

18. Lincoln's First Public Address, March 9,1832, *Lincoln Writings*, 223.

19. Stuart Bruchey, *Enterprise: The Dynamic Economy of a Free People* (Cambridge MA: Harvard University Press, 1990), 322.

20. Application for a Patent, May 22, 1849, *Lincoln Writings*, 325.

21. Mark R. Wilson, *The Business of Civil War: Military Mobilization and the State, 1861–1865* (Baltimore: Johns Hopkins University Press, 2006).

22. Proclamation for Thanksgiving, October 3,1863, *Lincoln Writings*, 783–84.

10. TURNING POINTS

1. William Hesseltine, *Lincoln and the War Governors* (New York: Alfred A. Knopf, 1955).

2. Herman Hattaway and Archer Jones, *How the North Won: A Military History of the Civil War* (Urbana: University of Illinois Press, 1991), 266.

3. Abraham Lincoln to General Carl Schurz, November 24, 1862, *Lincoln Writings*, 735.

4. Abraham Lincoln to Henry Halleck, November 27, 1862, *Lincoln Works*, 5:514–15.

5. James M. McPherson, *Tried by Fire: Abraham Lincoln as Commander in Chief* (New York: Penguin, 2008), 164.

6. Noah Brooks, *Washington in Lincoln's Time* (New York: Century, 1895), 56.

7. Abraham Lincoln to Joe Hooker, January 26, 1863, *Lincoln Works*, 6:78–79.

8. Abraham Lincoln to Joe Hooker, June 5, 10, 14, *Lincoln Works*, 6:249–50, 257, 273.

9. George Meade proclamation, July 4, 1863, *Official Records*, ser. 1, vol. 27 pt. 3, p. 567; Michael Burlingame and John R. Turner, eds., *Inside Lincoln's White House: The Complete War Diary of John Hay* (Carbondale: Southern Illinois University Press, 1997), 62.

10. Henry Halleck to George Meade, July 7 (two dispatches), July 8 (two dispatches), 1863, *Official Records*, ser. 1, vol. 27, pt. 3, p. 82–83, 84–85.

11. Abraham Lincoln to George Gordon Meade, July 14, 1863, *Lincoln Works*, 6:327–28.

12. Henry Halleck to George Meade, July 14 (two dispatches), 1863, George Meade to Henry Halleck, July 14, 1863, *Official Records*, ser. 1, vol. 27, pt. 1, pp. 92–94.

13. Don E. Fehrenbacher and Virginia Fehrenbacher, eds., *The Recollected Words of Abraham Lincoln* (Stanford CA: Stanford University Press, 1996), 292.

14. Brooks D. Simpson, *Ulysses S. Grant: The Triumph over Adversity, 1822–1865* (Boston: Houghton Mifflin, 2000), 184–85.

15. Abraham Lincoln to Isaac Arnold, May 26, 1863, *Lincoln Works*, 6:230.

16. Abraham Lincoln to Ulysses Grant, July 13, 1863, *Lincoln Works*, 6:326.

17. Abraham Lincoln to James Conkling, August 26, 1863, *Lincoln Writings*, 779–80.

18. Robert S. Henry, *"First with the Most" Forrest* (Westport CT: Greenwood, 1974), 152–57.

19. Henry Halleck to William Rosecrans, July 7, 1863, *Official Records*, ser. 1, vol. 23, pt. 2, p. 518.

20. Abraham Lincoln to William Rosecrans, August 10, 1863, *Lincoln Works*, 6:377–78.

21. *Grant Memoirs*, 274–334.

22. Eugene Murdock, *Patriotism Limited, 1862–1965: The Civil War Draft and the Bounty System* (Kent OH: Kent State University Press, 1967); Eugene Murdock, *One Million Men: The Civil War Draft in the North* (Madison: University of Wisconsin Press, 1971); James W. Geary, *We Need Men: The Union Draft in the Civil War* (DeKalb: Northern Illinois University Press, 1991).

23. Adrian Cook, *The Armies of the Street: The New York Draft Riots of 1863* (Lexington: University Press of Kentucky, 1974), 174–76, 178–80, 194–95. See also Iver Bernstein, *The New York City Draft Riots* (New York: Oxford University Press, 1990).

24. Opinion of the Draft, August 15, 1863, *Lincoln Writings*, 771.

25. Wood Gray, *The Hidden Civil War: The Story of the Copperheads* (New York: Viking, 1942); Frank Klement, *Dark Lanterns: Secret Political Societies, Conspiracies, and Treason Trials in the Civil War* (Baton Rouge: Louisiana State University Press, 1984); Oscar A. Kinchen, *Confederate Operations in Canada and the North* (North Quincy MA: Christopher Publishing House, 1970); Larry E. Nelson, *Bullets, Ballots, and Rhetoric: Confederate Policy for the United States Presidential Contest of 1864* (Tuscaloosa: University of Alabama Press,1980).

26. Frank L. Klement, *The Limits of Dissent: Clement L. Vallandigham and the Civil War* (Lexington: University Press of Kentucky, 1970).

27. Abraham Lincoln to David Corning, June 12, 1865, *Lincoln Works*, 6:260–69.

28. David Herbert Donald, *Lincoln* (New York: Simon and Schuster, 1995), 443–44.

29. For a brilliant analysis, see Gary Wills, *Lincoln at Gettysburg: The Words That Remade America* (New York: Simon and Schuster, 1992). See also William E. Barton, *Lincoln at Gettysburg: What He Intended to Say; What He Said; What He Was Reported to Have Said; What He Wished He Had Said* (Indianapolis: Bobbs-Merrill, 1930); Louis A. Warren, *Lincoln's Gettysburg Address: "A New Birth of Freedom"* (Fort Wayne IN: Lincoln National Life Foundation, 1964); Glenn LaFantasie, "Lincoln and the Gettysburg Awakening," *Journal of the Abraham Lincoln Association* 16, no. 1 (Winter 1995): 73–89.

30. Philip Van Doren Stern, ed., *The Life and Writings of Abraham Lincoln* (New York: Modern Library, 2000), 786–87.

11. TOTAL WAR

1. Richard E. Beringer, Herman Hattaway, Archer Jones, and William N. Still, *Why the South Lost the Civil War* (Athens: University of Georgia Press, 1986), 247.

2. Herman Hattaway and Archer Jones, *How the North Won: A Military History of the Civil War* (Urbana: University of Illinois Press, 1991), 501–33; Mark E. Neely, "Was the Civil War a Total War?" *Civil War History* 37 (March 1991): 5–28; Archer Jones, *Civil War Command and Strategy: The Process of Victory and Defeat* (New York: Free Press, 1992); Daniel E. Sutherland, "Lincoln, John Pope, and the Origins of Total War," *Journal of Military History* 56, no.4 (October 1992): 567–86.

3. *Grant Memoirs*, 168–69.

4. Burke Davis, *Sherman's March* (New York: Vintage Books, 1980), 109.

5. William Lee Miller, *President Lincoln: The Duty of a Statesman* (New York: Alfred A. Knopf, 2008), 367.

6. Joseph T. Glatthaar, *The March to the Sea and Beyond: Sherman's Troops in the Savannah and Carolina Campaigns* (New York: New York University Press, 1985), 130.

7. William Sherman to Ulysses Grant, November 6, 1964, *Official Records*, ser. 1, vol. 30, pt. 3, p. 660.

8. Mark Grimsley, *The Hard Hand of War: Union Military Policy toward Civilians, 1861–1865* (New York: Cambridge University Press, 1995).

9. Abraham Lincoln to William Rosecrans, November 19, 1864, *Abraham Lincoln Papers at the Library of Congress*, Manuscript Division, American Memory Project, http://memory.loc.gov/ammem/malquery.html.

10. *Grant Memoirs*, 338.

11. Tyler Dennett, ed., *Lincoln and the Civil War in the Diaries and Letters of John Hay* (New York: Dodd, Mead, 1939), 178–79.

12. Ludwell H. Johnson, *The Red River Campaign: Politics and Cotton in the Civil War* (Baltimore: Johns Hopkins University Press, 1958); Gary Dillard Jones, *One Damn Blunder from Beginning to End: The Red River Campaign of 1864* (Lanham MD: SR Books, 2003).

13. *Grant Memoirs*, 433, 372–434.

14. *Grant Memoirs*, 440; Jean Edward Smith, *Grant* (New York: Touchstone, 2001), 305.

15. Ulysses Grant to Henry Halleck, May 11, 1864, *Official Records*, ser. 1, vol. 36, pt. 2, p. 627.

16. Abraham Lincoln to Ulysses Grant, August 17, 1864, *Lincoln Writings*, 822.

17. James McPherson, *The Battle Cry of Freedom: The Civil War Era* (New York: Oxford University Press, 1988), 756–60; Hattaway and Jones, *How the North Won*, 614–15.

18. Hattaway and Jones, *How the North Won*, 606.

19. Hattaway and Jones, *How the North Won*, 607.

20. Richard S. West, *Mr. Lincoln's Navy* (New York: Longmans, Green, 1957); Robert Carse, *Blockade: The Civil War at Sea* (New York: Rinehart, 1958).

21. McPherson, *Battle Cry of Freedom*, 378–82.

22. McPherson, *Battle Cry of Freedom*, 761.

23. Hattaway and Jones, *How the North Won*, 505.

24. Phillip Shaw Paludan, *The Presidency of Abraham Lincoln* (Lawrence: University Press of Kansas, 1994), 218.

25. Dudley Taylor Cornish, *The Sable Arm: Black Troops in the Union Army, 1861–1865* (Lawrence: University Press of Kansas, 1987); Joseph Glatthaar, *Forged in Battle: The Civil War Alliance of Black Soldiers and White Officers* (Baton Rouge: Louisiana State University Press, 1990).

26. Glatthaar, *Forged in Battle*, 10.

27. Abraham Lincoln to James Conkling, August 26, 1863, *Lincoln Works*, 6:409.

28. Abraham Lincoln to James Conkling, August 26, 1863, *Lincoln Works*, 6:409.

29. Abraham Lincoln to Charles Robinson, August 17, 1864, *Lincoln Works*, 7:499–501.

30. Frederick Douglass, *The Life and Times of Frederick Douglass* (New York: Collier Books, 1962), 346–49.

31. Miller, *President Lincoln*, 276.

32. Proclamation, July 31, 1863, *Lincoln Works*, 6:357.

33. Speech at Baltimore, April 18, 1864; Abraham Lincoln to Edwin Stanton, May 17, 1864, *Lincoln Works*, 7:302, 345–46.

34. Robert Lee to Ulysses Grant, October 1, 3, 1864; Ulysses Grant to Robert Lee, October 2, 4, *Official Records*, ser. 2, vol. 7, pp. 906–7, 909, 914.

35. James G. Randall, *Constitutional Problems under Lincoln* (Urbana: University of Illinois Press, 1951); Harold M. Hyman, *A More Perfect Union: The Impact of the Civil War and Reconstruction on the Constitution* (New York: Alfred A. Knopf, 1973); Philip S. Paludan, *A Covenant with Death: The Constitution, Law, and Equality in the Civil War Era* (Urbana: University of Illinois Press, 1975); Herman Belz, *Lincoln and the Constitution: The Dictatorship Question Reconsidered* (Fort Wayne IN: Louis Warren Lincoln Library, 1984); Mark E. Neely, *The Fate of Liberty: Abraham Lincoln and Civil Liberties* (New York: Oxford University Press, 1991); William M. Wiecek, *Equal Justice under Law: Constitutional Development, 1835–1875* (New York: Oxford University Press, 1991); Herman Belz, *Abraham Lincoln, Constitutionalism, and Equal Rights in the Civil War Era* (New York: Fordham University Press, 1998).

36. Address to Congress, July 4, 1861, *Lincoln Works*, 4:426.

37. Abraham Lincoln to Erastus Corning and Others, June 12, 1863, *Lincoln Works*, 6:267.

38. Reply to Emancipation Memorial by Chicago Christians, September 13, 1862, *Lincoln Works*, 5:421; Michael Burlingame and John R. Turner, eds., *Inside Lincoln's White House: The Complete War Diary of John Hay* (Carbondale: Southern Illinois University Press, 1997), 217–18.

39. Abraham Lincoln to Albert Hodges, April 4, 1864, *Lincoln Works*, 7:281.

40. Abraham Lincoln to Erastus Corning, June 12, 1863, *Lincoln Writings*, 761.

41. Abraham Lincoln to Benjamin Butler, August 9, 1864, *Lincoln Works*, 7:487–88.

42. David Herbert Donald, *Lincoln* (New York: Simon and Schuster, 1995), 305.

43. Paludan, *Presidency of Abraham Lincoln*, 81.

44. Peter Irons, *A People's History of the Supreme Court* (New York: Penguin, 1999), 188.

45. Mark E. Neely, "The Lincoln Administration and Arbitrary Arrests: A Reconsideration," *Papers of the Abraham Lincoln Association* 5 (1983): 8, 6–24; Neely, *Fate of Liberty*, 130, 168–69, 173.

46. Burrus M. Carnahan, "Lincoln, Lieber, and the Laws of War: The Origins and Limits of the Principle of Military Necessity," *American Journal of International Law* 92, no. 2 (April 1998): 214, 213–31.

47. Carnahan, "Lincoln, Lieber, and the Laws of War," 216; Abraham Lincoln to Joseph Reynolds, January 20, 1865, *Lincoln Writings*, 668.

48. Robert I. Alotta, *Civil War Justice: Union Army Executions under Lincoln* (Shippensburg PA: White Maine, 1989), 30; Miller, *President Lincoln*, 337–50, 461–63.

49. William L. Barney, *Battleground for the Union: The Era of the Civil War and Reconstruction, 1848–1877* (Englewood Cliffs NJ: Prentice Hall, 1990), 212.

50. Katherine Helm, *The True Story of Mary, the Wife of Lincoln* (New York: Harper and Row, 1928), 230–31.

51. Abraham Lincoln to Isaac Schermerhorn, September 12, 1864, *Lincoln Works*, 8:1–2.

52. Edmund Kirke and James R. Gilmore, "Our Visit to Richmond," *Atlantic Monthly*, December 1864.

53. Herman Belz, *Reconstructing the Union: Theory and Practice during the Civil War* (Ithaca NY: Cornell University Press, 1969); William C. Harris, *With Charity for All: Lincoln and the Restoration of the Union* (Lexington: University Press of Kentucky, 1997).

54. Belz, *Reconstructing the Union*.

55. Proclamation of Amnesty and Reconstruction, December 8, 1863, *Lincoln Writings*, 790–93.

56. Proclamation Concerning Reconstruction, July 8, 1864, *Lincoln Writings*, 820–21.

57. Donald, *Lincoln*, 524.

58. James McPherson, *Tried by War: Abraham Lincoln as Commander in Chief* (New York: Penguin, 2008), 226.

59. John H. Cramer, *Lincoln under Enemy Fire* (Baton Rouge: Louisiana State University Press, 1948).

60. Ulysses Grant to Henry Halleck, July 31, 1864, *Official Records*, ser. 1, vol. 37, pt. 2., p. 558.

61. Abraham Lincoln to Ulysses Grant, August 14, 1864, *Lincoln Writings*, 428; Edward C. Kirkland, *The Peacemakers of 1864* (New York: Macmillan, 1927).

62. Smith, *Grant*, 380.

63. William F. Zornow, *Lincoln and the Party Divided* (Norman: University of Oklahoma Press, 1954); David Long, *The Jewel of Liberty: Abraham Lincoln's Reelection and the End of Slavery* (Mechanicsburg PA: Stackpole Books, 1994); John C. Waugh, *Reelecting Lincoln: The Battle for the 1864 Presidency* (New York: Crown, 1997).

64. John Eaton, *Grant, Lincoln, and the Freedmen* (New York: Longmans, Green, 1907), 186–91.

65. Jessie Ames Marshall, ed., *The Private and Official Correspondence of Gen. Benjamin Butler* (Norwood MA: Plimpton Press, 1917), 5:25.

66. Memo, August 23, 1864, *Lincoln Works*, 7:514.

67. McPherson, *Battle Cry of Freedom*, 804–5.

68. William C. Harris, *Lincoln's Last Months* (Cambridge MA: Harvard University Press, 2004).

12. WITH MALICE TOWARD NONE

1. Annual Address to Congress, December 6, 1864, *Lincoln Writings*, 833, 834.

2. Jean Edward Smith, *Grant* (New York: Touchstone, 2001), 389.

3. Abraham Lincoln to William Sherman, December 26, 1864, *Lincoln Writings*, 835.

4. *Grant Memoirs*, 483–89.

5. Doris Kearns Goodwin, *Team of Rivals: The Political Genius of Abraham Lincoln* (New York: Simon and Schuster, 2006), 690–91.

6. George Milton, *The Age of Hate: Andrew Johnson and the Radicals* (New York: Coward McCann, 1930), 145–48.

7. Second Inaugural Address, March 4, 1865, *Lincoln Works*, 8:116–17.

8. Charles M. Segal, *Conversations with Lincoln* (New York: G. P. Putnam's Sons, 1961), 382.

9. David D. Porter, *Incidents and Anecdotes of the Civil War* (New York: D. Appleton, 1886), 294.

10. James M. McPherson, *The Battle Cry of Freedom: The Civil War Era* (New York: Oxford University Press, 1988), 849.

11. Last Public Address, April 11, 1865, *Lincoln Writings*, 846–51.

12. For the best overview, see William Hanchett, *The Lincoln Murder Conspiracies* (Urbana: University of Illinois Press,1983). See also George S. Bryan, *The Great American Myth* (New York: Carrick and Evans, 1940); William A. Tidwell, James O. Hall, and David Winfred Gaddy, *Come Retribution: The Confederate Secret Service and the Assassination of Abraham Lincoln* (Jackson: University Press of Mississippi, 1988); Albert Furtwangler, *Assassin on Stage: Brutus, Hamlet, and the Death of Lincoln* (Urbana: University of Illinois Press, 1991).

13. Moorhead Storey, "Dickens, Stanton, Sumner, and Storey," *Atlantic Monthly* 145 (April 1930): 464; Frederick W. Seward, *Reminiscences of a War Time Statesman and Diplomat* (New York: G. P. Putnam and Sons, 1916), 256.

14. Howard K. Beale, *The Diary of Gideon Welles, Secretary of the Navy under Lincoln and Johnson*, 3 vols. (New York: W. W. Norton, 1960), 2:282.

13. REVOLUTION

1. James M. McPherson, *The Battle Cry of Freedom: The Civil War Era* (New York: Oxford University Press, 1988), 818–19; Nicholas Onuf and Peter Onuf, *Nations, Markets, and War: Modern History and the American Civil War* (Charlottesville: University of Virginia Press, 2006).

2. *Grant Memoirs*, 303.

3. McPherson, *Battle Cry of Freedom*, 854; Richard E. Beringer, Herman Hattaway, Archer Jones, and William N. Still, *Why the South Lost the Civil War* (Athens: University of Georgia Press, 1986), 451–81; Herman Hattaway and Archer Jones, *How the North Won: A Military History of the Civil War* (Urbana: University of Illinois Press, 1991), 721–32. For the recent estimate of 750,000 dead, see Guy Gugliotta, "New Estimate Raises Civil War Death Toll," *New York Times*, March 4, 2012.

4. For the most comprehensive overview of Reconstruction, see Eric Foner, *Reconstruction: America's Unfinished Revolution, 1863–1877* (New York: Oxford University Press, 1988). See also Kenneth Stampp, *The Era of Reconstruction* (New York: Knopf, 1965); Dan Carter, *When the War Was Over: The Failure of Self-Reconstruction in the South* (Baton Rouge: Louisiana State University Press, 1985); Brooks D. Simpson, *The Reconstruction Presidents* (Lawrence: University Press of Kansas, 1998).

5. Erwin S. Bradley, *The Triumph of Militant Republicanism* (Philadelphia: University of Pennsylvania Press, 1964); John G. Sprout, *"The Best Men": Liberal Reformers in the Gilded Age* (New York: Oxford University Press, 1968); Michael G. McGerr, *The Decline of Popular Politics: The American North, 1865–1928* (New York: Oxford University Press, 1986).

6. Charles Sumner, *His Complete Works* (New York: Negro University Press, 1969), 12:468–69; Foner, *Reconstruction*, 236; George W. Julian, *Speeches on Political Questions* (New York: Hurd and Houghton, 1872), 269–70.

7. Roger L. Ransom and Richard Sutch, *One Kind of Freedom: The Economic Consequences of Emancipation* (New York: Cambridge University Press, 1977); Claude F. Oubre, *Forty Acres and a Mule: The Freedmen's Bureau and Black Landownership* (Baton Rouge: Louisiana State University Press, 1978).

8. Foner, *Reconstruction*, 56.

9. George C. Rable, *But There Was No Peace: The Role of Violence in the Politics of Reconstruction* (Athens: University of Georgia Press, 1984), 224.

10. William S. McFeely, *Yankee Stepfather: O. O. Howard and the Freedmen* (New Haven CT: Yale University Press, 1968).

11. Foner, *Reconstruction*, 152.

12. Foner, *Reconstruction*, 145.

13. U.S. Bureau of the Census, *Historical Statistics of the United States: Colonial Times to 1970* (Washington DC: Government Printing Office, 1975), 382.

14. Eric L. McKitrick, *Andrew Johnson and Reconstruction* (Chicago: University of Chicago Press, 1960); Michael Perman, *Reunion without Compromise: The South and Reconstruction, 1865–1868* (Cambridge: Cambridge University Press, 1973); Albert E. Castel, *The Presidency of Andrew Johnson* (Lawrence: University Press of Kansas, 1979); James F. Sefton, *Andrew Johnson and the Uses of Constitutional Power* (New York: Little, Brown, 1980); Hans L. Trefousse, *Andrew Johnson: A Biography* (New York: W. W. Norton, 1989).

15. M. A. De Wolfe Howe, ed., *The Home Letters of General Sherman* (New York: Scribners' Sons, 1909), 373.

16. David H. Donald, *Charles Sumner and the Rights of Man* (New York: Alfred A. Knopf, 1970), 237–38.

17. Leroy P. Graf and Ralph W. Haskins, eds., *The Papers of Andrew Johnson* (Knoxville: University of Tennessee Press, 1972), 3:165, 7:226; Trefousse, *Andrew Johnson*, 236; John Hope Franklin, *Reconstruction after the Civil War* (Chicago: University of Chicago Press, 1961), 42.

18. Trefousse, *Andrew Johnson*, 247.

19. McKitrick, *Andrew Johnson and Reconstruction*, 428–38.

20. James M. McPherson, *Abraham Lincoln and the Second American Revolution* (New York: Oxford University Press, 1991), 16–18.

21. Ralph Andreano, ed., *The Economic Impact of the American Civil War* (Cambridge MA: Schenkman, 1962), 240–42, 227, 236; Donald B. Dodd and Wynelle S. Dodd, *Historical Statistics of the South, 1790–1970* (Tuscaloosa: University of Alabama Press,1973); Gavin Wright, *The Political Economy of the Cotton South: Households, Markets, and Wealth in the Nineteenth Century* (New York: W. W. Norton, 1978); Lee Soltow, *Men and Wealth in the United States, 1850–1870* (New Haven CT: Yale University Press, 1975); Claudia D. Goldin and Frank D. Lewis, "The Economic Cost of the American Civil War: Estimates and Implications," *Journal of Economic History* 35 (1975): 299–326.

22. Foner, *Reconstruction*, 255.

23. Richard H. Abbott, *The Republican Party and the South, 1855–1877: The First Southern Strategy* (Chapel Hill: University of North Carolina Press, 1986).

24. Foner, *Reconstruction*, 9.

25. Foner, *Reconstruction*, 352, 355; Michael Perman, *The Road to Redemption: Southern Politics, 1869–1879* (Chapel Hill: University of North Carolina Press, 1984).

26. Hans L. Trefousse, *The Impeachment of a President: Andrew Johnson, the Blacks, and Reconstruction* (Knoxville: University of Tennessee Press, 1975); Michael Les Benedict, *The Impeachment and Trial of Andrew Johnson* (New York: W. W. Norton, 1999); David O. Steward, *Impeached: The Trial of President Andrew Johnson and the Fight for Lincoln's Legacy* (New York: Simon and Schuster, 2009).

27. Jean Edward Smith, *Grant* (New York: Touchstone, 2001), 457.

14. NIGHT RIDERS AND BLACK CODES

1. First Inaugural Address, March 4, 1869, in *The Papers of Ulysses S. Grant*, ed. John Y. Simons et al. (Carbondale: Southern Illinois University Press, 1967–), 19:139–42.

2. Jean Edward Smith, *Grant* (New York: Touchstone, 2001), 509.

3. William Gillette, *Retreat from Reconstruction, 1869–1879* (Baton Rouge: Louisiana State University Press, 1979); Terry L. Seip, *The South Returns to Congress: Men, Economic Measures, and Intersectional Relationships, 1858–1879* (Baton Rouge: Louisiana State University Press, 1983); Michael Perman, *The Road to Redemption: Southern Politics, 1869–1879* (Chapel Hill: University of North Carolina Press, 1984); Richard H. Abbott, *The Republican Party and the South, 1855–1877: The First Southern Strategy* (Chapel Hill: University of North Carolina Press, 1986).

4. Allen W. Trelease, *White Terror: The Ku Klux Klan Conspiracy and Southern Reconstruction* (New York: Harper and Row, 1971); George C. Rable, *But There Was No Peace: The Role of Violence in the Politics of Reconstruction* (Athens: University of Georgia Press, 1984).

5. Ulysses Grant to George Thomas, July 6, 1866, in Simons et al., *Papers of Ulysses S. Grant*, 16:230–31.

6. Eric Foner, *Reconstruction: America's Unfinished Revolution, 1863–1877* (New York: Oxford University Press, 1988), 426, 129; Rable, *But There Was No Peace*, 86.

7. Trelease, *White Terror*, 43–44, 155–79.

8. Foner, *Reconstruction*, 454.

9. James McPherson, *Ordeal by Fire: The Civil War and Reconstruction* (New York: McGraw Hill, 2010), 560; Everette Swinney, "Enforcing the Fifteenth Amendment, 1870–1877," *Journal of Southern History* 28 (1963): 203–7.

10. W. E. B. DuBois, *Black Reconstruction in America* (New York: Harcourt, Brace, 1935), 30.

11. Foner, *Reconstruction*, 31.

12. Harold M. Hyman, *A More Perfect Union: The Impact of the Civil War and Reconstruction on the Constitution* (New York: Alfred A. Knopf, 1973); Robert J. Kaczorowski, *The Politics of Judicial Interpretation: The Federal Courts, Department of Justice, 1866–1876* (New York: Fordham University Press, 1985).

13. Robert D. Marcus, *The Grand Old Party: Political Structure in the Gilded Age, 1880–1896* (New York: Oxford University Press, 1971).

14. Dee Brown, *The Year of the Century: 1876* (New York: Scribners' Sons, 1966), 342.

15. Smith, *Grant*, 479.

16. Ari Hoogenboom, *Outlawing the Spoils: A History of the Civil Service Reform Movement, 1865–1883* (Urbana: University of Illinois Press, 1961).

17. Alexander B. Callow, *The Tweed Ring* (Westport CT: Greenwood, 1981); C. K. Yearley, *The Money Machine: The Breakdown and Reform of Government and Party Finance in the North, 1860–1920* (Albany: State University of New York Press, 1970); Margaret S. Thompson, *The "Spider Web": Congress and Lobbying in the Age of Grant* (Ithaca NY: Cornell University Press, 1983).

18. Chester Destler, *American Radicalism, 1865–1901* (New York: Octagon Books, 1963).

19. Ellen C. Dubois, *Feminism and Suffrage: The Emergence of an Independent Women's Movement in America, 1848–1869* (Ithaca NY: Cornell University Press, 1978); William Leach, *True Love and Perfect Union: The Feminist Reform of Sex and Society* (Middletown CT: Wesleyan University Press, 1989).

20. Barbara Epstein, *The Politics of Domesticity: Women, Evangelism, and Temperance in Nineteenth-Century America* (Middletown CT: Wesleyan University Press, 1981).

21. Ralph Andreano, ed., *The Economic Impact of the American Civil War* (Cambridge MA: Schenkman, 1962).

22. C. Vann Woodward, *Reunion and Reaction: The Compromise of 1877 and the End of Reconstruction* (Boston: Little, Brown, 1951), 63.

23. Ray Allen Billington and Martin Ridge, *Westward Expansion: A History of the American Frontier* (New York: Macmillan, 1982), 573–90.

24. Rendigs Fels, *American Business Cycles, 1865–1897* (Chapel Hill: University of North Carolina Press, 1959); Eric Hobsbawm, *The Age of Capital, 1848–1875* (New York: New American Library, 1979); Harry Screiber, Harold Vatter, and Harold Faulkner, *American Economic History* (New York: Harper, 1976), 202.

25. Lee Benson, *Merchants, Farmers, and Railroads: Railroad Regulation and New York Politics, 1850–1887* (Cambridge MA: Harvard University Press, 1955).

26. Foner, *Reconstruction*, 590.

27. C. Vann Woodward, review of *The Confederate Nation, 1861–1865*, by Emory M. Thomas, *New Republic*, March 17, 1979, 25–27. For an excellent analysis of the conservative counterrevolution, see C. Vann Woodward, *The Origins of the New South, 1877–1913* (Baton Rouge: Louisiana State University Press, 1961).

28. Smith, *Grant*, 571.

29. Foner, *Reconstruction*, 604.

15. FRONTIERS

1. For perhaps the best analysis of this theme, see Richard Slotkin's brilliant trilogy: *Regeneration through Violence: The Mythology of the American Frontier, 1600–1860* (New York: Harper Perennial, 1973); *The Fatal Environment: The Myth of the Frontier in the Age of Industrialization* (Middletown CT: Wesleyan University Press, 1985); *Gunfighter Nation: The Myth of the Frontier in Twentieth-Century America* (Norman: University of Oklahoma Press, 1992).

2. Robert F. Berkhofer, *Salvation and the Savage: An Analysis of Protestant Missions and American Indian Response, 1787–1862* (Lexington: University Press of Kentucky, 1965); Dale Van Every, *Disinherited: The Lost Birthright of the American Indian* (New York: Morrow, 1966); Bernard W. Sheehan, *Seeds of Extinction: Jeffersonian Philanthropy and the American Indian* (Chapel Hill: University of North Carolina Press, 1973); Brian W. Dippie, *The Vanishing American: White Attitudes and U.S. Indian Policy* (Middletown CT: Wesleyan University Press, 1982); Robert M. Utley, *The Indian Frontier of the American West, 1846–1890* (Albuquerque: University of New Mexico Press, 1984); Francis Paul Prucha, *The Great Father: The United States Govern-*

ment and the American Indian (Lincoln: University of Nebraska Press, 1986); Philip Weeks, *Farewell My Nation: The American Indian and the United States, 1820–1890* (Arlington Heights IL: Harlan Davidson, 1990).

3. William R. Nester, *The Arikara War: The First Plains Indian War, 1823* (Missoula MT: Mountain Press, 2001).

4. Robert M. Utley, *Frontiersmen in Blue: The United States Army and the Indian,1848–1865* (Lincoln: University of Nebraska Press, 1981); Robert M. Utley, *Frontier Regulars: The United States Army and the Indians, 1866–1891* (Lincoln: University of Nebraska Press, 1984).

5. Interior Secretary Columbus Delano testimony, January 10, 1874, in U.S. House Committee on Military Affairs, *Report to Accompany the Bill (H.R. 2546)*, House Report 384 (Washington DC: Government Printing Office, 1874), 99, 169.

6. Speech to Indian Chiefs, March 27, 1863, *Lincoln Works*, 6:151–52.

7. Kenneth Carley, *The Dakota War of 1862: Minnesota's Other Civil War* (Minneapolis: Minnesota Historical Society Press, 1976).

8. Carley, *Dakota War of 1862*, 6.

9. David A. Nichols, *Lincoln and the Indians: Civil War Policy and Politics* (Columbia: University of Missouri Press, 1978), 87.

10. Carol Chomsky, "The United States–Dakota War Trials: A Study in Military Justice," *Stanford Law Review* 43, no. 1 (November 1990): 1–26.

11. Nichols, *Lincoln and the Indians*, 118.

12. Ulysses S. Grant, First Address to Congress, December 6, 1869, in *A Compilation of the Messages and Papers of the Presidents*, ed. James D. Richardson, 20 vols. (Washington DC: Government Printing Office, 1897–1917), 7:38.

13. Ulysses S. Grant, Second Inaugural Address, March 4, 1873, in Richardson, *Compilation of the Messages and Papers*, 7:222.

14. Henry F. Fritz, *The Movement for Indian Assimilation,1860–1890* (Westport CT: Greenwood, 1963); Robert Winston Mardock, *Reformers and the American Indian* (Columbia: University of Missouri Press,1971); Robert H. Keller, *American Protestantism and United States Indian Policy, 1869–1882* (Lincoln: University of Nebraska Press, 1983).

15. Glyndon Van Deuson, *William Henry Seward* (New York: Oxford University Press, 1967); David H. Donald, *Charles Sumner and the Rights of Man* (New York: Alfred A. Knopf, 1970).

16. Ulysses S. Grant to George H. Stuart, October 26, 1872, in *The Papers of Ulysses S. Grant*, ed. John Y. Simons et al. (Carbondale: Southern Illinois University Press, 1967–), 23:270.

17. Allan Nevins, *Hamilton Fish: The Inner History of the Grant Administration* (New York: Dodd, Mead, 1937).

18. Louis A. Pérez, *Cuba between Empires, 1878–1902* (Pittsburgh: University of Pittsburgh Press, 1982); José M. Hernández, *Cuba and the United States: Intervention*

and Militarism, 1868–1933 (Austin: University of Texas Press, 1993); Louis A. Pérez, *Cuba and the United States: Ties of Singular Intimacy,* 2nd ed. (Athens: University of Georgia Press, 1997).

19. Nevins, *Hamilton Fish,* 191–92.

20. William Javier Nelson, *Almost a Territory: America's Attempt to Annex the Dominican Republic* (Newark: University of Delaware Press, 1990).

21. David P. Crook, *The Alabama Claims* (Ithaca NY: Cornell University Press, 1975); Reginald Stuart, *United States Expansionism and British North America, 1775–1871* (Chapel Hill: University of North Carolina Press, 1988).

22. Herman Melville, *Moby-Dick,* ed. Harrison Hayford and Hershel Parker (New York: W. W. Norton, 1967); Michael Paul Rogin, *Subversive Genealogy: The Politics and Art of Herman Melville* (New York: Alfred Knopf, 1983); John Bryant, *A Companion to Melville Studies* (Westport CT: Greenwood Press, 1986); Andrew Delbanco, *Melville: His World and Work* (New York: Alfred Knopf, 2005); Clare L. Spark, *Hunting Captain Ahab: Psychological Warfare and the Melville Revival* (Kent OH: Kent State University Press, 2006).

23. Mark Twain, *"The Innocents Abroad" and "Roughing It"* (New York: Library of America, 1984); Everett Emerson, *Mark Twain: A Literary Life* (Philadelphia: University of Pennsylvania Press, 2000); Fred Kaplan, *The Singular Mark Twain: A Biography* (New York: Doubleday, 2003); Hamlin L. Hill, ed., *Mark Twain, The Gilded Age and Later Novels* (New York: Library of America, 2002).

24. Mark Van Doren, ed., *The Portable Walt Whitman* (New York: Penguin, 1973).

25. Louis Menand, *The Metaphysical Club: A Story of Ideas in America* (New York: Farrar, Straus, and Giroux, 2001).

26. Ralph Waldo Emerson, *The Essential Writings of Ralph Waldo Emerson* (New York: Modern Library, 2000).

27. Hampton Slides, *Blood and Thunder: The Epic Story of Kit Carson and the Conquest of the American West* (New York: Anchor Books, 2006), 311–21. Here again, see Richard Slotkin's brilliant trilogy: *Regeneration through Violence, Fatal Environment,* and *Gunfighter Nation.*

28. Roderick Nash, *Wilderness and the American Mind* (New Haven CT: Yale University Press, 1982), 115, 114.

16. EIGHTEEN SEVENTY-SIX

1. For overviews, see Robert M. Utley, *Frontier Regulars: The United States Army and the Indians, 1866–1891* (Lincoln: University of Nebraska Press, 1984), 236–95; Paul L. Hedren, ed., *The Great Sioux War, 1876–77* (Helena: Montana Historical Society Press, 1991); Jerome Greene, ed., *Battles and Skirmishes, 1876–1877* (Norman: University of Oklahoma Press, 1993). For works that provide good overviews but concentrate on Custer's role, see Stephen Ambrose, *Crazy Horse and Custer: The Parallel Lives of Two American Warriors* (New York: Doubleday, 1975); Evan S. Connell, *Son of the Morning Star: Custer and the Little Bighorn* (San Francisco: North Point

Press, 1984); Louise Barnett, *Touched by Fire: The Life, Death, and Mythic Afterlife of George Armstrong Custer* (Lincoln: University of Nebraska Press, 2006); James Donovan, *A Terrible Glory: Custer and the Little Bighorn; The Last Great Battle of the American West* (New York: Little, Brown, 2008).

2. Dee Brown, *The Year of the Century: 1876* (New York: Scribners' Sons, 1966), 14.

3. John Bigelow, ed., *The Letters and Literary Memorials of Samuel J. Tilden* (New York: Harper and Brothers, 1908), 1:271.

4. Keith Polakoff, *The Politics of Inertia: The Election of 1876 and the End of Reconstruction* (Baton Rouge: Louisiana State University Press, 1973); C. Vann Woodward, *Reunion and Reaction: The Compromise of 1877 and the End of Reconstruction* (Boston: Little, Brown, 1951).

5. Eric Foner, *Reconstruction: America's Unfinished Revolution, 1863–1877* (New York: Oxford University Press, 1988), 570.

6. James McPherson, *Ordeal by Fire: The Civil War and Reconstruction* (New York: McGraw Hill, 2010), 588.

7. Rutherford Hayes, *The Diary and Letters of Rutherford Birchard Hayes*, 5 vols. (Columbus: Ohio State Archeological and Historical Society, 1922–26), 3:47.

8. Foner, *Reconstruction*, 581.

9. Foner, *Reconstruction*, 582.

17. LEGACY

1. Richard E. Beringer, Herman Hattaway, Archer Jones, and William N. Still, *Why the South Lost the Civil War* (Athens: University of Georgia Press, 1986); Richard E. Beringer et al., *The Elements of Confederate Defeat: Nationalism, War Aims, and Religion* (Athens: University of Georgia Press, 1989); Herman Hattaway and Archer Jones, *How the North Won: A Military History of the Civil War* (Urbana: University of Illinois Press, 1991); William W. Freehling, *The South vs. the South: How Anti-Confederate Southerners Shaped the Course of the Civil War* (New York: Oxford University Press, 2001); Armistead L. Robinson, *The Bitter Fruits of Bondage: The Demise of Slavery and the Collapse of the Confederacy, 1861–1865* (Charlottesville: University of Virginia Press, 2005).

2. John Russell Young, *Around the World with General Grant: A Narrative of the Visit of General U.S. Grant, Ex-president of the United States, to Various Countries in Europe, Asia, and Africa in 1877, 1878, 1879*, 2 vols. (New York: American News, 1879), 2:354.

3. James G. Randall, *Lincoln the Liberal Statesman* (New York: Dodd, Mead, 1947); Allan Nevins, *The Statesmanship of the Civil War* (New York: Macmillan, 1962); John Thomas, ed., *Abraham Lincoln and the American Political Tradition* (Amherst: University of Massachusetts Press, 1986); Mark E. Neely, *The Last Best Hope of Earth: Abraham Lincoln and the Promise of America* (Cambridge MA: Harvard University Press, 1993); Philip Shaw Paludan, *The Presidency of Abraham Lincoln*

(Lawrence: University Press of Kansas, 1994); David Herbert Donald, ed., *Lincoln Reconsidered: Essays on the Civil War Era* (New York: Vintage, 2001); William Lee Miller, *President Lincoln: The Duty of a Statesman* (New York: Alfred A. Knopf, 2008).

4. Louis A. Warren, *Lincoln's Youth: Indiana Years, Seven to Twenty-One* (New York: Appleton, Century, Crofts, 1959), 225.

5. T. Harry Williams, *Lincoln and His Generals* (New York: Alfred A. Knopf, 1952); Allan Nevins, *The War for the Union*, vol. 1, *The Improvised War, 1861–1862* (New York: Charles Scribners' Sons, 1959).

6. George W. Julian, *Personal Recollections, 1840–1872* (Chicago: Jansen, McClurg, 1884), 201.

7. John G. Nicolay and John Hay, *Abraham Lincoln: A History* (New York: Century, 1890), 5:155–56.

8. Abraham Lincoln to Don Carlos Buell (copy to Henry Halleck), January 13, 1862, *Lincoln Works*, 5:98–99.

9. James M. McPherson, *Tried by War: Abraham Lincoln as Commander in Chief* (New York: Penguin, 2008), 268.

10. Abraham Lincoln to General Henry Halleck, September 19, 1863, *Lincoln Writings*, 782–83.

11. Jean Edward Smith, *Grant* (New York: Touchstone, 2001), 171.

12. Charles Bracelen Flood, *Grant and Sherman: The Friendship That Won the Civil War* (New York: Farrar, Straus, and Giroux, 2005).

13. *Grant Memoirs*, 175–76.

14. James M. McPherson, *The Battle Cry of Freedom: The Civil War Era* (New York: Oxford University Press, 1988), 328.

15. McPherson, *Tried by War*, 42.

16. Edward Hagerman, *The American Civil War and the Origin of Modern Warfare: Ideas, Organization, and Field Command* (Bloomington: Indiana University Press, 1988).

17. David D. Porter, *The Naval History of the Civil War* (Secaucus NJ: Castle, 1984).

18. Stephen R. Wise, *Lifeline of the Confederacy: Blockade Running during the Civil War* (Columbia: University of South Carolina Press, 1988).

19. Beringer et al., *Why the South Lost*, 55, 56.

20. Beringer et al., *Why the South Lost*, 247.

21. Michael Fellman, *Inside War: The Guerilla Conflict in Missouri during the American Civil War* (New York: Oxford University Press, 1989), 23–24.

22. Fellman, *Inside War*, 88.

23. Hattaway and Jones, *How the North Won*, 17–18.

24. Alice Fahs, *The Imagined Civil War: Popular Literature of the North and South, 1861–1865* (Chapel Hill: University of North Carolina Press, 2001).

25. McPherson, *Battle Cry of Freedom*, 306–7.

26. Paludan, *Presidency of Abraham Lincoln*, 198; McPherson, *Battle Cry of Freedom*, 600.

27. McPherson, *Battle Cry of Freedom*, 608.

28. McPherson, *Battle Cry of Freedom*, 792, 799, 802.

29. Ira Berlin, Barbara J. Fields, Thavolia Glymph, Joseph Reidy, and Leslie Rowland, eds., *Freedom: A Documentary History of Emancipation*, 3 vols. (New York: Cambridge University Press, 1982); Louis Gerteis, *From Contraband to Freedman: Federal Policy toward Southern Blacks, 1861–1865* (Westport CT: Greenwood Press, 1973).

30. Robert E. Lee to Andrew Hunter, January 11, 1865, *Official Records*, ser. 4, vol. 3, pp. 1012–13.

31. Beringer et al., *Why the South Lost*, 392.

32. David M. Potter, *The Impending Crisis, 1848–1861* (New York: Harper and Row, 1976), 29–50; Bruce Levine, *Half Slave and Half Free: The Roots of Civil War* (New York: Hill and Wang, 2005); Elizabeth R. Varon, *Disunion!: The Coming of the American Civil War, 1789–1859* (Chapel Hill: University of North Carolina Press, 2008).

33. For an excellent overview of how traditional southerners then and thereafter justify their rebellion and war against the United States, see Edward L. Ayers, *What Caused the Civil War: Reflections on the South and Southern History* (New York: W. W. Norton, 2005). See also David Blight, *Race and Reunion: The Civil War in American Memory* (Cambridge MA: Harvard University Press, 2001).

34. For the best, though ultimately flawed, argument that emphasizes economic divisions between North and South, see Charles Beard and Mary Beard, *The Rise of American Civilization* (New York: Macmillan, 1927). For a broader view that embraces social as well as economic divisions while dismissing slavery as the war's cause, see Arthur C. Cole, *The Irrepressible Conflict* (New York: Macmillan, 1934). For an excellent critique of this view, see Eric Foner, *Free Soil, Free Labor, Free Men: The Ideology of the Republican Party before the Civil War* (New York: Oxford University Press, 1995).

35. Frederick Douglass, "There Was a Right Side in the Late War," in *Frederick Douglass: Selected Speeches and Writings*, ed. Philip Foner (Chicago: Lawrence Hill Books, 1999), 632.

36. Second Inaugural Address, March 4, 1865, *Lincoln Works*, 8:333, 4:434n.

37. Eric Foner, *A Short History of Reconstruction* (New York: Harper and Row, 1990), 193.

38. Charles Sumner to John Bright, August 5, 1862, in *The Selected Letters of Charles Sumner*, ed. Beverly Palmer (Boston: Northeastern University Press, 1990), 2:122.

39. Annual Address to Congress, December 1, 1862, *Lincoln Works*, 4:438, 5:537.

40. Earl J. Hess, *Liberty, Virtue, and Progress: Northerners and Their War for the Union* (New York: Fordham University Press, 1997); Susan-Mary Grant, *North over South: Northern Nationalism and American Identity in the Antebellum Era* (Lawrence: University Press of Kansas, 2000); Mark Voss-Hubbard, *Beyond Party: Cultures of*

Anti-partisanship in Northern Politics before the Civil War (Baltimore: Johns Hopkins University Press, 2002).

41. Frederick Douglass, *The Life and Times of Frederick Douglass* (New York: Modern Library, 1994), 785–86.

42. Philip S. Foner, ed., *The Life and Writings of Frederick Douglass* (New York: International Publishers, 1950–55), 4:309–19.

43. Wilbur Zelinsky, *Nation into State: The Shifting Symbolic Foundations of American Nationalism* (Chapel Hill: University of North Carolina Press, 1988); Seymour M. Lipset, *American Exceptionalism: A Double-Edged Sword* (New York: W. W. Norton, 1996); Grant, *North over South*; Melinda Lawson, *Patriot Fires: Forging a New American Nationalism in the Civil War North* (Lawrence: University Press of Kansas, 2002); Susan-Mary Grant and Peter J. Parrish, eds., *The Legacy of Disunion: The Enduring Significance of the American Civil War* (Baton Rouge: Louisiana State University Press, 2003).

44. Books D. Simpson, *The Reconstruction Presidents* (Lawrence: University Press of Kansas, 1998), 188.

45. James M. McPherson, *Abraham Lincoln and the Second American Revolution* (New York: Oxford University Press, 1991), 13.

46. Dee Brown, *The Year of the Century: 1876* (New York: Scribners' Sons, 1966), 248.

47. For perhaps the best analysis of this theme, see Richard Slotkin's brilliant trilogy: *Regeneration through Violence: The Mythology of the American Frontier, 1600–1860* (New York: Harper Perennial, 1973); *The Fatal Environment: The Myth of the Frontier in the Age of Industrialization* (Middletown CT: Wesleyan University Press, 1985); *Gunfighter Nation: The Myth of the Frontier in Twentieth-Century America* (Norman: University of Oklahoma Press, 1992).

48. Theodore Calvin Pease and James G. Randall, eds., *The Diary of Orville Hickman Browning*, 2 vols. (Springfield: Illinois State Historical Library, 1925–33), 1:600.

49. Alan M. Kraut, ed., *Crusaders and Compromisers: Essays on the Relationship of the Antislavery Struggle to the Antebellum Party System* (Westport CT: Greenwood Press, 1983); David F. Ericson, *The Debate over Slavery: Antislavery and Proslavery Liberalism in Antebellum America* (New York: New York University Press, 2000); Mason I. Lowance, ed., *A House Divided: The Antebellum Slavery Debate in America,1776–1865* (Princeton NJ: Princeton University Press, 2003).

50. Zelinsky, *Nation into State*.

51. Edward Pessen, "How Different from Each Other Were the Antebellum North and South?," *American Historical Review* 85 (December 1980): 1119–49; James L. Huston, *Calculating the Value of the Union: Slavery, Property Rights, and the Economic Origins of the Civil War* (Chapel Hill: University of North Carolina Press, 2003); Jonathan Daniel Wells, *The Origins of the Southern Middle Class, 1800–1861* (Chapel Hill: University of North Carolina Press, 2004).

52. Nicolay and Hay, *Abraham Lincoln*, 10:302.

INDEX

For the reader's convenience there are entries for arts and literature; associations; battles (non–Civil War); Civil War; corporations; forts; Indian chiefs; Indian tribes (by region); Abraham Lincoln; newspapers and publishers; philosophy; Reconstruction; religion; rivers; schools; treaties and agreements; United States, pre-1860; wars (non–Civil War); and women's rights. Cities and towns are grouped with their respective states, and countries are grouped with their respective continents or regions.